D0927485

Lucille Lortel

The Queen of
Off Broadway

Alan Fontaine

Lucille Lortel in 1995

Lucille Lortel

The Queen of Off Broadway

ALEXIS GREENE

LIMELIGHT EDITIONS · NEW YORK

First Limelight Edition   March 2004
Copyright © 2004 The Lucille Lortel Foundation, Inc.

Published in the United States by
Proscenium Publishers Inc., New York

Interior design by Rachel Reiss

Manufactured in the United States of America

LIBRARY OF CONGRESS CATALOGING-IN-PUBLICATION DATA

Greene, Alexis.
Lucille Lortel : the queen of Off Broadway /
Alexis Greene.-- 1st Limelight ed.
p. cm.
Includes bibliographical references and index.
ISBN 0-87910-302-7
1. Lortel, Lucille. 2. Theatrical producers and
directors--United States--Biography. I. Title.
PN2287.L653G74 2004
792.02'32'092--dc22

2004000492

For Gordon Richard Hough

Acknowledgments

*T*his biography could not have been written without the archival legacy left by Lucille Lortel, who collected hundreds of documents and photographs about her productions and her theatres. Nor could it have been written without the cooperation of the Lucille Lortel Foundation, which generously provided me with access to Lucille Lortel's papers.

I am enormously grateful to Dr. Mary C. Henderson, the Lortel Estate's historian, who encouraged, prodded, advised and always stood by me throughout my research and writing, and to three dedicated and skilled archivists—Camille Dee, Donna Lewi, and Francesca Pitaro—who patiently answered my questions and let me work side-by-side with them. I owe a debt of thanks to Mary Ellen Rogan, senior archivist of the theatre collection at the New York Public Library for the Performing Arts, who graciously gave me a desk in the Rose Building, which became my home away from home.

Other librarians across the country aided me as I searched collections for answers to some of the mysteries of Lucille Lortel's life and career. I owe particular thanks to Gail Malmgreen at New York University's Tamiment Institute Library and Robert F. Wagner Labor Archives, for she helped me as I pored through the vast archives of Actors' Equity

Association. I also thank Cathy Hemming and Joel A. Weiner for their invaluable assistance.

Lucille Lortel crossed paths with hundreds of people during her lifetime, many of whom willingly spent hours talking to me about their friend and colleague. But I give special thanks to Mimi Bochco, Vincent Curcio, Ben Sprecher, and Sandra Starr, who allowed me to pick their memories several times over.

Finally, I must thank my extraordinarily patient publisher, Mel Zerman; Dale Ramsey, who first came to me with the idea of writing about this feisty, charming and contradictory lady; and Cynthia Cooper, for reading the manuscript and giving me her invaluable advice.

To my husband, Gordon Richard Hough, no words can express my gratitude for his love and support.

Contents

1. A Young Woman of the Theatre · · · · · · · · · · · · · 1
2. Breaking In · · · · · · · · · · · · · · · · 21
3. An Unlikely Marriage · · · · · · · · · · 53
4. The Making of a Producer: The White Barn Theatre · · · · 79
5. A Theatre in Greenwich Village · · · · · · · · · 113
6. The Queen of Off Broadway · · · · · · · · · · · 133
7. Passages · · · · · · · · · · · · · · · 191
8. On Her Own · · · · · · · · · · · · · 217
9. Of Renewal, Honors and Gifts · · · · · · · · · · 241
10. A Walk on Broadway · · · · · · · · · · 277
11. On the Wings of a Dream · · · · · · · · · · · 305
    Afterword · · · · · · · · · · · · · · · · · · 327
    Bibliography · · · · · · · · · · · · · · · · 333
    Notes · 337
    Index · 359

CHAPTER 1

A Young Woman of the Theatre

*O*ne mild Sunday night in Westport, Connecticut, in July 1947, eight actors sat on a platform in the second story of what had once been a country barn. Above them were wooden rafters and around them a rudimentary stage set: black drapes, a couple of circus posters strung up with wires, a round patio table big enough for a telephone and a few other stage props. The cast held scripts, from which they read intently, occasionally getting on their feet to play a scene. Their focus was a torrid drama about circus life called *Painted Wagon*, written by a spunky former actress named Elizabeth Goodyear and a handsome leading man named Philip Huston, who hoped their play would be Broadway-bound.

The script, as it turned out, was unmemorable, and years later even Goodyear acknowledged that this overwrought story of romance and revenge "wasn't very good."

But the circumstances surrounding its first public reading proved noteworthy. The invited audience of show business folk and well-to-do Connecticut residents, crowding eagerly if uncomfortably on metal folding chairs, were witnessing the first steps of a new theatre. And the feminine, slightly smiling dark-haired woman who welcomed them from the stage, who had willed it all to happen, was embarking upon a new life.

Indeed, perhaps without realizing it herself—for she tended to act instinctively—Lucille Lortel, at the age of forty-six, had found the career through which to express her talents and needs. As a theatre producer and owner, first at the White Barn in Westport and later Off Broadway at the Theatre de Lys, she would employ her intuitive knowledge of theatre, her taste for the offbeat, her charm, sociability and considerable energy. Abetted by her husband's wealth, Lucille Lortel's innate determination to go forward would translate into fearlessness, enabling her to take artistic risks that made her a leader of a burgeoning Off-Broadway movement during the 1950s and '60s and one of the few women of her generation to be a significant player in New York City theatre.

During her career, she would often display a confounding mixture of traits: enormous financial generosity as well as seemingly unwarranted stinginess; loyalty to unknown artists as well as effusive admiration for celebrities; skill at promoting her productions and an equally fervent desire to promote herself. At bottom, however, two forces drove her existence: a love of theatre and a craving for recognition.

Lucille Wadler was born on December 16, 1900, at 153 Attorney Street, a bustling, congested neighborhood of shops and airless five-story tenements on Manhattan's Lower East Side. Dr. Ben Friedman, filling out the birth certificate two months later—a common practice at a time when babies were born at home and the first weeks of their lives were uncertain—wrote that the new infant's name was "Lucel," a spelling in keeping with the Germanic backgrounds of the girl's parents, Anny and Harris Wadler. Polish Jews, they had been born in Austria, which, arm-in-arm with Russia and Prussia, had sliced up Poland in 1797 and devoured it.

The origins of Lucille's family, like those of many who immigrated to the United States during the nineteenth century, are mostly forgotten. Also like many immigrants and first-generation Americans, the Wadlers and their children distanced themselves from their history, stressing where they had arrived rather than the poverty or religious persecution from which they fled. Certainly once Lucille was a producer, she never talked publicly about her family's background, and even close friends knew little about that aspect of her life. Perhaps she did not know the complete story herself.

If Lucille had described her history, she would have told that her maternal grandfather, Heiman Moskowitz, came to the United States from Krakow during the 1880s, arriving at Castle Garden in the Battery, off the tip of lower Manhattan. Built in New York harbor as a fort in 1807, Castle Clinton, as it was originally called, had been acquired by the city and renamed Castle Garden. In 1839, when the Battery was still an elegant park, the building had been transformed into a theatre and eight years later had become an opera house. Courtesy of that ebullient impresario, P.T. Barnum, the Swedish soprano Jenny Lind made her American debut there in 1850.

But over the years the Battery's elegance had diminished. In 1855, the hall where the Swedish Nightingale once sang was converted into the Emigrant Landing Depot, to accommodate waves of Irish, Italian and East European immigrants. Until Castle Garden was closed and its operations moved to Ellis Island, in 1892, more than seven million people trudged across its hard floors, to find their way to the sweatshops of the Lower East Side or, able-bodied but apparently without skills, to be sent to the interior of the country to work on farms or in mines.

Heiman Moskowitz must have been good with his hands, for he played the fiddle and eventually worked as a jeweler, making settings and repairing watches. Still, he began life in the United States toiling in a coal mine in Pennsylvania, where he made enough money to send for his wife, Dibvra Minz, and their children, including Anna Lee, or Anny, who had been born in 1876. All together, Heiman and Dibvra would have six daughters who survived: Anny, Victoria, Helen, Mildred,

Sophie, and Rose; and two sons: Isidore, who became a violinist, and Philip, who played the piano. Lucille's family possessed an artistic bent.

At some point Heiman, Dibvra and their children arrived in New York City, but exactly when and where are unknown. By 1894, when eighteen-year-old Anny married twenty-two-year-old Harry Wadler, she was living at 218 East 115th Street and Harry lived about two blocks away; they were in a section of East Harlem where Jews, Irish and Italians rented what were called "cold flats," because the only heat came from the kitchen stove. It is reasonable to assume that at eighteen Anny was still living with her parents, but in the City Directory for 1894–95, one finds "Hyman Moskowitz, watches" at the opposite end of the city—downtown at 150 Attorney Street—and soon after at 153 Attorney, where Anny and Harry were living when Lucille was born. It seems Heiman had originally lived on the Lower East Side and then, like many Jews, had moved uptown. He rode the clattering elevated railway from East Harlem to the Bowery and walked to Attorney Street to his shop.

Eventually Heiman and Dibvra moved even further uptown, to the Mott Haven section of the Bronx, where New-Law tenements let in more light and air than their fetid predecessors in Manhattan, and where an apartment sometimes had steam heat, hot water and its own bathroom. Three of Anny's sisters and their husbands were already living there. Lucille's cousin Martine Lund, who was born in 1909, recalled growing up on Concord Avenue and 141st Street and visiting "Grandpa" close by. She remembered as a child seeing Heiman sitting by a window in his apartment, fixing watches and surrounded by cuckoo clocks.

Lucille's paternal grandparents, Meier Wadler and Augusta "Gussie" Polimer, made the arduous voyage across the Atlantic to New York City around 1882, when their son Harry was about ten years old. Little is known about Meier, who died before the end of the century. But Gussie was a force to be reckoned with. Born in Galicia in 1849, Tante Geldshe, as her family in Poland called her, married three times, first when she was fifteen. She had at least two other children with Meier—Annie and Willie—and after Meier died, she married one Max Cohn and raised another family. Her last child, Miriam, a pianist who occasionally accompanied Lucille's brother Mayo during his violin concerts, was born in 1897, when Gussie was around forty-eight years old. A stocky woman who wore her hair in a bun and spoke with a slightly clipped East European accent, she embodied the energy and stamina essential for survival in her new country.

There is an undated photograph of Anny and Harry Wadler on Table Rock at Niagara Falls. They look incongruously formal and overdressed, posing for the camera while apparently sitting on a bench atop a pile of stones. The photographer undoubtedly shot the couple in a studio against a backdrop of rocks and bushes, a technique that was popular late in the nineteenth century. Anny wears a fur coat and fur-trimmed hat, and her hands disappear into an enormous fur muff on her lap. Harry, who inherited his mother's stockiness, sits staring at the camera, his legs slightly apart. He holds a homburg in his left hand and a cane in his right, and there is a dapper cut to his coat. Their faces lack expression, but they project an intriguing combination of old-world ornateness and new-world aspirations.

Anny and Harry were married by a rabbi on November 9, 1894. Whatever else brought them together, they shared a determination to improve their economic and social place in the world.

But the change in their fortunes took awhile to accomplish, for they had a growing family to feed and shelter. Anny gave birth to Mayo on October 5, 1895; Ruth was born on October 14, 1898; Lucille in 1900; and Seymour Leonard came into the world on October 20, 1902. Between 1895 and 1903 the Wadlers moved at least five times, ending up, in what must have felt like a frustratingly circular journey, at the same sort of cold flat in East Harlem where Anny and Harry had lived before they married. Harry, who gave his occupation as "tailor" on Lucille's birth certificate, was striving to set up a cloak business, probably at first by contracting to sew for manufacturers of ready-to-wear men's clothing. At the same time that he was moving his family, he was uprooting his shop, entering into temporary partnerships with other cloak makers as well as trying to keep a company in his own name. But gradually he climbed out of the ghetto, and by 1906, "Harry Wadler, cloaks" was at 37 East 18th Street, near the "Ladies' Mile" of fashionable department stores like Arnold Constable and Lord & Taylor. Soon, in fact, Harry would shift to manufacturing ladies' dresses.

Lucille's childhood world included crowded apartments that were stifling in summer and icy in winter. But there were also the smells of home-cooked food, the sounds of her relatives' pleasant jumble of Yiddish, German and English, the twang of her grandfather's fiddle, and the melodies that glided from Uncle Isidore's classical violin. For a few summers there were trips into the country. Lucille once told Vincent Curcio, who became the White Barn's general manager in 1979, that her earliest memory was of going to Moodus, Connecticut, when she was about five years old. She remembered sailing up a river, and a farmer and his wife who arrived in a hay wagon to meet the boat and allowed Lucille to ride on top of the wagon all the way to their farm. For five-year-old Lucille, it was an idyllic experience.

When it came to their children, Anny and Harry centered their aims and expectations on Mayo, a pressure that the dark-haired, dark-eyed youngster absorbed, rigorously imposed on himself and ultimately hated. Guided by his Uncle Isidore, Mayo had begun to play the violin when he was three, and when he was about eight he took part in a recital at the 1,000-seat Carnegie Lyceum Theatre, in the stately brick building that housed Carnegie Hall (press releases would later brag that this youthful performance actually took place *in* Carnegie Hall). The esteemed German violinist Willy Hess was leading the Boston Symphony Orchestra at the time, and Isidore, who often assisted Hess, invited him to hear Mayo play. Impressed by the boy's talent, Hess sponsored Mayo's admission to the Royal Academy in Berlin, and when the German virtuoso returned there in 1909, he took Mayo with him. Accompanied by Hess and Isidore, Lucille's thirteen-year-old brother sailed to Germany to become a concert violinist.

Ruth, Seymour and Lucille could not help but realize that Mayo was both the family's star and their mother's favorite. He was the one who presumably would bring glory to the Wadlers. Perhaps in response, Ruth eventually retreated into her own creative world, while Seymour, unable to compete with his older brother in either physical attractiveness, personal style or talent, floundered pitifully. Lucille, like her mother, cherished Mayo—she saw him as a true artist—but she would supplant him as the family's success story.

Around the time that Mayo went to Germany, Anny and Harry moved their family to 140th Street, joining Anny's sisters in Mott Haven. Anny most likely did not relish living in the Bronx—she was always more ambitious than the rest of her family. But she was also practical, and with Mayo abroad, the Wadlers remained in the Bronx for five years, while Harry prospered and paid the bills. Then in September 1914, war stirred across Europe, and the family sailed to Germany to retrieve Mayo, who returned with them to New York at the beginning of October. As though to celebrate the homecoming and provide a suitable base from which to launch his older son, Harry moved his family into a twelve-story apartment building at 448 Riverside Drive, near 117th Street. Two years later he ensconced them in the cream-colored, thirteen-story Hamilton at 420 Riverside Drive, on 114th Street, in a third-floor apartment with a sumptuous view of the Hudson River. Fifteen-year-old Lucille could proudly invite friends to visit and just as proudly tell them that her father was president of his own company, Gem Dress House, at 11 East 26th Street.

If Anny and Harry shared a desire to rise in the world, their success, according to anyone who knew either of them, was due to Anny. "Harry didn't have much personality," recalled Isidore's son, Paul Moss, who was born in 1916 and grew up not far from Lucille on the Upper West Side. "My aunt ran the show. She was dominating."

Like Harry's mother, Anny was a survivor. When she and Harry separated during the 1920s, a result of her husband's business failures and extramarital affairs, Anny went to work selling insurance for the Equitable Life Assurance Society, and Lucille always credited her mother with holding the family together. Well into her children's adulthood, "Mama" took charge of ensuring that they were making good. When Mayo returned from his European tour in the 1920s, typed letters went out over Anny's name to rich acquaintances, inviting them to a Musicale being held in Mayo's honor. Mayo's older daughter, Carolyn "Lynne" Mayocole, recalled her mother describing how Anny would regularly usher Mayo, Ruth, Lucille, and Seymour into a private meeting after Sunday dinner at Lucille's home in Westport, even when Lucille and her brothers and sister were in their forties. "Anny would call them together, and there would be some kind of summing up of how progress was going." The way her mother told it, Lynne assumed that Anny had been holding these sessions for years.

As for Harry, Lucille's cousin Paul Moss called him "a bad penny." Portia Waldman Laveman, Gussie's granddaughter by Max Cohn, knew Harry after he and Anny had separated and described him as "a womanizer" who "used to have affairs with his models in the garment industry." After his business failed, he would visit Gussie and Portia's mother in the Bronx and plead poverty, but after Gussie died in 1934, they lost track of him.

Still, while the Wadlers were together, Harry was concerned about the future success of his children and could inspire anxiety. In Berlin, Mayo wrote in his diary on November 28, 1913, that he returned to his

pension to find a letter from "Papa" and Isidore, ". . . in which are written their dreams of me becoming a Great Artist, which makes me feel
very depressed, as that state seems to be so very very far off. But nonetheless their faith in me stimulates me to work harder."

As for Lucille's interaction with her father, a hint emerges in a photograph taken when Harry visited her at camp: both perch on a wooden
railing, both look relaxed and are smiling at the camera and leaning toward each other. All her adult life, Lucille liked to bask in the company
of attentive men, and men were always more important beings than
women in her estimation. It is easy to imagine that at some point she
idolized her father.

But after she grew up, Lucille had minimal contact with Harry, shut-
ting his betrayals and embarrassing financial failure out of her life. Even
close friends never heard her speak about him, or only in passing. During
the 1940s, her father must have reconciled with Anny and his children, for
suddenly a balding, paunchy man with a drawn face appears in informal
photographs taken at Westport. But whatever flair Harry Wadler once
possessed had vanished. Lynne Mayocole remembered "a sad, quiet, little gray man" who didn't seem capable of much. "My grandmother was
such a presence, that you never questioned that she was uniquely responsible for her children. What did she need somebody else for? She never
seemed as though she was a half of something that had gone lacking."

The move to Riverside Drive was a shrewd one for an aspiring middle-
class family. In the last quarter of the nineteenth century, the section of
Manhattan along the Hudson River had begun to attract the attention
of New York City's developers. Frederick Law Olmsted, the imaginative
landscape architect who had designed Central Park, was asked to create
a boulevard with broad carriage ways and sidewalks that would extend
north along the river from 72nd Street. This avenue would camouflage

the railroad tracks, dredges, and piles of stone and dirt that a feverishly industrial nation had thrown up along the waterfront. On top of Manhattan's rocky cliffs, the boulevard would be a charming place from which to view a magnificent river and the picturesque Palisades on the opposite bank. By 1908, the newly named Riverside Drive and Park stretched to 145th Street.

Mansions flowered along the lower sections of Riverside Drive; above 110th Street, the Morningside Heights area was an outlying region thought fit mainly for asylums and orphanages. But as developers shifted their attention from the East Side of Manhattan to the West, that real estate suddenly looked enticing. In 1891, Columbia University announced plans to move to 116th Street and Broadway from its site at 49th and Madison Avenue. A year later, the cornerstone was laid for the towering Cathedral of St. John the Divine. The Interboro Rapid Transit began service beneath Broadway in 1904, and with the subway promising a twenty-minute ride downtown, grand apartment houses—the new style of urban dwelling—began to rise on the Upper West Side.

By the time the Wadlers moved to Riverside Drive, they were in good company, or at least on the fringe of it. The East Side might house the elite of New York, but the Upper West Side attracted well-off businessmen, millionaires like the aggressive newspaper mogul William Randolph Hearst, who lived in the top three floors of the Claremont at Riverside Drive and 86th Street. For Anny and Harry, who were neither rich enough nor socially prominent enough to live on Fifth Avenue, or in the luxurious apartment houses that began to line Central Park West, the imposing building at 114th Street demonstrated considerable accomplishment. They had wrested prosperity from the rough terrain of American commerce.

Certainly life on Riverside Drive was comfortable for Lucille and her family. Anny often went horseback riding, and Lucille and Ruth could promenade along the gently curving drive, stopping to watch the yachts gliding down the Hudson. The girls always wore the sharpest styles, for

Harry would bring them dress samples from work. Some summers Lucille went to camp, and occasionally Anny rented a house in Long Beach, a largely Jewish resort on the Atlantic shore of Long Island. Mayo had his own motorcar, and there was a car with a chauffeur for the family.

Lucille and Ruth formed a bond that they sustained for the rest of their lives. When they were in their teens and twenties, Ruth was Lucille's confidante; years later, Lucille would be Ruth's protector. Physically, they could have been mistaken for twins when they were young women: they were nearly the same height and both had dark hair and curvaceous figures, although Lucille always complained that her legs were too heavy. But emotionally they were opposites. Lucille was outgoing, like her mother, while Ruth was introspective. "Ruth was Lucille in pastels," said Lynne Mayocole.

The girls escaped the degree of pressure their parents imposed on Mayo. Still, it would be hard to imagine that Anny and Harry didn't have expectations for their attractive, creative daughters. "Anny was grooming them," said Mimi Bochco, who met Ruth during the 1930s and eventually became one of Lucille's closest friends. "Like the typical Jewish lady who was going to marry her daughters to millionaires, to doctors, lawyers, that sort of thing." At one point Anny and Harry tried to steer Ruth toward being a musician, but early on she demonstrated a talent for drawing and painting and eventually she became a portrait artist. They sent her to the Horace Mann High School for Girls, at that time a laboratory school for Teachers College at 120th Street, within walking distance of home. It would not have escaped Anny and Harry's notice that Ruth's Class of 1917 included girls with last names like Schwab and Van Raalte, whose families were among the most affluent on the Upper West Side.

Lucille's formal education was erratic. In her teens, she attended the Myron T. Scudder School at 59 West 96th Street near Columbus Avenue, then she went to The Clark School for Concentration, a small private school founded by a teacher named Thomas F. Clark, located on

West End Avenue near 72nd Street. But either she did not take Clark's regimes to heart or something else in her life, possibly an intense round of parties, interfered with studying. During her last semester she was failing French, and the school complained that she was chronically late, as well as absent nearly every afternoon during the spring term. The administration sent Harry a letter warning that if Lucille did not buckle down she would fail her June examinations and not be able to get into college, and it recommended intensive study at home. There is no record of whether Lucille completed Clark, although she subsequently attended Adelphi, a young liberal arts college that had been started in Brooklyn. But she suffered from both claustrophobia and heart palpitations, and after fainting one day on the subway, she refused to go back.

If Lucille was a middling student, she won high marks from her friends for charm. Letters from girls at camp and school gushed that "Lu" was the only one who listened to them and understood their inmost thoughts. Their only complaint was that "lazybones" never answered their letters; indeed all her life, Lucille was a terrible correspondent. Taking the lead from Anny, who was observed dancing and partying well into her eighties, outgoing, flirtatious Lucille took to socializing with childlike enthusiasm. According to Mimi Bochco, "You could wake Lucille up in the middle of the night and she would come to a party." After Mayo returned from Germany, the girls' social world expanded to include musicians, actors and visual artists to whom their handsome, sophisticated brother introduced them. In 1918, he made his New York debut at Aeolian Hall and shortly afterward did his first American tour. His circle included a dashing violinist and future conductor named Arthur Fiedler, who had been a fellow student in Berlin; the violinist Leopold Godowsky, Jr., son of a world-famous pianist; a Polish-born violinist, Rudolf Bochco, and Max Rosen, an American violinist who was a childhood friend of the burgeoning composer George Gershwin and his songwriter brother, Ira. Lucille and Ruth met them all.

In 1900, when Lucille Wadler was born, American theatre was a sprawling, rude, vital business. From Broadway to Main Street, melodramas to vaudeville, it was the country's chief form of entertainment.

New York City was the commercial theatre's engine. In 1900 eager theatregoers could visit dozens of playhouses during a season, beginning with the Star, formerly the famous Wallack's Theatre, at 13th Street and Broadway, and continuing uptown until they stopped, dazzled, at 45th and Broadway. There the New York Theatre and the Criterion occupied Oscar Hammerstein's former Olympia Music Hall and Lyric Theatre, an entertainment palace decorated with minarets and columns that fronted on an entire city block.

Plays were often trivial, but just as often filled with passion and romance. Stars compensated where literature failed. During the season of 1900–01, fragile, winsome Maude Adams beguiled audiences playing the title role in Edmond Rostand's patriotic drama *L'Aiglon*, while Junoesque twenty-one-year-old Ethel Barrymore made a sensation acting the vivacious Italian opera singer Madame Trentoni (of Trenton, New Jersey), in Clyde Fitch's romantic comedy *Captain Jinks of the Horse Marines*. The magnificent Richard Mansfield, at forty-six one of the last of the nineteenth-century's great actor-managers, played Shakespeare's Henry V, in one critic's words, "as a king who was half warrior and half saint."

Most theatre people know the moment they fell in love—the production that swept them into a magical world, the performance that riveted them. Strangely for somebody who adored theatre, Lucille never recounted a specific time, place or production. She told Vincent Curcio that she had first wanted to be a dancer but had decided it was not for her. She used to tell interviewers that as a young girl she always wanted to be an actress, especially in the movies. Photographs of Lucille when she was a teenager show her reveling in her thick, long dark hair and adopting sultry Theda Bara-like poses, the sort that an innocently sexy girl with fantasies of movie stardom might strike.

Anny or one of her relatives definitely took the children to the theatre; Mayo remembered being taken to amateur night in a vaudeville house on 125th Street and Lenox Avenue, when he was seven or eight years old. After the family moved to Riverside Drive, they could easily walk or ride to the theatres on the Upper West Side, for by 1920 more than two dozen legitimate and variety houses ranged all the way from Columbus Circle at 59th Street to Cathedral Parkway at 110th. Later, when Lucille played opposite Sessue Hayakawa in *The Man Who Laughed*, she would perform in one of them: B.F. Keith's Riverside Theatre at Broadway and 96th Street.

But for a star-struck girl, theatre's glamorous heart lay along Broadway from 13th Street to Times Square. Writing around 1915, the theatre critic Walter Prichard Eaton observed,

> Here, at night, the Great White Way—which, to be sure, is golden—stretches north to the tower of the Times Building between and beneath a splendour of electric advertisements that mocks the dark. Electric chariots race overhead. Great figures clad in incandescent underclothes spar one with the other, proclaiming the flexibility of the weave. A gigantic kitten sports with a perpetually unwinding ball of somebody's yarn. Brilliant signs announce farces and operas and musical comedies, and once in a blue moon the name of Shakespeare may make itself known in gold. Meanwhile along the walk passes an endless throng of men and women bent on pleasure, and through the roadway rolls an endless stream of cabs and motor cars, jewels and white shirt bosoms flashing within.

After the Adelphi disappointment, Lucille told Anny and Harry that she wanted to be an actress. Needless to say, they were not pleased by the idea. Actresses lived helter-skelter existences, and their reputations for sexual looseness generally kept them from the sort of marriage which her parents had envisioned for their daughter. But Lucille, who had developed a will as strong as her mother's, insisted enthusiastically, and Anny and Harry allowed her to audition for Franklin Haven Sargent, the president of the American Academy of Dramatic Arts.

Sargent, a former professor of speech at Harvard University, had established the Lyceum School of Acting in 1884 with the director and manager Steele MacKaye and the theatre manager Daniel Frohman. But when his colleagues moved on to other projects, Sargent set up the New York School of Acting, later renamed the American Academy of Dramatic Arts—the first school of actor training in the United States. By 1920 the Academy had taken over the 1,000-seat Carnegie Lyceum Theatre, a handsome basement auditorium beneath Carnegie Hall, at 57th and Seventh Avenue, and several floors in an adjoining building. It had absorbed its only real competition, Charles Frohman's Empire Theatre Dramatic School, and earned a reputation for delivering students into the professional theatre and the youthful film industry (Cecil B. DeMille was an early graduate). No doubt this last attracted Lucille and was a favorable mark from her parents' viewpoint. According to the persuasive catalogue, the Academy did not promise to do the impossible—"to teach all the art of an Edwin Booth in two short years"—but it assured that the training would enable a student to "find his proper place and rank as an actor, to test his powers in all modes of dramatic expression, and to train his imagination to be in sympathy with the joy and pathos, heights and depths of that humanity he is to interpret."

On January 15, 1920, a nervous Lucille met Sargent, who most likely heard her audition in his office, where he could watch her intently through his pince-nez. In the audition book, Sargent jotted Lucille's age (19), her height (5′4″) and her weight (119 pounds). He also made the following observations, in accordance with a list of attributes that the Academy evaluated in prospective students:

> Coloring: dark
> Proportions: good
> Physical condition: good
> Personality: good
> Stage presence: good (small)

He noted her previous training: dancing.

There is no record of Lucille's audition pieces that day. As to her stage potential—"Reading, Spontaneity, Versatility, Characterization, Distinction, Pantomime, Dramatic Instinct, Temperament, Intelligence, Imitation, Recitation, and Imagination"—Sargent wrote "fair" next to "Distinction" and scrawled "fairly good" in pencil across the whole page. Then he wrote "good ingenue type" and "should make up well," and signed his initials. He had accepted Lucille into the Academy; she entered that January as a Junior, the first rung of the two-tier program.

It is hard to know the nature of the training that Lucille received. In the Junior Course, which lasted six months and cost $400, a student took physical, vocal and stage training, this last consisting of stage mechanics, stage business, make-up and costuming; classes in dramatic literature and dramatic analysis "to suggest to the students the means of reproducing their own emotional experiences for the purposes of presenting them on the stage"; and training in physical, vocal and stage expression, culminating with performances in "examination plays" in the Carnegie Lyceum Theatre, when the faculty judged whether a student should return for the Senior Course.

The Academy's purported intention was to prepare actors for the newly realistic plays that were slowly moving into the American theatre. But many of the teachers Lucille encountered were former actors with roots in the nineteenth-century stage and the acting style developed by the Frenchman François Delsarte, who formulated laws of stage expression based on a rigid correlation between emotion and pantomimed gesture.

One instructor, a 5-foot-2-inch actor and director with fierce, arching eyebrows—Charles Jehlinger—wanted to move the Academy away from Delsarte's rules, although in what direction was not always obvious. He would become legendary as a tough, often acid-tongued instructor and an inculcator of acting maxims, such as these collected by Eleanor Cody Gould, who was a Junior at the Academy in 1918:

> Every character has a heart, brain and soul. You are the servant of the character; the character is not your servant.

> The eyes to the balcony rail gives the natural position to the head.

> You must understand the motive of the character, what the character is trying to do. Then do it in the most charming, womanly manner possible.

When Sargent died in 1923, "Jelly" took charge and reigned over the young actors Rosalind Russell, Spencer Tracy, Kirk Douglas, and many others who went on to fame and fortune. According to her friend Anna Strasberg, Lucille said that she trained under the often celebrated, sometimes vilified, Jehlinger. He probably had a hand in her final public performance at the Academy.

Lucille liked hearing the music that seeped from behind the doors of the Carnegie Hall studios as she went up and down the marble stairs to classes. With her fellow students, she sat in the dressing rooms backstage and learned to apply stage make-up. She drilled to enunciate clearly and project her voice, which was pleasantly low for a young woman. When she had the chance, she tucked her feet under her and nestled into a seat in the Carnegie Lyceum's balcony, to watch the rehearsal of a Broadway play. The deep, fifty-foot-wide stage was popular with productions headed for the Great White Way.

At the end of the Junior Course, Lucille and forty-one fellow students qualified for the six-month Senior Course (also $400), which included what the catalogue described as "experimental" challenges for the Senior Class stock company. In an arrangement that sounds much like what Lucille later organized at the White Barn, these productions were performed once in the evenings in the Carnegie Lyceum, for members of the Academy and an invited audience. For these "Dress Rehearsals," as the programs called them, Lucille got to play several meaty parts: a second ingenue role that required feistiness as well as sexual allure, and two character turns that gave her a chance to stretch her range. She was a stenographer named Violet Landsdowne in *Girls*, a vacuous, slightly titillating three-act comedy by Clyde Fitch about three roommates who swear off men (in a bit seen in dozens of comedies from Broadway to Hollywood, Violet stands on top of a ladder while a canny gentleman holds it from below). In a scene from Edward Knoblauch's sentimental drama *My Lady's Dress*, Lucille played a hunchbacked cockney girl who makes artificial flowers to survive, and she was cast as a cranky, self-pitying and tearful resident of an old ladies' home in a one-act comedy by Alice Brown, *Joint Owners in Spain*.

But the Academy's ultimate goal was to usher its graduates into the commercial theatre. The high points for the Senior Class were afternoon productions open to the public and the press at the superb New Lyceum on West 45th Street, a 900-seat house with two balconies built for Daniel Frohman in 1903. Attended by producers and talent scouts, these performances were a young actor's chance to be noticed.

Of her class's ten productions at the Lyceum, Lucille participated in only four, and what must have been particularly disappointing for an aspiring actress, only two roles were sizable or distinctive enough to show her off. One, on January 28, 1921, was the part of a scheming parlor maid, who robs her elderly employer, in a one-act melodrama *Two Crooks and a Lady*. Lucille had to be tough, jealous, fearful, and remorseful in quick succession. The critic for the Chicago-based *Musical Leader* opened his review with words that might both have pleased an actress receiving her first notice and privately distressed a young woman who did not want to live in her older brother's shadow:

> Mayo Wadler's sister, Lucille Wadler, reveals talent different from that of her brother, who has made a name for himself as a violinist here and abroad. She gave evidence of fine sensibility, subtlety of feeling and an understanding of values...

The other flashy part was Clariel, the Swallow, in Gabriele D'Annunzio's poetic drama *The Honeysuckle*, a strained tale of love, evil and revenge. Presented on Monday afternoon March 21, 1921, *The Honeysuckle* seems an eccentric choice for the Senior Class's tenth and final showcase, even if this was an American première. The three acts of suspected murder, guilt and recrimination feel endless, the language is self-indulgently extravagant and, in the English translation by Cecile Sartoris and Gabrielle Enthoven, exceedingly cloying. That girl-symbol The Swallow, who cannot lessen the anguish of her sister, Audain, asks

> What would I not do to cure my Audain? I think I would even give her my happiness, if it were possible....If I were really a swallow I would go away and fetch her that unknown him that one waits for always; who, before he came to me, dwelt in the corner of the golden sky, whence come the swallows certain evenings...

But as she would reveal at the White Barn Theatre, and even more so when producing Off Broadway, Lucille had an affinity for plays that were novel in style or content. And the role, which required an actress who could be "light and vivacious as a bird," offered Lucille a chance to draw on her dancing and demonstrate her physical grace. Intuitively she also drew on deep affection for her own sister. This time the critic from *The Musical Leader* really did have something to write about:

> Lucille Wadler, an exquisite little creature, had an astonishing op-
> portunity in the part of the Swallow, a nick-name for a petted lit-
> tle sister in the first flush of her youth and love. Miss Wadler
> seemed to be inspired, and as she darted to and fro, first with kisses
> and then with flowers, she warranted the name. While the role en-
> tailed all that simplicity and a natural flow of affection might do
> for a slip of a girl, there was one crucial moment when the child
> gazed upon her sleeping sister who had become a mental and
> physical wreck; there Miss Wadler arose to the situation with more
> than passing skill and feeling and of understanding for the profes-
> sion she has selected.

The critic for *The Morning Telegraph*, while calling *The Honeysuckle* a "turgid, dour, oratorical, vague and most depressing piece at best," wrote, "Lucille Wadler, the Swallow of the play, disclosed great personal beauty, a fine girlish exuberance and an unaffected and frank manner. That marked her performance as one of the best, certainly the pleasan-test, of the afternoon."

The next day, at three o'clock in the afternoon at the Lyceum, Lucille Wadler was graduated from the American Academy of Dramatic Arts.

CHAPTER 2

Breaking In

O ne month later, on April 20, 1921, Lucille, Ruth, Seymour and Anny stood on a deck of the R.M.S. *Olympic* and watched the buildings of lower Manhattan recede to a gleaming speck as the great liner churned slowly toward the open sea. They were going to Europe.

The ostensible reasons for the trip were to visit Mayo, who was playing concerts all over the Continent, and for Lucille to study acting. "My brother was studying in Europe and thought I should too," she told the journalist Markland Taylor in a 1983 interview for the *New Haven Register*. She also told interviewers that the Broadway producer Sam Harris had seen her work at the Academy and was interested in her, but that her parents insisted she go abroad.

There may have been other motivations behind Anny's departure with her children. Harry's womanizing and the state of his business affairs had caused a rift in the family, and Anny would be away from her husband for two years.

It might have benefited Lucille's acting career if she had stayed in New York, where she could capitalize on her complimentary reviews and her connections with the Academy. She was twenty years old, an age by which contemporaries like Helen Hayes and Eva Le Gallienne, not to mention less talented women, were already on Broadway.

But if Lucille was concerned or angry about forfeiting an aggressive start to her career, her letters from the *Olympic* gave no hint of it. She had been to Europe only once before—on the brief trip to Berlin with her parents when she was thirteen, to bring Mayo home. Now the prospect of France, Austria and Italy excited her.

The *Olympic,* which the White Star Line had launched in 1910 as a sister ship to the *Titanic,* had been stripped during the war and used to carry troops. But now her opulent furnishings again decorated the grand rooms. Lucille ate dinner in the 114-foot-long Louis Seize dining saloon and roamed the ship's promenades, which seemed wide as European boulevards. She wrote the young pianist Marvine Maazel that she relished her shipboard schedule: exercising in the gym in the morning, strolling on deck in the afternoon, and at night lazing about in a steamship chair beneath an immense, star-dappled sky. With a combination of naïve boasting and conscious titillation, she informed Maazel that "the men are so nice to me. The [gym] instructor thought I was good looking. He told me some of the men were talking to him about me. Isn't that funny? I think the real reason is because I wear those black bloomers and all the other ladies wear their skirts . . ."

When not daydreaming about Europe, she was juggling the ardent attentions of Maazel and Leopold Godowsky, Jr., whom she had left pining for her in New York.

Like Mayo, the dark-haired Maazel was a child prodigy. Born in 1899 in Russia, where his mother was a singer and his father a pianist, he came to the United States with his family at the age of two, studied with his father and at fourteen became a protégé of the world-famous Austrian pianist and composer Leopold Godowsky. By nineteen Maazel had been a soloist with the Metropolitan Opera House orchestra and made his New York debut at Aeolian Hall.

Dark-haired, jowly Leopold Godowsky, Jr., was born in Chicago in 1900, where his father was performing; six weeks later, the family returned to Vienna, and Leo lived in Europe until he was fourteen and a half, studying the violin under his father's hypercritical glare. Then when World War I broke out, the Godowskys fled to America and settled in New York City. At the private Riverdale Country School in the Bronx, Godowsky met Leopold Damrosch Mannes, a young pianist with a musical pedigree equal to his own and an equally fierce enthusiasm for photography. After graduation, Mannes left for Harvard University to study physics and musicology, and Godowsky hied to the University of California, where he majored in physics and chemistry while playing the violin with the San Francisco and Los Angeles Philharmonic orchestras. He had returned to New York a few months before Lucille graduated from the American Academy.

Maazel was hard-working, disciplined and puritanical. Godowsky was brilliant, self-confident and seductive. Their rivalry for Lucille had been under way for some time and intensified when she sailed for Europe. "Beloved," Godowsky wrote after Lucille left,

> The bliss that was mine for a while, no treasure could buy. You lightened my despair. I felt the touch of two warm lips to mine. Your shimmery hair rippled over my eyes. I felt your soft body close to mine. Two white, gentle arms stole around me with passion confessed. You were mine for one moment of bliss. But alas it was only a dream. If loving is but dreaming, then let me never wake.
>
> Come back, Sweetheart, to me.
>
> L.

Both saw Lucille off on the ship and showered her with presents. Responding to Maazel's gifts in an unusually long (and unpunctuated) letter, Lucille teased him mercilessly, playing one against the other as she would frequently later in life with both men and women.

> On board R.M.S. "Olympic"
> Friday 22 1921

This is the 3rd day and still not sea sick, pretty good for a delicate thing like myself n'est-ce-pas.

Well, Marvine how many more surprises are you going to spring upon me. Isn't it good enough that you gave Ruth a fountain pen? Why give me one also; but that wasn't enough you had to give me another to write to my friends. I think they're beautiful I'm so thrilled with this silver one *with* which I am writing to you now.

I don't miss you as much as I thought I would. In fact I hardly miss you at all. How can I because everything about me comes from you. The first thing in the morning I use your comb, then comes all your nail files at once (Really kid, I almost cried with laughter when all those files popped out. However I was wise enough to take a few with me and Frances [Gershwin] gave me a beautiful manicuring set.)....After that's accomplished I take one of your mouchoires and perhaps a pin and then up for breakfast In the afternoon I have you with me again. Your writing tablet on my lap and your beautiful fountain pens. Then last but not least I use your rouge and lip stick for dinner. (I know you wouldn't like that but they came from you and you can't help minding that so much.)

Before retiring I read your letter, a chapter from Balzac and that ends the day with Marvine occupying most of it. So you can see I haven't much time to miss you; and what's more I like it much better this way. I don't want to miss you. This way I feel that you are with me.

I wrote to Leo telling him I didn't want him to change his attitude from that friendship feeling which he said he felt. By his letters I am a little worried and fear that my good intention one night must have renewed his old feelings. I've written quite plainly to him so that he shouldn't misunderstand my actions. I'm afraid it will upset him a great deal but please don't mention this to him . . .

To Godowsky she wrote a soft, youthfully serious letter:

Monday 25.1921

Leo,

Of all things I just reminded myself I forgot to thank you for your charming gifts. It was very lovely of you but quite unessessary [*sic*]. You gave me this beautiful pencil and it was foolish of you to go to all that trouble to get me that big box of Sherry's and that lovely red rose.

It was so pretty I hated to see it die so I was going to press it. But then I didn't like to spoil it by pressing it so I kept it all alone in my stateroom (the other flowers I had put on our dining table) It lasted longer than any of the others and when it was really dying out I wore it in my hair Now I am playing the funeral march for it

It is really sad thinking about it, so similar to life. First it was a beautiful red rose in full bloom and now it is withered and dried without a speck of its former beauty

So many things in life can be compared to this . . .

Really Leo your steamer letters frightened me. But when I think in what kind of mood you were in when you wrote them I can understand it a little. I am sure you aren't in that kind of mood now. So I shall not feel uneasy in writing to you the way I feel . . .

Godowsky pulled ahead in the race. When Lucille expressed concern about the tone of his letters, he apologized smoothly, reassuring her that "I love you for your sincere and noble character." He told her that he was probably sailing in June, to go "automobiling" through Central Europe and Italy, and would arrive in France in August. In fact in June he reached Paris and hastened to the address on the Rue Marbeau where Mademoiselle Lucille Wadler and her family were staying. During the next few days—"happy days," Godowsky later wrote, that "will live with me throughout my life"—he and Lucille strolled in the Bois de Boulogne, and Lucille again reprimanded him for not keeping his emotions in check.

Indeed on July 1, after Leo had traveled on to Austria, Lucille wrote, with a combination of teasing and youthful sincerity, that

> ... it is very sweet of you to miss me but if it is going to make you feel depressed and melancholy don't do it. You know Love often turns to Hate. So just think terrible things about me (all the things you don't like) and they sure are enough and then you will soon hate me and will feel much better about it. After that feeling is over we can start again and be life long friends. It is a wonderful feeling to feel that one has a real friend. Lovers can be had anytime but, it is only a friend that one can depend upon to stick and be true ...

Maazel soon learned about the romance, largely from Lucille's own letters. By turns Maazel scolded her, implored her to love him and disparaged Godowsky, accusing him of being a seducer. Maazel's letters were sometimes twenty-three-page marathons of recrimination followed by apologies and extravagant adoration, none of which appealed to Lucille. Adding to his dismay, she showed his words to Leo. Things came to a head in late July and early August, when Leo joined Lucille and her family at the seaside resort of Dinard, where Mayo was playing the violin at a reception attended by the Queen of Rumania. Sitting on a curb-stone in Dinard, Lucille angrily wrote Maazel, tersely defending her boyfriend against rumors of sexual escapades:

> Don't believe what you said about Leo. It is all false. You can be-lieve [it] if you want but, I prefer to believe Leo & he wouldn't lie to me. Don't be so glad to accuse people. He told me all the flirta-tions they had on the boat but he did not do what you think . . .

As Lucille sensed, Maazel's truth-telling was self-serving and self-righteously judgmental. But part of Maazel's frustration was that he imagined Lucille frolicking rather than improving herself as an artist, as he was trying to do back in New York and had done all his life. Unfor-tunately his way of expressing concern was to chastise. "Do you fail to realize that you are ruining the best in you by laying yourself open to a danger that no one but myself seems to worry about," he queried in Sep-tember. Free-spirited Lucille did not yet possess the focus that drove Maazel, Godowsky and Mayo. Maazel unwittingly aroused a tension that would infuse most of Lucille's significant relationships with men: she would engage their advice and guidance but want to maintain inde-pendence from their control. Maazel was controlling.

By accusing Godowsky of immoral behavior, Maazel had also proved disloyal, and Lucille prized loyalty. As artists and fellow pro-ducers would learn, once she committed to a person or project, she re-mained steadfast long after others would have jumped ship. Conversely she responded icily to infidelity. She punished Maazel by not writing for about two months and never really renewed their friendship. Dur-ing the next year Maazel's mournful, loving notes became fewer. He eventually settled in California, married, changed his first name to Marvin, and sustained a respectable if unspectacular concert career. They barely corresponded.

Lucille and Leo probably did not have an affair that summer of 1921. For all her flirting, Lucille was sexually inexperienced. The two were the same age, but emotionally and sexually Lucille was younger—and naïve about Godowsky's sophistication. Also Anny was around to ensure her daughter's virginity, and Lucille, despite a rebellious streak, was more middle-class than bohemian.

Godowsky returned to the States, while Lucille remained in Europe, and there is no record of further romantic involvement. Lucille headed toward theatre, Godowsky toward photography. In 1922, he and Mannes opened a color-film laboratory in New York, a venture that would eventually win them the backing of the Eastman Kodak Company and in 1935 lead to the development of Kodachrome film. Godowsky would become a millionaire. In 1930 he married Frances "Frankie" Gershwin, who was the sister of George, Ira and Arthur, had had a minor career as a singer and dancer, and whom, ironically, Lucille had known since she was a teenager. It was undoubtedly for the best. Self-absorbed Leo would not have been encouraging or tolerant of Lucille's producing career.

Ruth, too, was having a romance that summer of 1921. In New York the year before, Mayo had introduced her to a tall, lean Spanish-born painter named Francis Coradal-Cugat, and they had begun seeing each other. In July, Cugat, as his friends called him, sent Ruth a two-word telegram: "Come home." "Coming," she wired back, and on July 27 sailed for New York. There she found Cugat waiting for her, and also discovered that her father's personal and business affairs were even more uncertain than when she had left in April. Having little money of her own, she moved into Uncle Isidore's and Aunt Bertha's apartment, a five-story walk-up on the corner of Columbus Avenue and 87th Street where she slept in the living room. Despite Ruth's distress about the problems at home, in November she wrote an encouraging letter to her younger sister, who was now in Vienna studying acting and immersing herself in the city's rich cultural world. It was the sort of loving reassurance that endeared Ruth to Lucille:

> Dearest, Darling—Lu—
>
> I'm so glad you are observing so much and learning—absorbing and what not—all to make you a very great person—and to know that you are my sister. That is the happiest thought I have. I was particularly careful not to mention in any of my letters how much I care for you—miss you and long, long desperately for you. Every night I dream that you are back and together we are working. Sometimes I imagine if I could only tell you these things I'd feel better. But I don't wish to influence you. I want you to stay there and learn. You'll know that you'll never get another chance to see these places. And I feel that when you do come back I will enjoy and appreciate you all the more.
>
> The penciled letter you copied from Dad, sounds worse than what really is. I seldom see him—which means quiet and peace. He probably thinks I write mother all the dirt that goes on but I wouldn't, not because I'm afraid of him—but I do not wish to annoy her. You'll never regret it darling—if you spare her any annoyance. Even if friends are lacking there still she can enjoy it. Here *everything* will be lacking. As I said he probably thinks I write about him so he tries to invent things about me ...

Ruth also teased Lucille affectionately about her younger sister's attempt to offer financial advice. With Harry's finances in disarray, and less money coming from New York, Lucille was apparently trying to restrict herself to spending no more than ten cents a day and suggested Ruth do the same. But as Ruth pointed out, ten cents in Germany meant perhaps thousands of marks; in New York City it bought one bus fare.

Marvine Maazel had been right. During the summer Lucille had given little thought to her acting career, although she had snagged a bit of publicity. In Trouville, the English-French *Daily Mail* ran a photograph of Lucille posing in a beach chair near one of the resort's elegant striped tents. They shot her smiling happily at the camera, her thick hair blowing haphazardly around her shoulders, sporting the bright colors which she loved to wear: "Miss Wadler, of the New York Dramatic Academy, taking her morning sun-bath in an orange bathing dress and a red silk wrap."

But when fall came, she was studying with Arnold Korff, an American-born character actor who had grown up in Austria and performed in both the United States and Europe. With connections to the avant-garde theatre director Max Reinhardt, and the outstanding stage and film actor Emil Jannings, Korff probably helped Lucille make a contact in the German film industry. In December Ruth wrote that she had heard Lucille was "working on a picture in Berlin" and asked for details, since Lucille had reverted to her habit of being a reluctant correspondent. The picture to which Ruth referred was *Peter der Grosse,* or *Peter the Great,* a silent feature released in 1922 that starred the thirty-seven-year-old Jannings as the Russian tsar. Lucille was only an extra—a lady-in-waiting. But she must have found this taste of movie-making a delicious appetizer, especially in company with an actor of Jannings' stature. She could feel that, in a small way, it vindicated her choice of a career.

If *Peter der Grosse* led to any significant film work for Lucille, she never spoke about it. Following the example of Mayo and her mother, she constantly collected clippings and photographs about herself, and she surely would have preserved a notice or mentioned it to reporters in later years. Instead she spent much of 1922 exhausting herself to the point of illness with concert-and theatre-going, parties and late nights spent with new friends and attentive young men. Maazel, had he known, would have lectured her severely.

But she did make one other film in Berlin: a two-reeler called *Freddys Liebestod*, or *Freddys Lovedeath*, produced by the American Continental Film Association, directed by John D. Reldaw with Siegfried Dessauer and released in May 1923. The title hinted that this was comedy, perhaps in more ways than one. Under the name "Lucy Larkin," a demure Lucille played the lovely Dolly, whose fiancé Freddy may have killed himself and might be writing her from beyond the grave. And while there really was a German director named Siegfried Dessauer, upon closer inspection the name "Reldaw" spelled backwards becomes "Wadler," suggesting that Mayo, Anny, Lucille, and even Seymour took matters into their own hands and made this film.

Seymour returned to the States in July 1922 with the intention of going into business. He would have no success. Bright but increasingly adrift psychologically, he was always to be odd man out in the Wadler family. He was the eccentric Wadler, the one who obsessed about nutrition and lectured his relatives on their poor eating habits while secretly going down to the Lower East Side and gorging on cheesecake. In 1966 he founded a short-lived Marriage Museum near Lincoln Center, although his own marriage to a woman more than thirty years younger was falling apart, largely because he was abusive. During the 1950s and '60s he survived by working for Mayo's public relations agency and living off the income from a trust established by Lucille's husband.

After Seymour sailed home, Anny and Lucille remained in Europe with Mayo for another six months. There was no urgent reason to come back, according to Ruth's letters. On June 8, 1922, Ruth reported to Lucille in uncharacteristically acerbic fashion that she had dropped in on their father's shop, to show him photographs of Anny and Lucille taken in Europe and return some reviews of Mayo's concerts:

> ... It was the first time in (5) five months that I had any communication with him / either by phone, letter, or sight. In other

words he was dead to me for 5 months *or* twenty (20) weeks. At
last I saw him.

I acted as though it was so natural for me to see him. I merely
said, Hello Dad, here are some pictures & criticisms. He made
some cheap remark that "if he were younger he'd propose to
mother." Well nothing else was said and I was about to go.... .
Then I said you needed some clothes. He asked me to pick them
out for you. There wasn't much of a selection. After that I waited
for him to say something but he didn't so I said goodbye and I left.
He never even suggested that I take some rags for myself. Later he
called Bert [Bertha] and asked me to come and get some for myself. I couldn't take much as there wasn't anything decent. So that
was the first time in all this while that I came in contact with him.
The next day... Dad came up, paid Bert & myself a visit. It was
like entertaining a stranger. I really had no feeling for that man
who neglected even the most common considerations a father has
for a child.

Dismissing her father, Ruth, now twenty-four, turned her attention to
painting and to Cugat, whom she married in a civil ceremony at the Municipal Building on November 28, 1922. Two months later, on January
26, 1923, Lucille and her mother sailed back to New York.

When she imagined the name "Lucille Wadler" on a marquee, she did
not like it. For one thing, it was too much like "Lucille Watson," a character actress who had also graduated from the American Academy of
Dramatic Arts. She wanted a name that caught the ear and eye, was easy
to remember and recognize. One day soon after Lucille returned from
Europe, she, Ruth and the Romanian-Jewish writer Konrad Bercovici

sat around inventing stage names, and out of the dozens they thought up, she chose "Lucille Lortel," liking its alliterative sound.

The first time Lucille saw her new name in print was in a magazine of the rag trade called *Apparel Producer*—promotion most likely arranged by Harry. The blurb below her photograph, a graduation picture, announced that "Lucille Lortel, talented young American actress, recently arrived from Europe where she featured in notable film creations, will shortly appear in Broadway stage production."

Lucille and Anny returned to 420 Riverside Drive, but Lucille had been away from home for nearly two years, and the changes she confronted were enormous. Her family was scattered. Her father was no longer around on a regular basis. Mayo was in Europe. Ruth and Cugat were living in an apartment at 556 West 156th Street with Cugat's brothers Albert, Henry and Xavier, the future band leader.

Soon she would face the reality that the comfort she had known since she was a teenager on Riverside Drive had evaporated. For the rest of the 1920s, she and Anny, and sometimes Seymour, would live in a series of small apartments on the Upper West Side, while her mother worked at Equitable and Lucille made the rounds of producers' offices. One day her friend and fellow actor Luther Adler asked to borrow five dollars. He said, "I have to have this money," and so she loaned it to him. And through the years she would see him and she would say, "You know, that five dollars . . . " And one day he told her, "You know, Lucille, I'm never going to pay you that money back." And she said, "Why not?" And he said, "Because I want you to remember how young and how poor we all were when we started out."

People who knew Lucille long after she married and became wealthy were alternately amused or scathing about her bursts of frugality, or as some pointedly described it, her tightness with a dollar. "Tight as the skin on an onion," was how Hope Alswang described it. She might ask an acquaintance to share a cab after the theatre, but she would not contribute to the fare. As producer of the White Barn, she fought Actors' Equity Association long and hard to preserve an agreement by which she made a fixed annual donation to Equity Library Theatre, instead of paying her performers. Food in the White Barn's kitchen was under lock and key, so an actor wanting an emergency sandwich at two in the afternoon was out of luck.

The frugality sometimes resembled hoarding. Her friends observed in later years that she often scooped plates of petits fours into her pocketbook at receptions and took packages of food home from restaurants and parties. But rather than eat the food immediately, she would keep the parcels in her freezer for months. They theorized that she was behaving from some long-ago deprivation.

Perhaps she was expressing a fear of never having enough and wanting more, or a desire to hold onto and control what she already possessed—anxieties that had developed during childhood when Harry and Anny moved the family from apartment to apartment and struggled financially. Or possibly at some point during her growing up Lucille absorbed the trait from her mother. When Anny took charge of buying food at Lucille's estate in Westport, during the fifties and early sixties, she was known to send someone out for a quarter pound of cheese and weigh it on a scale to make sure nobody had cheated her.

Whatever the sources of Lucille's behavior, she could not have felt secure during the 1920s. Columns of scribbled figures referring to rent and telephone bills testify to her attempt to budget and live within limited means.

But Lucille also possessed determination, charm and energy, qualities that an ambitious actress needed in order to compete with the hundreds of other young women who aimed to be the next Hazel Dawn or Jeanne Eagels, two of the most popular stage actresses of that era.

In the 1920s, the usual way for an actress to find work was to go from one producer's office to another and try to talk her way past the secretary. If she was fortunate, she might have a letter of introduction from another producer, a well-known actor or one of the few agents who handled the unknown. The veteran dramatic agent Wales Winter recommended Lucille for a couple of shows. "Are you casting today?" would be Lucille's first question, and if the answer was no, down the stairs she would go and on to the next office. Or she might receive a tip that one of the Selwyn brothers or A.H. Woods or David Belasco was auditioning, and she would rush to the theatre to see if she could read for them.

Once in a production, Lucille had to use her wits to survive financially and artistically. If the show were out of town, sometimes producers provided transportation, but not always. Out of her meager weekly salary, Lucille might have to pay for bus or train fare, meals and a room in the local hotel or boardinghouse. If a part called for contemporary clothes, she was expected to provide them. Actors' Equity did not yet require producers to pay performers for rehearsal, but since there was usually little rehearsal anyway, that hardly mattered. Performers received sides—pages of script with only their cues and their lines. Chances are Lucille saw only one full script during her acting career, for *The Man Who Laughed,* the one-act melodrama in which she toured with Sessue Hayakawa. As for holidays, if Lucille were unlucky enough to be touring at Christmastime, she might get the day off but she would not be paid. Perhaps the memory of Christmases on the road influenced Lucille when she produced Off Broadway; she was known to keep a show running during the holidays, even if it was not doing well.

She first appeared on stage professionally the week of May 5, 1924, with the Proctor Players in Albany, New York. Founded by Frederick Francis Proctor, a one-time circus performer who owned chains of vaudeville theatres, largely in New York state, the Proctor Players operated out of the famous Harmanus Bleecker Hall, which seated more than two thousand people and boasted, among other things, a painted asbestos curtain depicting Henry Hudson's ship the *Half Moon* arriving at the site of the future city of Albany.

Lucille's contract called for her to play roles "as cast" for at least ten performances a week (there were matinees almost daily), for which she received her transportation and $50 a week. During three weeks with the Proctor Players she drew minor parts, but parts that exploited her sexual allure. She played Gypsy Montrose, one of several chorus girls with hearts of gold in Avery Hopwood's 1919 comedy *The Gold Diggers,* and she was a film actress named Dot Madison in *The Demi-Virgin,* Hopwood's 1921 farce about a movie star whose marriage is interrupted on her wedding night. In the opening of *Demi-Virgin,* which takes place at the fictional Laska Motion Picture Studio in Hollywood, Dot plays a model who is auditioning for an artist. The action called for Lucille to wear a one-piece black bathing suit and green marabou cape. Turning her back to the audience, she gathered the cape about her, looked over her shoulder and winked knowingly, and let the cape slip down around her shoulders. At another point, Dot suggests a card game called Stripping Cupid, which ends with her in her underwear.

Lucille felt excited to land a professional acting job and to be taking care of herself. But knowing her family's high expectations, and being a proud person in her own right, she was self-conscious about the smallness of the roles and the quality of the plays. This was not, after all, high art. During one performance, she scribbled a note to her family on the back of a program:

> Dearest folks. Am at the matinée between the acts. Here is a clipping of the cast and some program. Am having great fun in this performance. Wish you could be here. Don't be disappointed if you don't see any separate criticism of me. They can't criticize everyone

just the main characters. Gee Mom. I wish Ruth & you could see me just once in this. Don't bring anyone else not even Mayo.

Anny probably accompanied Lucille to Albany to see her safely settled in, but it is unlikely that she saw her daughter act; she was in New York waiting to hear if Mayo was returning from Europe. On May 4, she wrote Lucille in her misspelled English "Say kidd I miss you terribly." But with her usual tactlessness where Mayo was concerned, Anny weighed a visit to Albany against her son's arrival. "It all dipends upon what news I get about Mayo. I would allmost rather be with you. so you can imagen how I feel."

In June, Lucille traveled to the manufacturing city of Lewiston, Maine, for two weeks with the newly formed Twin City Players. Started by one Joseph Lawren with a playwright and Columbia University professor named J. Kenyon Nicholson, the Players opened to high hopes and a sold-out crowd at Lewiston's Music Hall. "The boxes," wrote a local reporter, were "draped with the national colors" and "filled with friends, one being given over to the mayoralty party from Auburn," Lewiston's urban twin across the river.

That first week the company presented *My Lady Friends*, a light comedy written in 1919 by Emil Nyitray and Frank Mandel and soon to become the basis for the musical *No, No, Nanette*. "Lucile Lortelle [*sic*]," wrote a reviewer, was one of three young women who "made the most of lesser parts."

The second week, the Players offered *Kick In*, Willard Mack's 1914 drama about New York City lowlifes and the tough-talking police who put them away ("kick in" was slang for "give up"). Acting a sharp-tongued, supposedly "retired" shoplifter named Memphis Bessie, described in the script as "dressed up like a house, flashy and in very bad taste," Lucille got the chance to sling some smart lingo, as in this moment in Inspector Garvey's office:

GARVEY:... Benny's in trouble.

BESSIE: My Gawd—so is Europe. Why bother me with it?....

GARVEY: You ought to be tickled to death, it's breaking the way
it is, for you.

BESSIE: Oh, I am. I am so happy I could dive through a port
hole and never muss my hair...

Unfortunately Twin City's second week in Lewiston was also its last.
The good people of that town, supposedly avid theatregoers during the
winter, did not take to drama during the summer. A farewell article in
the *Lewiston Journal* conveyed the future plans of company members:

Miss Lortel goes back to New York. She has an offer to go into a
musical comedy "The Purple Cow," inspired by Gellett [*sic*]
Burgess verses, and will have four songs for which she means to
prepare herself by taking singing lessons this summer. She also has
a chance at the Marigny Theatre with the only English-speaking
stock company in Paris, but thinks she prefers to remain on this
side of the water.

The offers may have existed—a musical based on the famous poem by
Gelett Burgess *was* produced that fall in Washington, D.C.—and they
suggest that Lucille was trying to climb to higher theatrical ground:
Burgess, who lived in San Francisco, was reputed to be a literary aes-
thete. At any event, it sounded good. At twenty-three, Lucille had mas-
tered an out-of-work actress's cardinal rule, which was to talk as though
great opportunities were just around the corner. She was also learning
how to promote herself to the press.

By the end of August she had signed with the Myrkle-Harder Players
to tour six plays in repertory around New York and New Jersey. Once
again the vehicles were vapid Broadway hits, and as in Albany she

worked hard for her money: eight performances a week, sometimes more, and a different play each day. But she earned $60 each week, ten dollars more than she had made in Albany, and she drew larger parts.

She made her Broadway debut on February 23, 1925, at the Selwyn Theatre on West 42nd Street. The play was a windy item called *Two By Two*. Produced by Jessy Trimble, Inc., and written by one John Turner and a veteran character actress named Eugenie Woodward, it purported to be a comedy about an attractive widow left waiting at the Marriage License Bureau, while her young second-husband-to-be elopes with her daughter. A suave unknown actor named Howard Lindsay played the traitorous boyfriend. Lucille was one of several women in the License Bureau, along with a future film star, Una Merkel.

The production had had two performances at the Stamford Theatre in Connecticut, and in the opinion of New York reviewers should not have pressed its luck. The disgruntled *Variety* critic called it "premature and abortive as a Broadway attraction." The critic for the *American* declared that it "lacked one solitary bright line." The playwright John Turner was really Miss Jessy Trimble, and although the director, Clarence Derwent, tried manfully, he could not get "the two little old ladies" as he called the authors to cut reams of superfluous dialogue. Sixteen performances after *Two By Two* marched onto Broadway, it exited.

Despite the abrupt end to Lucille's Broadway debut, the adventure ultimately paid a dividend. Derwent, a gentlemanly British-born actor and director, became Lucille's friend and a crucial supporter. During the 1940s and '50s, when he was president of Actors' Equity and then of the American National Theatre and Academy (ANTA), he would ease Lucille's way with both the union and ANTA.

Given *Two By Two*'s fast demise, it is easy to understand why Lucille never mentioned it in later years. Describing her acting career to the press, she always asserted that her Broadway arrival occurred in the

Theatre Guild's production of George Bernard Shaw's *Caesar and Cleopatra*, which opened on April 13, 1925, at the new Guild Theatre on West 52nd Street. Undoubtedly she also believed that the production's stars added luster to her own reputation. The lean-faced British actor Lionel Atwill played Caesar, and the diminutive (and miscast) Helen Hayes acted Shaw's mischievous Egyptian queen.

Lucille's account of her participation came with a good story, one which she loved to tell. "I did the harpist. I had very beautiful hands then," she told playwright Corinne Jacker, who taped an interview with her during the 1980s. "Then I played the strumpet on the wharf. Philip Moeller, who was the director, had five men following me and gave me a line to say which George Bernard Shaw did not write. And Moeller said, 'Do it very quickly.' I was supposed to say to these men following me—and one was Harold Clurman, who was also assistant stage manager—I was supposed to say, 'No, no, no, I'll have nothing to do with you.' But of course that was my big moment. I wasn't going to say that fast. So I stopped in the middle of the stage and said it very slowly: 'No—no—no. I'll have nothing to do with you.' Moeller said, 'Will you stop that? Do you want Shaw to get after me? Get off stage fast, or I'll cut the line out.' And that was my big moment in the Theatre Guild."

Caesar and Cleopatra finished its six-week run at the end of May, and Lucille made the rounds. Broadway producers, then as now often lacking in imagination, looked at the shapely dark-eyed actress and typed her as a sultry foreigner or a sullied woman, preferably both. "I had long dark hair, and they always engaged me for exotic parts," Lucille told an interviewer years later. That August she went into David Belasco's popular production of Willard Mack's *The Dove*, a torrid melodrama set in Mexicana, Mexico, which had reopened at the Empire after several weeks' hiatus before its national tour. Staged by the great Belasco himself, it starred the stout character actor Holbrook Blinn and a twenty-seven-year-old sensation named Judith Anderson. Lucille was cast as

Inez, a decorative female in a den of South-of-the-border iniquity called Brayfield's Gambling House.

When the show traveled to Philadelphia she went along but, believing there was no chance of a larger part, and feeling that it was better to stay in New York than vanish from sight with a long tour, she left the production before it moved on to Cleveland. It was a risky choice; by October most new productions were already cast. The middle-aged Blinn, who had found Lucille a sympathetic listener for his romantic troubles, wrote her a letter of introduction to Robert McLaughlin, whose allegorical spectacle *The Pearl of Great Price* had been waiting off stage for years. Nothing came of it. In December she had a bit of luck: the producer A.H. Woods used her as one of the "mice," or prostitutes, in John Colton's new melodrama, *The Shanghai Gesture*, which was playing Newark and Atlantic City, New Jersey, before coming into New York. But Woods fired his leading lady, the tempestuous Mrs. Leslie Carter, and the production closed in Jersey to regroup. In February 1926, at the last moment, Lucille went into Owen Davis's adaptation of F. Scott Fitzgerald's *The Great Gatsby*, in which she played a flapper and, if nothing else, got to pose provocatively in a bathing suit. *Gatsby* closed suddenly in May, but by then Lucille had gotten a break.

One Man's Woman was not the sort of drama that Mayo or anybody else with literary taste would have championed. Written and produced by a mediocre talent named Michael Kallesser, it was set on a sugar planta- tion in Hawaii and involved a romance between the plantation's misog- ynist boss, Kenneth Regan, and a woman with whom he falls in love only to discover one drunken night that she works in a brothel. Lucille played the plantation owner's daughter, Clara Rathboone, who loves Ken but learns to accept defeat gracefully. Louis Kennel's elaborate settings in- cluded a volcano, which erupted at the moment Ken is smitten.

The critics gleefully sharpened their pencils. "It is still raining South Sea island plays," jeered Frank Vreeland of the *Telegram* on May 26.

" 'The Half Caste' had no sooner closed at the National Theatre than 'One Man's Woman' opened last night at the Forty-eighth Street, discarding the yacht of the earlier play but apparently taking over some of the ukulele scratchers..."

Brooks Atkinson, who had recently been appointed drama critic at the *New York Times,* complained that "the banalities of old-time theatricalisms drenched the situations, the lines and the characters. And the jaded first-nighters, in a holiday mood after a dreary season, giggled, cackled, snorted, guffawed and expressed a perverse pleasure in many discourteous fashions."

The astounded reviewer for the *Evening Graphic* predicted that the drama was "destined for a short stay." He was wrong. Not only had it sold out during a pre-Broadway week at the Werba Theatre in Brooklyn, but despite the giggles of the opening-night crowd, it ran for 158 performances on Broadway, ensuring Lucille at least $75 a week for many months.

Lucille herself received little mention in the reviews—the critics spent most of their words damning the script. But her softly smiling face, ringed with dark hair and a white ribbon—photographed, sketched, silhouetted—appeared in so many newspapers so frequently, a reader would have thought she was the star.

With an ingratiating charm and an instinct for cultivating men in a position to help her, Lucille had made a friend of the show's clever press agent, Richard Maney, who was doing everything *he* could to keep the show open.

In his 1957 autobiography *Fanfare,* Maney wrote that "press agentry is no business for people with nerves." He had none. "By such dodges as matinees 'For Women Only,' and by stressing its carnal content, I contributed to the twenty-week run of *One Man's Woman,* one of the most odious plays ever loosed on Manhattan Island," he wrote. Eventually he would be known as the greatest flack of them all. But in 1926 he just wanted to make a salary and earn a reputation for keeping a show running. Lucille wanted publicity. He placed items about her every chance he got.

Certainly the publicity helped her social life. She lived with her mother in an apartment so tight and crowded she was embarrassed to invite dates inside, but she liked parties and dancing too much not to enjoy herself. Each night when the curtain came down on *One Man's Woman,* Lucille and her friends piled into taxis. They headed for bashes in Greenwich Village, and when those tired they drove up to Harlem to hear Luckey Roberts' band at Connie's Inn or, if their escorts were flush, stepped into the swank Cotton Club for the enlivening sounds of Andy Preer's Syncopators. The federal government's prohibition against alcohol, rather than inhibiting people's fun, seemed to stimulate it. Lucille usually drank little—she hated heavy drinking—but like many another pretty actress in her twenties, she spent a good part of each night slipping in and out of speakeasies.

As for socializing with her family, Lucille missed Ruth and Cugat, who had moved to California in 1925. But that year Mayo had finally returned from Europe, and Lucille and Anny saw a good deal of him. To his mother's deep disappointment, but possibly to Mayo's secret relief, his concert career had waned. A fine technician, he lacked that intangible brilliance which makes an extraordinary artist. He was also a proponent of modern music, a taste that did not endear him to traditional symphony orchestras.

One day in 1926 he walked over to the Capitol Grand Theatre, a movie palace at Broadway and 51st Street managed by a showman who called himself Major Edward Bowes. Mayo expected to be hired as a solo violinist with the Capitol's resident orchestra, an ensemble of symphonic dimensions that played during the daily showings of silent films, elaborate stage shows and for a radio broadcast every Sunday morning. Instead, the musical director, David Mendoza, asked him to be an assistant conductor with Eugene Ormandy. Mayo had never held a baton before, but he watched for two weeks and then went into the pit. He intended to take the job for a few months; he stayed eighteen years. Along the way he changed his name to Waldo Mayo, as though to separate himself from that earlier identity into which he and his family had poured so much effort and expectation.

On October 2, 1926, the volcano in *One Man's Woman* erupted one last time. Lucille was not out of work for long, however. A quick study, and determined to take whatever came her way if she could get on stage, she often went into shows on short notice after they had been running a while. At the Eltinge on November 3, she stepped into the part of a vivacious maid who dances the Charleston in William Anthony McGuire's affable comedy, *If I Was Rich*. The following February at the Princess Theatre, she took over the leading role of Elsa, the chief siren in William Francis Dugan's and H. F. Maltby's *The Virgin Man*. The comedy's plot was trivial enough: a sexually innocent Yale undergraduate meets three sophisticated women in the big city and barely escapes a fate worse than death. But *Virgin Man* had attracted a measure of notoriety. On February 9 the New York City police had descended on the Princess and, as part of a sweep intended to root out indecency in the theatre, hauled the cast and playwright Dugan to jail for violating that section of the Penal Code which forbade production of "obscene and immoral plays." Other supposedly offensive items raided that night were Mae West's comedy *Sex* and *The Captive*, Edouard Bourdet's drama about a young girl's passionate love for an older woman. *Virgin Man's* cast and playwright posted bail and eventually appeared at a trial before three judges in the Court of Special Sessions, where they and the producers were found guilty, fined and given suspended sentences. Benefiting from the publicity, *Virgin Man's* ticket sales jumped, even though its original leading lady, Dorothy Hall, left the show (she told one newspaper that she believed in censorship). Lucille stepped into the role. Elsa was obviously an attention-getting part, and Lucille got to spend a good deal of time in silky underclothes, kissing and caressing the determinedly unresponsive Yalie. She went into the production "on less than twenty-four hours notice," according to a squib in a New York daily, and "didn't miss a single cue."

Meanwhile, John Colton's *The Shanghai Gesture* had opened on Broadway.

Colton had scored a sensation in 1922 with *Rain,* which he adapted with Clemence Randolph from Somerset Maugham's story of a missionary who encounters a prostitute on a Pacific island. His new melodrama transported audiences to another exotic realm—Shanghai, China, in the 1920s—in four acts teeming with sex, racism and retribution.

The central figure is obsessive, conniving Mother Goddam. Born a Manchu princess, she abandoned her heritage years earlier for a love affair with a British trader named Guy Charteris, by whom she had a child. Charteris deserted her to marry an Englishwoman and literally sold his Chinese lover down the river to the junk men. Charteris' wife died in childbirth, and he has raised a girl whom he supposes to be their daughter, Poppy.

Now Goddam runs the Angry Dragon, the largest brothel in the world, a place of tiered galleries where the "mice" sit in cages and sing seductively to the men who look them over. She plots revenge against Charteris, who has become one of the richest businessmen in Shanghai. Inviting him to a formal dinner, she sells a girl in front of his eyes as he once sold her and afterward informs him that the girl is his English daughter, whom, long ago, she snatched from his home and replaced with their own, knowing that Charteris would raise the child in an elite European world.

But the revenge is on Mother Goddam. The beautiful Poppy visits the brothel that night in the company of her Japanese lover Prince Oshima. The young woman's avid degeneracy disgusts Mother Goddam. Then, when Poppy and Charteris accidentally come face to face, Goddam learns to her horror that Poppy is the daughter Charteris has brought up. Revolted by what the girl has become, Goddam strangles her and sends her tumbling down the giant Green Stairway of the Angry Dragon. At the end, in a gesture of acceptance and remorse, she gives Charteris back his true English daughter.

Florence Reed, an illustrious actress with a penchant for what were then called "Oriental" parts, had replaced Mrs. Leslie Carter as Mother Goddam. Reed's costumes alone inspired awe. She wore elaborate head-dresses and brocade gowns with ropes of pearls that dripped to below her knees. Her black hair was pulled tightly back from her face, made up in stark white except for dark, slanting eyebrows and a pointy, red mouth. She looked vacant and sinister. When Mother Goddam rose at the dinner to denounce Charteris, and Reed spat out the angry woman's avenging words, delighted audiences erupted in thunderous applause. At the end, when Mother Goddam chased Poppy up three rows of galleries and then pushed her down the stairs, Reed filled the hall with sobs and lamentation.

Her bravura performance, the opulent settings and Guthrie McClintic's astute direction made *Shanghai Gesture* a hit on Broadway and on the road. Actors and actresses trooped to see it, eager to study up the meaty parts in case they received a call.

A.H. Woods called Lucille in August 1927 and hired her at $200 a week to go to Kansas City, Missouri, to act Poppy opposite Reed's Goddam. On September 25, Lucille boarded a train in Manhattan, and on the twenty-seventh she was rehearsing with the company. Five days later she opened at Kansas City's Shubert Theatre.

Poppy was the best role of Lucille's career. On the surface the character is a well-bred English girl, all proper speech and manners. Underneath she longs for sensual gratification. When Poppy enters in Act I, the playwright describes her as "exquisite as a summer morning. Everything about her spells youth and *beauté de diable*. She is small, slender, willowy and graceful—a gentlewoman to the tips of her fingers, yet there is an alien something in her brunette beauty, something a little odd and fantastic." Feminist critics would have called Poppy a male fantasy, for beneath the ladylike veneer lives a wild creature who drinks, smokes opium and wants a man's sexual freedom. "Oh, I am a bad one!" she drunkenly tells Mother Goddam in one of the play's daringly frank moments.

> Yes, I'm a bad one! That's what I want to be!—want to live my life like a man! All most women ever get is the same four legs in a bed always—always!—That's marriage! Ugh!—Horrible! Low—I wouldn't stand it—not one minute!

The part gave Lucille an opportunity to show off her range. In Act I she had to be demure, in Act III Poppy passionately throws her arms around Oshima and makes love to him, then smokes opium and passes out. By Act IV Lucille played a staggering, drugged wreck, who confronts Goddam with all the venom she possesses.

It should have been an exceptional opportunity for an actress. The play received low grades from moralizing critics, but audiences cheered the turbulent action. Lucille's notices were complimentary, if not ecstatic. The *Kansas City Star* observed that "Lucille Lortell [*sic*] ... won a deserved hand of approval in her big scene in the third act." *The Independent*'s critic wrote, "Lucille Lortell gave the part full measure," and the reviewer for the *Kansas City Times* wrote,

> Lucille Lortell is Poppy, the unprincipled (to put it mildly) girl in the case and handles two most difficult scenes in a manner that rescues them from the unpleasant, not to say offensive, taste they well might leave were they played by a less capable actress. Miss Lortell is pretty, too, and that is always a help.

But Lucille's memories of the stint were unpleasant. Nobody had taught her how to fall without hurting herself, and she was often black and blue. "I remember bouncing down those goddamn stairs every night," she told Vincent Curcio. More importantly, she did not get along with Reed. Lucille missed cues, which understandably upset the star, who gave her "a very strong talking to about that." Lucille continued with the tour to St. Louis but not beyond. Quite possibly Reed had her fired. In any case Poppy was not Lucille's sort of part. The so-called "bad" women Lucille played were usually seductive or tough on the outside. Poppy was lascivious to her core.

Early in 1928 Lucille went out on the Keith and Orpheum vaudeville circuits with *The Man Who Laughed,* a dreadful sketch by Edgar A. Woolf that headlined the handsome, thirty-nine-year-old silent film star Sessue Hayakawa. The Japanese-born actor played jealous Otoya, who, once left for dead in Nagasaki, now searches the world for his lover, a half-Japanese, half-Spanish dancer named Rosieta. He finds her at last in a run-down lodging house on the Barbary Coast, where she is the captive of the thug named Jim who had almost murdered him. Otoya feels like killing Rosieta. But weeping on her knees, she declares her love for him, and with one quick throw of his knife he kills Jim instead. Sweeping Rosieta up in his arms, he curses "the dirty dog, lying there to die upon the floor" and goes out "laughing—laughing—laughing!!!!"

Vaudeville had always provided actors with chances to work between legitimate engagements; brief plays shared the bill with singers and dancers, comedy turns and animal acts. For Hayakawa, who had left Hollywood around 1922 and returned to the stage, vaudeville was an excellent showcase, for he wanted to prove that he could speak well enough to work in talking pictures.

The tour was ideal for Lucille, too, and in later years she spoke about it as the pinnacle of her acting career. Although she once again played an exotic, she played her at the Palace Theatre in New York City, the top vaudeville house in the nation. The only woman in a cast of four, Lucille felt like a star acting opposite a star. She received fan mail on the road, and at her request, the production's management wrote Van Raalte & Co. and asked the famous lingerie manufacturer to supply Lucille with stockings "at a wholesale rate," because "the action of the piece is such that regardless of the quality of the stocking, two pair on an average are used weekly," and "she insists that your hose is the only kind she can wear." Lucille and the debonair Hayakawa got along splendidly, cutting up between performances and palling around. Lucille always maintained that their flirtatious behavior was to cover up Hayakawa's real affair: at the time, the married Hayakawa was seeing an actress named Ruth Noble, with whom he had a child.

The tour took Lucille north to Canada and west to California, where she visited Ruth and Cugat, who were living in West Hollywood. In the sunlight of California, Ruth was painting freely. An exhibition of her work in Los Angeles showed impressionistic, color-drenched views of the jagged Sierra Madre Mountains and delicate landscapes of barren sycamore trees in Malibu. She also painted several female nudes, but their expressionless faces belied their fulsome bodies, suggesting emptiness and depression within.

In New York Cugat had worked in the art department of Vitagraph's motion picture studios. In Hollywood he was an art director for Douglas Fairbanks, Sr., at United Artists, and Ruth had even appeared in a few films. Their involvement with the film industry rekindled Lucille's yearning to get into movies, and in the summer of 1928 she wrote to David Mendoza, Mayo's well-connected musical director, asking if he could help her do just that. In response to her cross-country plea, Mendoza wrote:

> Your letter to hand (right hand) and I promise you I will do everything in my power to enable you to get into the movies. Though

why you should want to, in God's name, I don't know, especially as
you still claim to be a virgin.

However, fortunately there happens to be in New York just now
the brother of Norma Shearer with whom I have had occasion to
do some work—and quite a charming fellow. As soon as I get an
opportunity, I will try to get a letter from him either to his sister or
his brother-in-law, who is none other than Irving Thalberg, the big
shot at the studio.

There is no record of whether Lucille met Thalberg or anybody else
at Metro-Goldwyn-Mayer. But back in New York in 1929 she did make
the fifteen-minute film of *The Man Who Laughed.* Called *The Man Who
Laughed Last,* it was one of the earliest movies to have sound recorded on
discs, and she was enormously proud of it.

The Man Who Laughed was Lucille's last significant acting job on the
stage. In 1929 Lucille again dove into New York's night life. She was
seen at the opening of the new Romany Marie's on Washington
Square, mingling with artists like the Japanese sculptor Isamu Noguchi
and the Russian sculptor Alexander Archipenko. She regularly joined
the throng at George and Ira Gershwin's adjoining penthouses on
Riverside Drive.

Lucille and Anny had moved into a small apartment in the respectable Mayflower Hotel, at 60th Street and Central Park West, and
the rest of the family had also settled temporarily in the city. Mayo, now
concertmaster for the Capitol orchestra, had met a sculptor and former
actress named Frances Grace Jones, and they were living a few strides
from Central Park on West 72nd Street, in a residential hotel called the
Oliver Cromwell. Ruth and Cugat had returned from California and set
up their easels in an urban aerie at the opposite end of West 72nd Street,
overlooking the Hudson River. North light poured into their thirteenth-
floor penthouse, and there Cugat and Ruth painted. Under the name

Ruth Ramon, Lucille's sister earned money drawing elegantly gowned women for R.H. Macy advertisements and sketching celebrities for the entertainment pages of the *New York Post*.

When the stock market plummeted in October 1929, Broadway producers shivered in their fur-collared coats. Lucille had trouble finding work. She appeared in a short-lived farce, *For Ladies Only*, which played the Brandt's Carlton Jamaica Theatre in Queens in 1930 but never came into Manhattan. That year she also made several short films at the Brooklyn studios of the Vitaphone Corporation, which Warner Bros. and Western Electric had formed in 1926 to explore a sound-on-disc system that could synchronize words and images (the system was abandoned around 1931 in favor of sound-on-film). One was *Grounds for Murder*, which featured the limpid-eyed stage actress Phoebe Foster and poked fun at a married woman's devotion to murder trials, while *Everything Happens to Me* was a comic short directed by Arthur Hurley, who had staged Sigmund Romberg's 1926 Broadway musical *The Desert Song*. *Gypsy Code*, another marvel from Edgar A. Woolf, starred well-muscled Roy D'Arcy as the gypsy Demetru. Lucille, costumed in the loose-fitting bodice and skirt that were somebody's idea of gypsy garb, earned $250 playing his wife, Maria.

Lucille did not give up her acting career—it was not in her nature to give up. But she had to face that she was nearly thirty years old and had not become the star she dreamed of being. She had considerable assets for a performer: beauty, grace, vivacity. "She had a sense of theatre," observed the dancer and choreographer Donald Saddler, who became a good friend during the 1980s. "Maybe it was because of the era she came from, when ladies came to the doorway and paused for a moment before they entered a room, for she did know how to make an entrance."

But she had weaknesses. The film *The Man Who Laughed Last* shows an actress who conveys little expression through her face or eyes and makes conventional, stagy gestures. She suffers from comparison with Hayakawa, who had perfected stillness and understatement on the screen.

From the beginning of her professional career, Lucille had been cast as the vamp and the coquette. She had little choice. Like hundreds of actresses during the 1920s, she fed Broadway's appetite for sexually enticing women in suggestive plots. She knew the material was poor, but she did not resist. The roles enabled her to earn a living and brought her a certain amount of attention. Her languorous, physically revealing publicity photographs demonstrate that, if anything, she promoted this image. But she must have felt that it was becoming a difficult image to maintain, for she had begun to take five years off her age.

Theatre itself was being forced to grow up. "Wall Street Lays an Egg," screamed the famous *Variety* headline after the stock market crashed, and theatre tumbled with it. The number of legitimate houses outside New York declined, and consequently so did the tours that had kept hundreds of actors employed. Vaudeville had already been losing the battle to radio and talking pictures, and with the deepening economic depression would become extinct. As for Broadway, never again would it overflow so cheerfully with silly comedies and seething melodramas.

· · · **CHAPTER 3** · · ·

An Unlikely Marriage

"If you closed your eyes, if you listened to him," said Lynne Mayocole, "he was the handsomest man in the world. He was witty, he
was melodic. He was anything other than what you saw when you
looked at him."

Louis P. Schweitzer was born February 5, 1899, in the Ukraine, to Vera
Gorodnitzky and Peter J. Schweitzer, an educated, affluent businessman
whose father, Joseph, had imported paper from France to Odessa. Shortly
after Lou was born, the Schweitzers fled Russia's anti-Jewish pogroms,
escaping across Eastern Europe and finding safety in France. Early in the
twentieth century they came to the United States. An affectionate poem
called *Lou's Saga,* written by Lou and Lucille's friends to celebrate his
forty-fifth birthday, lightheartedly described this daring trek:

> *Lou looked at that cold Russian winter*
> *After which he quickly got inter*
> *The plush lined seat of his gold plated droshky*
> *With the mink on top*
> *He droshkied West in quite a commotion*
> *From France, he droshkied over the ocean . . .*

In more down-to-earth terms, Peter J. Schweitzer established and bought companies to import and mill paper—carbon paper and the tissue paper that radio manufacturers used for insulation—in Malaucène, France, which was about twenty-five miles northeast of Avignon, and in Jersey City, New Jersey. In the United States, Peter, Vera and their five children—three sons and two daughters—lived first on Edgecombe Avenue in Harlem, then on Ridge Boulevard in Brooklyn. Around 1918 they moved to an apartment building at West End Avenue and 73rd Street, diagonally across from the cream-colored granite castle owned by Charles Schwab. Lou was living there when he met Lucille.

The Schweitzers were better off than the Wadlers and they were more politically engaged. Like the Wadlers they were secular rather than observant Jews, but they dedicated themselves to the Zionist movement to set up a Jewish national state in Palestine. Peter J. Schweitzer was chairman of the Palestine Foundation Fund and the largest individual contributor to that cause. Between 1917 and 1922, when he died of acute appendicitis at the age of forty-eight, he had given $400,000 to the Zionist movement. He and Vera visited Palestine in 1921, and he laid the foundation stone for a hospital in Tiborias, to which he gave $50,000. At Schweitzer's death, his funeral cortege wound more than three miles from his home to 55 Fifth Avenue, the headquarters of the Zionist Organization of America. Rabbi Stephen Samuel Wise, a leader of the American Zionist movement and a famous proponent of Reform Judaism in the United States, was a pallbearer.

When her husband died, stout, indomitable Vera became president of Peter J. Schweitzer, Inc. She also became first president of the Palestine Light House of the Blind in Jerusalem, and for her philanthropic work in Malaucène, the French made her a Knight of the Legion of Honor.

Lou absorbed his parents' political outlook and philanthropic commitment to what, in 1948, would become the nation of Israel. He also fashioned for himself a liberalism centered around the Bill of Rights.

Few liberties meant more to him than freedom of speech, which he himself had exercised since the age of fourteen when he learned to operate a ham radio and use the airwaves to talk with radio buffs around the world. For Lou, amateur radio was more than a hobby; it was a love affair.

He was brought up to enter his family's business. With an eye toward the intricacies of paper manufacturing, he studied chemical engineering at the University of Maine in Orono, where fellow students nicknamed him "Kaiser," apparently finding a resemblance between his personality and that of Germany's omnivorous ruler. "If you want to see egoism personified and symbolized," went a college yearbook entry, "take a look at 'Kaiser.' " After he was graduated in 1919, he and William Schweitzer, one of his two younger brothers, worked at their father's paper mill in Malaucène and went back and forth as much as possible between France and the United States. Around the time Lou and Lucille were married, he received a second engineering degree from the University of Grenoble.

Most likely Lou met Lucille in 1930, for his hurricane of a courtship has the turbulent feel of sudden romance. One of Lou's private names for Lucille was "Mrs. Moonlight," a reference to the eternally youthful heroine of a drama which had opened on Broadway that September and which, quite probably, they had seen together. As to how they met, Lucille recalled a prosaic beginning. She had been invited to Bridgeport, Connecticut, for a friend's first wedding anniversary and was told that somebody named Louis Schweitzer would pick her up to take her to the party. Lou was strongly attracted to the dark-haired, dark-eyed woman with the low voice and pleasurable laugh, and the two began seeing each other.

To Lucille's friends, the couple must have looked like the personification of beauty and the beast. Lou had heavy features and a thick-set body—at 5 feet 7 inches he was only slightly taller than Lucille—and although he was only thirty-one, his reddish-brown hair was thinning on top. He bore a startling similarity to Harry at around the same age.

He was not Lucille's fantasied ideal. He was not in the theatre, not any sort of an artist. Lucille was always impeccably dressed and groomed; Lou's clothes always looked slightly rumpled, and he smoked constantly, which Lucille hated. Lucille loved to dance; Lou did not. But he liked to sing to her: "Something to remember you by," an Arthur Schwartz tune that seductive Libby Holman crooned in the 1930 revue *Three's a Crowd*. He had an open, genial smile, an inventive sense of humor and, on the surface anyway, an enveloping self-assurance. Lucille found a flair and a larger-than-life aura about the man, even in the jaunty angle at which he wore his hat or gripped a pipe with his teeth. And there was definitely style, as well as romance and intensity, about the way he pursued her. Certainly no one else in her crowd had a boyfriend who proposed marriage during a transatlantic telephone call, as Lou did early in 1931.

Perhaps to her own surprise, Lucille accepted him. As she once coyly explained, "It was harder and harder to get the sort of parts I wanted. And it was spring." She might have added that the American economy was suffering the coldest winter of its history, that she was nearly thirty-one and unmarried and, other than acting, had no means of supporting herself.

Whatever her impulse, she did not share Lou's eagerness. Among other things, after watching her father betray her mother, she distrusted marriage and husbands. Ten years later, when her own marriage was severely strained, she wrote Lou, "... you know what I think of married men—they stink with very few exceptions."

But Lou desired her. Toward the end of February 1931, he was sailing for France to wind up his studies in Grenoble and enjoy a brief vacation, and he fervently wanted to get married before he left. Lucille demurred. She feared that would mean involving their families or incurring their families' displeasure if the couple went down to City Hall without telling anyone. Anny, who was about to take a trip to Cuba, knew nothing of these schemes, and Lucille was torn between wanting to keep Anny out of her private life and feeling compelled to tell her. So Lucille put Lou off, sending him a birthday telegram on February 5 and affectionately teasing that "you persist in behaving like a spoiled child."

Less than two weeks later, Lou sailed by himself. Frustrated and lonely, he wired Lucille on February 17 from the S.S. *Europa*, urging her to join him in France and marry him there. The cablegrams sped back and forth as fast as Western Union could deliver them, with Lucille admonishing him to "Be patient my sweet." On February 19 a disappointed and miserably seasick Lou responded in a letter, "God kid you must have a lot more patience than I have" and vowed that "This vacation will do me absolutely no good unless I see you soon as I can't get my mind off you a second and I won't be happy until I see you again."

Lucille tried to put him off one more time, suggesting that she sail after her mother returned to New York. But Lou was not standing for any more delays. On February 23 he wired from Paris that he wished she would leave on the *Europa* March 5; if not, he would embark for the States on March 7. Feeling the determination in Lou's words, and wanting to avoid a confrontation with her family if he returned in that mood, she finally gave in to his ardent insistence and cabled him that same day: "If you really want me sail Europa I will."

There followed a flurry of activity. Lou, ecstatic, bought her a cabin-class ticket and wired her to get a passport and French visa. Unable to find a birth certificate, and with her mother away, she had to ask her father to vouch for her citizenship and vital statistics; Harry obligingly took five years off her age. A passport was issued on February 27 and a visa on March 2. On her passport photograph, Lucille scrawled "Lucille Wadler prof. known as Lucille Lortel." She enlisted Ruth and Cugat in the preparations, saying only that she was to meet Lou in

France and go on a trip. Shopping and packing had to be done. She took her fur coats, for the Atlantic crossing would be cold in March and in addition because the newly built *Europa,* North German Lloyd's flagship, was supremely luxurious. Her friend Amalie Baruch, in whom she had confided the marriage plan, arranged an appointment with Margaret Sanger, the revolutionary advocate for birth control. "I was very naïve in those days," Lucille told the reporter Kitty MacVickar in 1989, when she was presenting a one-woman play about Sanger at the White Barn Theatre. "I believed a woman should be a virgin until marriage." Just before she sailed, Lou wired that he had passed his exams. On March 5, shortly after midnight, the *Europa*'s whistles sounded, she slowly backed away from her pier, and tugs nosed the grand liner out of the shimmering New York harbor and pointed her toward the Atlantic.

When Anny returned from Cuba on March 12, Ruth and Cugat met her at the pier and cooked up a story about Lucille still being asleep at the Mayflower. Anny was bubbling about a Chinese doll she had bought for Lucille, and Ruth wrote her sister, "Really kid you would think that you were about 6 years old the way she acted." As Lucille had expected, Anny was less than delighted when she arrived at the hotel and learned that her precious daughter had taken off without telling her. She tried to make Lucille feel guilty. "You certainly played a trick on me," she wrote, and continued in her slightly misspelled and badly punctuated English:

> You can't imagine what a disapointment it was to come home and find you gone. The last few days of my trip inspite of the wonderful time I had, I just could not wait until I reached home to see you–Ruth I felt heart sick. It is no use stressing on it as it wont change matters now....Please darling dont worry about me or anything just try and be happy yourself thats all that matters.

But Anny's unsubtle recriminations were in vain; her letter did not catch up with Lucille until she had returned to New York. In the meantime, the *Europa* was steaming toward Le Havre. "Welcome home," Lou lovingly radioed on March 13, as the ship prepared to dock.

Lou adored Lucille. He adored her femininity, her luxuriant hair, her body, which he found voluptuous—"Volly," or "Volley" as he sometimes spelled it, was another of his private names for her. He was thirty-one and aspired to make more of himself. In the letter in which he complained to Lucille of loneliness and *mal de mer*, he noted ruefully that he had run into a former classmate, who "has gone a good deal further in life than I have, being married for eight years and the proud father of two little girls." He believed Lucille would understand his ambitions and help realize them.

Lucille was not deeply in love, nor attracted sexually. But she liked Lou's quirky humor, even if she sometimes found his eccentric pranks embarrassing. She responded to his fearlessness and independence and to his adoration. She trusted his directness and lack of pretension. At a moment when her career and the economy were faltering, when Lou was pressuring and home was a cramped apartment with her intrusive mother, she behaved as she often did in her life: accepted things as they were and went forward.

"She and I used to talk about Lou," said Mimi Bochco. When the White Barn was up and running, Lucille and Mimi would often relax in Lucille's living room after a show—they would take a couple of apples and paring knives from the kitchen, sink into their favorite chairs, put their feet up and eat and giggle and talk. "She would tell me a lot about his background," Bochco recalled. "About his mother, who was a matriarch really and held the family tight. Lucille was not in love with Lou. There is a difference between being in love and loving. I think she loved him later on, because he was so good to her and so indulgent."

But Lucille often veiled what was going on inside her. Perhaps after years of marriage she did not remember early moments of tenderness, such as the note she sent to Lou's cabin on Sunday, March 22, during their return trip to the States:

> Darling
>> Everyone is at church and the weather is punk. No more news
>> except that I love you je vous aimes & ich liebe dich jo te amo and
>> if I knew anymore to write them down I would
>>> Your volley.

They had hoped to marry in Paris, but it turned out that French law required a six-week residency. So one week after Lucille arrived, she and Lou turned around and headed back to New York on the *Leviathan*, the giant flagship of the United States Lines.

Lou probably suggested the shipboard wedding. Not one to give up, and having come so far, he was unlikely to let an irritating glitch like Gallic law interfere with his wooing. The man who would later surprise his wife with such gifts as a Venetian gondola and a New York City taxicab could easily arrange a wedding at sea.

Commodore Albert B. Randall was a warmhearted fellow and, with only 586 passengers on a ship that could sleep more than 2,000, this promised to be an easy crossing. He and his crew threw themselves into the job of staging the impromptu event. A generous passenger donated a gold bar from his watch fob, and the chief engineer, one James J. Fagan, hammered the metal into a wedding band (Lou had not come prepared).

On Monday at 8 P.M., March 23, as passengers gathered in the cavernous dining room, the ship's orchestra played Mendelssohn's "Wedding March," and Lucille, graceful in a softly draped white evening gown, with no adornments other than a strand of pearls and a rose corsage, stood beside Lou while Commodore Randall pronounced them husband and wife. Afterward the ship provided a "Nuptial Feast" for the couple and eight guests, including Randall and the purser. The menu featured Beluga Malossol caviar with blinis, consommé Carmen, filet of sole Otero, breast of capon, Waldorf salad, bombe commodore and wedding cake. There was no champagne. The *Leviathan* being an American ship, and Americans being under the dry thumb of their government's prohibition against alcohol, no wine was allowed, not even to celebrate a marriage.

Lucille and Lou look almost solemn in their wedding photograph. Perhaps after weeks of commotion, they were simply exhausted. Commodore Randall gave them the Royal Suite, but Lucille, unsure for some reason about the legality of the ceremony, refused to make love until they were married on American soil. Lou must have been mystified by this strait-laced behavior from his flirtatious, party-going wife, who had once posed in nearly transparent gowns for publicity photographs. "She was really a puritan in so many ways," said Mimi Bochco. "I thought she was naïve about sex. As a young, beautiful actress, you would imagine she would have had some experience. But I don't think so." Fog added to Lou and Lucille's tension on Wednesday, March 25, when it kept the *Leviathan* from docking at her pier, and she had to anchor off Staten Island for an additional twenty-four hours, until the weather cleared and the tide was right. By that time, the press knew that Lucille Lortel, actress, had married Louis Schweitzer of 270 West End Avenue, and reporters, as well as friends and family, greeted a smiling bride and slightly disgruntled groom as they strode off the ship on Thursday. Years later Lucille recounted that they were also wed in a civil ceremony, as Ruth had been, but there is no record of that. On Friday March 27 a rabbi married Lucille Wadler and Louis Schweitzer at the Hotel Mayflower. She gave her age as twenty-five.

At first they lived in a room at the Hotel St. Moritz on Central Park South, then they shifted to the Shoreham Hotel, at 33 West 55th Street between Fifth and Sixth Avenues. It was not until January 1, 1932, that they moved into their first real home, a ninth-floor apartment at 55 Central Park West, between 65th and 66th Streets, only three blocks from Anny at the Mayflower. Lucille, who wanted an apartment with a view, could look out her living room windows and see the dramatic expanse of the park. Lou signed the lease for Peter J. Schweitzer, Inc; the rent was $1,700 a year, or $147.47 a month for the first nine months. Perhaps because there was a depression and this was a renter's market, a year later Lou was able to renegotiate for $125 a month. They would live there until 1936.

They discovered that neither knew what each expected from the other in their marriage.

Lou, as he had promised, was working hard to make something of himself. He and his brother William intended Peter J. Schweitzer, Inc., to dominate the lucrative cigarette paper industry. At the time, every cigarette smoked in the United States came wrapped in paper imported from France, and despite the Depression enveloping the United States—or perhaps because of it—millions of people were lighting up. *Time* magazine announced in April 1931, that "Two young U.S. paper men, Brothers Louis and William Schweitzer, stand ready to challenge France's old monopoly. In Elizabeth, N.J. they have a factory ready to turn out cigaret paper." According to the March 25, 1931, issue of *Business Week*, the Schweitzers were using "linen rags of the finest type," put through a lengthy process to produce cigarette paper that was stronger and purer than that of foreign competitors and used a "mineral filler" which caused the paper to burn slowly and steadily.

Lou was driving back and forth to New Jersey and keeping long hours at the plants. He wanted to find his beautiful wife at home in the evenings; Lucille wanted to go to parties. But if she went to parties by herself, Lou would telephone to make sure she was there. He wanted children, she did not—not yet anyway. He certainly did not want her to be an actress. "Lou was very jealous of it," Lucille told Corinne Jacker in the 1980s. "He wanted her all to himself," observed Mimi Bochco.

Her husband was exerting the sort of control which always made Lucille chafe. What is more, he was insisting that she give up aspects of her life that brought her the most pleasure and also gave her an identity. From Lou's perspective, his wife was selfishly rejecting her new role.

Lucille tried to circumvent Lou's demands and please him and herself at the same time. She sought radio work that would not take her from home at night. Films tended to rehearse and shoot during the day, so once again she auditioned for the two-reelers she had been making before she married. In April 1932, Warner Bros.' Vitaphone Corporation paid her $50 to play a "Woman Acrobat" in a film called *Stage Struck,* which she rehearsed and shot one Saturday in a studio at 220 West 43rd Street. Around this time she probably made a comic short with the former vaudevillian George Givot, known as "The Greek Ambassador," whose signature turn was portraying a Greek immigrant fracturing the English language.

Then, without telling Lou, in August 1932 she accepted the part of a French maid in the Theatre Guild's production of *The Man Who Reclaimed His Head,* a heavily symbolic drama by Jean Bart, the nom-de-théâtre of the actress and dramatist Marie Antoinette Sarlabous. Claude Rains starred as a journalist with socialist leanings, and Jean Arthur played his wife; the young director was a former Theatre Guild stage manager named Herbert J. Biberman. Lucille's role was minor but she did get to dance.

As the opening neared, and Lucille had to attend evening rehearsals and performances, she told Lou about the $75-a-week job, and he ordered her to pull out of the production. Proud and angry, she refused, and Lou assuaged his own anger by going down to the Broadhurst on West 44th Street after every rehearsal, to take her home.

The production opened on September 8, 1932, and Lou sent her a punning telegram: "Hope you maid good." Four nights later she was dancing on the set's revolving stage, and as she was pulled toward the edge, she tripped and fell, spraining her right ankle and bruising her spine and back (she filed for workmen's compensation and received $100 from the producers). Capping the unhappy experience, *Man* closed after twenty-eight performances. Lucille made a lifelong friend in Biberman, who, with his wife, the film actress Gale Sondergaard, would be black-listed by Hollywood as a Communist during the 1950s. But she must have felt a pang of sadness when she walked out of the stage door for the last time, as though she were leaving a part of herself behind.

Perhaps their marriage's storminess had shocked them a bit, for they began trying to accommodate each other's schedules and desires. Lou still kept a strenuous routine, but they went out at night. The states repealed Prohibition in 1933 and, coincidentally, that year Francis Cugat's brother Xavier and his band began to play the Sert Room in the towering new Waldorf-Astoria at Park Avenue and 50th Street. The Depression that drove millions of desperate Americans to bread lines did not really touch Lou and Lucille. Still, with Vera Schweitzer controlling the amount of money Lou made, the couple lived on a tight budget, which Lucille, who paid the household bills from an account at the nearby Corn Exchange Bank Trust Company, tried to keep on track with meticulous entries on their checkbook stubs. When they gave parties, she told Vincent Curcio, "I'd say to people, 'What would you like, scotch or bourbon?' And I'd go out to the kitchen, and I'd have one bottle and I'd pour it out of the same bottle. Nobody ever knew the difference."

Her party-giving was more successful than her stabs at keeping house, which evoked the Clyde Fitch comedies in which she had appeared early in her career. She tried to cook but burned the food. She hated housekeeping. For most of their married life, they would employ a maid, a cook or both, and in New York City they would live in hotels.

On Saturday, March 18, 1933, Lou left for England on a trip that would also take him to France, to find markets for Schweitzer cigarette paper. He planned to be gone for over a month. Lucille remained at home; she had hurt her arm, and Anny stayed with her. It was the first time the couple had separated for any lengthy period since they were married, and the trip coincided with their second wedding anniversary. But they realized that they needed distance from each other.

"I don't have to tell you that all the time my thoughts will be of you," Lou wrote from the M.S. *Lafayette* on the first day out. "I hope the trip will do us both good. You from the point of health and the work you want to do and me from the point of view of business." He wrote her nearly every day he was at sea, reporting about celebrities on board as well as potential business contacts for himself. At times he wrote about the sort of thing that was bound to needle her, such as the evening he and an acquaintance, Sidney Matz, danced with two young women Matz knew. But usually Lou expressed devotion, mingled, as was his way, with a touch of sarcasm. "Volly dear you don't know how much I love you and how lucky I feel to have you for my wife. The thought of you gives me a belief in myself I never had before and you'll make a man of me yet." On Thursday, March 23, when he walked into the dining room for supper, he found a cake and a split of champagne on his table from Lucille.

Perhaps to make it up to Lucille, who relished travel, in 1934 Lou took her on trips to Bermuda and Canada, and in June 1936, they sailed to the French and Italian Rivieras for the honeymoon they had missed five years before. Around that time they also moved to 40 West 67th Street, to a dark apartment in a nine-story building diagonally across from the Hotel des Artistes, which, as its name implied, was in the heart of an artistic neighborhood on the Upper West Side.

They arrived at a sort of compromise about Lucille's acting. Lou did not object to her performing on radio, which was not only his favorite

medium but also did not require theatre's lengthy rehearsal or performance schedule. Her low voice and fairly distinct enunciation made her a
natural, and in 1935, Ben Gross, the popular radio columnist for the
Daily News, wrote that "Lucille Lortel . . . is drawing applause for her dramatic portrayals on WHN."

In 1936, the Home of the Daughters of Jacob, a charitable organization for elderly women of which Vera Schweitzer was president, hired
Lucille to act in their sentimental dramatic serial, *The House on the Hill.*
The fifteen-minute program, which aired on WHN Tuesday nights at
8:15, starred Jennie Moscowitz, who was famous for playing sympathetic
Jewish mothers in the Yiddish and English-speaking theatres; the serial's
characters were from working-class backgrounds, and the roles required
dialects. *The House on the Hill* went off the air in February 1937, but during 1936 and 1937, the Columbia Broadcasting System periodically hired
Lucille to participate in *Dear Columbia,* a half-hour morning program that
invited listeners to send in questions, to which the network supplied comments and answers (she earned $10 to $15 a program). She kept auditioning for radio work well into 1939.

When Lucille later described her life from 1931 to 1947, she often summarized her feelings by saying that she thought she would go "nuts" because she did not have enough to do. She was existing in a wasteland
dotted with trips, parties, the occasional acting stint, and even a try,
around 1940, at going back to school.

There was more distress than she admitted. Although she looked
softer and more womanly than ever, letters from friends during the late
1930s and early '40s repeatedly asked if she was happier than when they
saw her last, and one from Carl Reifenberg, a homosexual German-
Jewish writer and émigré whom Lucille met through Ruth, indicates that
in 1939 he urged her to leave Lou. For a long time Lou was possessive,
then he suddenly distanced himself, and Lucille panicked and wondered

if she had a marriage or not. Without work of her own to engage and reward her, the marriage had become her focus.

Lou's devotion often expressed itself through anxiety and jealousy. He cabled her regularly when he was away, alerting her to when he had arrived at his destination, where he was staying and when he was coming home. But sometimes worry about how his beautiful wife was occupying her time in his absence got the better of his judgment. "By the way," he wrote from London during that lengthy business trip in 1933, "there's one reason I'm glad you're not with me. There are more good looking men here in one block than there are in the whole of the city of New York. But then again you always said that you didn't like good looking men. However I want you to stay away from the homely ones too."

He was aware of his problem—Lucille made him aware—and occasionally he made fun of himself, like the time he gave her a necklace with a gently joshing note, "You don't like me around your neck so wear this."

He willingly offered her anything she wanted, except what she deeply missed: the freedom to act in the theatre. He understood that she needed to see her family, he sympathized that she needed to get away from the apartment during the baking New York City summers, and most summers Lou provided for Lucille and her mother to go to the seashore. In late August 1935, Lucille, Anny and Ruth—her two "older sisters" as Lou good-humoredly and astutely called them—packed themselves off to a kind of health camp called Reilly's SunAire Farm in Oak Ridge, New Jersey. Another time, at Rosedor, twenty miles north of Manhattan in Irvington-on-Hudson, she and Anny diligently consumed quantities of milk, a feat that elicited much kidding from Lou. These were just two of many health regimens and spas that Lucille would patronize during her lifetime in a never-ending battle to lose weight. Most likely Lou paid everybody's bill, as he would always do for Lucille's relatives—and as Harry had failed to do. By 1941 Lou was sending Anny a regular check.

Lou even seemed to understand Lucille's need to work at something, although he teased her about it. In a rhyming note which began, "I never thought I would like a girl as much as you," he mused

> The only thing that I regret is that you haven't got a job as yet. But I'm not the kind of mope who easily gives up hope. And when you finally get some work I know your duty you won't shirk. Cause then I know you'll do your best to see I get a much needed rest. So go look around you've got my best wishes and when you get it why I'll wash the dishes.

Lucille tried to acclimate herself to his behavior. "To a crazy guy," she wrote on a gift card, "who happens to be married to a crazy wife for living with him. Love—Volley." And one Christmas: "To Lou— Merry Xmas and please dear try & be a little sane the next year because I cant keep up with you. Your still (in spite of you) devoted Mrs. Moonlight."

On March 20, 1938, following a gallbladder operation, Vera Schweitzer died at Mount Sinai Hospital at the age of fifty-seven, and Lou and Lucille's lives changed dramatically.

With his mother's death, Lou became president of Peter J. Schweitzer, Inc. Status and wealth both required and allowed for a more comfortable manner of living, and that year they moved into a five-room apartment on the seventeenth floor of the mammoth, twin-towered Century Apartments, which fronted an entire block between 62nd and 63rd Streets on Central Park West. The rent was $2,600 a year, or $216.67 each month.

That year they also looked for a country home. Mayo, who had been appointed conductor of the Capitol's orchestra and was also involved with the lucrative *Major Bowes' Original Amateur Hour* on the radio, had bought property in Stamford, Connecticut, and moved there in 1936. And even though Lucille loathed Frances—years later, in a letter to her friend Blanche Marvin, Lucille described Frances as "a cold bitch of a woman"—she wanted to be near her brother and his new baby, Carolyn. Unable to find a house she liked in Stamford, Lucille picked one in Westport, only about twenty-two miles away. Lou bought it for $30,000.

In 1938, Westport was a New England town with an artists' colony in its midst. Fifty miles from New York City and reachable by the New York and New Haven Railroad, since the 1920s it had been a haven for painters, illustrators and cartoonists, writers and actors, who either made careers in New York City but wanted to live away from the bustle, or wanted a second home during the summer. On June 29, 1938, the first seventeen and a half miles of the picturesque Merritt Parkway opened, stretching from the New York border to Norwalk, Connecticut, and by 1940 was complete, ensuring even easier access for city dwellers who wanted to retreat behind low, rambling stone walls or sun themselves at Compo Beach. After World War II, cozy Westport became a mecca for the media and theatrical elite. Well-heeled New York advertising executives, film and theatre producers, radio and television personalities soon joined the exodus to the town on the Saugatuck River. The CBS Radio commentator Quincy Howe and his wife bought property adjoining the Schweitzers' on Cranbury Road, and Howe's daughter Tina, who later became a playwright, remembered sneaking onto the Schweitzers' land with her brother when she was a youngster, and her brother tormenting her by swinging her in the Schweitzers' enormous hammock.

Westport did not welcome Jews. Well into the 1930s, Westport's Real Estate Board had an unspoken policy of not selling or renting to Jews or African Americans, and neither group could become members of the local country club. But while Lou and Lucille were aware of the prejudice, it does not seem to have bothered them; they were in the vanguard of a Jewish migration that would increase during and after the war, and Lou would eventually help build the town's first synagogue. More important from Lucille's point of view, the town offered a theatre: the Westport Country Playhouse.

Their new home was called Fayreweather and had been built in 1935 by Forrest Wilson, a writer who in 1942 would receive the Pulitzer Prize for a biography of Harriet Beecher Stowe. Situated on 18.6 acres, the property was bordered by Newtown Avenue on the West and on the South by Cranbury Road, from which a long driveway entered the land, then crossed over a ribbon of Stony Brook and wound around and up a knoll to the two-story clapboard house. Pin oaks, black alders and gray birch grew on the land, and there were blueberries. The house's most attractive feature was a living room with pine floorboards and pine paneling from an eighteenth-century New Hampshire house, and a roomy bay window opposite a substantial fireplace.

The impetus to buy a country place had come from Lucille, but Lou took charge of the project. He hired Westport architect Edwin L. Howard to enlarge the kitchen and the dining area and build an enclosed porch off the living room, and he set about constructing tennis courts and damming the brook to create a pond deep enough for swimming. While Lucille shopped at W. & J. Sloane in Manhattan to decorate the master bathroom, he outfitted a pine-paneled walk-in bar off a corner of the living room where they planned to put a grand piano that belonged to Anny. When their decorating spree was complete, the result was a comfortable hodge-podge: partly rustic, partly suburban chintz.

Lucille could not know it at the time, but their most valuable purchase would be a two-story barn, which they bought at a nearby farm shortly after the United States entered World War II, reassembled not far from the house and painted white. They intended to keep horses, but feed was hard to come by during the war, so they turned the barn's second story into a playroom, installed a ping pong table and an upright piano, and stored machinery downstairs. They changed the spelling of the property's name to "Fairweather."

About this time, it seems, Lucille made her first attempt to produce theatre rather than act in it. On February 11, 1941 she wrote Carl Reifenberg, who was now living in Rio de Janeiro, that she had tried to start a stock company but that the project had fallen through, and so she had come to Hollywood, Florida, to nurse her disappointment.

In Florida, the distress with which she had been living expressed itself through depression and neediness. She was supposed to have gone with Lou, but at the last moment he pleaded work—he was trying to open two new mills and there was a paper convention to attend—and she took her sister instead. "Bon voyage honey," he wired her to the Orange Blossom on February 7, an hour before the train pulled out of Pennsylvania Station. "And have fun for both of us."

As early as 1937, Anny had started vacationing in Hollywood, Florida, the "Dream City" that an adept salesman named Joseph Wesley Young had built in the 1920s near Miami Beach, at the start of the Florida land boom. But this was Ruth's and Lucille's first trip. They stayed at the Hollywood Beach Hotel, where, Lucille wrote Lou, she was running into many New Yorkers and Westporters whom they knew, including Leo and Frankie Godowsky and the Gershwin matriarch, Rose. One night she and Ruth drove to Miami Beach to hear Xavier Cugat. When it was not raining, Lucille took a tennis lesson or played golf, and she had a massage every day "to keep the weight down."

Feeling dispirited and lonely, she wrote Lou an uncharacteristically long, pleading letter on Monday, February 17, three days after Valentine's Day:

Lou dear—

Received your letter yesterday I felt so blue all day Friday
because I hadn't heard from you. I thought I would get a letter
then or that you would telephone. When I didn't hear from you
Saturday, I tried to get you by phone but you weren't home. On
Sunday your letter came so I felt better—you see it was five days
since I spoke to you or got any news—telephone me at least
once a week. I am always in my room at seven oclock getting
dressed for dinner. I don't usually go down to the diningroom
before 8:30.

She was reverting to the kind of intense partying in which she had in-
dulged when she was a teenager and during her trip to Europe in 1922.
The scrawled, rambling letter, with its run-on sentences and lack of
punctuation, sounded as though she were writing it after a long, dizzy
night. She described how, one evening, she and the brother of her friend
Sadie Gilman had gone out gambling, how on another day she had gone
to the races and won on a horse named Playhouse, how she was not getting to bed until after three every night but, because she was not drinking much, she still looked well. She urged Lou to call Anny, whom she
had heard was feeling lonely.

Tell her that you heard from me and that Ruth & I look and feel
like a million dollars & that we are the nicest and bestlooking here.
You know you can put it on but it happens to be the truth.

The only trouble with us is that all the married men are trying
to make us and all the others are either too old or too young for us
to be interested in and you know how I hate what I think of married men—they stink with very few exceptions I now am beginning to feel the way I use to about men and marriage—never
again How's by you . . .

If Lou felt baited or hurt, he restrained himself and on February 20 responded only with humor and light sarcasm:

> I received your letter yesterday and believe me I didn't think you had it in you. How did you ever write such a long letter? And such an intelligent and philosophical one too.
>
> So you have developed into a gambler. My, my you'll be taking to drinking next. And as for your observations on marriage I too will never get married again. It's too much trouble making out checks every week...

Undoubtedly Lou was working hard, but perhaps for the first time since he married Lucille he was also playing hard to get. For somebody who so regularly sent telegrams, telephoned and wrote letters, his communiqués had clearly dwindled. Maybe he was angry with Lucille for being away from home for five weeks, or frustrated by their sexual incompatibility, or simply annoyed that she wanted things only on her terms. Worried about his remoteness, Lucille wrote in desperation to Lou's sister Elizabeth Licht, in Riverdale, New York, a woman with whom she was not close, and begged for information about what could be causing her husband to withdraw. The letter was full of scratched out words and exposed such deep anxiety that most likely Lucille did not send it.

> Look honey I am leaving Sunday March 16th & arriving Monday March 17 at 3:30. Is it at all possible for me to see you before Lou comes home that night. Ever since I told him I was coming home he seems so cold. I am staying on a week longer than I expected but as far as he is concerned it seems too short. (I'd rather not write all the things he said. All I know, his voice & attitude over the phone isn't very conducive to coming home)— ... one of

the things that puzzles me is. He said if I stayed longer he *might* be able to get away at the end of the month for 10 days. I told him if he would come right away O.K. but that I didn't care to stay that long. Everyone I knew was leaving and I would rather come home and go away with him when he can get away. He said in that case he would go away himself on a cruise. I said I would go with him but he said it would be too expensive to take me...I also told him...I wanted to be with him on our anniversary & didn't he want to be with me that day he didn't answer that....He didn't once say he missed me & wished I was back...

In her February 11 letter to Carl Reifenberg she had written that perhaps she needed to end the marriage after all, as he had suggested a year and a half earlier. He wrote back on March 8, changing his advice:

> ...you two still have too much in common, you still understand each other in numerous ways, you still need each other. So it's better to find a "modus vivendi" and carry on. I know I told you differently, when I was there, but you are right and I am rong [*sic*]. So try to make the best of it, times are difficult enough for every one, without ourselves trying to create new difficulties to add.

Lucille and Lou did celebrate their tenth wedding anniversary together, with champagne and a group of friends. "The first ten years are the hardest Volley," Lou wrote on the card that accompanied a pair of earrings, "so now your troubles are over. Wear these to-night Mrs. Moonlight with all my love." When Lucille next wrote to Carl Reifenberg, she reported that things were going more smoothly. Reifenberg wrote back on August 21, "What made me really happy, was the atmosphere that came out of your letter. This atmosphere of quiet, content happiness, some thing, that was so very far away from you, when I first met you....I am glad you found back to your work, I am glad you so thouroughly [*sic*] enjoy your beautiful property in Westport..." The work Reifenberg refers to may have been another rebellious excursion into acting: in May and June 1941, Lucille took a part under an assumed name in a drama about capitalism's abuses called *Zero Hour* by George Sklar and Albert Maltz, which played some performances in the Transport Workers Hall at 153 West 64th Street.

For the time being, Lou and Lucille seemed to have reconciled, although there were still underlying problems. In 1942, they were wrestling with their childlessness, and a cousin, Louis Berlin, wrote Lucille about an opportunity to adopt. Lucille wrote back on July 6:

> Dear Louis
>
> I appreciate your thinking of me and your suggestion sounds very tempting, but unfortunately your letter came today, and I do not see my husband until the weekend. Speaking to him on the telephone isn't very satisfactory. He says he wouldn't think of adopting any child unless he could first see it as he feels it will be taking too much of a risk. So I am afraid I will have to say no in this instance. I probably will have to get a child through an institution where my husband will have the opportunity of seeing it and at the same time get used to the idea. It seems a shame to let such a good opportunity pass. but naturally, without my husband's consent nothing can be done.

Lucille would always say that her theatres were her children. She felt about them the way a dramatist feels about a play, an artist about a painting—that she had given birth to them and raised them to thriving adulthood through love and hard work.

But how much tension the absence of actual children caused Lucille and Lou is unknown. In later years she sometimes said that she had wanted children, at other times that she had not, which was easier to believe—few people described Lucille as maternal. She was too self-absorbed and wished to preserve an image of herself as sexually alluring rather than motherly. But one cannot imagine Lou, so sensitive where matters of masculinity were concerned, liking the idea of adopting someone else's child. For him it would have been a public admission that he had failed. Hope Alswang, the older daughter of Lucille's good friend, designer Ralph Alswang, remembered a Christmas around 1985 when Lucille, who was holding Hope's infant son on her lap, said, "You know, I wanted children, and we didn't have them. And when I talked to Lou about adopting, that's when he started having affairs."

By 1942, whatever theatre plans Lucille harbored, World War II postponed. Mostly she passed the war in New York and in Westport, where Lou, ever attentive to her needs, had a chicken coop built to provide her with fresh eggs, one of many items that government-imposed rationing made scarce. But even gas rationing did not impede their enjoyment of the country, where they kept a car, a boat and a dog who soon became Anny's dear companion. Lou had erected a radio tower and built a shack not far from the house, outfitted with state-of-the-art amateur radio equipment. His call letters were W1BE—two-letter call signs indicated an early pioneer of amateur radio—and he spent pleasant hours contacting other short-wave enthusiasts around the globe. By now they also had a housekeeper, an African-American woman named Rosamund "Rozzie" Bennett.

Always closely involved with her family, Lucille was particularly concerned about Mayo. He and Frances finally married in 1940 and had another daughter, Penelope, and in 1942 Mayo had built a lavish home on their property in Stamford. But by 1943 they were estranged and wrangling in Connecticut Superior Court about temporary alimony, lawyers' fees and their children's custody. Subsequently both parents fell ill, Frances with a perforated ulcer and Mayo with what the gossip-hungry Connecticut newspapers described as a nervous breakdown. Lynne Mayocole was seven in 1945 and recalled "my awareness that my father had had a heart attack. I remember him lying in bed, very weak, shaking, and I remember being curled up next to him." Perhaps there was truth in both interpretations. *Major Bowes' Capitol Family Hour* had gone off the air in 1941, and *Major Bowes' Original Amateur Hour* had expired in 1945. Although Mayo sought out other radio opportunities, by the age of fifty he had turned from playing and conducting music to writing children's books about musicians. "That may also have been the ending of his music career," said Mayocole, "which had been his whole life."

Ironically, at one point it seemed that Lou and Lucille might become adoptive parents after all. A possible outcome of the fierce custody fight was that Carolyn and Penny would be awarded to Mayo, who, since he was making little money and living in a small Manhattan apartment, suggested giving the children to Lucille and Lou to raise in the comfort of their Westport estate. But the judge awarded custody to Mayo's wife. According to Leo Nevas, who was involved in the legal tussle on Mayo's side, Lou paid the settlement.

During World War II, Lucille began to establish a network of Westport friends and connections. There were Charmé and Charles Speaks from Columbus, Ohio, who would become active supporters of the arts in Westport and throughout Connecticut. There were John Davis Lodge and his wife Francesca Braggiotti. Lodge, a lawyer and a descendent of one of Massachusetts' politically stellar families, had married a dancer, gone to Hollywood with her and become an actor there and on Broadway. In 1941 he moved his family to Westport, where the flamboyant Francesca grew a Victory garden and rode into town with a horse and carriage, to save gas. "She and Lucille got on like a streak," said Francesca's daughter Lily Lodge, who also became an actress. John Lodge would be elected to Congress in 1946 and in 1950 become governor of Connecticut.

Lou and Lucille took part in local bond rallies, and one Saturday evening in September 1942 hosted a supper party and auction for Russian Relief on their property. The guest list included a mixture of New York and Westport celebrities and neighbors: Lily Pons; the conductors André Kostelanetz and Fritz Reiner; Leo and Frankie Godowsky, who had bought property in Westport in 1938; Erwin Piscator, the German director who headed the Dramatic Workshop at the New School of Social Research, where Lucille often saw productions, and his wife Maria-Ley; the Arthur Gershwins; Xavier Cugat and his wife; the Clifton Fadimans; Mr. and Mrs. Benjamin A. Javits. The comedian Danny Kaye, who was one of the entertainers, looked around the barn at one point and said, "You know, this could make a nice little theatre."

CHAPTER 4

The Making of a Producer:
· The White Barn Theatre ·

W ith the Depression, a sea change washed over the American theatre. Broadway producers dug into shallower pockets than during the high-flying 1920s. Two hundred and forty-two productions opened on Broadway during the 1929–30 season; only seventy-five during 1940–41. Audiences also had less money to spend—or were spending it at the movies—and their numbers declined.

Oddly, during those ten years the quality of the plays was extraordinarily high, as though American playwrights, surrounded by economic and social despair, finally had material for a uniquely American drama and nothing to lose by writing about their country as they saw it. In the fall of 1931, the Theatre Guild produced Eugene O'Neill's *Mourning Becomes Electra*, fourteen acts and six hours of a self-destructive American family seen through the prism of Aeschylean tragedy. New writers like Sidney Kingsley, Jack Kirkland and Clifford Odets, whose *Awake and Sing!* portrayed an unsparing social truth, helped generate a fiercely realistic style of American performance. Directors like Harold Clurman, Elia Kazan, Robert Lewis, and Lee Strasberg emerged, to influence American theatre for generations.

Then, just as suddenly as the serious playwriting of the 1930s appeared, it seemed to vanish. Wartime patriotism discouraged social criticism. With Americans fighting for democracy in Europe and Asia, the spurt of daring plays diminished to a trickle. Established writers like Kingsley and Maxwell Anderson failed to come up to their previous artistic levels. Robert Sherwood turned to speech-writing for President Franklin D. Roosevelt, and Odets moved to Hollywood to pan for gold. O'Neill retreated behind illness. Of well-known playwrights, only Thornton Wilder explored new dramaturgical realms with his adventuresome satire *The Skin of Our Teeth* in 1942. And only one new voice sang imaginatively and poetically: Tennessee Williams. His sensitive, autobiographical *The Glass Menagerie* barely made it to Broadway in 1945. It had been really in the realm of musical comedy that Broadway made headlines during the war years, when Rodgers and Hammerstein's *Oklahoma!* burst on the scene in 1943 like a patriotic tonic.

After the war, America returned to prosperity. But the costs of producing on Broadway rose, making it harder for a serious drama to survive. Against this background, Lucille sought to invest in productions, a move natural for someone with money, theatrical connections and the gradually forming desire to produce. In 1945 she put $1,200 into Oscar Serlin's production of *Beggars Are Coming to Town*, a three-act drama about gangsters by Theodore Reeves, who had written the screenplay for *National Velvet*. The production came with a good pedigree: direction by Harold Clurman, sets by Jo Mielziner, costumes by the talented young designer Ralph Alswang. Strong actors like Herbert Berghof, E.G. Marshall and Lucille's old friend, Luther Adler, headed the cast. But Reeves was better at writing about youngsters training a horse for the Grand National than about Prohibition mobsters. *Beggars* closed after twenty-five performances, returning only $16.82 to Lucille on her investment and later an additional $400 when Serlin sold the movie rights to Hal Wallis.

Lucille probably tried to involve herself with the Westport Country

Playhouse. She and Anny, who spent a good deal of time at Fairweather, regularly attended opening nights, and Lucille often hosted an opening night party at the house. But Lawrence Langner, who had founded the Theatre Guild in 1918 and started the Playhouse in 1931 with his wife Armina Marshall, had no call for a neophyte producer. Lucille found more opportunity at the Ridgefield Summer Theatre, a purportedly commercial enterprise run by a trio of actors that included the one-time Broadway star Alexander Kirkland, who had been married to Gypsy Rose Lee. As she did later with the American National Theatre and Academy, Lucille first involved herself on a social level—she is listed in a 1947 program as the "Subscription Committee" for Westport—and she probably contributed money. The program also lists her as a "Production Assistant," possibly because she enlisted Mayo's aid selecting music for a production of *Rip Van Winkle* and because she helped with casting.

But investing in other people's projects was not as rewarding as starting her own. In 1941, when Lucille had felt that Lou was distancing himself from her, she panicked. In 1947, when Lou, as Lucille once wrote her friend Blanche Marvin, was "in Paris . . . making hanky-panky," she started a theatre.

The impetus for the White Barn Tryout Theatre, she told Tere Pascone of the *Bridgeport Sunday Post,* was a backers' audition she had attended at somebody's New York apartment. The place was crowded and hot. It was hard to see or hear the actors, let alone focus on the script for which the producers were trying to raise money. Lucille left, she told Pascone, thinking she could easily do the same in Westport and more comfortably besides.

By early June, encouraged and assisted by Mayo and a public relations man named Irwin Nathanson, who had a summer home nearby, she had installed a temporary platform stage on the barn's second floor, hung a few lighting instruments and set up folding chairs. As she told Pascone, "Waldo [Mayo] lives in New York, comes out to Westport

week-ends. He contacts producers there, and I arrange everything else at
this end." The playwrights or potential producers were supposed to pick
up the cost of rehearsals in New York, pay the actors and provide transportation to Westport; Lucille would furnish the theatre, the audience
and feed the cast. A press release dated June 10, 1947, went out on stationery for the White Barn Tryout Theatre, mangled syntax and all:

> I wish to announce that the WHITE BARN THEATRE in Westport is
> now available for try out performances or readings of new plays.
>
> Do you have a play which you intend to produce this fall, and
> would you like to introduce it before an invited audience for one or
> more evenings this summer? My friends and I may be disposed to
> participate financially in your New York production. Many of New
> York's first night audiences are summer residents here, and one of
> the most discriminating audiences in the Metropolitan area.
>
> The WHITE BARN THEATRE was recently built for entertain-
> ment purposes and seats about one hundred and fifty people. The
> simple stage and lighting equipment is suitable to informal per-
> formances. However, whether it be a reading or more finished
> presentation, is entirely at your discretion. The theater is situated
> one mile from the Merrit Parkway, and two and a half miles from
> the station.
>
> If you are interested, please write or call me at the above ad-
> dress, or call my associate in New York, Waldo Mayo (Columbus
> 5-7750).
>
> Sincerely,
> Lortel Productions

Philip Huston and the actor Canada Lee approached Lucille with a
script. Huston and Elizabeth Goodyear, an actress turned professional
fund-raiser, had written a melodrama called *Painted Wagon,* about an

American soldier who changes his identity after the war and joins the circus, to elude a wife he hates. With Broadway in mind, they offered the pivotal role of the circus's animal trainer to Lee, who in 1941 had played murderous Bigger Thomas in the stage adaptation of Richard Wright's novel *Native Son*. "I don't think *Painted Wagon* was a very good play, to be perfectly honest," Goodyear said when she was in her nineties. "But it was a vehicle at that time for Canada, and Canada was hot. I think Lucille realized that." Lucille, in fact, had often brought Lee as her guest to opening nights at the Westport Country Playhouse.

If Lucille was being canny, she was also displaying gumption by bringing an African-American actor, even an acclaimed one, to perform in racist Westport. With this gesture she aligned herself with the majority of Actors' Equity Association, which at that time was boycotting discriminatory theatres and hotels and would take up the cudgels that summer against the National Theatre in Washington, D.C.

Huston, who directed the reading, cast himself as the former GI and asked a pretty, relatively untried eighteen-year-old named Nancy Franklin to read the part of the circus owner's daughter, with whom the ex-soldier falls in love. He cast a young actor named Kurt Cerf, who was teaching at Piscator's Dramatic Workshop, and used an assortment of established character actors, including Francesca Braggiotti's debonair brother Stiano. "I was told that this was the first play of this new theatre, which was only going to do new plays," said Franklin, who remembered the whole experience as "dazzling for someone just starting out." She recalled rehearsing in New York and being driven to Westport on the day of the reading, a Sunday. She was not too dazzled to notice that Lee had a glass eye, "which fascinated me, and a very rich voice and kind of played the star," that Huston "did look dissolute," and that Lucille was "gracious and lovely" when speaking to the audience from the stage.

For weeks Lucille had called friends and neighbors in Westport and New York, exhorting them to come. She had never produced a staged reading but she knew how to throw a good party, and instinct told her that this gathering must be convivial and stimulating. A turnout of more than a hundred people rewarded her effort. Establishing a White Barn tradition, she sat at a table near the barn's first floor entrance, and audience members stopped to sign their names and addresses in an outsized guest book and receive their tickets, before streaming up a flight of outdoor stairs to the improvised theatre.

That first night the audience included a smattering of everybody: critics like Vernon Rice from the *New York Post* and Fred H. Russell from the *Bridgeport Post*; Nat H. Greenberg, whose family owned a department store on Main Street; theatrical agents William Liebling and Audrey Wood; film actress Lilli Palmer; Lily Javits, mother of New York Representative Jacob Javits. Even Rosamund, the Schweitzers' housekeeper, signed the book. Later readings attracted more industry people, but this first time out, Lucille was glad to fill the house.

"The thought of speaking in public frightens me," Lucille once said. Throughout her career, Lucille remained anxious about talking in front of others in a formal situation, afraid that she would forget what she was supposed to say. But shortly after 8 P.M., wearing a bold print dress with a flattering scooped neckline, she stepped onto the stage and received the warm applause of the cast and the audience. If she felt nervous, she also felt proud that she was able to bring together so many congenial, interested people for a worthwhile purpose. Although she could not have articulated it to herself or anyone else, she sensed that she was stepping into a new role, one that would give her authority and status. After sixteen years she was in the theatre again, and the theatre was hers.

The room was hot, and during the two intermissions the audience flowed outside for air. When the reading was over, people walked downstairs to the first floor, to cool off with soda and beer, make themselves miniature ham and Swiss cheese sandwiches on rye, talk about the play and mingle with the cast. Then the director and his actors went back to the city. But Lucille and Mayo stayed up late, talking about how to proceed, and Lucille pored over the names in the guest book, identifying with a penciled notation whether this person was a producer, that one an agent, another a director. This, too, would become a ritual, for audiences were contacts whom she would invite again or call upon to work at the White Barn.

Painted Wagon never reached Broadway. "It died a natural death," said Elizabeth Goodyear. But press coverage of the White Barn promised a good run.

"Something new in the way of a summer theatre was recently opened by Lucille Lortel with the assistance of her brother, Waldo Mayo," wrote Vernon Rice in the *New York Post* on July 29. "It's called the White Barn..."

Rice, who would become a prime booster of the Off-Broadway movement, found the heart of Lucille's experiment:

> Miss Lortel probably doesn't know it, but she is performing playwrights a service. The good points come out under the Lortel tryout conditions, but the bad ones shine like a beacon light on a dark night. Mr. Huston and Miss Goodyear are probably at their typewriters right now, polishing and rewriting scenes and speeches, whose defects they had been totally unaware of at the beginning of the try-out performance. It's no place for those with wobbly scripts, who use the theatre just as a means to raise some quick and easy money. A microscope couldn't bring out blemishes more clearly.

Before the next reading on August 17, of a mystery by Jay Victor called *Beloved*, Lucille set about improving her theatre. She installed a cooling system and additional seats, laid a flagstone terrace and provided chairs so that people could sit outside. Inside on the ground floor she set up a green room, with couches and a counter for serving drinks and food. Workmen carved an additional driveway onto the property from Newtown Avenue and added a small parking area behind the barn.

Several people who attended the first reading gave Lucille scripts, and soon the White Barn's dance card was filled for the rest of the summer. At Audrey Wood's recommendation, Lucille presented *No Casting Today,* a musical revue with lyrics by a public relations consultant named Alex Bennett Kahn and music by William Provost. The audience received a ballot and voted its favorite songs and performers, one of whom was a newcomer with a lovely, pure soprano named Jo Sullivan.

If trouble with Actors' Equity signified professional recognition, then Lucille achieved it sooner than she expected. By the time she set about presenting her fourth reading on August 31, of Warren Silver's heavily philosophical romance, *House on the Hill,* Equity had gotten wind of the White Barn Tryout Theatre. The union let Lucille know that, unless she adhered to Equity's rules for readings—that there be neither rehearsals nor stage, that performers not move off their chairs and that each actor receive $5 for the effort—she could no longer offer readings with union members. Either that or pay each actor two weeks' salary. For Silver's play she withdrew the Equity people and used young, nonunion actors, and for the summer's last two staged readings she harked back to her radio experience and told the visiting directors to cast radio performers. Thus it was that on Sunday, September 14, a fragile, blonde twenty-three-year-old radio and television actress named Eva Marie Saint, who lived on Kissena Boulevard in Queens, appeared in *Ivory Tower,* a comedy about a congresswoman with a strong resemblance to Clare Boothe Luce.

So also began the White Barn's tangled relationship with Equity. On September 2 Lucille and Mayo, in his role as the White Barn's managing director, appeared before the Equity Council. According to the Council minutes, the two "stated that they had devised a plan for the trying out of new plays for authors or prospective producers that was more than a reading...in that it required [actors] to take direction and act against a scenic background after rehearsal for a day or more." Most likely they voiced the thoughts that Mayo expressed in a statement published on September 9 in the trade publication *Actors Cues*.

> THE WHITE BARN is hoping to get Equity to permit actors to Act, scripts in hand, during its stage readings.
>
> Like any other audition, talent buyers expect to see an actor act, just as they see a dancer dance and hear a singer sing. Without the freedom to act, an actor's opportunity with the producers and agents in the WHITE BARN audiences is completely lost.

They asked Equity to fix a special rate for this special kind of reading and the rehearsal it required.

Lucille and Mayo were advocating the sort of staged readings which one day would become accepted in theatres all over the country, and which Equity would issue rules to cover. But in 1947 the Council was unimpressed and, after the pair left the meeting, voted down their request. Much to Lucille's and Mayo's irritation, Sam Zolotow reported on September 3 in the *New York Times* that "one exasperated councilor characterized the plea as an attempt to get actors to work for nothing." The pair sent Zolotow a lengthy letter defending their position and invited him to the White Barn.

Preferring charm and persuasion to confrontation, Lucille revived her friendship with her former director Clarence Derwent, who was president of Actors' Equity and had chaired the Council meeting. On September 14 Derwent was among the more than one hundred and twenty-five people who saw *Ivory Tower* and he was photographed with Lucille while signing in. Indeed, in the spring of 1948, fired by the news that the American National Theatre and Academy was going to resuscitate its dormant Experimental Theatre Invitational Series, and considering the White Barn an experimental endeavor, Lucille conveyed to

Derwent that she believed Equity had granted permissions to the Invitational Series which it was disallowing the White Barn.

Despite Equity's ruling, Lucille was basking in the Tryout Theatre's success. Suddenly the White Barn was news. The Westport press lavished praise. *Variety* ran an article on September 10, 1947, "Readings of plays for potential angels—which are normally dull affairs in someone's crowded living room or a dingy rehearsal hall—have been transformed by a stage-struck (and wealthy) Connecticut matron into Sunday evening events with something of the excitement and glamour of a Broadway first night." *Ivory Tower* was supposedly heading for Broadway, and Lucille was interviewed on radio programs and made Cholly Knickerbocker's gossip column in the *New York Journal-American*. She even drew good press for a bit of psychodrama. On Sunday afternoon, October 5, Lucille opened her theatre to Dr. J. L. Moreno, who demonstrated his psycho-dramatic techniques for treating patients; the audience included Philip Huston, Stella Adler and Harold Clurman.

Throughout that first summer, Lucille reveled in the newfound pleasure of bringing together untried plays, unknown actors and potential backers. On Sunday mornings she drove to the train in a station wagon, to meet actors arriving from New York. Back at Fairweather, she saw that they received breakfast—orange juice, eggs, jelly doughnuts—that coffee flowed all day in the green room and the cast received an early dinner. She let directors scavenge her house for props and furniture. At night she greeted the audiences and mingled with them after the reading, leaning on the counter in the green room and chatting about theatre. She became increasingly confident and assertive, and her whole manner grew more animated.

According to Lucille, Lou learned about the White Barn while he was in Paris, from a *Variety* article picked up by European newspapers. In September he wrote her from France and offered advice and complete financial support. But Lucille, who suspected he was having an affair, was not beguiled. "Dear Lou," she responded pointedly,

Thanks for all the help and interest you had given me in the "White Barn Theatre."

I do hope that when you return—you will bring with you the Lou—with all his ideas and devotion—that I loved

Your

Lucille

Based on Lucille's hints and confidences, Mimi Bochco always believed that her friend also had a love affair that summer. True or not, Lucille was so angry with Lou by the time he returned to Westport that she would not let him into the house and made him sleep in an apartment over the garage.

Buoyed by the enthusiastic press, Lucille headed energetically into her 1948 season, but with a difference. Gone were the mediocre properties of the previous summer and in their place were a couple of stylistically experimental plays with literary merit. Alfred H. Tamarin, formerly the Theatre Guild's publicity chief and now East Coast publicity director for United Artists, brought her Sean O'Casey's poetic urban drama, *Red Roses for Me*, which was yet to be produced professionally in the United States. Tamarin and Lucille formed a joint venture to mount an $80,000 Broadway production in the fall and, hoping to attract partners, they enlisted John O'Shaughnessy to direct a reading with Kim Hunter, using her day off from playing Stella in *A Streetcar Named Desire*. To Tamarin's and Lucille's deep disappointment, they could not raise the money.

Canada Lee and a young producer named Mark Marvin brought William Saroyan's surrealist *Jim Dandy*, which they hoped to take to Broadway. The cast included Lee and a comic actor with a rubbery face named Zero Mostel, who fell and broke his left leg the week before the reading and, with his leg in a cast, performed sitting in a wheelchair. There was a play called *A-Day* by the screenwriter Robertson White, about eleven people forced to live one thousand feet underground in preparation for an

atomic explosion. And at the last moment, Lucille added a postseason surprise: Hoagy Carmichael's Broadway-bound musical revue, *Alive and Kicking*, which treated the audience to the jazzy vocalizations of the Golden
Gate Quartet. Lucille told Fred Russell of the *Bridgeport Post* that it would
be "a delightful change of pace." She invested in it herself.

That yen for a change of pace led Lucille during the spring of 1949 to
go to France and England to mine the theatre scenes there. After all, she
told herself, other theatrical producers made this pilgrimage; why
shouldn't she?

Perhaps, too, she aspired to make the White Barn more than a spot
for backers' auditions, no matter how glorified. *Variety* had characterized
her as a rich matron, a description that dogged her for the rest of her career. "I would not like my rich friends to think I play with this," she once
told Eloise Armen, who was publicity director at the White Barn in 1977.
"I want them to think I'm a professional." But she could not have a commercial theatre on her property—the residential zoning laws were pro-
hibitive. And in any event, Lou, with whom she had partially reconciled
and who was financing this enterprise, did not want to undertake an operation that would have to compete with the Westport Country Playhouse, which sat more than six hundred people and offered elaborate,
star-filled productions. So she shrewdly cast about for another approach,
one that would suit her eclectic and offbeat taste, entertain her audience
and bring herself professional recognition.

In addition, while the Tryout Theatre's press coverage was excellent,
attendance fluctuated, sometimes dipping below one hundred. It must
have occurred to her that there were only a finite number of potential
backers who would traipse to readings in Westport, and that by pursuing
investors she was losing the theatre people about whom, in her heart,
she cared the most.

And she still had to find a way of dealing with Equity. Although the
actors in *Red Roses for Me* had received the required $5 payment, nobody

had applied to the union for permission, and two days after the reading both Shaughnessy and Tamarin had been compelled to appear before the Council to defend their gaffe. Equity, she felt, was cramping her style.

In February 1949 she opened an office for Lucille Lortel Productions at 400 Madison Avenue, about ten blocks from the Plaza Hotel at Fifth Avenue and 59th Street, where she and Lou were now living. And on March 26 she and Lou sailed for Europe on the *Queen Elizabeth*. Intending to go to Paris and London, with a brief stop in Zurich, she canvassed friends for the names and phone numbers of theatres and dramatic agents, which she carefully wrote in pencil at the back of her pocket-sized address book. Erwin and Maria-Ley Piscator gave her letters of introduction to the French playwright Marcel Aymé and the actor and director Jean-Louis Barrault.

They arrived in Paris on April 1 at two o'clock in the morning, slept and then walked to the Café de la Paix. For Lucille and Lou, seeing Paris together for the first time since the war was as much about repairing their marriage as it was a chance for Lucille to find plays. They went for walks on the Champs Élysées, ate at Prunier, Maxim's and the Ritz, went to nightclubs and snacked in their hotel room in the early morning hours. On Wednesday, April 6, they saw Marcel Aymé's *Lucienne and the Butcher,* and Lucille scribbled in her travel diary that she "liked it," and she saw Armand Salacrou's *L'Archipel Lenoir*. But generally she did not care for the French plays. They left Sartre's *Les Mains Sales* at intermission; she noted in her diary that "Lou wanted to go" and that she "enjoyed N.Y. production much better." She attended fashion shows at Dior and Jacques Fath, and shopped: two coats and two dresses for herself; perfume for Mrs. Piscator; on a side trip to Switzerland, she bought watches for her brothers, for Ruth and Cugat, and for "mom and dad," who were nominally sharing an apartment on West 73rd Street. But in terms of plays, Lucille wrote to Ruth, "I have as yet not found anything."

She need not have gone further than London, where they arrived on

April 25. There she met Mary Grew, a diminutive and once glamorous former actress, who, among other things, was guiding the acting career of her eighteen-year-old niece, a dark-haired beauty named Claire Bloom. Grew introduced Lucille to London's club theatres, particularly the New Boltons, run by Peter Cotes, the Lindsay, and the Sunday Night Club Theatre, whose director, actress Hazel Vincent Wallace, would become a good friend.

Club theatres, in which Lucille saw a model for the White Barn, had emerged before and after World War II as an alternative to commercial theatres. Intimate theatres that supported themselves by private membership, the club setups presented plays shunned by the conservative West End, London's equivalent of Broadway. Most importantly the club theatres circumvented the Lord Chamberlain's office, which for hundreds of years had read every play that was to be produced on the public British stage and vetoed production, or suggested cuts, if it deemed a work morally or politically unfit. Club theatres produced O'Neill's *Desire Under the Elms* and Lillian Hellman's *The Children's Hour,* both of which had fallen beneath the Lord Chamberlain's axe.

Lucille did not need to avoid that sort of censorship. Film, more than theatre, was subject to restraints, primarily from the Hays Code of the Motion Picture Association of America but also, beginning in 1947, from fear of the House Un-American Activities Committee, which was scouring the content of Hollywood movies for Communist propaganda.

But she saw in the club theatre a way to acquire a stable and fee-paying membership, give plays fully-staged productions and, because it would not seek to make a profit, hopefully avoid Equity's scrutiny. Eager to put her new idea in motion, on May 6 she and Lou sailed for New York on the R.M.S. *Caronia.*

Back in the States, in a May 31 report for *Show Business,* she praised the club theatres and suggested that Equity fall in line with its British counterpart:

... In England I was particularly interested in the Club Theatres. Like the White Barn Theatre in Westport, these Club Theatres situated off London's West End, also try out new plays. But instead of an audience of backers, such as we invite to the White Barn, these club theatres rely wholly upon subscribers' memberships. They strive to be self-supporting, but some need the assistance of wealthy patrons.

The Theatre Union considers the Club Theatres as private, non-commercial undertakings and do not prohibit the actor taking these club jobs or put any obstacles in the way of limiting the best possible productions.

The Bolton Theatre has 9,000 members. The club membership entitles the members and their guests to use the Club-room and Bar at the rear of the Theatre, which is open every day. The subscription for membership is one guinea ($5.00) annually with an initial entrance fee of ten shillings and sixpence. (Approx. $2.00)

Like the White Barn there is also an enthusiastic spirit and interchange of opinion between cast and members in the social rooms after the performance.

I hope that we too at the White Barn might be able to achieve the larger scope and advantages of London's Club Theatres. Toward this end the cooperation of Actors' Equity and the support of theatre loving people is essential.

Lucille transformed the White Barn into an American version of a British club theatre. First she altered the physical space. The German émigré Hans Sondheimer, who was technical director for the recently formed New York City Center Opera Company, created a permanent stage. Lucille installed lighting equipment, new drapes, a better cooling system.

The slightly smaller theatre now accommodated around 135 seats, of which Lucille set aside 100 for members and 35 for special guests such as critics, agents, producers, or anybody else she chose to invite. She sent form letters to prospective members and personally interviewed several who were interested, finally arriving at a group that included rich and not-so-rich friends from New York and Westport, local artists, and theatre people. Membership dues were $10 a couple, which entitled the pair to buy a five-performance subscription for $15; single tickets were $2. All members were promised free admission to special events like movies and discussions.

With members, she could now rely on an audience whom she knew personally and, since they had to present membership cards to receive their tickets, she was able to draw up a seating chart in advance and control who sat where at each performance, which was as vital to her as arranging the table for a dinner party. And woe to anyone who left at intermission. "She knew where I was sitting," said Leo Nevas, "and she'd call the next day. She watched. That seat was empty."

The newly renamed White Barn Club Theatre operated more like an arts center than simply a theatre. Following her inclination for variety, Lucille offered a taste of everything. The 1949 season opened with Federico Garcia Lorca's romance, *The Love of Don Perlimpin and Belisa in the Garden*. The following week came a prerelease screening of an avant-garde Scandinavian film. The next entry was an event Lucille dubbed the White Barn Varieties, for which she drew performers as different as the comedian Roger Price, whose act she had seen at the Blue Angel; a Chinese bass-baritone named Yi-Kwei Sze, who was in the United States prior to his Carnegie Hall debut; and because she loved dance, two modern dancers from Katherine Dunham's company and the Haitian-born dancer and singer Josephine Premice.

From England's Lindsay Club Theatre, Lucille imported Shirley Cocks' drama *Gingerbread House,* about a young artist dominated alternately by his mother and a homosexual attorney. Possibly on advice from Mayo, who was still the White Barn's managing director, she brought the Lemonade Opera's American premiere of Felix Mendelssohn's *The Stranger*, which the company performed outdoors. Despite the cool evening, the audience sat on chairs arranged in rows on the flagstone terrace, and the singers stood on a miniature portable stage, set up on a gentle grassy rise in front of the terrace.

Politics, too, had its moment at the White Barn that summer, despite Lucille's frequent avowal that she was not a political person. After the performance of *The Stranger*, Jacob Javits and Clarence Derwent spoke briefly, to advocate for Javits' bill in congress calling for federal support of a national foundation to serve the performing arts. Among other things, this was Lucille's gesture of personal public support for the sixty-five-year-old Derwent, who, arriving back from England by plane on July 17, had been detained at La Guardia Field for six hours by U.S. immigration officials and grilled about possible Communist affiliations. As a British citizen heading an American union, a staunch supporter of racial integration in the theatre and an opponent of the Red Scare hysteria overrunning the country, Derwent was unfortunately a natural target of anti-Communist hatemongers.

That same year, Lucille even considered a fall season, momentarily anyway. In New York, she had trekked to a scruffy loft beneath a Yugoslav hall at 40th Street and Eighth Avenue, where a non-Equity group called the People's Drama Company was performing *They Shall Not Die*, a drama about the Scottsboro case that had once been mounted unsuccessfully by the Theatre Guild. Its director, Gene Frankel, had infused the play with raw immediacy. "Lucille saw it, liked it and wanted to support it," Frankel recalled. "I was really flabbergasted by the invitation." Lucille brought them to chilly Westport for one performance in November.

Was Equity swayed by this experimentation? More likely Derwent, who had allowed Lucille to print his name on White Barn stationery as an advisor, discreetly exerted pressure behind the scenes. Equity Library Theatre (ELT) was struggling financially at the time, and someone—

possibly Derwent, possibly Lucille, who brought ELT's production of T.S. Eliot's *Murder in the Cathedral* to the White Barn on July 9, 1950—devised a plan that would provide money for ELT and at the same time solve the White Barn's dilemma.

The union's records show that on July 25, 1950, Willard "Bill" Swire, who was then assistant executive secretary of Actors' Equity, made a proposal to the Council on Lucille's behalf: she was to be allowed to use Equity actors and rehearse them as much as ten days, if she paid each one a token fee of $10, covered the cost of room and board in Westport, travel to and from Westport, and donated $125 to ELT for each White Barn production. Swire had already secured ELT's consent. With this agreement, by 1951, Lucille was often adding a Saturday night dress rehearsal to which an audience was invited, but Equity avoided counting that as a performance.

In fairness, it would have made no sense for the White Barn to operate according to a commercial summer stock agreement, which in 1950 required that actors be paid a minimum of $50 a week for eight performances. But undoubtedly Equity was giving Lucille a break at actors' expense. Michael Tolan, who appeared at the White Barn in 1954 in *Here Is the News,* found it "quite amazing that Equity allowed us to be paid nothing" and wondered, "How did she get away with this?"

But most actors accepted the arrangement in exchange for an opportunity to be seen. Lucille quickly acquired a reputation for drawing television and film producers, theatre directors, talent agents and New York reviewers to her Sunday nights. "I was not at the beginning of my career, but close to it," said Sada Thompson, who performed in Paul Shyre's *U.S.A.* in 1953, winning raves from the critics. "And I went to Westport with the hope that something more was going to come from it." Anne Meacham first worked at the White Barn in 1955, when she played opposite the veteran actress Ruth Chatterton in Ettore Rella's drama *Sign of Winter.* "Anytime an actor performs with a good company and director and play—it is an advantage to be seen by professional theatre people such as some who came to the White Barn," she commented years later. "However," she added carefully, "it was a certain kind of luxury to work there without—fee." Lucille did pay companies whose productions she brought to the theatre whole: $100 to the Tibor-Nagy Marionettes for two performances in 1950; $200 for the Young Ireland Theatre Company in 1952; $150 in 1953 to Geoffrey Holder and his Trinidad Dancers.

But Lucille could be cavalier about an artist's sacrifice. In 1957, when Douglass Watson wanted to stage Kafka's *Metamorphosis* for the ANTA Matinee Series, of which Lucille was artistic director, he rented a rehearsal studio out of his own pocket. "He was not a wealthy actor," said the drama critic Henry Hewes, who was executive director of ANTA's Greater New York Chapter at the time, "and I suggested to Lucille that we reimburse him for the rehearsal space. She said, 'Oh no, no, no, actors want to do this, and it's for their pleasure I'm doing it.' " Despite producing the work of numerous British playwrights, she rarely paid these authors' fares to the United States to see their work, nor in the early years did she pay for the right to present their work if she could avoid it. It was as though she needed to see that an artist, or anybody else who wanted money from her, was resolute and in some measure self-reliant before she supported them.

At times, in fact, her giving seemed to the recipients like an exercise in control. She had always given money to Ralph Alswang, who, according to his daughter Hope, was notoriously bad at managing money, and when Betty and Ralph Alswang died during the 1970s, leaving Hope and her husband to raise her brother, Ralph, Jr., who was only a teenager, Lucille gave money for the boy's boarding school and college. "She asked to see me after my father died," said Hope, "and she said she would help with Ralph, Jr.'s schooling. But it wasn't like she just wrote the check every year and I could count on it. There would be years when Vincent Curcio would say, 'She's in a bad mood and she thinks your letter was rude; write her another letter.' She was generous but she was also irrational and erratic."

But Lucille's support, when she believed in and cared for someone, was unquestioning. The gift might be lighthearted, like throwing a wedding reception at Derwent House for Geoffrey Holder and his bride Carmen de Lavallade. Or it might be vital, like enabling the Irish actor Milo O'Shea to remain in the United States legally. O'Shea was touring the country with the Young Ireland Theatre Company when he received an offer to work on Broadway. "I was on a visitor's visa," O'Shea recalled, "and I needed to get permission to work here and I needed sponsors. I told this to Lucille and Lou, and they said, 'Don't worry, we'll be your sponsors.' "

Often she gave without being asked. In 1977 Mimi Bochco's husband, Rudolph, was bedridden with cancer in California, and Bochco could only afford to hire a nurse at night. Lucille sent her enough money for nurses around the clock. The director Marshall W. Mason recalled that, during the late 1980s and early '90s, he was living in California, struggling to obtain film work, and sometimes could barely meet his rent. Lucille on occasion would send him a $5,000 check. Of course once he did ask—for $6,000—and when she sent the money she wrote that $5,000 of it was a gift, the rest she expected him to repay.

With the Equity problem resolved, Lucille moved on to the pleasanter tasks of improving and promoting the White Barn. From 1950 through 1955, she strengthened its profile. Each year, it seemed, she introduced something new, whether it was cosmetic, like putting Cugat's woodcut of the theatre on the program's cover, or structural, like incorporating in 1951 as the private, charitable White Barn Theatre Foundation. John Lodge, who had been elected state governor the previous November, probably helped arrange that Connecticut grant Lucille the necessary charter. The Foundation's purpose was now officially "The furnishing of an opportunity for new playwrights, directors, actors and designers to exhibit and develop their talents pertaining to the theatre."

Thus did the White Barn Club Theatre quietly transform into the White Barn Theatre. The new status ensured that Lucille and Lou could deduct their own expenses as contributions and raise money to support the operation, which by 1952 was reportedly costing Lou between $20,000 and $30,000 a year. Now the White Barn was officially a non-commercial enterprise. As Lucille once told *New York Herald Tribune* reporter Don Ross, "I'm not in the theater business to make money."

Lucille, Clarence Derwent and Albert A. Dickason, of the University of Bridgeport's Drama Department, were the Foundation's first three directors. Dickason, a congenial, well-organized man who preserved hopes of writing and directing plays professionally, saw the White Barn as a credit that could further both his academic and commercial careers. In him, Lucille saw somebody who could run the White Barn's Summer Apprentice School, which she had initiated in 1951 and for which she charged each apprentice $150 for the eight-week season.

Depending on one's outlook, there was either an irritating sloppiness or an appealing looseness to Lucille's operation. The summer roster often did not coalesce until the last moment. The curtain rarely went up on time, for she allowed no production to start until she felt everything was ready. But she offered an astute blend of the old-fashioned and the new, the irreverent and the conventional, the European and the American.

Audiences might see a 1911 Somerset Maugham drama called *Loaves and Fishes*, which she had caught that April in a revival at the New Boltons. Even Maugham, writing Lucille, said "I should have thought that by now it was entirely dated." Or they might see a young American company called the Touring Players, a group founded in 1946 by the actresses Lisabeth Blake and Peg Murray. In 1952 Blake and Murray came to the White Barn with three one-acts: *Londonderry Air*, by the well-known children's book author Rachel Field, portrayed a charming tramp and the servant girl he woos; Ellen Violett's adaptation of Gertrude Stein's *Brewsie and Willy* dramatized war's disturbing aftereffects; Violett's version of Shirley Jackson's potent short story, *The Lottery,* demonstrated the horror of mob violence. A subscriber distressed by the darkness of these plays could be consoled later in the season by Lawton Campbell's three-act melodrama, *Elizabeth, The Bachelor Queen,* a romance about Elizabeth I of England and Robert Dudley. And if they did not care for *that,* they could at least admire Nancy Wickwire's magnetic performance as Elizabeth.

Sometimes Lucille chose to produce an actor more than a script. In 1953, after nearly twenty years of making films, gnomish, white-haired, sixty-two-year-old Sam Jaffe found himself pursued by the anti-Communist witchhunt and could no longer find work. He wanted to re-turn to the legitimate theatre as Noah in André Obey's allegorical 1931 drama *Noah: The Voyage of the Ark.* Lucille, who knew Jaffe from Westport, and knew that her audience liked him as a film star and remembered him as a stage actor, scheduled it. Unfortunately, during the Saturday night dress rehearsal, which was essentially a performance, Jaffe col-lapsed onstage from the July heat in the middle of the third act. His fel-low actors got him to his feet—Jaffe was taken to the hospital—and the rest of the performance was canceled, leaving disconsolate subscribers to wander downstairs to the green room and munch aimlessly on sand-wiches and cake. Despite the disruption, the *Variety* critic managed to write a review, citing "heavy-handed pacing" and an "amateurish" pro-duction but praising Jaffe's "sensitive, appealing performance."

Three weekends later, at the opposite stylistic pole from Obey's phi-losophizing, Lucille presented Paul Shyre's adaptation of John Dos Pas-sos' sweeping social novels, *U.S.A.,* with its verbal portraits of national icons like Isadora Duncan, Rudolf Valentino and the Unknown Soldier. Shyre, who also directed, wove together biography, newsreels and fiction using recitation, blackout sketches and minimal props. Adopting an ap-proach that, during the 1960s, would become a popular tool of story theatre, Shyre asked his five performers to act out the newsreel sequences. Audiences were alternately engrossed and bored, and the *Show Business* critic Rita Hassan, a Westport resident, suggested "judicious cutting." But she added, "Now and then the piece is evocative. Outstanding is the reading by Sada Thompson. Without movement, talking conversationally, there were one or two moments when the actress succeeded in becoming the fabulous Isadora herself."

Critics, while encouraging, often did not know what to make of Lucille's potpourri. *Variety*'s scribes were looking for plays with commercial possibilities, but rarely found them on Cranbury Road. Fred Russell of the *Bridgeport Post*, one of the more provincial reviewers, expressed shock when he believed a play went over the line morally. Covering an adaptation of Georges Simenon's novel *The Snow Was Black*, about a prostitute's son, in 1954 Russell grumbled, "Had the story been told with even the slightest touch of finesse the impact might have been less repulsive." For Vernon Rice at the *New York Post*, Lucille could have dispensed with everything except the avant-garde. Cajoled in August 1951 into covering the *White Barn Revue*, a musical by Albert Dickason about a group of youngsters taking over a theatre, a stunned Rice wrote,

> Everybody went around telling everybody else, "Isn't it wonderful" to think many of them have never been on a stage before and they did it all in three weeks. Me, I'm a middle-of-the-road guy. Apprentices have to get experience, and Miss Lortel's are fortunate that they are getting theirs in front of such sympathetic and understanding audiences. The fact that a baby walks, however, is only remarkable to the baby and to its parents. The casual bystander can only consider walking rather commonplace.

But Rice was not running a summer theatre. The apprentice productions were open to the public, not just to subscribers, and they were enormously popular with audiences who came to see their children. These exuberant amateur romps received more press coverage than anything else Lucille presented. It might have astounded Rice to learn that, during the summer of 1951, Lucille also participated in Celebrity Day in honor of the town of Norwalk's 300th birthday, appearing on a kind of quiz show at the Norwalk High School with Armina Marshall of the Westport Country Playhouse and Manfred Lee, author of the *Ellery Queen* murder mysteries. She rarely turned down a public opportunity to be introduced as the producer of the White Barn and was too smart to ignore her community.

She tried to walk in the fledgling steps of the American Shakespeare Festival Theatre and Academy. For years, Lawrence Langner had dreamed of an American playhouse patterned after the sixteenth-century Globe Theatre, where many of Shakespeare's finest plays were first performed. Since Langner had a home in Westport and already ran one theatre there, he thought the town would be an ideal place for his dream to become reality. John Lodge, Connecticut's governor, endorsed the venture. Langner engaged a Westport architect to draw up plans in 1951 and he established an office and fund-raising staff in town. Committees were formed to spread the word and find support.

In 1952, Lucille opened her living room at Fairweather to a meeting of the Authors', Writers' and Publishers' Committee. Lily Lodge, the governor's daughter, explained a model of the proposed building. The director Margaret Webster talked about America's need for a world-class Shakespearean stage. Lucille probably would have participated more if asked. But the good people of Westport rejected Langner's vision—the theatre was finally built in Stratford, Connecticut—and the Schweitzers' involvement eventually consisted of contributing dollars. As Lucille undoubtedly realized, Langner's reach extended to a powerful network of financiers and politicians, beside whom the Schweitzers, for all their money, could not compete. "My feeling," said the actress

Paula Laurence, whose husband, Charles Bowden, managed the West-port Country Playhouse, "was that Lucille and Lou, for good reason, decided they would help if it was something that interested them, but they weren't going to try to get into areas where they clearly weren't being welcomed with open arms. They were going to run their own op-eration. And I applauded that."

To find plays for the White Barn, Lucille would go anywhere. It was an aspect of her personality that endeared her to designer Ralph Alswang. "He adored her," said Hope Alswang. "Daddy always said, the thing that was great about Lucille was that she'd climb ten flights of stairs, go to any dirty loft, do anything to see theatre." Hope never found Lucille as sympathetic as her father did. "But I'm not in the theatre. What is this theatre obsession, that they would drag each other to see all of this avant-garde?"

Lucille preferred seeing plays or hearing them read aloud to reading them herself, long before difficulties with her eyes would make reading hard if not impossible. "She did not read scripts," averred Rita Fredricks Salzman, a former actress who met Lucille in the 1940s through Equity Library Theatre. Certainly Lucille went to considerable lengths to hear a play. It annoyed producer Basil C. Langton, who wanted Lucille to con-sider an adaptation of André Gide's *Symphony Pastoral*, that she insisted on a special reading in 1958. "Couldn't you use the tape, or send the script to your board, or would you like me to talk to them about it and read pas-sages," he wrote her somewhat querulously. Later, in the 1970s, actors would have to troop to her apartment at the Sherry-Netherland to read aloud the scripts that producers wanted her to consider.

"The idea of someone looking for new playwrights and adoring plays and not reading them makes you smile," said Marian Seldes, who starred in *Gertrude Stein and a Companion* at the White Barn and often was called upon to read plays at the Sherry. "But if she heard the plays, she would respond to them. I think it's brilliant."

The closest Lucille came to explaining the reason for her approach was one rainy day in 1993, at a reception in the Westport Public Library honoring Sam McCready's bio-bibliography of her. There were not many people there, but she felt among friends and was unusually relaxed, and someone in the audience asked about Athol Fugard. "I find reading Fugard is very simple," she said, turning around in her seat to answer the question. "I find it difficult to read a lot of plays. I have to go over and over. But not Fugard. Even now I could read a Fugard play."

But no matter how many plays she saw, during the first half of the 1950s it was difficult to find startling new scripts, especially home-grown ones. A goodly amount of the innovative work Lucille presented was in the realms of music and dance. In 1952 she brought the Baltimore-based Hilltop Musical Company and its production of Hugo Weisgall's opera *The Stronger*, based on Strindberg's play and conducted by Weisgall, who was a significant American composer. The following summer she offered the United States debut of Paul Curtis' American Mime Theatre.

In June 1953 Lucille was a celebrity judge on the Dumont Network's television program *Stage a Number*, which showcased aspiring performers. A lithe, six-foot-six dancer named Geoffrey Holder had recently arrived from the Caribbean with his steel band and had auditioned for the impresario Sol Hurok, who declined to give him or his group a job. So one day Holder and his company found themselves performing on *Stage a Number*—and won. "My dear Mr. Holder," Lucille said to him afterward, "I love your band very much. Would you like to perform at the White Barn Theatre?"

Paula Laurence never forgot the July 5, 1953 evening Holder first danced at the White Barn. "In those days," she said, "Lucille had a natural outdoor theatre that was ravishing. It was the Fourth of July weekend, and our house guest was an old chum of mine named Bill Hawkins, who was the drama critic on the *New York World-Telegram and Sun*. Lucille had invited us to her Sunday night, and this evening she was presenting Holder, who had never danced in this country before, and she was having an exhibition of his paintings in the green room.

"We were outdoors on the terrace, this beautiful expanse of lawn with a little hill. There was a clump of birch trees, and in the middle of it was this extraordinary figure. Seven feet tall, this glorious thing, and he had his arms outstretched. He seemed to be wearing a couple of necklaces and some tight pants, and you could see a figure in white through the trees, a woman named Scoogie Brown, a wonderful dancer. It was just an enchanting evening." As Lucille had doubtless hoped, Hawkins rhapsodized about Holder in print and, said Laurence, "Geoffrey was off and running."

Promotion was all-important to Lucille. Confident and aggressive in that arena, which required action more than analysis, she enlisted a series of assistants and secretaries to saturate the Connecticut and New York newspapers with press releases. Drawing on her experience as an actress, she parlayed any event into an announcement: upcoming productions; her trips to Europe to find plays; the parties she threw; her involvement with New York-based theatre groups like ANTA and New York productions in which she had a financial interest; the celebrities in the audience at the White Barn, for she had learned the knack of sending a list of famous guests to newspapers ahead of time. She carried press releases and newspaper clippings in her pocketbook, to hand out to anybody whom she felt ought to know about her theatre. Articles and reviews were pasted religiously in scrapbooks, which she proudly brought forth when talking to reporters or being interviewed by radio hosts like Barry Gray, Eva Gabor and Maggi McNellis. She easily cultivated journalists and critics, inviting them to her parties at Fairweather and the Plaza in New York City—even giving Christmas presents to a select few.

Fearless about inviting notable guests, whether she knew them or not, she scored publicity coups when they appeared. On August 19, 1951, the acting Irish consul and the Irish vice consul were on hand when the Young Ireland Theatre Company performed Lady Gregory's *The Rising of the Moon* and W.B. Yeats' *The Words Upon the Window Pane.* Writing to the American composer Gian-Carlo Menotti in Mount Kisco, New York, on July 1, 1952, Lucille mentioned that she had read an article by him in the *New York Times* magazine and thought he might be interested in hearing Weisgall's opera. He could bring a guest, she added. Menotti arrived with a young conductor named Thomas Schippers. Naturally the two musicians were photographed picking up their tickets. Visiting stars, whether they liked it or not—and some did not—could always expect to be photographed with Lucille, and the Westport newspapers ran the pictures. Lucille and her theatre were good copy.

Of the many talented people Lucille drew into the White Barn's orbit in its early years, the most valuable was Ralph Alswang. A hulking, handsome man who towered over her, Alswang knew all aspects of the professional theatre: directing, producing, designing sets, costumes and lighting. Also he had worked in television, until he was blacklisted. He moved his family from New York City to Weston in 1951, when he was thirty-five years old. "All I remember," Hope Alswang recalled, "from the time we lived in Connecticut, is that Ralph was at the White Barn every weekend. For him, it was wonderful having this theatrical experience around the corner. The Westport Country Playhouse wasn't very intriguing—it was doing more conventional things. This was an experimental theatre that gave him a lot of pleasure."

In Alswang Lucille found a counselor, especially in the area of design. Although the White Barn had advanced from its tryout days, when a set meant a bed or table on stage, aesthetically stimulating productions were hardly the theatre's signature. Productions looked haphazard, and black drops seemed to be the background for every play. Sets for the apprentices' productions were thickets of heavy furniture borrowed from local antique shops. Lucille had dealt with the problem by presenting plays that required minimal sets and lighting, which also reduced costs. Actors in contemporary works usually wore their own clothes.

The turning point was Alswang's redesign of the stage itself. In 1954, he devised a plan that widened the stage to twenty-six feet and more importantly deepened it to thirty feet. A new back wall contained a sliding door that could open to reveal treetops and sky, or close to permit the use of rear projections thrown from an elevator platform outside the theatre. Alswang's adjustments also allowed for a hundred and fifty-six permanent seats.

Lou supervised the expansion and technical installations. He also purchased state-of-the-art equipment in the relatively youthful field of television and set up a closed-circuit viewing system and a projection television, on which he watched some of the earliest televised sports events.

That summer critics actually complimented the designs, which they had hardly ever done before. Reviewing Franz Spencer's political comedy *The Happy Ant-Hill*, Bryson Randolph in the *Westporter-Herald* praised Richard Merrell's "imaginative, highly stylized, multi-level setting," as well as "the occasional better-than-average lighting, the mood-setting rear-projection effects and the fluid groupings by director Steve Zacharias." The rather schematic satire drew a parallel between ants and human beings living in Eastern Europe under a variety of governments, and Merrell's concept reflected the playwright's intention. "The set," wrote Harold Hornstein in the *Westport Town Crier*, "consisting of the cellar, garret and living quarters of a home, was used as a microscopic field for observing the seamy habits of man under three regimes—capitalist, fascist and Communist. As the regimes change, the occupants of the luxurious living quarters change. Under capitalism, the landlord occupies the living quarters; under fascism, a couple of thieves; under communism, the janitor becomes a commissar who reaches the best part of the house."

Merrell designed sets for the three new plays that originated at the White Barn that season. Unfortunately he was gone the next summer, but he had helped the White Barn cross a threshold.

There was another change in 1954. Needing to house the actors who, thanks to Equity's decision, now spent longer rehearsal periods at the White Barn, Lucille looked about for a place to buy. She also wanted to provide accommodations for African-American actors, who could not find lodging in discriminatory Westport and often were forced to stay in run-down hotels in Norwalk. Near Fairweather stood a mansion that had once belonged to a wealthy manufacturer named Walter Lissberger. A formidable two-story pile built during the nineteenth century, it offered at least ten bedrooms, many of which could accommodate two beds; a swimming pool; and it was only a seven-minute walk from the theatre. At the end of March, the White Barn Theatre Foundation purchased the property for $28,500, although it was clear that Lou put up the money. Lissberger's nephew, a film producer named Eliot Hyman, reportedly donated $500 to refurbish the sun porch as a dining room. On the lovely warm evening of June 13, Lucille hosted cocktails and a dinner to dedicate Derwent House, as she called it in honor of her good friend. Derwent and his sister, Elfrida, an actress, were the first guests.

Photographs began to cover the walls of the green room at the White Barn, photographs of Lucille with the celebrities who came there from New York, Connecticut and Hollywood. Leo Nevas noticed that Lou was not in any of the shots.

The White Barn was Lucille's world, and with its success, the balance of her marriage had changed, at least publicly. Nevas remembered that at parties and other gatherings, she could always be seen talking animatedly with groups of people, while Lou stood on the outskirts, his shirttails hanging out, an Old Gold cigarette dangling loosely between the fingers of his left hand. On Sundays, when Lucille was seeing to actors, Lou would hole himself up in his radio shack and talk to fellow hams around the world. Actors who worked at the White Barn often wondered who the strange man was, slouching about the property looking frumpish and wearing a battered, peaked straw hat.

The actor George Morfogen, who studied at the theatre with Eva Le Gallienne during 1956 and '57, remembered "a stone-faced" and "unavailable man," who was "not a very effusive person." But Anne Meacham remembered "a genial man. At one end of the lobby was Lou's television control booth, and Lou was delighted when someone was truly interested."

Lou involved himself in his wife's enterprise in ways that made him feel comfortable and did not impinge on the attention that he knew she wanted. He helped out with the sound for various productions. When the Young Ireland Theatre Company performed at the White Barn in 1951 and 1952, Lou arranged for the thrilled actors to talk via shortwave radio to their relatives and friends in Dublin. As Milo O'Shea recalled, Lou "got on the blower" and "I spoke to my parents. It was wonderful." Not in the best of health—he had been diagnosed with diabetes in 1945—Lou was never more content than when absorbed in his electronic toys.

It was public knowledge that Lou supported the White Barn financially, but that he steered the theatre toward smart business practices was less widely known. Angry though Lucille might have been by Lou's affairs, and determined though she was that the world know this was her theatre alone, she relied on and trusted his business expertise. Lou, for his part, wanted to ensure that his wife's theatres were managed in a way that would never embarrass her or lose money unduly. Herbert Sturz, whom Lou hired in 1960 to help establish the Vera Foundation, recalled many instances when Lucille would phone her husband at the office, to ask advice about this or that move she was about to undertake.

Sometimes Lou simply stepped in quietly, as in 1951 when he wrote a letter to his rich friend Benjamin Sonnenberg, a public relations expert, and asked if he "could get some publicity" for an opera called *Comedy on the Bridge* that Lucille was presenting. Lou also observed that the White Barn needed a trustworthy and knowledgeable person to take charge of the theatre's technical side, so he brought in Arthur "Art" Murray, who had worked for him at a Schweitzer paper plant in New Jersey. Now the White Barn's technical director, in 1954 Murray moved his wife, Genevieve, and their children to Westport permanently, to help the Schweitzers year-round.

At other times Lou intervened more forcefully. He guided Lucille's strategy for responding to Actors' Equity in the early 1960s. When Paul Berkowsky managed the Theatre de Lys from 1964 to 1976, "things were negotiated through Lou," said Berkowsky's widow, Sheala. "If Paul had any problems or he wanted a week off—even when it came to negotiating contracts for the theatre—Lou had to be in on it. He had to know everything." Sheala Berkowsky believed that "it didn't make any difference to Lucille. Lou was a successful businessman, she relied upon him to do the right thing." But like Leo Nevas, Paul Berkowsky noticed that photographs taken at the White Barn and the Theatre de Lys never included Louis Schweitzer. "Paul used to say that to her all the time," Sheala recalled. " 'That's all right, darling,' Lucille would tell Paul. She didn't want to come out and say, 'Well, this is me, this isn't him.' "

By the mid-1950s, Lucille was the center of her family both financially and emotionally. Not only was Lou supporting Anny, but he began setting up living trusts for Mayo, Seymour, and Ruth and Cugat. Harry had died in 1955 with little fanfare: the obituary notice in the *New York Times* simply read "beloved husband of Anna, devoted father." Lucille wanted Ruth near her in Westport, and in 1960 Lou bought them a house called Cranbury Farm close by on Partrick Avenue. There Ruth and Cugat eventually became recluses, painting and tending their myriad cats.

After involving himself in the beginnings of the White Barn, Mayo had removed himself from the scene. Most likely he realized that Lucille wanted this territory for herself and, as Lynne Mayocole summarized it years later, that his sister had become "the family standard-bearer." He tried producing television but finally he started his own public relations firm, an enterprise in which he seemed to find satisfaction. During the 1950s he married a former model and in 1960 they had their first son.

At the end of the 1954 season, Lucille could look around the White Barn and see enormous growth. From a toddler that offered readings of plays with pretensions to Broadway success, the White Barn had quickly developed into a young adult presenting full productions of artistic merit. Responding to her eclectic taste, the White Barn had evolved into a center offering plays, operas and dance. More changes still were in the offing—endowed with unflagging energy and restless by nature, Lucille sought change, at least during this point in her life. Ralph Alswang joined the board of directors in 1955. That summer Lucille brought two other notable people on board: actress Eva Le Gallienne, who lived in Weston and gave classes at the White Barn in acting Ibsen, Shakespeare and Chekhov; and Leo Miller, who took charge of publicity and would remain with the White Barn for eighteen years.

Lucille was now a producer, with a style that suited her. A stickler for detail, she paid attention to casting, publicity and public relations, seating arrangements, the care that the actors and other artists received once they arrived at the White Barn, the upkeep of Derwent House. But once a play was in rehearsal, whether in New York City or Westport, she largely left the director and the actors alone. "She would drift in occasionally," recalled Robert Glenn, who staged *Shakespeare in Harlem* at the White Barn in 1959 and later directed at the ANTA Matinee Series. "And she usually sat in on the dress rehearsal. But she didn't say, 'Do this' or 'How about this?' None of that." Where the art was concerned, she felt more comfortable staying nonjudgmentally behind the scenes.

Some directors appreciated that approach. Lucille "provided a co-coon" was how Glenn described it. "She's what I call a good producer," said Ira Cirker, who staged *Gertrude Stein and a Companion* at the White Barn and Off Broadway. "She just shut up and paid the bills." To others, like Gene Frankel, Lucille's style validated their assumption that she was a rich lady playing. "I felt she had no idea about theatre," he said. "I felt she had enthusiasm—the need to be part of it."

But Geoffrey Holder interpreted that enthusiasm as the essence of Lucille's worth. She had transported him to Westport and made the inspired suggestion that he dance outdoors. "The producer is a magician who puts the ingredients together to create magic," he said. "She is the person who sees the whole circle. The important thing was: it was Lucille's thought, it was Lucille's idea, to present me. She saw something in me, and out of that she got it together and presented it to America."

The White Barn had its own style and its own audience. "Artsy-craftsy," was how Elizabeth Stearns, a stage manager and lighting designer who apprenticed there in the mid-1950s, described the ambience. "We did little shows," said Stearns. "It was not mainstream. But it was very elitist, so that Marilyn Monroe would show up, and Actors Studio people would show up." The largely Jewish subscribers saw themselves as politically liberal and intellectually curious, and if the productions were never as elaborate as those at the Westport Country Playhouse, audiences legitimately told themselves that the content was more stimulating.

Lucille Lortel had cajoled, promoted and willed the White Barn Theatre into thriving existence. It was time to take the next step.

CHAPTER 5

A Theatre in Greenwich Village

*T*here had always been alternatives to Broadway. During the first decades of the twentieth century, a defiant group of non-commercial Little Theatres sprung up around the country. In New York City, this movement emerged in 1915 as the Neighborhood Playhouse on Grand Street and the Washington Square Players in Greenwich Village, one of whose members, Lawrence Langner, would later lead the Theatre Guild and the Westport Country Playhouse. The Provincetown Players left their original home on Cape Cod in 1916 to come to New York and establish a theatre on MacDougal Street, where they introduced their star dramatist, Eugene O'Neill, to Gotham. Edna St. Vincent Millay, the poet and Greenwich Village bohemian, commissioned scenic designer Cleon Throckmorton to convert a nineteenth-century farm building on Commerce Street into a theatre that opened in 1924 as the Cherry Lane. These art theatres bloomed for a time, then wilted as their talented playwrights, directors and designers were drawn into the American theatre's mainstream. In the 1930s leftist theatres arose to replace them, and during the 1940s the imaginative German director Erwin Piscator, who had developed agitprop staging techniques, established an experimental base with his Dramatic Workshop at the

New School of Social Research. But his was an exception. With the arrival of World War II, alternatives to Broadway generally evaporated.

When the war was over, a fresh generation of theatre artists felt locked out by Broadway's style, values and financing, and turned, perhaps because of its lingering bohemian aura and its low rents, to Greenwich Village—that profusion of oddly angled, narrow streets between Broadway and Greenwich Street, bounded by 14th Street to the north and Spring Street to the south. The area became the crucible for a new theatrical movement: Off Broadway.

Critic and journalist Stuart Little, who chronicled Off Broadway from his perch at the *New York Herald Tribune,* traced the movement's beginnings to an actor-driven company called New Stages, which took over a shuttered movie house at 159 Bleecker Street, not far from Washington Square. There, on December 21, 1947, the group presented Barry Stavis' *The Lamp at Midnight,* a drama about the astronomer Galileo. The following February they mounted a bill of one-acts that included Jean-Paul Sartre's *The Respectful Prostitute,* which blasted racism in the American South.

Spurred by overflowing audiences, who had read that *Prostitute* was sexy and sensationalist, the production moved to Broadway, but New Stages, unable to match that notoriety in subsequent productions, folded soon after. Other groups sprang up, though. A company called Interplayers unlocked the old Provincetown Playhouse during the summer of 1948 and soon introduced audiences to an incandescent actress named Kim Stanley. By 1949, five companies had formed the Off-Broadway League of Theaters, to negotiate contracts with an Actors' Equity that considered Off-Broadway salaries almost too meager to recognize.

In 1950 an intensely shy, Panamanian-born director named José Quintero and a former law-student named Theodore Mann transformed an awkwardly shaped nightclub space on Sheridan Square into an arena stage where the audience sat on three sides. They called it, quite simply, the Circle in the Square. Their first production, in 1951, was Howard Richardson and William Berney's exotic romance, *Dark of the Moon*, about a witch boy in the Smoky Mountains who falls in love with a beautiful human girl. But in July 1952 it was their revival of Tennessee Williams' *Summer and Smoke*, which had failed on Broadway in 1948, that brought Circle in the Square and Off Broadway their first significant critical recognition. Graced by the delicate but intense performance of Geraldine Page as the repressed Alma Winemiller, and staged by Quintero with an achingly sensitive awareness of the play's sexual tensions, *Summer and Smoke* sold out Circle in the Square for months. "As staged by the talented new director José Quintero," wrote the critic John Gassner, "*Summer and Smoke* represented a triumph of atmosphere and theatrical poetry over all the mediocre realism that gluts the market place of tired Broadway showmanship."

In the fall of 1952 a man who called himself William de Lys opened a 299-seat theatre at 121–123 Christopher Street.

From the start, Billy de Lys, as he was known, was a mystery. He seemed to have arrived from nowhere and he described a colorful personal history. That he had been born in Pittsburgh and was around thirty-six-years old appeared to be true, but as to the truth of his adventures en route to New York, this was anybody's guess. He boasted that his father went by the name of Bill Walters and was half of the vaudeville team of Walters and Kane; that he himself had once fought in Pittsburgh as a lightweight and had worked in circuses, carnivals and puppet shows as a clown and advance man; that he had owned his first sideshow, a wax museum, when he was around eighteen; that he had run a "geek" show, a combination wild man and animal show, where the main attraction was a fellow who ate live rats and snakes; that he had run summer theatres in Wisconsin. He claimed to have done a four-year stretch as a sailor in the Pacific, where he had nurtured the idea of opening what he told one reporter would be a "theatrical art center . . . for the newer creative talents of the East." Of middle height, he wore his dark hair slicked down and he favored bow ties. Lucille Lortel, who undoubtedly met him when he visited the White Barn one evening in July 1952, to see William Harrity's play *Dogface Sonata,* thought he was a pimp.

Certainly de Lys was an entrepreneur, and when a young drama critic named Harold S. Stern told him about a building that might make a good theatre, he went to look at it. Near the northeast corner of Christopher and Hudson streets, diagonally across from where tiny Bedford Street jutted into Christopher, stood a dilapidated movie theatre, the Hudson Playhouse—journalists referred to it as a "grind house," because it used to run films nearly twenty-four hours a day. The boarded-up two-story building was a dispiriting reminder that this pleasant street of small shops had grown shabby over the years. Still, to de Lys the Hudson looked promising. He took a seven-year lease on the building from its owner, Ralph N. Voorhis, on February 7, 1952, at an annual rent of $4,200 and proceeded to gut it.

His plans were as fluid and extravagant as his résumé. At first he called his operation the American Comedia Theatre. Then in January 1952, even before he had secured his lease, he announced that the Comedia would be patterned after the English club theatres. Lucille told Corinne Jacker, "A chap came to me by the name of Bill de Lys and he said, 'I would like to ape what you're doing at the White Barn and call it the Club Theatre on Christopher Street.' " Brochures for the Theatre de Lys, as he eventually called it, offered three levels of membership: for $2, a General Member could attend all functions, provided he or she paid admission; for $150, an Associate Member would have one seat in the elegant loge for all events "at no admission charge"; a $250 Joint Membership afforded the same perks for two.

In exchange de Lys promised a gargantuan roster of delights: ten plays; the Dance de Lys; a Jazz Art Series; a Concert Series; something called "International Varieties"; Theatre de Lys, Jr., which were to be Saturday performances for young audiences; and an Opera Series. The ten plays, each of which was to run four weeks, were to include entries like *Sodom, Tennessee* by the pair who had written *Dark of the Moon*, described as "The Sodom and Gomorrah biblical tale transposed to the hill country of Tennessee," and *The Man with a Couch*, by one Lyn Smith, touted as "a rollicking farce dealing with the bawdy escapades of a pseudo-psychiatrist."

De Lys had questionable taste in plays but surer aesthetic judgment about his new playhouse, which, promoter that he was, he portrayed in highfalutin terms. Hiring designer Harry Baum, de Lys alternately announced that the theatre would be modeled after a Japanese Kabuki theatre then, as he put it, a "Comedia" stage, but in any case would have an open-sided stage that jutted into the house. Red seats replaced the Hudson's battered ones. He named the small balcony the Kabuki Lounge and outfitted it with tables and loveseats where he planned to serve coffee during performances and allow patrons to smoke. A state-of-the-art lighting and sound booth at the rear of the balcony replaced the movie house's projection booth. Unfortunately de Lys cared more about what audiences could see than what they could not: the redesign allowed no space above the stage for flying scenery, and the dressing rooms—which *were* over the stage—were a row of stalls. "They were open cubicles," said Jane Connell, who played Mrs. Peachum in *The Threepenny Opera* in 1955. "We could barely sit next to each other and make up." Reports circulated that the renovation had cost from $125,000 to $140,000, although where and how de Lys had raised the cash was undetermined. He told the *New York Times* that he had spent $95,000 of his own money, and supposedly the theatre had 2,700 members by the time it was scheduled to open on September 29, 1952. De Lys had bragged that he would attract twice that number.

For his inaugural production de Lys chose to mount *Frankie and Johnny*, a musical play that the film director John Huston had written around 1928 in a moment of youthful weakness. Based on the legendary folk ballad of two doomed lovers, it had been performed in 1929 as a puppet play, but de Lys had hired a team to musicalize it anew. The opening had been delayed and rescheduled for October 27, a Monday, but it was found that the date coincided with the first night of *My Darlin' Aida* at the Winter Garden, a lavish pre-Disney musical based on Verdi's opera and set in the American South during the Civil War. So on Tuesday, October 28, at 8:30 P.M., after one preview and almost a month later than originally planned, *Frankie and Johnny* and the Theatre de Lys officially opened.

Both Lucille and her husband were in the audience that night, for Lou, although he rarely accompanied Lucille to the theatre in New York, was as curious as anyone to see what the *Wunderkind* from Pittsburgh had wrought. The theatre impressed them: the seats were comfortable, the sight lines excellent, the acoustics good. But like the critics whose nearly universal pans appeared the next day, Lou and Lucille could only laugh and cringe at what they saw on the lovely stage. John McClain of the *New York Journal American* wrote that "what [William de Lys] has put onto the stage of the Theatre de Lys shouldn't happen in the auditorium of Shelby Junior High School..."

William Hawkins at the *New York World-Telegram and Sun* mentioned "a gruesome interlude involving a song called 'I'm Full of Alkali' by a female dipsomaniac who is graphically seasick, which represents the bottom of some subdued invention and taste."

"The results are fairly frightening," Walter Kerr managed to sputter in the *New York Herald Tribune*. For proof, he cited the line, "Him so lovin' and tender and her so base vile."

Perhaps this *Frankie and Johnny* intended to spoof the famous legend, in a way that camp theatre artists of the next decade would have known how to achieve. The male chorus wore pink shirts and black pants, and the female chorus wore black bras and pink pants. In the *Morning Telegraph* of October 30, Whitney Bolton complained that the production was not only "candied up with some fake ballet costumes, it is as stylized as a gargoyle and no one in it ever talks plain or walks simply. If a man stands at the bagnio bar, he strikes an attitude. If a dame walks across the stage, it is an angular attitude."

Even de Lys, who seemed as shocked as the critics, thought the production was terrible. Press agent Max Eisen, who was handling publicity, remembered that de Lys walked outside during intermission and told everyone standing on the sidewalk that he was firing the actors. The next day he announced that he had closed the show.

De Lys told the press that he still hoped to produce *Sodom, Tennessee,* but then disappeared from the scene as mysteriously as he had arrived, leaving creditors and unions furious in his wake. From time to time *Variety* ran a squib on his whereabouts—he tried to produce again in New York around 1957, was supposed to open a theatre-cabaret in New Orleans' French Quarter in 1962 and turned up in Los Angeles in 1975. But William Schmitt—for that was his real name—part con artist, part visionary, never again created anything as lasting as the theatre he built on Christopher Street.

Lucille always contended that Lou first thought of buying the Theatre de Lys the day after they saw *Frankie and Johnny.* "My husband," she told Corinne Jacker, "said, 'I'm going to get that theatre for you, and maybe you won't have to be a house mother. You wouldn't have to sleep ten actors, feed the actors, and it would also give a chance to the plays that you feel could go further and give them a longer run.' " Even if that was Lucille's way of staking an early claim to their purchase, buying the de Lys would have been a natural impulse for Lou. The charming theatre was of manageable size and conceivably could be profitable if operated smartly. He probably realized that after the fiasco of *Frankie and Johnny,* de Lys could not afford to keep the theatre going. If he bought his wife a theatre in Manhattan, Lou thought, she might close the one in Westport.

As for Lucille, she had never stopped trying to produce in New York. Although she was unable to interest enough backers in *Red Roses for Me,* she continued to put money into productions on and off Broadway. Just a year earlier, in October 1951, she was one of several sponsors who helped Luther Greene, a Broadway producer and the husband of leading lady Judith Anderson, to bring over the English staging of Christopher Fry's new verse drama, *A Sleep of Prisoners*. Lucille, who produced *Prisoners* in association with Greene, put in $5,000 of the $20,000 needed to open Fry's dignified work about four prisoners of war, which they presented in St. James' Church at Madison Avenue and 71st Street and later toured briefly. Lucille had no intention of giving up the White Barn, but she did not object to acquiring a base in New York.

In the meantime, the Theatre de Lys was without a leader. In November 1952, the John Post Construction Corporation, which had worked on the renovation but never been paid in full, acquired the lease to the theatre from de Lys. Finally, on March 6, 1953, the building's owner, Ralph N. Voorhis, assigned the lease, liens and violations to John Post Construction. Post knew nothing about theatre, so he hired Max Eisen, de Lys' former press agent, to book productions (Eisen in turn often hired himself out to do publicity for the shows he booked).

During the next twelve months, the de Lys housed the sort of presentations that epitomized Off Broadway's scrappy exuberance. There were classics and revivals staged on shoe-string budgets. There were new American plays of middling quality produced with outstanding actors. Fueled by the innovative training of the Actors Studio, young performers surged Off Broadway, willing to work for Equity's excruciating Off Broadway stock minimum of $25 a week. The cast of Calder Willingham's *End As A Man*, which Claire Heller produced at the de Lys in September 1953, included a bevy of Studio-trained future stars: Pat Hingle, Anthony Franciosa, Albert Salmi, Mark Richman, and Ben Gazzara.

Then on March 10, 1954, the de Lys hosted the opening of Bertolt Brecht and Kurt Weill's *The Threepenny Opera*.

Threepenny Opera was Brecht and Weill's adaptation of John Gay's eighteenth-century musical satire *The Beggar's Opera*. It had been Brecht's first success in Germany when it opened in Berlin in 1928. Brimming with his sardonic lyrics and Weill's edgy, jazz-tinged music, the opera was both entertaining and intelligent, theatrical and politically sharp. Set in London at the time of Queen Victoria's coronation in 1838, but sounding more like Berlin in the 1920s, it is what one character calls "an opera for beggars." It chronicles the love affairs and crimes of an urban underclass of whores, thieves, murderers, and pimps, who jauntily imitate the betrayals, greed and moral hypocrisy of the middle-class that looks down on them. Its hero Macheath, or Mack the Knife, robs, murders and seduces with flair. In the Berlin production, Weill's wife, Lotte Lenya, memorably sang the role of the whore Jenny Diver.

At first, *Threepenny* did not fare so well in the United States. In 1933, the year Brecht left Germany to avoid Nazi persecution, a misguided version opened on Broadway and closed thirteen performances later. The only other significant productions had occurred in 1946 and '48, at the University of Illinois and at Northwestern University, with the libretto and lyrics translated by Desmond I. Vesey and Eric Bentley respectively. Then in 1952 Lotte Lenya sang Jenny for the first time in English at Brandeis University, in a concert version translated and adapted by the American composer and librettist Marc Blitzstein and conducted by Leonard Bernstein. By then Brecht had returned to Europe and was living in East Berlin; Weill had died in 1950.

Enthusiastic producers thronged Blitzstein, eager to stage his adaptation if only they could make changes. Billy Rose wanted to soften Brecht's cynical happy ending, in which Macheath is saved from hanging. Blitzstein, backed by Lenya, refused, and a year and a half after Brandeis, *Threepenny* still lay on his desk.

But around that time a young director named Carmen Capalbo and his business partner Stanley Chase started hounding Blitzstein for permission to stage and produce the opera. And after Blitzstein's other options fell through, and after he and Lenya assured themselves that Capalbo understood the piece and would stage it as adapted—for nobody was going to direct *Threepenny* without Lenya's consent—they gave the precious script over to the two men. Capalbo and Chase had rented the de Lys for a show that never happened; instead, on March 10, 1954, they installed *Threepenny*.

The de Lys was a fortuitous choice artistically. The small open platform allowed actors to come downstage and speak or sing directly to the audience, as Brecht and Weill had conceived. "It's a wonderful theatre to play in," said Jo Sullivan Loesser, who sang Macheath's naïve young wife Polly Peachum. "Perfect for this piece." The theatre's drawbacks—no fly space, little room for an orchestra—became advantages. William Pitkin's evocative designs provided an expressionistic gray and brown backdrop of Victorian London. The eight-piece band conveyed the aura of "threepenny opera" better than any full orchestra could.

Reviews were generally positive, especially from the *New York Times*. "The score of 'The Threepenny Opera,'" wrote critic Lewis Funke on March 11, "is...one of the authentic contemporary masterpieces." As for the production, he found that "The company...is young, full of vigor and goodwill....From time to time it is difficult to avoid being conscious of a lack of bite and style. But this only indicates how much lurks in this opera." The *Times'* Brooks Atkinson thought it one of the best productions of the season. Performances were sold out for twelve weeks and undoubtedly could have been extended if Eisen had not already scheduled another production.

While Eisen was booking the de Lys, Lou Schweitzer was quietly buying it. Two days before *Threepenny* opened, on March 8, he acquired an option to purchase the 121–123 Christopher Street building from Ralph Voorhis. Shortly afterward, he negotiated with John Post to buy the theatre's lease. They reached an oral agreement on March 23, and Lou immediately called a delighted Lucille at her office. That night they celebrated their twenty-third wedding anniversary with a lively party at the Plaza Hotel, and Post personally congratulated Lucille on being the theatre's new owner. But when the party ended at around two in the morning, Max Eisen, who had come as Post's guest, emerged as though he were a villain in a melodrama and warned Lou that others were interested in acquiring the right to operate the theatre—and could well get it.

Eisen's comments unsettled Lou, and he secured his acquisition of the building. Lawyers drew up a contract of sale in July, and on August 26, Lou bought it for $60,000, immediately transferring title to Lortel, Inc., a corporation he had formed on August 12. Among the documents that Voorhis turned over were those pertaining to John Post Construction Corporation's assumption of the lease between Voorhis and William de Lys. Post Construction had assigned the lease to a company called Senior Estate, Ltd., which Post and his sister owned and through which they operated the theatre. Senior Estate began paying rent to Lortel, Inc.

But Eisen had been busy, too. He had developed a fondness for the de Lys and was himself the interested party with which he had threatened Lou. Scraping together money from friends and relatives, on April 1, eight days after Post congratulated Lucille at the Plaza, Eisen had paid Post $11,000 to buy 50 percent of the stock of Senior Estate. Now Eisen and his newly-formed syndicate had voting power in Senior Estate and owned a half-interest in the sublease. The press agent believed that he was in a position to quash a sale if and when it took place.

During the next months, Lou and Lucille gave Eisen little thought, and on September 25, they left for a luxurious cruise to the Mediterranean on the S.S. *Caronia*, stopping at exotic ports like Alexandria and Haifa. When the ship finally docked in Southampton, they remained in Europe, not sailing home until November 27. Upon their return, Lou entered into final negotiations to buy the lease from Senior Estate, seemingly the only item that stood in the way of Lucille's complete control of the theatre, and purchased it on March 16, 1955 for $37,500. Altogether he had spent nearly $100,000 to buy the Theatre de Lys for his wife.

He did not know that he was buying a lawsuit as well.

Eisen testified later to being surprised when, on March 23, the *New York Times* announced that "pending the signing of papers today, everything has been agreed upon for Lucille Lortel to assume full charge of the Theatre de Lys." But Eisen's public response came so quickly, it seemed he must have been expecting the news and perhaps even waiting for it so that he could take action. At nearly the same time that Lucille announced her acquisition, Eisen announced that he was taking legal steps to thwart it. Both of their press releases arrived at the *Daily News* on the same day. Within two weeks, Eisen sued, complaining that Post had not asked—or received—his formal permission as a 50 percent stockholder in Senior Estate. He served notice on Lou to restrain him from using the theatre.

The case went before Justice Henry Clay Greenberg of the Supreme Court of the state of New York on May 9, 1955. At the outset, Greenberg asked if the press agent would settle for money, a standard offer that presumably came from the defendants. Eisen, an irritating, slippery, but feisty plaintiff, declined.

The outcome hinged on the judge's interpretation of Section 20 of New York State's Stock Corporation Law. Essentially this held that, if a corporation sold assets outside the regular course of its business, it needed the written consent of all the stockholders. But what was Senior Estate's regular course of business? Was its business real estate, as its certificate of incorporation indicated—and as Post and Schweitzer maintained—in which case nobody needed Eisen's written approval? Or was its actual business running the theatre, as Eisen maintained, in which case a real estate sale would be outside the normal course of operations and would require a stockholder's formal okay? After taking trial testimony without a jury, the judge proceeded to rule that written consent was not necessary and on May 17 dismissed Eisen's complaint. Eisen was furious.

Lucille went into her ninth summer at the White Barn believing that she now owned one of the finest theatres in New York City. Lou testified in court that she had been less upset than he about the prospect of losing the de Lys, but it is hard to imagine she would have taken the loss and embarrassment lightly. Perhaps she simply assumed, as she usually did where Lou and business were concerned, that he would solve the problem. She was unusually happy that summer. Not only was she proud owner of the de Lys, but Ruth and Cugat had returned to the States after a lengthy stay in Europe and were taking a house in Westport. Lucille looked forward to having her beloved sister nearby.

When the news of the court's decision became public, congratulations had poured in to Lucille, as had proposals from producers eager to use her new space. She sent news of her acquisition to her theatre friends in England, and Hazel Vincent Wallace wrote back that "the thought of your project with the Theatre de Lys makes me feel quite dizzy with excitement, and I do hope you have a wonderful time planning it all."

Since coproducing *A Sleep of Prisoners,* Lucille had devoted most of her energy to the White Barn and had been wary of backing commercial productions. Now, with the Theatre de Lys ready to receive plays, she looked about seriously for a drama that might have a life Off Broadway. Six new plays dominated the White Barn's roster that summer of 1955, suggesting that Lucille was forming a way to use the venue as a testing ground for New York. In September she would tell Don Ross of the *New York Herald Tribune,* "I consider the De Lys simply an extension of my activities at the White Barn. Now I can give a good run to plays that I think deserve it."

The two most important entries for Lucille that season were Charles Morgan's *The River Line* and Ettore Rella's *Sign of Winter.* The first she saw as the most likely prospect for a New York transfer, the second came with the theatre and film star Ruth Chatterton.

Charles Morgan was an English novelist and playwright and had been drama critic for the *Times* of London. While fighting in World War I, he had been captured and held prisoner in Holland for four years, an experience that he possibly drew upon for *The River Line*, which he wrote first as a novel and then adapted. A carefully conceived three-act play— part drawing-room drama, part psychological melodrama—it focused on three veterans of 'The River Line,' an escape route for Allied agents and downed airmen that operated in occupied France during World War II. Now it is 1947, and the three friends—an American, an Englishman and his French wife—are tormented by their decision to execute a fellow soldier whom they had suspected of being a German spy. "The author," wrote the reviewer for the *Westport Town Crier*, "is concerned not only with an intriguing mystery—were they right or wrong, was the victim really guilty or not?—but with the ethical justification for such an act of violence, and its psychological effects on the perpetrators."

The play had been produced at the 1952 Edinburgh Festival and then had run for two years in London, where Britain's fresh memory of the war, and Paul Scofield's performance as the American, turned this overly soul-searching play into a hit. The Theatre Guild had optioned the script, but never produced it; Lucille, who had seen the play in London, believed in it.

At the White Barn, she made the production a family affair. Cugat designed the settings, which alternated between the garden terrace of the Englishman's upper-middle-class home and the granary in France where the compatriots hole up in 1943. Ruth's dignified portrait of Anny decorated the set, and Ruth herself, looking demure in a peasant blouse, her gray hair up in a bun, posed in front of the painting for pre-show publicity. The excellent cast included Paul Shyre, Peggy Feury, Zohra Alton (later known as Zohra Lampert), and James Lipton. Kim Stanley's husband, Curt Conway, supervised the production.

If Lucille wanted confirmation that the play had commercial

possibilities, she received it. The reviewer for the *Town Crier* wrote, "The play . . . is considerably closer to popular in its appeal than many of the White Barn's admittedly esoteric offerings. It would not be hard to imagine Mr. Charles Morgan's excitingly written drama as a substantial Off-Broadway success next season—perhaps at Miss Lortel's own Theatre de Lys?"

The *Variety* critic, whose appraisal carried more weight, wrote, " 'The River Line' is a three-act drama with one brilliant act. A problem play with a provocative and engrossing theme it seems a doubtful prospect for Broadway success, but might be a strong entry for Off Broadway. Despite its flaws, 'River Line' is the best new play that Lucille Lortel has presented at her White Barn Theatre, and she has given it an excellent production." Lucille took an option on the script.

Perhaps because she had given up her own stage career, Lucille was awed by actors and actresses who attained the sort of recognition she had wanted. Such a one was Ruth Chatterton. On Broadway at eighteen and a star at twenty, she progressed to a rewarding if brief film career. She retired from the theatre in 1951 to write novels and had last performed in 1954, when she played Gertrude to Maurice Evans' Hamlet for NBC television. Whatever the project, Lucille would not have thought twice about saying yes when Chatterton, now sixty-one and living fairly close by in Redding, chose to return to the theatre on the stage of the White Barn.

Chatterton herself had selected Ettore Rella's play for her comeback. An American poet of Italian and Albanian descent, Rella had written in blank verse about an impoverished, drunken widow desperate to keep her family together, a dishonest Southern politician (Ian Martin), the widow's daughter (Anne Meacham), and the daughter's African-American lover (Rai Saunders). Meacham said that she "found the depth and complications of this relationship way ahead of its time." But two weeks of rehearsal were not enough for the director to corral

Rella's sprawling, pretentious work. The agent Hartney Arthur, who attended the Sunday night performance, remembered thinking that Chatterton was "very courageous" but had made a "grave mistake," since she was unsure of her lines. If true, the reviewers were kind. Rita Hassan wrote in *Show Business*, "It was apparent [Chatterton] believed deeply in the play and the writing, for she brought to it all her acting skill." Ira Bilowit, also in *Show Business*, wrote that Chatterton "ably maintains and projects the appearance and determination of a drunken, disappointed widow, who is first and finally a mother who cares." They saved their venom for the script.

Bad or good, at the Saturday performance on August 27 the audience was probably more intrigued by a celebrity in their midst. Her blonde hair pinned haphazardly in a twist, and wearing a simple sleeveless white blouse and black skirt, Marilyn Monroe arrived at the White Barn escorted by the writer Norman Rosten and by Henry Rosenfeld, identified in a local newspaper as the "dress king." Lucille sat demurely behind the table as Monroe leaned over to sign the guest book. Nan Kruelewitch, who was an apprentice that summer from the Friends School in New York City, remembered that during the intermission everyone stared at the exquisite film star, who stood downstairs in the Green Room talking with the Schweitzers' housekeeper, Rosamund Bennett.

Less enthused about *Sign of Winter* than *The River Line*, but not wholly decided, Lucille took a one-month option. But by that time, the show which would reopen the de Lys under her management was already booked.

Lou had not been so sanguine as his wife about the status of their ownership. Shortly after Justice Greenberg ruled in Schweitzer's favor, Eisen indicated he would file an appeal. It also worried Lou that the de Lys was dark. Productions that had rented the theatre under the previous management had finished their runs—the last entry, Patricia Joudry's *Teach Me How to Cry*, closed May 15. While Lucille was engaged in Westport with the White Barn, nobody was in charge of booking the house.

What happened next is unclear. Did Lucille come up with the idea of bringing *Threepenny Opera* back to the de Lys, or did Carmen Capalbo and Stanley Chase? According to Lucille's version of events, the director Herbert Machiz had come to her office as far back as March 1955, told her that Lotte Lenya said he could direct a production of *Threepenny* and asked if Lucille would produce it at the de Lys. Soon after, according to Lucille, Capalbo and Chase came to her office asking if they could use the de Lys to rehearse a series of plays they were producing on Broadway at the Bijou Theatre; supposedly Lucille suggested reviving *Threepenny*.

Capalbo's version involved his running into Lou during the summer of 1955—where is not certain—and Lou asking if the director had any suggestions for what Lucille could book into the theatre. Capalbo, a persistent man, suggested bringing back *Threepenny Opera*, with himself directing and he and Chase producing again. The pair still had the scenery and costumes in storage. Lucille agreed, but Capalbo always asserted, "It was Lou Schweitzer and us."

Lucille always invited people with whom she planned to do business to come to the White Barn, and on Sunday, July 31, Capalbo and Chase went up to see Gene Frankel's staging of *Père Goriot*, which Joan Littlewood had adapted from Balzac's novel. After this, on August 16, a letter of agreement was signed between Louis Schweitzer and Threepenny Productions, represented by Carmen Capalbo and Stanley Chase, with Lou guaranteeing to pay $2,400 to Lortel, Inc., to cover the theatre rental for the first four weeks; the agreement provided for the amount to be paid back, unless the show closed before four weeks were up. In consideration of this advance, Threepenny Productions agreed to pay Schweitzer 10 percent of the producer's share of the net profits for the entire run after expenses and payments to investors.

A second letter of agreement, also dated August 16, 1955, made between Capalbo and Chase and Lucille Lortel, confirms

Lucille Lortel will receive "in association with Lucille Lortel" billing in connection with the production of THE THREEPENNY OPERA at the Theater de Lys, in large preliminary display advertisements controlled by Carmen Capalbo and Stanley Chase, and houseboards used in the Theater de Lys.

Miss Lortell [*sic*] shall have no participation in profits, or any other rights in connection with the production. Lucille Lortel to receive equal prominence in billing and also in distribution of all advertising and publicity.

In 2002, the lawyer Floria V. Lasky, who represented Capalbo and Chase in 1955 as a member of the firm of Fitelson and Mayers, said, "My hunch, if I were to reconstruct, is that agreement number two was in consideration for agreement number one. Carmen and Stanley agreed to give Lucille billing for Schweitzer giving four weeks rental. But Schweitzer also exacted a percentage of the profits. As a producer, you give away profits sooner than you give away gross."

Thus did Lucille begin a tradition, which would continue with few exceptions until her death, of receiving the billing "in association with" for any production that rented her theatre on Christopher Street.

Had the show really run only four weeks, the discrepancies in Lucille's and Capalbo's stories about bringing back *Threepenny* might have meant little. But when it opened for the second time on September 20, 1955, largely with the original cast in leading roles—Jane Connell replaced Charlotte Rae as Mrs. Peachum—reviewers gladly welcomed it back. Lewis Funke, covering the production again for the *New York Times*, wrote " 'The Threepenny Opera' is back at its original stand and everybody should give a vote of thanks."

The show would play 2,611 performances over seven years, making it at that time the longest-running musical in theatre history. And since it was installed at Lucille's theatre, and since Lucille received "in association with" billing and wielded more influence than either Stanley Chase or Carmen Capalbo, it was she who became identified with *Threepenny* as its alma mater and producer, a legend that she encouraged and ultimately believed. "The problem is," said Ben Sprecher, who became general manager of the de Lys in 1981 and was working for Lucille at the time she died, "Lucille sometimes took credit for things she didn't do. She did not produce *The Threepenny Opera*. But the world will remember that she did, because that's the publicity spin she put on it. And nobody knows who Carmen Capalbo is."

Chase turned to producing film and television; Capalbo continued to work in theatre—among other things, he staged and coproduced in 1970 the Brecht-Weill opera, *The Rise and Fall of the City of Mahagonny*. But he never again directed or produced anything so successful as *Threepenny*, nor did he forgive Lucille for what he described as her "poaching"on his and Chase's work and *Threepenny*'s reputation.

At almost the same time that *Threepenny* was embarking on its marathon, Max Eisen filed his appeal against Louis Schweitzer and Senior Estate in the Appellate Division of New York Supreme Court.

And this time he won. On March 29, 1956, the five justices handed down a unanimous decision that ordered Schweitzer to return the sublease to Senior Estate, and Post to return the money from the sale to Schweitzer. They had found that, whatever the certificate of incorporation stated, running the theatre was Senior Estate's core operation and the lease could not be sold without Eisen's written consent. The sale, they declared, was void.

The reversal both angered and distressed Lucille and Lou. Although the court's decision did not threaten their ownership of the building at 121–123 Christopher Street, if the decision stood, it would take away their right to operate the theatre and produce there, at least until Senior Estate's sublease ran out in 1959. Conceivably the decision could threaten the run of *Threepenny Opera* if it was upheld after an appeal and if Eisen wanted to bring in another production. Attorneys for Schweitzer and Senior Estate immediately sought relief from New York State's highest court, the Court of Appeals in Albany.

Lucille submerged her anxiety in the White Barn that summer. The stress took its toll on Lou. One burningly hot Sunday he was having lunch by the pool at Derwent House, avidly discussing the pros and cons of the Marxist and capitalist political systems, when he suffered a mild heart attack and had to be sped to the hospital. But with rest he seemed to recover, and although it took more than a year for Eisen v. Post to come up on the Court of Appeals' calendar, Lou and his attorneys pulled out all the stops. To Eisen's disgust, they were able to secure friend of the court briefs from, among others, the president of the New York State Title Association, who predicted "chaos within the real estate community" if the decision favoring Eisen were allowed to stand. When the case finally came before the Court of Appeals on May 8, 1957, lawyers for Schweitzer and Senior Estate tore the previous decision apart.

At the end of the year, on December 6, five of the seven judges ruled for Schweitzer and Senior Estate. Lou had fought hard and won. Eisen could really go no further. In 1961 he and his syndicate received and accepted 50 percent of the lease's sale price, which, after legal expenses, came to about $6,000—a loss. Although it was really Post who had betrayed Eisen—Post, after all, had sold him stock in Senior Estate—the press agent's bitterness centered on Lou and Lucille. He always asserted that he was up against a well-connected millionaire and attorneys whose influential clients were interested in standing by their own.

Meanwhile, Lucille had her Off-Broadway theatre.

· · · · · · CHAPTER 6 · · · · · ·

The Queen of Off Broadway

---

*H*ad it not been for *The Threepenny Opera*, there might not have been an ANTA Matinee Series. With *Threepenny* keeping Lucille from mounting major productions at the Theatre de Lys, she found another outlet for her desire to present experimental work: the American National Theatre and Academy, or ANTA.

The dream of ANTA was born in 1931 in Philadelphia, where the conductor Leopold Stokowski had brought together prominent citizens to advocate for the sort of arts movement that had once started the city's renowned symphony orchestra. The notion of a Civic Repertory Theatre emerged, then the concept of a National Theatre chartered by the Congress of the United States. Moneyed leaders joined the cause, notably the financier Otto Kahn, who actually selected the name American National Theatre and Academy. According to ANTA's secretary and first historian, George Freedley, these influential folk went to Washington, D.C., and bent the ears of every representative and senator who would listen, until the seventy-fourth Congress finally passed Public Law 199, in 1935 granting a federal charter to create a people's theatre called the American National Theatre and Academy.

Unfortunately, these well-meaning and influential people neglected

133

to ask the government for funding. Or as Clarence Derwent once put it to Rube Dorin of the *Morning Telegraph,* "We got the charter but not the money."

According to Freedley's history, the American National Theatre and Academy sought no funds, "because it was thought that it would be unwise to ask official support for the organization before it had had a chance to grow and show its own strength." But such a gentlemanly attitude quickly proved foolish. Within a year of the organization's founding, the government funded the Federal Theatre Project, which completely overshadowed ANTA. Then the United States entered World War II. All together, the American National Theatre and Academy did not function for eleven years.

In 1946, director, producer and World War II veteran Robert Breen spurred the dormant organization into life in a now-or-never moment. He and Robert Porterfield, a fellow GI who had founded the Barter Theatre in Virginia, aimed to establish a National Theatre Foundation modeled in part on the Arts Council of Great Britain. The Foundation, Freedley wrote, "will be to the theatre what Rockefeller, Carnegie, Guggenheim and other philanthropic foundations are now to other fields of the arts and sciences." Supported by this Foundation, Freedley enthused, "ANTA would bring the best plays to the largest possible number of people at the most reasonable prices."

For a few years ANTA adopted Breen and Porterfield's idea, although once again the organization rejected asking the federal government for dollars, preferring to raise support from private sources instead. As this was a time when the government was uninterested in subsidizing the arts, it was probably the only viable approach. But it would prove to be one of ANTA's fatal mistakes.

Still, the reconstituted American National Theatre and Academy attempted to be a resource for the American theatre. It arranged for guest artists to work with university and community theatres, and provided technical advice and a personnel service. For two seasons ANTA sponsored an Experimental Theatre, which produced noncommercial plays on limited budgets, and then in 1950 the group launched a sequel called the ANTA Play Series. ANTA served as the United States Centre of the International Theatre Institute. The organization's aims were monumental: nothing less than unifying American theatre and bringing excellent, affordable productions to all Americans would do.

Lucille became interested in ANTA around the time she started the White Barn. In June 1947 she was receiving the ANTA Newletter—four poorly typed pages—and a copy of the bylaws, on which she checked the artistic purposes that appealed to her, including, "The stimulation of public interest in the Drama as an art belonging to the Theatre and to Literature and thereby to be enjoyed both on the Stage and in the Study." Before she discovered the British club theatres, she and Mayo focused on the model of ANTA's Experimental Theatre, which staged plays that Broadway would never have touched for hundreds of subscribers.

Like others involved with ANTA after the war, Lucille used the organization to meet people who could further her career, for its enormous board read like a who's who of the American stage. At the beginning she offered her services as a patron and hostess. In 1950, when ANTA bought the Guild Theatre on West 52nd Street and raised money to pay the mortgage and renovate the building, Lucille endowed an orchestra seat for $1,050. The next year, she chaired the Gifts Committee for the ANTA Theatre Ball, an elaborate event at the Plaza Hotel that displayed jewels donated by the likes of Katherine Cornell and Gloria Swanson, to be auctioned by the Parke-Bernet Galleries. Along with socialites and theatre personalities such as Mrs. Angier Biddle Duke, the Duchess of Windsor and Cornelia Otis Skinner, Lucille was listed in the *New York Times* as hosting a pre-ball dinner party. For a raffle that night, she donated a new Cadillac worth $4,500, which she had previously won at a raffle for the Heart Fund.

ANTA rewarded her contributions. Early in 1952 Lucille became a founding member of its newly formed Greater New York Chapter and, to no one's surprise, she was elected to the Chapter's board of directors. "Anybody with any sense would have put her on the board," said Marjorie L. Dycke, who headed the drama department at the High School of Performing Arts and served on ANTA's national board. "Lucille loved theatre and had the money to back it."

At times during the summer of 1952, the White Barn resembled ANTA's Connecticut outpost. The author of *Elizabeth, the Bachelor Queen,* C. Lawton Campbell, was honorary chairman of ANTA's board, and Nancy Wickwire, the production's star, had recently received an ANTA scholarship. Richard Harrity, whose *Dogface Sonata* Lucille presented in July, was supposed to produce an ANTA television series the following fall. Lucille regularly invited ANTA board members to her Sunday nights, and that October she was elected to the board of the national organization and soon afterward to the executive committee. Minutes show that she rarely talked. "She listened," said Marjorie Dycke, "and when something came up that she thought she could contribute to, she contributed."

The New York Chapter wanted to establish an acting company, and in 1954 Lucille served on a committee that considered various proposals, none of which materialized. The idea resurfaced shortly after *Threepenny Opera* reopened in September 1955. At an executive committee meeting of the national organization on November 14, Mrs. H. Alwyn Inness-Brown, the cool, trim socialite who was the New York Chapter's president, reported on plans "to get together a group of very well-known actors, many of whom have expressed interest, to produce plays at the Theatre de Lys. This would also include readings and workshop productions and, it is hoped, may lead to the establishment of a permanent resident company."

Like the impulse for remounting *Threepenny,* the birth of the ANTA

Matinee Series is cloaked in competing stories and personalities. "I had the idea of using the de Lys for this matinee series that would be done by the New York Chapter," recalled the former *Saturday Review* drama critic Henry Hewes. He described the sort of concept that only a critic would invent: "The original idea was that people who had done performances in the past would come and talk about the performances and give us a sample. That developed into the theatre series."

Lucille told Corinne Jacker, "I was on the board of ANTA, and ANTA wanted to do big things. They wanted to do a series at the City Center, and so I said, 'In the meantime, until you've raised your money, you could have my theatre, and why not do it during the run of *Threepenny* on a Tuesday matinee, while actors that are performing on the Broadway stage and Off Broadway still could do something.' "

Whoever conceived the idea, from the start Lucille held the title of artistic director of the Matinee Series and she became permanently identified with it. The Series allowed her the kind of freewheeling, eclectic producing that she loved—the kind of producing she had hoped to do at the de Lys before *Threepenny* came along—and she plunged in enthusiastically. Susan Komarow, an ANTA volunteer who assisted Hewes, remembered the first time she met Lucille in ANTA's offices at 1545 Broadway. "She came in with a rush, in a flourish," Komarow said. "She was wearing an *Ile de France* hat, a kind of quirky felt fedora with an S.S. *Ile de France* ribbon. She was very different than I thought she'd be. Not glamorous at all. In a way, she was very friendly. She was bossy of course, but not immediately."

The experiment came together with the sort of speed that only enthusiasm and energy generate. The actress Mary Morris, who had played Abigail Putnam in the Broadway premiere of O'Neill's *Desire Under the Elms,* had since become a formidable acting teacher at the Carnegie Institute's School of Fine Arts in Pittsburgh. She had previously staged Felicia Komai's adaptation of Alan Paton's novel *Cry, the*

Beloved Country and she brought the play in and offered to direct it again. And on Tuesday, May 15, 1956, at two-thirty in the afternoon, Lucille and Henry Hewes inaugurated their project with a concert reading. On a stage which was bare except for *Threepenny*'s backdrops, an extraordinary cast that included Morris, Clayton Corbin, Henderson Forsythe, Earle Hyman, and Rosetta Le Noire read Komai's searing verse drama about a Zulu pastor and his son Absalom.

"Mary was the narrator, black man, white man, black woman—all these characters," recalled Hyman, who played Absalom. "She looked rather like a grande dame, but the poor darling was almost blind. Her eyes were very tiny and she wore thick glasses. She stood on the side of the stage and set the scenes." Hyman remembered, "You could hear the crying in the audience. Not just women but men."

"Scores were turned away for lack of seats," wrote George Freedley in the *Morning Telegraph*. "It is a pity a second reading could not be arranged ....Earle Hyman, a brilliant young actor, starred and certainly deserved it. It was a highlight of the Off-Broadway season."

At the Greater New York Chapter's annual membership meeting on June 18, Hewes reported that *"Cry, the Beloved Country* ... proved to be a moving and exciting experience, and personally I felt that this single afternoon justified our existence." With huzzahs ringing in their ears, Lortel, Hewes and Inness-Brown determined that, in the fall, the New York Chapter would stage a season of matinees.

Lucille departed for Fairweather for the summer. In the mornings she and Lou would sit outdoors and eat breakfast and read the newspapers. At night Anny, who was in charge of organizing meals, ruled the dining table, while Lou sat and ate quietly, the inevitable ashtray and cigarette at his side despite his doctor's orders against smoking. When Lucille's actors invaded his property, he retreated to his radio shack or to the television room at the back of the theatre.

Despite the scare of Lou's heart attack and worry about the status of the de Lys, Lucille was busier than ever and thriving on the pace. She reverted to her mixture of musical events and plays that summer, bringing in Richard Stuart Flusser's After Dinner Opera Company and its productions of Gerald Cockshott's *Apollo and Persephone* and Richard Chanler's *Pot of Fat*. New plays included Nicholas Biel's *Sound on the Goose*, directed by Frank Silvera, and Arnold Perl's adaptation of *I Knock at the Door*, the first volume of Sean O'Casey's autobiography, which Lucille considered coproducing.

She still wanted to mount *The River Line*, but knowing that *Threepenny* was filling houses at the de Lys, she pursued other theatres. Although she disliked going into the hot city during the summer, on August 23 she met with Sanford Friedman to talk about coproducing Morgan's drama Off Broadway at the Carnegie Hall Playhouse. Morgan's agent was dubious, but Lucille told Friedman that she had enlisted Henry Hewes, who was going to London, to persuade him.

Back at the White Barn, she watched Anna Sokolow's Theatre Company on Sunday, August 26, and Eva Le Gallienne's senior class presenting scenes from Shakespeare, Ibsen and Chekhov on September 1 and 2. Recognizing that Le Gallienne still needed professional and monetary support, but also that her presence heightened the White Barn's reputation, Lucille had again asked the actress to give classes and perform; that summer Le Gallienne acted Mrs. Alving in her own adaptation of Ibsen's *Ghosts*.

The actress called Lucille "God fairy," said Eloise G. Armen, Le Gallienne's friend and, in later years, her caretaker. Whenever Le Gallienne needed money, she went to Lucille for teaching or putting on a play, and Lucille paid her whether enough students enrolled or not. "Le Gallienne was very grateful to her," said Armen, "but laughed at her. We all did. Fondly. Lucille was so out front about everything. She loved the publicity and didn't make any pretense about, 'Oh, dear, what a fuss.' " Le Gallienne's biographer, Helen Sheehy, believed that the actress considered Lucille something of a dilettante, although as Paula Laurence said, "I don't see how anyone could call Lucille a dilettante. She worked too hard."

Returning to Manhattan after Labor Day, Lucille dove into arranging the first season of the Matinee Series with Henry Hewes. "Five Tuesday Afternoons of Off-Beat Theatre" announced the flyer that went out from ANTA's office to potential subscribers. A ten-dollar, tax-deductible subscription entitled a subscriber to a ticket for five matinees. Another ten dollars bought membership in both national ANTA and the Greater New York Chapter, a subscription to *Theater Arts* magazine and the Chapter's stylish, over-sized newsletter, *Chapter One*. Clearly one of the Matinee Series' aims was to gain national and local members.

On the afternoon of October 23, 1956, Peggy Wood stood on the stage of the Theatre de Lys at two-thirty and introduced the 1956–57 Matinee Series, as she would each season for the next ten years. A few minutes later, Helen Hayes inaugurated the Series with *Lovers, Villains & Fools*, a pastiche of Shakespearean poetry and dramatic scenes. Hayes' Equity company bore the lion's share of the performance, although the well-beloved star narrated the concert-style presentation and performed a little. Wearing a black velvet suit trimmed with white ermine, and a white ermine hat, the diminutive actress introduced the program, comparing the scenery-less de Lys to Shakespeare's Elizabethan stage. Then she spoke lines from the Chorus of *Henry V*. At the end, she gave Puck's final speech from *A Midsummer Night's Dream*.

By contrast, *U.S.A.* offered a modern brand of theatre on December 18 and enabled Lucille to fulfill her promise of bringing productions from the White Barn to the de Lys. Since staging his adaptation of the Dos Passos novel at Westport in 1953, Paul Shyre had cut and polished. With Norman Hall directing a new cast—Sada Thompson was the only actor from the earlier production—critics cheered. "John Dos Passos' 'U.S.A.' came vividly and thrillingly to life yesterday at the Theatre de

Lys," wrote the critic for the *New York Post* on December 19. "If Paul Shyre's concert-reading versions of books continue to be as consistently successful as they have been," crowed the *New York Times* reviewer, "it is conceivable that some people may begin to prefer exclusively the spoken word of the theatre to the written one between covers..." January 22, 1957, had Lucille bringing Eva Le Gallienne reciting two short stories by Oscar Wilde, *The Birthday of the Infanta* and *The Happy Prince*, which the actress had performed at the White Barn in 1955.

"We booked anything that we thought interesting," Henry Hewes recalled. "Douglass Watson wanted to do the Kafka *Metamorphosis* as a dance drama, and we did that, along with his adaptation of Maeterlinck's *Pelleas and Melisande.*"

Hewes himself staged *Hamlet* in late January, with the Irish actress Siobhan McKenna, who was appearing on Broadway at the time in Shaw's *St. Joan*, playing the melancholy prince. Hewes cut the scenes in which Hamlet was not directly involved, placed McKenna in front of a screen on which he projected a variety of images, then positioned actors such as Earle Hyman, Beatrice Arthur, Clarence Derwent, William Ball, Ellis Rabb and Joyce Ebert behind curtains at either side of the screen. Unseen, they spoke to McKenna on stage.

McKenna certainly looked the part, with her black hair cropped short for playing Joan, but Lucille found it pretentious. She told Corinne Jacker years later that it "was an ego trip for Siobhan McKenna, who stood in front of the curtain spouting, and all these great stars behind her with their voices coming out." The critics agreed.

The Series concluded its first season with the sort of conventional, star-studded entries that were guaranteed to bring subscribers back the following year. Peggy Wood performed a concert reading of Shaw's *Candida* on March 28, and three weeks later Dame Sybil Thorndike and her husband Sir Lewis Casson presented the American premiere of their Dramatic Recital, a collection of excerpts from the world's literature.

Critics congratulated the Series for offering work more innovative than anything Broadway would have touched, even if they caviled about a particular Matinee. For instance, after seeing *U.S.A.*, *Variety*'s critic commented that, "Desirable as this repertory objective may be, shouldn't such a theatre be built on a broader base than the benign but limited patronage of the lorgnette set?" But that was not the sort of criticism to which Lucille, who dismissed negative reviews anyway, paid attention. For her, it mattered that the first season had been a stimulating mixture of the familiar and the groundbreaking, of stars and youthful talent, of European classics and new American work. Range and surprise would be the Series' signature and the key to its popularity. An audience never knew exactly what to expect at any performance, and for most of the Series' life, the critics as well as the general public responded to that wide-open approach.

Elsewhere Lucille's 1956–57 season had provided more mixed rewards. While the fate of the Theatre de Lys was still undecided, that of *The River Line* had been all too certain. Lucille, Sanford Friedman and Henry Boettcher had finally produced Morgan's drama at the Carnegie Hall Playhouse on January 2, 1957, with Lucille putting up $10,500, half the capitalization. Stuart Vaughan directed the handsome production, which was designed by Wolfgang Roth. Almost unanimously, critics praised the acting, particularly the performances of startling, red-haired Beatrice Straight as the French wife, Gene Lyons as the American soldier troubled by the murder they committed, and Sada Thompson as a girl with whom he falls in love. But equally unanimously the critics had difficulty with Morgan's writing. Some found it outright dull. Others, like Kerr at the *Herald Tribune* and Atkinson at the *Times*, believed that Morgan's overcivilized style mirrored his view of a postwar world retreating behind an overcivilized façade.

These were not reviews to keep a production open. *River Line,* the play that Lucille probably would have brought into the de Lys had *Threepenny* not come along again, closed on January 13 after fifteen performances. She lost almost her entire investment.

On the personal front, Lou had apparently recovered from his heart attack, and in late February and most of March, in between Matinee performances, the couple relaxed at Harbor Island Spa in Miami. The Schweitzer family had made a firm offer on January 28 to sell both Peter J. Schweitzer, Inc., and a partial interest in the Schweitzers' French company, Papeteries de Mauduit, to Kimberly-Clark, the giant paper goods manufacturer. These deals brought the Schweitzer brothers and sisters 735,000 shares of Kimberly-Clark common stock, $4,000,000 in cash and put Lou at ease about his companies' future.

To Lucille's relief, Lou's improved health and victory with the de Lys brightened his spirits, and his eccentric side reemerged. Lucille often worried when she could not find a taxi at night in the out-of-the-way parts of the city where she attended theatre. One day an employee of Lou's was riding in a cab and noticed that the driver's name was Louis Schweitzer. Lou contacted the Hack Drivers' Bureau, located the man, who lived in the Bronx, and made him an offer he apparently could not refuse. Lou would buy a car, convert it to a taxi and split the proceeds with Louis the cabdriver, provided the cabdriver would be available to take Lou's wife wherever she needed to go. The cabby agreed, and Lou purchased a gray SL190 Mercedes-Benz (cost: $4,000), a taxi medallion (cost: $17,000) and eventually had the built-in radio tuned permanently to 99.5 FM, the wave length of WBAI, a radio station that he also purchased in 1957. Lucille not only traveled safely but in style.

On April 24, Lou and Lucile sailed on the *Queen Mary* for Europe, where Lou's whimsical mood continued. During an excursion to Venice, he convinced the association of gondoliers to break a 450-year-old rule and allow an outsider to own a gondola, and for $1,000 the *gondolieri* built him one, with "Lucille" inscribed on the stern. Lou always urged his globe-trotting friends to seek out a gondolier named Bruno and take a free ride, although sometimes he sent them a bill upon their return. Hazel Vincent Wallace and her sister spent two days in Venice during the summer of 1965 and she wrote Lucille that they "were simply thrilled to be piloted by such a wonderfully handsome and dignified signore and to be in a gondola called Lucille."

In London, Lucille discovered that the theatre community was gasping about the premiere of Jean Genet's *The Balcony*, directed by Peter Zadek, which had opened in April at the modest Arts Theatre Club. Set in a fantastical brothel run by the queenly Madame Irma, *The Balcony* pits totalitarianism against a passionate but impotent revolution. Madame Irma helps men indulge their fantasies of power; at her brothel, they dress up as a general, a bishop and a judge and are catered to by women who are both subservient and punitive. Eventually, to help her friend the Chief of Police quell the revolution, Madame Irma actually impersonates the queen and asks her clients to take on publicly the roles they have been acting out privately.

Supposedly the Arts was immune from the predations of the Lord Chamberlain's censorship; nonetheless, the play's setting—and the vicious satire of church and state—proved too tempting for that conservative office, and it had insisted on cuts. Out went supposedly blasphemous references to Christ, the Virgin, the Immaculate Conception, and Saint Theresa. Out, too, went the pivotal scene in the brothel in which Roger, the revolutionary, castrates himself. Genet watched a dress rehearsal with his translator Bernard Frechtman and, understandably furious, created havoc. Barred from the Arts, he returned home to Paris, leaving a *cause célèbre* in his wake and a production that, good or not, became a must-see. And so Lucille, Lou and Hazel Vincent Wallace trooped to see it. In a letter to playwright Meade Roberts about a year later, Lucille asked if he had read *The Balcony*. "It is very unusual," she wrote. "And I found it fascinating." Many years afterward Wallace remembered, "I was really rather shocked by [the play] but you took it on the chin so well that I didn't like to say so!!"

By June, Lucille and Lou were in Paris, where they arranged to meet the *enfant terrible* in person at the Ritz. With Lou translating in his excellent French, Lucille conversed with Genet. Later she told friends that she found the playwright appealing and shy. Lou paid him $500 for a one-year option on *The Balcony,* and they sailed back to New York with what was undoubtedly one of the hottest properties in the avant-garde theatre.

Although the White Barn did not open that summer until August 4, Lucille had assembled some of the most innovative work her theatre had presented. Corinne Jacker directed her adaptation of Katherine Anne Porter's story *Pale Horse, Pale Rider,* and Terese Hayden staged the American premiere of the drama about an aged poet that she had brought to Lucille—English playwright John Whiting's *Saints Day*.

On August 24 and 25, Lawrence Arrick directed the first American production of Eugene Ionesco's dark farce, *The Chairs,* with Jenny Egan and Roberts Blossom as the elderly couple who invite a crowd of possibly imaginary guests to hear the great message that the Old Man is leaving for humanity. Amazingly, of the New York critics, only Henry Hewes from *The Saturday Review* attended that weekend, which left it to local reviewers to grapple with Ionesco's absurd world and Arrick's too realistic staging of it. Myrtle M. Couture, in the *Westport Town Crier and Herald*, wrote

> Even the weather on Sunday evening conspired to conjure the audience at Lucille Lortel's White Barn Theatre into a mood befitting the workings of the failing minds of an old man (95 years old)

and an old woman (94 years old) who are pursuing the last years of their frustrated existence on a lonely island.

...the rain came down in torrents, pattering the roof of the White Barn with a dismal rhythm, intermingled with the weird half tones of appropriate mood music composed and directed by Donald Marsh...

The play, which takes place entirely within the minds of the aged couple, certainly cannot be described as pleasant entertainment, though it may be described as an audaciously realistic presentation. And, after all, that is true theatre.

All the frustrations, disappointments, hopes and fears which have formed the life of the couple find easement at the last in "play pretend." Thus the play is actually a psychiatric study.

In particular to those who have had experience in dealing with the confusion which all too often besets the aged, the tragi-farce was such an accurate depiction as to create a mood of depression which like a nightmare lingered long after the performance ended.

With her enthusiasm for juggling several enterprises at once, that summer of 1957 Lucille was also looking forward to Paul Shyre's adaptation of *I Knock at the Door,* which she, an attorney named Howard Gottfried and Shyre were producing at the Belasco near the end of September (she had never produced Arnold Perl's adaptation of the previous summer). In 1956, Shyre and the director Stuart Vaughan had presented two well-received performances of *I Knock at the Door* at the YM-YWHA, and Shyre and Gottfried had gone to Lucille with the idea of producing a run of forty-eight performances. "It was her money that made it possible," Vaughan said.

Even as a limited run, it was a risky choice for Broadway. O'Casey's plays had not had much luck getting produced in the United States. They were intricate and expensive to mount and, as their author proudly knew, politically subversive. When The Playhouse in Houston, Texas, staged *Red Roses for Me* in 1951, the Catholic community protested loudly, almost closing the production. Then there was O'Casey himself: quick to anger, blunt-spoken and nearly blind, he was not easy to work with, even a continent away.

Shyre's adaptation of *I Knock at the Door* was O'Casey diluted, but it gave appreciative audiences a taste of this great Irish writer. The cast of six, which included Aline MacMahon and Staats Cotsworth, read at least thirty roles, all the while sitting on high stools in front of lecterns, with a blue cyclorama behind them. While some critics objected to the noncommercial look of what was still a commercial production, others, like Arthur Gelb of the *New York Times,* relished "the tenderness, the humor, the anguish, and above all, the poetry that sings from O'Casey's pages...stunningly evoked on the stage of the Belasco Theatre." Vaughan, Gelb wrote, "has directed with the ear of a musician, as well as the sure knowledge of a theater craftsman."

Lucille realized with pleasure that she was slowly achieving status as an Off-Broadway producer. She had always received offers to rent out the de Lys, but as artistic director of the Matinee Series, and since producing *The River Line* and *I Knock at the Door,* she was being sought in a different way. Owning the rights to *The Balcony* made her even more desirable. Undoubtedly some of her popularity stemmed from her money. But it was also becoming clear that she lavished it on unorthodox scripts in which few commercial producers were willing to invest, especially to that degree. Thus David Ross, who ran the Fourth Street Theatre, sounded her out to coproduce Brendan Behan's controversial play about capital punishment, *The Quare Fellow,* and John C. Wilson wrote her that he had optioned two new Tennessee Williams plays, which the dramatist wanted done Off Broadway. "Would you rent me your theatre? or even if you wished—care to co-produce?" he wrote in September 1957. "I can assure you that they are *very* 'avant-garde' and might intrigue you . . . " Lucille, who almost always responded to such inquiries by first stating what she herself was busy doing—in this case, *I Knock at the Door*—asked for a script. (Wilson produced the plays, *Something Unspoken* and *Suddenly Last Summer,* with Warner LeRoy.) Even if she sensed that some queries were patronizing, she was enjoying her identity as an Off-Broadway producer and the position of being out in front of the crowd in terms of theatrical taste. At the end of the 1957–58 season, the *Village Voice* Off-Broadway Awards, known informally as the Obie Awards, gave Lucille a Special Citation "for fostering and furthering the spirit of theatrical experiment through the distinguished ANTA Matinee Series at the Theatre de Lys." It was the first of literally dozens of personal honors that she would receive during her lifetime.

The theatre community also noted that plays produced in the Matinee Series often transferred to commercial Off-Broadway runs. After Lucille moved *Pale Horse, Pale Rider* from the White Barn to the Matinee Series in October 1957, Bradley Phillips and David Wheeler moved it to Off Broadway's Jan Hus Theatre, although it survived for only forty performances, to Katherine Anne Porter's deep disappointment. "I live in a world of highly specialized people," she wrote Lucille from her home in Southbury, Connecticut. "The wide reaches of popularity are not for me or, usually, not for them! In spite of the failure to make a season of it, I still am glad the play was done."

Neil McKenzie's *Guests of the Nation,* on a Matinee Series bill with Edna St. Vincent Millay's *Aria da Capo* in May 1958, fared better. In addition to praising the acting of Tom, Liam and Patrick Clancy, of the Irish singing group the Clancy Brothers, Arthur Gelb wrote in the *Times* "Perhaps the most poignant aspect of yesterday afternoon's twin bill . . . is that it was a one-performance venture. 'Guests of the Nation,' deserves to be seen by many more people than could be crowded at the matinee into the cozy theatre on Christopher Street." A dramatization of Frank O'Connor's vivid short story, it involved a pair of young Irish nationalists guarding a couple of English hostages in 1921. The four find that they like each other, a troublesome sentiment when the Irish have to shoot their captives. In June, McKenzie and the producer Paul E. Davis transferred *Guests of the Nation* to the Theatre Marquee, where it played for 102 performances. In the interim it won a *Village Voice* Obie Award for Best One-Act Play.

The following October, at an ANTA executive committee meeting, Lucille expressed her feeling that "it was a pity for a production such as 'Guests of the Nation'... to be lost to us and be picked up by another producer who derives the benefit." The New York Chapter wanted to explore ways for taking productions further, possibly with tours to colleges. In principle, the executive committee supported the idea; in practice, what with other demands on national ANTA's limited resources, it never happened. Two years later, in 1960, the Library of Congress in Washington, D.C., through its Gertrude Clarke Whittall Poetry and Literature Fund, would invite the Matinee Series to present two one-acts in its Coolidge Auditorium. From then on Lucille took matters into her own hands and almost every year fed the Library with morsels from the Matinee's table.

When the Matinee Series had begun, director Terese Hayden had urged Lucille not to offend the unions, as she had done at the White Barn. But, as in Westport, Lucille wanted the best deal that she and ANTA could negotiate with Equity; the New York Chapter's production budget was meager, and Lucille did not want to come to its aid more than absolutely necessary. The actors in *Cry, the Beloved Country* had each received $35, but Lucille and the New York Chapter found that rate expensive and during the first full season they paid actors little or nothing. That was a situation Equity could not let stand, and as of October 1957, the union wanted the Matinee Series to pay each actor $15 for a rehearsal week and $30 for the performance. Lucille and the Chapter sought a concession. In December, for W.H. Auden's *Christmas Oratorio* and e.e.

cummings' *Santa Claus,* Equity had allowed the actors to rehearse and perform for $20; Lucille asked to continue that scale.

Believing that additional persuasion might be helpful, she turned to her stalwart knight Clarence Derwent, and on January 7, 1958, Equity's president emeritus went before the Council to plead the Series' case. Not surprisingly, Equity agreed to the $20 rate, which stayed in place until 1960. At national ANTA's annual membership meeting in May, Lucille thanked Derwent "for his historic plea before Equity Council which melted all hearts and secured for us those concessions essential to our continuance."

That New York's best actors agreed to rehearse and perform for this ludicrous sum, and that directors and playwrights received no money at all, reflected the art form's age-old tradition of putting dedication above remuneration. But it also indicated the Series' prominence. "The Matinee Series had a considerable reputation," said the director Stephen Porter, who, with Ellis Rabb, adapted and staged Sophocles' *Philoctetes* and André Gide's modern *Philoctetes* for the Series in January 1959. "People saw those things and talked about them. It was early in the Off-Broadway movement, and lots of people were struggling to get started or do projects."

Even in the mid-1960s, when Off Off Broadway was taking up the experimental role that Off Broadway had filled, the Matinee Series remained a respected platform. There, in December 1965, Michael Kahn staged Adrienne Kennedy's surreal one-act *The Owl Answers*. "Lucille had asked me to direct it at the White Barn the previous August and then she brought it to the Matinee Series," said Kahn years later, when he was artistic director of the Shakespeare Theatre in Washington, D.C. "Joe Papp saw it and liked it and asked me to direct *Measure for Measure* in Central Park, and that was really the start of my career. The Series had a nice reputation. It was certainly a step up from Caffe Cino," said Kahn, referring to Joseph Cino's famous coffeehouse with its 8-by-8-foot stage. "And Lucille was legendary."

Increasingly the Matinee Series belonged to Lucille in spirit and direction. The notion of a repertory company evaporated, and the presentations evolved from readings to rehearsed and staged productions with minimal sets. Before the start of the 1958–59 season, Henry Hewes resigned as the New York Chapter's executive director, to seek a higher-paying job in addition to his post at the *Saturday Review*. At one point Lucille's office issued a guideline for the Series that included submitting ideas to her, after which, "They will be reviewed by an appointed committee." For many years in fact the playbills listed a "Matinee Theatre Series Committee" composed of socialites like Mrs. Nicholas "Pansy" Schenck and Mrs. Anthony A. Bliss, who was formerly an actress, and theatre people like Peggy Wood and Blanche Yurka. But the Committee was Lucille.

With Hewes gone, Lucille's only competition for authority and recognition was Mrs. H. Alwyn Inness-Brown, the president of the New York Chapter.

Except for their need to be in charge, the women were poles apart. Virginia Inness-Brown was a WASP listed in the Social Register; Lucille was Jewish and her parents had been immigrants. Tiny, slim Inness-Brown leaned toward navy suits and dresses, matching Tiffany pins and earrings, and pearls. Lortel, now almost fifty-seven, had grown plump and by comparison seemed almost working class in her brightly colored skirts and blouses. At the one-year anniversary party for *The Balcony*, she sat at a table, one hand wrapped around a can of Ballantine, the other holding a paper cup. "When I first saw Lucille at a function for ANTA," said Susan Komarow, "I was amazed that she was dressed up, with jewels and everything else. I always saw her in the context of the de Lys, and you were not going to put on fancy outfits there." By all accounts Inness-Brown knew nothing about theatre; to

ANTA's growing number of critics, she epitomized the nonprofessional, upper-crust element they deplored.

In press releases, feature articles and minutes of ANTA meetings, the two women jockeyed for control and public acknowledgment, although each was careful to give the other her due. "They didn't like each other," observed the director Robert Glenn, who worked closely with Lucille as the Matinee Series' coordinator from 1959 to 1961. "They did not personally get along, although I never was present at any actual animosity between them." Ultimately Lucille prevailed in this duel; among other things, she oversaw the publicity that went out for each Matinee, including the placement of her name in press releases. As Terese Hayden said, "You could never imagine that Lucille would invest herself in something and that somebody would bump her. She had too many resources."

"Lucille had the upper hand," Susan Komarow said. "She had the theatre."

When not organizing the Matinee Series, Lucille was considering other producing options. During the fall of 1957, the British director Peter Brook visited New York and Lucille talked with him about staging Genet's *The Balcony*. The thirty-two-year-old Brook, who had acquired a superior reputation staging Shakespeare and modern dramatists like Christopher Fry and Jean Anouilh, was slated to direct the Paris premiere that winter.

But Brook was elusive. He told her that he would rather not commit himself until she saw the Paris production, at which point he would also be in a better position to decide whether he wanted to direct the American one. He wrote her from Europe on November 11 that he was immersed in studying the play, and that Genet was "doing a number of major revisions to the script." He would let her know when the Paris opening was set.

With the judgment of an increasingly experienced producer, on November 20 Lucille wrote Genet's translator, Bernard Frechtman, "At present feeling he is the best director for the play I would rather wait and do it right, than just do it." In the meantime, she was getting offers from other directors, including Alan Schneider, a talented, forty-year-old American who had recently been staging the work of Samuel Beckett. Schneider also wrote her on November 11, to suggest, "If Peter Brook turns out not to be available when you're ready for THE BALCONY, I'd be interested in your considering me . . ."

Indeed in Paris *The Balcony* was having difficulties. First there was trouble finding a theatre. Then, when the Théâtre Antoine agreed to produce, a typical Genet brouhaha erupted. For some reason Simone Berriau, who ran the Théâtre Antoine, enraged Genet; Genet called her a whore; Berriau handed the script over to the police, who essentially warned that if she put the play on, they would shut her theatre down. Brook would finally direct the French premiere of *The Balcony* in May 1960—but Lucille's American production would beat it by two months.

With Genet on hold, Lucille turned to O'Casey.

Sean O'Casey had written *Cock-a-Doodle Dandy* in 1949. A vivid comedy that poked merciless fun at Irish bigotry and sexual intolerance, it was the dramatist's favorite play. In 1950 Margo Jones had staged it at her theatre in Dallas, and in 1955, the Yale School of Drama had produced it in New Haven. But despite interest at different times from the director Robert Lewis and the producer Lawrence Langner, potential New York productions had languished. Paul Shyre was the only American who aggressively pursued the rights.

Shyre visited O'Casey at his home in Torquay, England, in August 1957, and the playwright gave Shyre the go-ahead. By January 1958 Shyre was hoping for a fall production and by July had contacted Lucille about investing. Lortel, Shyre and Howard Gottfried, the triumvirate of *I Knock at the Door*, searched for a theatre—*Threepenny Opera* was still an immovable force—and they chose the Carnegie Hall Playhouse, with an out-of-town tryout in Toronto. At O'Casey's suggestion, Philip Burton was directing.

If any publicity is good publicity, then Lucille and her colleagues could not have wished for a better trial run than Toronto. The play ignited a furor among those Catholics who considered it blasphemous. They stood in front of Toronto's Playhouse Theatre during intermission, asserted that the comedy should be banned and threatened the actors. At one Saturday night performance two men leapt up during the third act and shouted "you're a liar" when a dying girl returns uncured from the shrine at Lourdes and rejects miracle healing.

The opening in New York, on November 12, 1958, displayed no fireworks, either in the audience or, judging by the cool reviews, on stage. Brooks Atkinson, who was devoted to O'Casey's writing, admitted sadly that the largely American cast did not grasp the "Celtic tone" of the play. O'Casey was severely disappointed, as was Lucille. But the experience was by no means a loss, for she met O'Casey's wife, Eileen, who flew to New York in November to see the production and stayed until December in Lucille's one-room apartment at the Hampshire House.

The two women were the same age but they could not have been more different. Eileen O'Casey had been an actress and a beauty, but she had given up the theatre to raise three children and dedicate herself to her husband's art, serve as his eyes and nurse him through bouts of illness. More recently she had nursed their son Niall until his death of leukemia in 1956 at the age of twenty-one. Eileen and Sean O'Casey, who often turned down lucrative offers if they jarred his sense of artistic rightness, were always strapped for money.

But Lucille and the extraordinarily modest Eileen got along, possibly because Eileen was self-effacing and warmly appreciative of Lucille's generosity. They went to a production of O'Casey's *Shadow of a Gunman* at the Actors Studio. Together they saw Brendan Behan's *The Quare Fellow* at the Circle in the Square. Lucille took Eileen, Paul Shyre and the actor Will Geer, who was in *Cock-a-Doodle Dandy*, to a lunch at Sardi's hosted by the Woman Pays Club, a long-established organization for financially independent women in which Lucille was a member.

On the night before Eileen flew home, Lucille threw a party for her at the Hampshire House. It was a typical Lucille Lortel event, crammed with more theatrical celebrities than Eileen probably wanted to meet: Lillian Gish; Lee and Paula Strasberg; their daughter, Susan; Jessica Tandy; Agnes de Mille; Marc Blitzstein and many more. Lucille was also celebrating Anny's eighty-second birthday, and there was a gathering of the Wadler clan. Mayo, Ruth and Cugat, Seymour and his pretty, shy Italian wife, Lisa Glauber, were in attendance when a birthday cake made a dramatic entrance at midnight. It probably frustrated Lucille that, with all the famous people milling around, the ones whom Eileen wrote to ask about when she returned home were Seymour and Lisa. And of course Lou. "I have thought of you & Louis so much & your kindness," Eileen wrote from Torquay on December 3. "This was so warm & gracious . . . ; to give & let the receiver feel he is hardly receiving such great kindness is rare."

Robert Glenn was a tall, strapping Texan in his late thirties, a director "from the sticks" as he put it, when he first came to New York early in 1959. Through New Dramatists, an organization formed in 1949 to nurture American playwriting, he had received a six-week Ford Foundation grant to be attached to the Broadway production of *Look After Lulu*, an adaptation of a Georges Feydeau farce being directed by Cyril Ritchard. Glenn watched rehearsals, went through the try-out in New Haven and the opening in New York. But when it was over, he wanted to know what to do next. "How can I do things Off Broadway?" he asked the people at New Dramatists. "Well, there's Lucille Lortel, who owns the Theatre de Lys," they said. "Do you have any script or project you could submit to her?"

Glenn did. In Dallas he had directed the Little Theatre, one of the first African-American theatre groups there. "I couldn't find scripts for them," he recounted, "so I put together some of Langston Hughes' poetry, some music and called it *Shakespeare in Harlem,*" a title borrowed from one of Hughes' books of poetry. From back home in Texas, he sent Lucille a copy. Lucille wrote him to come to New York, although she did not offer to pay his way. "We'll do it," she said.

Glenn returned to the city in 1959 with hardly any money and camped in Lucille's office at 111 West 57th Street, working there by day and sleeping in an armchair at night. "I had talked with other people, and they said, 'Well, she's a little tough,' " Glenn recalled more than forty years later. "But she wasn't to me. She came to rehearsals, both at the White Barn and later when we did it for the Matinee Series, and she just loved it." Glenn discovered that Lucille reserved most of her toughness for employees like secretaries and assistants, whom she often chastised unsparingly and publicly. "She got pretty sharp," said Glenn. "I was sometimes embarrassed just sitting there."

Glenn knew no black actors in New York, but Lucille ran casting notices, and he used Lucille's office and the de Lys for auditions. The ten actors he selected included Isabel Sanford, who in the 1970s would become familiar to television audiences through the situation comedy *The Jeffersons,* and Godfrey Cambridge, who would become a popular television comedian. In 1959 they were at the beginning of their careers.

Shakespeare in Harlem ran under an hour, so for the White Barn's performances on August 29 and 30, Glenn added a kind of olio at the top of the bill, including a turn by none other than Butterfly McQueen, who had portrayed the squeaky-voiced maid Prissy in *Gone with the Wind*. "A friend of a friend of a friend knew her," he said.

But Hughes' poetry was paramount. "Each character, occasionally a group," wrote a reviewer named Leslie Latham, "picked out of the dark by spotlights. All representative people in Harlem, simple but articulate, shown mostly in situations of frustration: the frustration redoubled because of their colour. Even beneath the flashes of humour, the momentary escapes in jazz, the universalities of human reactions, each moves under that further shadow." The outstanding performance belonged to a young actor named Calden Marsh, with his rendition of "Theme for English B," a poem that portrayed a night student of English composition at Columbia University. "A student," said Glenn, "reminiscing about what he learned from his professor, what his professor learned from him, what they learned from each other. It was so tender, and Marsh was such a fine actor—it didn't stop the show in the sense of applause, but there was tremendous empathy in the audience."

That audience, Glenn remembered, was surprised by the slightly confrontational finish. "The play ends with part of 'Montage of a Dream Deferred,' " Glenn said. "And at that point the play takes a more aggressive approach. 'Good morning, Daddy. Haven't you heard?'—right to the audience. Some of the White Barn audience was going, 'Who me? I love Negroes. What do you mean?' That was remarked upon. For that time it was pretty aggressive, but soft compared to ten years later."

Lucille had made sure that Hughes was in the audience, and the poet came to the front of the stage after the performance, a smile lighting his pudgy face, and said a few words. Hughes later told the producer Stella Holt that *Shakespeare in Harlem* was "about the loveliest show I ever had."

One person who was not in the audience that weekend was Clarence Derwent. Lucille's longtime supporter and friend had died suddenly in his New York apartment on August 6 at the age of seventy-five. Lucille felt the loss sharply, but eminently practical about the present, she did not dwell on it. She asked Eva Le Gallienne to replace Derwent on the White Barn's Board of Directors, and the actress agreed. By the time *Shakespeare in Harlem* went up on August 29, Le Gallienne's name was on the playbill.

Shakespeare in Harlem opened the 1959–60 Matinee Series on October 27, with adjustments to the cast and, at the top of the bill, a morbid short play by Hughes called *Soul Gone Home*. Subsequently Glenn and Howard Gottfried took *Shakespeare in Harlem* Off Broadway to the 41st Street Theatre, between 6th and 7th Avenues, where, with yet another companion piece, *God's Trombones*, but without Godfrey Cambridge, it opened on February 9, 1960. Brooks Atkinson wrote a valentine: " 'Shakespeare in Harlem' is a garland of verses about the 'dream deferred' to which Lorraine Hansberry refers in 'Raisin in the Sun.' . . . the delicacy of feeling it discloses, the idiomatic music of the lines and the immaculate taste of the performance endow it with thoughtful beauty." With the success of *Raisin,* which had opened on Broadway in March 1959 and was still running, one would have thought that *Shakespeare in Harlem* could attract audiences. But the piece's modest nature—and the theatre's location, neither on Broadway nor in Off Broadway's usual stomping ground of Greenwich Village—may have discouraged ticket-buyers. The production closed after thirty-two performances.

Glenn was too optimistic to be disappointed for long. For him, Lucille's invitation had opened a world and a career. "Through my work with her and meeting other people, everything good came to me—working in Canada, theatres in Atlanta—all through connecting with her and New York ANTA."

Glenn was just the sort of attractive but unknown talent whom she enjoyed encouraging. By the beginning of 1960, she had him coordinating the Matinee Series, possibly as a way to ensure he had a salary, however small, for he was still living out of her office. In January she asked him to take over the direction of Ionesco's *Victims of Duty,* which was second on a Matinee bill with an adaptation of Dostoevsky's *Notes from the Underground*. On March 22, for that season's final Matinee presentation, he staged Sean O'Casey's one-act *Time To Go* and Paul Vincent Carroll's *The Coggerers*, which Lucille planned to take to the Library of Congress a week later. O'Casey's American agent, Jane Rubin, had told Lucille that *Time to Go* was a new play, and Lucille, who always wanted to stage premieres, was disappointed to discover later that it had been produced in New York in 1952. "Doesn't Sean have any new one-act plays that would be good for the series?" she wrote to Eileen O'Casey. In the meantime, aware of the O'Caseys' financial problems, she wished for the play's success. "I hope," she wrote, "that it will receive favorable notices so that there could perhaps be an Off-Broadway run, in which case, Sean could then get royalties."

As coordinator of the Matinee Series, Glenn read scripts and made recommendations. "I would say, 'This looks good' and send it to her in Westport or wherever, and she would have a secretary or someone else read it to her. I would write my capsule impressions on three-by-five cards and send these over to her." He recommended against her producing Genet's *The Blacks*. "I thought it demeaned blackness," he said.

Between 1959 and 1961, and then during the mid-sixties, when Glenn again worked at ANTA for a time, he and Lucille, by his informal count, went to hundreds of readings, auditions and plays. "She sat through not only plays but rehearsals, and presentations excerpted from these things," he said. "And many of these were not easy to sit through, not only from the way they were done but also because of the ideas they conveyed. She could sit through two or three a day. I rode in that taxi many times."

Glenn realized, "I was there basically, as I understood later, as her escort. She loved male escorts. And of course by that time I was fairly knowledgeable about the Off-Broadway community and so I was helpful."

He sometimes found the role embarrassing, especially when it involved Lucille's obsession with food. "I don't know if she came from a family that was deprived of food," Glenn recalled with amused astonishment, "but every place we went, when there would be any food—and I was always hungry—she would push her way up to the front of the line and want to eat first. She would say, 'Is the food served yet?' and she'd go right up and serve herself first. I didn't mind. I was behind her."

Both secure in himself and able to keep his long-range goals in view, Glenn admired Lucille's energy and ego. "From the very beginning," he said, "she was full of push. Ambition. For my project or anybody's project that she was enamored of." After *Shakespeare in Harlem*'s performances at the White Barn, she wrote to Hazel Vincent Wallace in England about getting the piece to the Edinburgh Festival. "How does one go about it?" she asked. And she added, "I think it would be a natural for the Royal Court or the Arts Theatre Club. It was sensational here."

"Of course, her name had to go on a project, no matter what," said Glenn. " 'Lucille Lortel this, Lucille Lortel that.' I never minded, because I understood that. When I went back to Dallas, I copied her, right down the line. I started a theatre in 1972—the Shakespeare Festival of Dallas—and my name went first. And I got that from her."

The press agent Howard Atlee often joked that "the two women in show business who used 'darling' most were Tallulah Bankhead and Lucille, and I got to work for both of them." He began handling press for the Matinee Series with the 1959–60 season, and like Glenn, he also understood Lucille's drive. "She never ceased to remind you that it was all hers," said the press agent. "Her idea, she's running it, and her name comes first on the press releases. Because Lucille Lortel was a name. And when you're selling tickets, you sell your star or your name, whether it's the playwright, your leading actor or actress. But in her case, it was always Lucille Lortel. I think that was from her acting days. Corner the press agent. Nothing wrong with doing that."

As at the White Barn, Lucille esteemed publicity, but by now she was more sophisticated. She was "detail oriented," said Atlee. Lucille might not know the Series' entire roster at the start of a season, but she scheduled enough plays ahead of time to give Atlee the lead time he needed. Then, using information she collected from critics, agents and colleagues, or based on her own knowledge, she would give Atlee the resources to write press releases. "You were going to get the full story from her," he said. "All the parts of the production, who was important, what they did before, why they were important. When she brought in Yukio Mishima, I remember coming into her office, and Lucille gave me the whole history. 'Well, darling, you know there's this great playwright in Japan now.' She would sell to me the way she would want me to sell to the public. She was very good about that."

She was, Atlee also noted, in the right place at the right time. The Matinee Series was searching for new European and American voices and so were a number of hungry newspapers and reporters. *"The New York Post,* that's where you went," said Atlee. "The *Post* remained sympathetic to anything that wasn't mainstream. Vernon Rice really discovered and made Off Broadway." In the fall of 1955, Dan Wolf, Ed Fancher and Norman Mailer started the *Village Voice.* "I have so many memories of jumping up the stairs to that office at Sheridan Square and sitting there while all that chaos was going on," said Atlee. "I had what they covered. Weekly newspapers like the *Village Voice* and the *Villager* wanted what I was selling."

The performance schedule helped, for it was unlikely that a critic had anything else to see on a Tuesday afternoon. But Lucille worked the hustings. Atlee assumed that she knew reporters and critics personally and probably called them on her own. "If she met somebody at the theatre who worked for a publication," he said, "particularly a publication which she respected, she would make sure that she talked to them, and then it was like she had known them all her life. She knew everybody at the *Times.* 'Send this to Gelb,' she would say. Savvy. Very savvy."

Her work paid off in reservations and full houses. Susan Komarow, organizing the subscribers' tickets, found to her dismay that, as at the White Barn, the seating arrangement was dear to Lucille's heart. Lucille and she each had a seating chart, and at least a week before the performance, Lucille would be on the phone to her or would show up at the ANTA office, to go over the names of subscribers, celebrities and critics who had made reservations. As at the White Barn, subscribers presented a card and received their actual tickets at the door. On Tuesdays, Lucille would meet Komarow at the de Lys around noon, and then the process of finalizing the seating would begin in dead earnest, often right until curtain time.

Komarow found this dance exhausting and ludicrous. But Lucille felt it was essential. It could pay off, she believed, in good reviews or a feature story or a star willing to act in the Matinee Series two months later. That the anonymous theatre-lover in her audience might get a worse seat as a result does not seem to have troubled her, and anyway by most reports the atmosphere at the Matinees was congenial, like a group of friends getting together every month or so.

Even when a Matinee had ended, Lucille did not consider her job done. After Lou bought WBAI-FM, which, he explained to newspaper reporters, he intended to run as an "Off-Broadway station" with controversial discussions and good music, Lucille instituted interviews with members of the audience. Alice Griffin, *Variety*'s Off-Broadway critic, and her husband John Griffin had a radio program called "Sidewalk Critics Review for WBAI." After a Matinee, they would stand in front of the de Lys, John wearing a portable two-reel tape recorder around his neck and Alice carrying the microphone, and they would nab well-known ANTA members and celebrities when they came out, ask their opinions of the production, then rush uptown to WBAI's studio in the Pierre Hotel and air the results. Impromptu though the interviews were, the interviewees usually understood their obligation to praise the play and the Series.

The next day, after particularly good reviews, Lucille would call Atlee. "I don't know if I can move this or not, darling," she would tell him, "but this is very good, we're going to do something with this."

By the summer of 1959, it was obvious to Lucille that Peter Brook was no longer in consideration to direct the American premiere of *The Balcony*. José Quintero at Circle in the Square became the leading contender for the job.

According to Ted Mann, who liked to downplay Lucille's role in the venture, she brought them the script with the idea of coproducing it. "I read the first three scenes," he said, "and thinking it was wonderful, I gave it to José to read. I read the rest of it, and he read the rest of it, and we decided to do it." According to Lucille's correspondence, Quintero had asked Lucille's good friend Audrey Wood to put his name forward, but whether that occurred before or after the trio began negotiating is unclear.

Quintero was not, at first glance, the most obvious choice to direct *The Balcony*. He had earned his reputation staging naturalistic plays, notably the moody, atmospheric work of Eugene O'Neill. At the end of the 1955–56 season he had received the Vernon Rice Award and a *Village Voice* Obie for bringing to life O'Neill's gargantuan *The Iceman Cometh;* the following season, he won lavish praise for his nakedly moving interpretation of O'Neill's autobiographical *Long Day's Journey into Night*. O'Neill's plays were not the raucous theatrical puzzles, the games of visual illusion, that Genet's were.

But they were saturated with language, as *The Balcony* certainly was. And there was another side to Quintero, that of the boy who had been raised a Catholic in Panama and knew both the pageantry and the hypocrisy of the Church, elements essential to Genet's script.

In the fall of 1959 Quintero had one other advantage over competitors: he had a theatre. And since *Threepenny Opera* still showed no sign of exiting the de Lys, a theatre was what Lucille needed. Lucille wrote Bernard Frechtman on October 30, 1959, "The use of the theatre is contingent upon his directing 'The Balcony'....I saw Quintero himself several days ago, and he assures me that he is most anxious to direct 'The Balcony' and will do his utmost to arrange his present commitments to enable him to do so this season."

That autumn Mann and Quintero were being forced to find a new location for the Circle in the Square, for their cherished home on Sheridan Square would soon be torn down to make way for an apartment building. Lucille hoped to persuade Mann to open his new space with the Genet—after all, this would be the French playwright's first production in the United States. But Mann had chosen Thornton Wilder's *Our Town* as the final production on Sheridan Square and decided to move that into the new theatre at 159 Bleecker Street, when it was ready on January 9, 1960. Lucille was learning that when she stepped outside her own theatre she frequently had to compromise, even if she was putting up all the money. But Lou had already paid Genet to extend their option, which by now they had held for two and a half years; it was time to make something happen. On January 20, 1960, Lucille Productions, Inc., and Circle in the Square signed a joint venture agreement to produce *The Balcony* and engage José Quintero to direct. The production was capitalized at $14,000, to be covered by Lucille Productions, and the billing would read "Lucille Lortel and Circle in the Square present..."

Quintero would soon say that *The Balcony* was the most difficult play he had directed at Circle in the Square. "It is not photography, but imagery," he told Gelb at the *Times*. "I don't think Genet is being sensational, and I am trying to stage the play very quietly. Of course, I think it may make some people wince; no one can be complacent when he sees and recognizes certain truths about himself. The play does hit very hard at several cherished areas—the armed forces, the game of politics, the law and even revolutionaries."

"We had a big problem with the play when we were in rehearsal," Mann recalled. "By the second week we realized that a lot of material was repetitive or diversionary. So we cut it. We cut the revolutionary character—the woman—which was like another play. Once we took that out, the play just sailed. I frankly don't remember that we ever asked permission."

Quintero may not have thought Genet was being sensational, but everyone else had sensationalism on their minds. Lucille did not have to worry about getting advance press for the March 3 opening. The author's reputation for rebelliousness, both theatrical and personal, preceded him. Gelb described him as an "incendiary dramatist." Lucille had invited Genet to the opening, and columnists wondered if he would come or, since he had a criminal record, even be allowed into the country if he did appear. Once here, would he create the kind of scene he had orchestrated in London? Charles McHarry at the *Daily News*, both astounded and impressed that Lucille would associate herself with a man of this type, wrote on January 29 that "lady producer Lucille Lortel reigns unopposed as Queen Mother of the Beatniks, the theatrical beatniks, that is." Genet did not show up.

The production looked spare but stunning on the new theatre's rectangular thrust stage. "A whorehouse is the image you come up with," recalled David Hays, who designed both the scenery and the lighting. "We took the ceiling—a low ceiling in that theatre—and hung it with any crazy thing we could, as if all these weird images funneled into this house of passion: chairs, crystal chandeliers, stepladders, dress dummies." The lighting isolated stage areas, faces and bodies. As Genet directed in the script, costume designer Patricia Zipprodt put the clients of Madame

Irma's brothel on cothurni, so that these would-be men of power towered over the prostitutes who accommodated their fantasies. As for the women, Zipprodt's costumes created their own sensation. The critic Stuart W. Little, in his 1972 book *Off-Broadway: The Prophetic Theater*, described "the long-legged Salome Jens as a provocative mount with leather haunches and a nylon spray tail that shook the air as her 'nervous legs and well-shod hooves' went into a spirited gallop around the general's favorite battlefield." He opined, "Quite possibly the whole 'leather look' in fashions in recent years may have derived from the use of the leather corselets and boots designed by Miss Zipprodt."

Luckily for the producers, a major snowstorm held off long enough for the critics to take their seats on opening night. But a white wasteland greeted the reviewers when they emerged from the theatre, and they had a bit of trouble getting to their papers in time to file their columns. Ted Mann remembered finding a lone taxi for Walter Kerr and wondering why he was being so gracious to somebody who was probably going to write a negative critique. Perhaps the weather interfered with their analytic abilities, for they offered up a slew of contradictory opinions. As Lucille wrote to Eileen and Sean O'Casey, "This got strange reviews." Some critics did not like the cuts or did not like it played in the round. Others simply loathed it outright: Kerr, with complete disregard for Genet's style, called it "a plaster-of-Paris play" in which "there are no people inside the costumes to make the transitions interesting." Several critics were bewildered but fascinated. Atkinson, usually so precise, gave himself up to generalities: "It would take a committee of alienists to define all the abnormalities contained in this witches' cauldron, and a committee of logicians to clarify the meanings. But anyone can see that M. Genet is a powerful writer able to document his point of view in imagery that is sharp, merciless and livid." Henry Hewes described it as "the most profound and the most poetic play of the current theatre season." Only Harold Clurman in the *Nation* dared suggest, "Genet belongs to a

category of artists who, while marginal to the mainstream of major work
..., retain a certain symbolic significance for their time. Such artists act
as a ferment..."

Clurman was right. Off Broadway needed Genet. *The Balcony*, with its
mesmerizing levels of illusion and reality, its intertwining games of sex,
power and politics, showed Off-Broadway audiences a chaotic, subversive, and cruel universe unlike any they had experienced in a modern
play. It opened a portal through which all the angry, theatrical, sensual
and darkly funny work of the 1960s, fine or terrible, could flow with a
new sense of freedom.

Lou wrote Frechtman on March 22 that the production was "selling
out every performance." At the 1959–60 Obie Awards, the three
judges—critics Richard Watts, Jr. of the *New York Post;* Robert Brustein of
the *New Republic;* and Jerry Tallmer from the *Village Voice*—gave *The Balcony* the award for Best Foreign Play, elevating it above Samuel Beckett's
Krapp's Last Tape, which they put in the "Distinguished Plays" category
with Edward Albee's *The Zoo Story* and Jack Richardson's *The Prodigal.*
Additional awards went to set designer David Hays; actress Nancy
Marchand, who played Madame Irma; and Jock Livingston, who played
the Envoy. *The Balcony* would run for 672 performances, the longest run
of any Off-Broadway play up to that time.

Lucille's connection to the play was by no means over—she would involve herself in the French production and other American productions.
But after the opening, she and Lou boarded a train to Florida for a well-
earned rest in Harbor Island Spa.

It was unlike Lou and Lucille to travel anywhere without a reserva-
tion. Perhaps after the intensity of *The Balcony* they simply left in a rush,
believing that, since they were well-known at Harbor Island, they would
easily get a room. To their surprise, no rooms were available. However,
the Spa's owner made a recommendation that appealed to Lou's sense of
whimsy. Why not rent or buy the houseboat that just happened to be

moored nearby? he suggested. That way, Mr. and Mrs. Schweitzer would always have a place to stay, and they could still have access to the Spa's health treatments and meals.

The houseboat needed paint, but it had a spacious living room with a corner suitable for Lou's radio equipment; two bedrooms; a kitchen; a bar on the bridge. It was a toy house, and they fell in love with it. Lou bought it as a twenty-ninth wedding anniversary gift, and they named it *Lucille's Showboat.*

They had grown closer since fighting for the de Lys, since Lou's heart attack, since working together to ensure that Lucille would acquire *The Balcony* and produce it to her advantage. Although Lou still sought sexual gratification elsewhere, the marriage had evolved into a stronger partnership where Lucille's career was concerned. Lou was determined that his wife make sound business decisions, and Lucille was able to recognize this as a sign of respect and a way to ensure the position she wanted.

In arenas where Lucille's career was not involved, Lou went his own way. In January 1960 he donated WBAI to the nonprofit Pacifica Foundation in California, a gift worth $200,000. He did so, *Time* magazine reported, because advertisers were finding the station too appealing and threatening his ideal of free radio. Lou believed that Pacifica, which already operated two commercial-free stations that depended only on contributions from listeners, would be a good home for WBAI.

One evening in 1960, Lou was at a cocktail party in Manhattan, talking to an employee of the city's Department of Corrections. He learned that hundreds of people, arraigned for crimes but unable to raise bail, languished in jails sometimes for more than a year while they waited for their trial dates to come around. New York City Prison Commissioner Anna Kross took Lou to visit a Brooklyn lock-up, where he spoke with inmates and proved to his satisfaction that the system discriminated against the poor. Lou hired Herbert Sturz to explore the situation further, and on the basis of Sturz' findings the two men developed a free bail system that would entitle most defendants to be released on their own recognizance pending trial. In 1961 Lou contributed $70,000 to start the Vera Foundation, which he named after his mother. In cooperation with New York University Law School, the Foundation set up the Manhattan Bail Project, and for more than two years a team of law students interviewed people awaiting trial in Manhattan Criminal Court and recommended release when possible. In 1964 New York City adopted Vera's procedures for all its criminal courts, and Lou's experiment set an example for the nation. President Lyndon Baines Johnson, upon signing the Bail Reform Act in 1966, cited "Mr. Louis Schweitzer, who pioneered the development of a substitute for the money bail system, by establishing the Vera Foundation and Manhattan Bail Project." That same year, after receiving support from the Ford Foundation, it would become the Vera Institute of Justice.

Lou had long ago accepted that Lucille, while proud of her husband's accomplishments, would rarely participate in them, and perhaps by now he even preferred it that way. He had adapted to her total immersion in theatre and found that the best way to live with her was to help engineer her success.

With that in mind, he aggressively pursued her desire to participate in the French production of *The Balcony*, which, after numerous delays, was scheduled to open May 18, 1960. In a March 22 letter to Frechtman, Lou stated, "Lucille is still very anxious to be one of the producers of 'The Balcony' in Paris," and by the middle of May, Lou had invested 10,000 francs. On June 10, they sailed to Europe on the S.S. *Constitution*. As always, this was a working trip for Lucille, and they stopped in Spoleto, Italy, where two plays that she had presented at the Matinee Series— Tennessee Williams' *I Rise in Flame, Cried the Phoenix* and Meade Roberts' *Maidens and Mistresses at Home at the Zoo*—were in the Festival of Two Worlds. But simply for pleasure they also returned to Venice. At the end of June, they arrived in Paris, and Lucille finally saw Peter Brook's rendition of *The Balcony*. By many accounts it was an elegant if flawed production; Marie Bell, one of the leading actresses of the Comédie Française, played Madame Irma as a grand lady, perhaps not the ideal approach. Genet did not see the production, but needless to say he was displeased with it.

While they were in Europe, Lucille's latest assistant back in New York, Joe Regan, continually sent her reports to keep her up to date on the progress of everything from cast replacements in *The Balcony* to the White Barn's performance schedule to why she had been booked into an Italian hotel as Mrs. Schweitzer instead of Lucille Lortel, a lapse about which she strongly complained.

Nineteen-sixty was another year when the White Barn season began late, but several entries demonstrated Lucille's instinct to experiment. On August 20 and 21, she presented the American premieres of three plays by Yukio Mishima translated by Donald Keene: *The Damask Drum; The Lady Saito* (originally titled *The Lady Aoi*); and *Hanjo*. Anne Meacham in *The Lady Saito* brought eroticism to the character of a mysterious stranger, who visits an ill woman every night in the hospital and eventually destroys her. The following weekend, Richard Barr directed Samuel Beckett's *Embers,* a play originally written for radio that had first been produced in 1959 by the British Broadcasting Corporation; *Nekros* by Harry Tierney, Jr., an American playwright living in England whom Lucille had taken under her wing; and the premiere of Edward Albee's *Fam and Yam,* a verbal jousting match between the Famous American Playwright—reportedly modeled on William Inge—and the Young American Playwright, modeled on Albee himself as boy genius of the American theatre.

But the most crucial event that summer was an incident which took place in September during the rehearsals of *Happy As Larry,* a 1946 comedy written in rhymed verse by Donagh MacDonagh and presented by the Irish Players. Formed in the mid-1950s by two Irish actors who had come to America—Helena Carroll, the daughter of the fine Irish dramatist Paul Vincent Carroll, and Dermot McNamara—the Irish Players were a bright company struggling to survive and they had brought MacDonagh's farce to Lucille in the hope that she would produce it Off Broadway.

According to the actor Felix Munso, who later filed a virulent complaint with Equity, after two weeks of rehearsal in New York City in what he described as a hot, "rather dirty and dingy hall" on West 42nd Street, the cast arrived at the White Barn on Friday, September 2, and were taken to Derwent House, where they were supposed to get lunch by the pool. In Munso's account, his fellow actors told him that there was not enough food to go around, and when Munso complained, one of Lucille's employees "literally *flung* a sandwich at me, told me to eat *that*, and when *that* was finished, he might see about more." Equity later determined that Munso himself had flung a tuna fish sandwich into the pool and accosted Lucille verbally.

"One of the reasons I liked Lou," said Helena Carroll years later, "was that when he came onto the scene, he said, 'You cannot talk to my wife like that.' Munso said, 'Why? Just because you have twenty million dollars?' And Lou said, 'You're wrong, bud. I've got forty million dollars.' " Coming from Lou this was undoubtedly humor, but to Munso it was one more example of arrogance. When the actors went back to the city after Sunday night's performance, the Irish actor and the Schweitzers did not part on warm terms.

Lou and Lucille believed they had simply lived through an awful weekend. They did not know with whom they were dealing. Munso was a talented comedian, but he had a history of bringing charges against management and fellow actors, which Equity, so far, had always dismissed as disruptive. New York producers kept an unofficial blacklist of troublemakers, and he was near the top. He once punched Michael Redgrave during a performance. In 1957, when he was not cast in George S. Kaufman's musical *Silk Stockings*, he wrote Kaufman, who was Jewish, "Since you seem to be fond of superficial physical impressions, I must tell you that I am also a great student of appearances: I know that you have two horns on your head." In St. Louis in 1959, he objected to the performance of an actor with whom he had to engage in a simulated fight. On Munso's part the fighting became so aggressive, the other actor was afraid to go on stage with him.

Returning to New York from Connecticut, Munso wrote Equity about what he deemed the White Barn's overly-long rehearsal time, only ten dollars pay, insufficient food, Lou's audio recording, and transmission of actors' performances over closed-circuit television without the actors' permission and without compensating them. Equity only investigated the recording complaint and, finding that Lou always erased the audio tapes, and that the televising was for the immediate audience, dismissed Munso's charge. But Lucille had not heard the last of him.

As far as she knew there was nothing to dampen her enthusiasm as she sailed into the 1960–61 season. Four of the White Barn's productions had been picked up for Off Broadway, and Lucille herself, despite the altercations at poolside, decided to produce *Happy As Larry*. This, the fifth year of the Matinee Series, promised to be its strongest. From the White Barn she brought the trio of Beckett, Tierney and Albee on October 25, and Gelb rewarded her by calling Beckett's *Embers* "a slow-starting, but ultimately absorbing, playlet—obviously a prelude to 'Krapp's Last Tape.' The protagonist is again an old man haunted by memories and loneliness. He is called Henry, but he is plainly Krapp without his tape recorder or his banana." With similar acuity Gelb dismissed Tierney's attempt as "overwrought" and Albee's as "a mildly diverting spoof."

On November 15, Lucille introduced New York audiences to two of Mishima's plays: *Hanjo* and *The Lady Saito*, again retitled to *The Lady Akane*, with Anne Meacham repeating her striking performance. Howard

Atlee remembered meeting Mishima and his wife at the Plaza, where "they were in Japanese robes, and very polite and bowing." Meacham had been distressed by the quality of Walt Witcover's direction at the White Barn, but when Lucille introduced her to Mishima at the dress rehearsal in New York, the actress asked a question about his play, and his answer clarified her performance the next day. Returning to her apartment after the Matinee, she was astounded and delighted to find twenty-four giant white chrysanthemums, which Mishima had sent her in appreciation. Meacham "plays the bizarre midnight visitor sinisterly and attractively," wrote Louis Calta in the *Times*. He called *The Lady Akane* "an eerie, baleful tale of psychological murder. The approach is surrealistic and the results are spine-tingling."

Lucille's autumn of avant-garde theatre concluded on a provocative note on November 29 with Eugene Ionesco's *The Shepherd's Chameleon* and a symposium, "Do Our Contemporary Playwrights Speak a Universal Language?" The week before, Ionesco, who had traveled to New York from Paris for the American premiere of *Rhinoceros* with Zero Mostel, had written and thanked Lucille "de tout cœur"—with all my heart—for the interest she had shown in his plays. It was because of her, he wrote, that productions of his earliest work had taken place in the United States. But he would not be able to attend, because he had to make a quick trip out of town and, to tell the truth, would prefer that she postpone the production until after *Rhinoceros* opened early in 1961; he was afraid if *Chameleon* received poor reviews, that might affect critics' response to the other, more important play. He might have added that, since *The Shepherd's Chameleon* was an attack on his critics, producing it could risk alienating the press. Lucille did not change the date, and despite a rumor that *Rhinoceros* producer Leo Kerz advised him not to appear, Ionesco arrived at the de Lys in time to take written questions from the audience.

Critics were alternately amused and stimulated by Ionesco's satire and, later, his remarks, which were translated on the spot by the critic and ANTA member Rosamund Gilder. "The curtain went up last week at Off Broadway's Theatre de Lys," wrote the reporter from *Time* magazine, "and there on the stage—in a play called *The Shepherd's Chameleon*, by French playwright Eugene Ionesco—was an actor playing a character called Ionesco, a playwright at work on a play called *The Shepherd's Chameleon*. Three more characters, each called Bartholomeus, turned up and began to unravel funny skeins of academic pedantry in argument with the playwright....

> The curtain went down, soon went up again, and there on the stage was Eugene Ionesco himself,... Through an interpreter he solemnly told his audience that the surrealists "nourished me," but that the three biggest influences on his work were actually Groucho, Chico and Harpo Marx. Answering written questions from the house, he picked up a cold potato that went "Do you think that the modern dramatic artist is essentially alienated?", thought it over and gave a perfect, two-syllable answer: "Oui, non."*

Taking it all more seriously was Stuart Little at the *Herald Tribune*, who reported

> Mr. Ionesco considered the accusation that he writes about people from "nowhere." He denied this, saying he wrote instead about people of "everywhere," that he wrote about the human condition not the social condition and that he wrote about everyone who "suffered, sorrowed, worked."... He went on to defend a free theater, one with a sense of humor and a feeling of lightness and gai-

---

* © 1960 TIME Inc. Reprinted by permission.

ety. The opposite of a nation with a free theater, he said, is a nation with concentration camps.

Shortly afterward, Lou and Lucille entertained Ionesco in Westport. Then they escaped to their houseboat, returning in time for Lucille to attend the first Matinee of 1961 on January 17: Richard Burton, Cathleen Nesbitt and Walter Abel reading selections of their choice during "An Afternoon of Poetry."

Howard Atlee recalled that Burton, who was starring on Broadway in the musical *Camelot,* was concerned because Cathleen Nesbitt felt ill, and the actor, who adored Nesbitt, considered canceling the performance. But the Matinee went on, bringing delight to an audience who probably would not have cared if the three had read the proverbial telephone book. Among Burton's selections that afternoon were poems by Rupert Brooke, Gerard Manley Hopkins and the mellifluous actor's fellow Welshman, Dylan Thomas. Lucille, seduced along with the rest of the audience, told Corinne Jacker, "Richard Burton's voice doing Dylan Thomas just went through my legs, it was such a thrill."

Concentrating on verse, the Series concluded on March 14 with readings of two dramatic poems by the American writer Conrad Aiken, *The Coming Forth by Day of Osiris Jones* and *The Kid.*

The spring felt promising. *The Balcony* had survived the winter doldrums, and to keep it going Circle in the Square ran it only on weekends, in repertory with Dylan Thomas' *Under Milk Wood.* Lucille and Lou threw a lively party in the Plaza's White and Gold Room to celebrate their thirtieth wedding anniversary. From Rome, Marc Blitzstein sent eight new verses to the tune of *Mack the Knife,* and Gerald Price, who had played the Streetsinger in the 1954 production, sang them to the couple, who laughed at Blitzstein's spoof of the producer and her indulgent husband:

Now she rarely / shops for diamonds.
No, the Lady / known as Lou
Tells the salesgirl: / "I want something
In a playwright; / maybe two.

"How's your Beckett? / How's Ionesco?
Is your Genet / in its prime?
How's your Blitzstein / out of Brecht-Weill?-
That should last me / quite a time."

Louis Schweitzer / said at breakfast:
"I suppose you'll / need some cash."
So Lucille bought / several theatres.
Did our boy say / something rash?

But the happy spring became a nightmare when Lucille brought *Happy As Larry* to the Martinique on April 25.

Why she decided to produce *Happy As Larry* Off Broadway is not clear. Helena Carroll recalled that Lou had watched the play in his television booth at the White Barn and liked it, and that Lucille had liked it too. But when Lucille and Lou later appeared before a special Actors' Equity committee, Lou explained that his wife had not really wanted to produce it, that she had urged the Irish Players to find another producer and only when they could not did she agree to support it.

One thing was sure: Lucille did not want Felix Munso in the cast, and the play went into rehearsal without him. But Carroll remembered that as opening night approached, the director, Michael Clarke-Laurence, and an anxious cast believed the production needed Munso's comic abilities if the quirky characters and extravagant action were to spring to life. They appealed to Lucille, who said in that case she would take her name off the production. Munso said he would not act in anything she produced anyway. Amid this turmoil, Munso rehearsed for one day and performed in one preview. But the morning of the opening he announced he would not go on, and it must have given him some sort of perverse satisfaction that, after the mostly negative reviews rolled in, Lucille closed the show one week later.

Trying to put this embarrassment behind her, Lucille went to Florida to get ready for the White Barn's 1961 season. Munso went to Equity. In June, at a regular Equity meeting in the ballroom of the Hotel Edison, Munso stood up and delivered a twenty-eight-page diatribe about what he thought was wrong with the union, its officers and certain producers, particularly Lucille Lortel. His litany repeated what he had written to Equity the previous fall, and he peppered this speech with derogatory comments about millionaires, rich wives and toadying union officials. At the end, Peggy Wood stood up and objected to the tone and content of Munso's accusations, but that only made her a target of his anger.

At this point Equity had no choice but to investigate the substance of Munso's charges, and the union appointed a special grievance committee, headed by actor Theodore Bikel, to sift fact from hyperbole. The committee investigated thoroughly, even placing Equity observers at the White Barn for every production that summer.

In recent years, Lucille had been open about the arrangement that Clarence Derwent brokered for her at Equity back in 1950. When a play went into rehearsal, each actor received a one-page agreement, which stated, "The performance will be presented as a benefit for the Equity Library Theatre and a contribution will be made by us to the said Equity Library Theatre, in an amount specified in a resolution of the Council of the Actors' Equity Association..." The agreement, which Equity later noted that Lucille was not even required to draw up, spelled out a ten-day rehearsal schedule and the ten-dollar payment. Lou, who had been keeping records of the contributions to ELT, many of which he had paid from an account at the Peter J. Schweitzer Foundation, produced evidence that since 1950 the White Barn had been donating $125 or more to ELT each summer.

On August 18, Munso appeared before Bikel's committee, which wondered, among other things, why he had signed the White Barn agreement that he later objected to so strenuously. On August 24, Lucille and Lou took their turn and to their surprise, the committee raised questions about the White Barn's operation prior to 1950. Lucille, who felt shocked by the whole experience, worried that she had not expressed herself well and sent a follow-up letter to Bikel on August 28:

> The sole purpose of operating the White Barn Theatre Foundation is to extend opportunities for writers, directors, and actors to appear in "showcases" where they will have the chance to experiment and perhaps be discovered by the agents and talent scouts who attend our performances. I feel this is a worthy effort, and my personal reward is the realization that a great roster of actors have received their initial opportunities at the White Barn Theatre.

Friends and colleagues sent letters to *Equity* magazine in support. "The White Barn," wrote Eva Le Gallienne, "is one of the very few places in this country where theatre people: actors, directors, singers, dancers and scenic-designers, are given an opportunity to experiment, in a congenial atmosphere and on a perfectly equipped stage, unhampered by the restrictions of Broadway. It is at once a laboratory and a showcase." Actress Carol Teitel wrote, "Having just had a very pleasant experience at Lucille Lortel's White Barn Theatre, I should like to make a statement about conditions there in answer to Mr. Felix Munso's recent charges....The housing and meals at Derwent House were delightful, and the attitude on the part of Miss Lortel and her staff toward the actors was one of respect and consideration." Audrey Wood was eloquent:

The moment [a playwright] types on the final page the curtain falls, he and his manuscript face the interpreters—the director—the actors—the designers—because only through these fellow artists can his work come alive before an audience and exist for them.

At exactly this period many playwrights endure an endless period of waiting. Broadway is no longer a place for taking chances on experimentation. Off-Broadway produces a few new plays each season but very often reproduces the produced play or the established European playwright. Universities throughout the country attempt a new work only when they can come with the cast. Stock companies in the true sense no longer exist and summer theatres—their replacements—delight in the small pleasure of reproducing the plays Broadway viewed during the previous season. Only Lucille Lortel's White Barn Theatre displays the imagination and courage to do a season of hitherto unproduced plays.

But Lucille needed the sort of advocacy that Clarence Derwent had provided, and that was unavailable. Equity knew it had to follow procedure strictly, especially with such an unpredictable personality as Munso stalking their every move. The Special Grievance Committee handed its findings and conclusions over to the Stock and Off-Broadway Committee, which made recommendations to the Equity Council. The Special Committee's report, which Lucille probably never saw but may have heard about—Lou had sent Richard Benter, who had directed at both the White Barn and the Matinee Series, to Equity meetings as a spy—sounded rather like parents admonishing a child for lapses the parents themselves had allowed:

> . . . While it was felt that there is, and should be, room for experimentation, there was unanimous dissatisfaction with the White

Barn setup as presently constituted. The feeling was strongly expressed that the White Barn's relationship with Equity suffered
gravely from a lack of definition. Not Mr. Munso alone but quite
a few other members had been dissatisfied; it seemed to the Committee that a half-hearted concession, embodying but few safe-
guards badly policed, serves little or no purpose. A total absence
of any regulations would have been preferable . . . .The pay-off to
ELT was also criticized in the sense only that, if any moneys are to
be distributed at all in connection with Equity, then they should
go to the member working there. A majority of the Committee
expressed the desire that a proper contract . . . should be negotiated
with the White Barn . . .

The Equity problem had distracted Lucille, but the White Barn had
gone forward. It presented only plays that summer, including work by
the arresting New York writer Lewis John Carlino and an Off-Broadway
playwright named Jack Dunphy; the American premiere of *The Typists*,
with James Coco as one of two ordinary but wistful office workers in
Murray Schisgal's quietly affecting one-act; and two plays by the French
avant-garde dramatist René de Obaldia. For the Sunday night performance of the Obaldia, Bikel himself was in the audience, perhaps making
his own observations of the White Barn.

Except for Schisgal's play, they would all go to the Matinee Series that
year. But first there would be a production about Bertolt Brecht.

The project started, according to Gene Frankel, who staged it, as an
exercise in Frankel's writing and directing class. There the tall, dark
Swedish actress Viveca Lindfors was working on a Brecht piece called
The Jewish Wife. "It was Viveca who was the prime mover in getting it
going," Frankel said. He and Lindfors' husband, the Hungarian writer
George Tabori, had become "chess friends," as he put it, and often got
together for a game at George and Viveca's home on East 95th Street. "I

was playing chess with George, and Viveca was stirring the pot and making noises about getting a production going."

The Jewish Wife is a stark, twenty-minute scene in Brecht's play *Fear and Misery of the Third Reich* (also known as *The Private Life of the Master Race*). Set in Frankfurt, Germany, in 1935, it shows a thirty-six-year-old upper-middle-class Jewish woman who is married to an Aryan surgeon. She calls her friends to let them know that she is going away, possibly for a few nights, perhaps a few months—and that she is leaving her husband behind. She rehearses the speech she will make to her husband when she leaves, and at the end of the scene, he comes in and urges her to go.

Frankel had worked at the White Barn, so he contacted Lucille, who was interested. But this was really Tabori's project. On October 21 he wrote her outlining his idea:

> I think the show should be called BRECHT ON BRECHT—His Life & His Art—Poems, Songs, Essays, Dialogues, Transcripts and Scenes. The first part of the show would be like a concert—songs and poems by him about the theater and himself, most of them totally unknown in this country except by a few aficianados [*sic*]. The second part would be the "Jewish Wife" . . . .
>
> I should be very happy to edit and arrange the first part of the show and even translate some of the stuff. [Eric] Bentley promised to help, and also Bertha Case, who represents the Brecht estate. I would do it gratis of course but ought to have some appropriate credit, such as "arranged by GT" or whatever you think fit. Once the material is collated we can try to get the best actors for the recital . . . .It would also be enormously helpful if you could ask Miss Lenya to participate as performer. If she is not available, she ought to give us permission to use some of the Weill songs.

Lucille did get Lenya, who did give them the rights to Kurt Weill's music. Tabori assembled the actors: Lindfors, George Voskovec, George Gaynes, Dolly Haas, Michael Wager, Eli Wallach and Anne Jackson. They rehearsed in Frankel's studio on MacDougal Street; Jackson recalled that Tabori arrived with a script but added selections as they worked. "He was a very disciplined writer. He had form, he had an idea—a recording of Brecht before the House Un-American Activities Committee would kick off the program."

Here was Brecht raging against the burning of books. Here also was Brecht musing on theatrical lighting, New York actors, casting. "The way people cast a play! As if all cooks were fat, all farmers tough and taciturn, all statesmen stately! As if all lovers were pretty!" Tabori did most of the translating—"a very good translator of Brecht, one of the best," Lenya told the author David Farneth. Even the translation of *The Jewish Wife*, while credited in the program to Eric Bentley, was increasingly Tabori's. "Bentley's was not muscular," said Frankel. "German has to be muscular, particularly that play, and between Viveca, myself and George, we didn't really use it."

There was no time to learn all the material before the performance on November 14, so they decided to hold scripts in their hands. "But it became the style of the production," said Frankel. Later, when *Brecht on Brecht* moved into the de Lys for a run, and the actors knew their lines, "they all had scripts as props," Frankel said, "because it was that impromptu feeling that I wanted to keep. It knit everything together. It was an event, and the event was a group of actors, with joy in their hearts and appreciation for a great artist, unveiling this work."

A gigantic photograph of Brecht hung at the rear of the stage, facing the audience and looking down in a sense on the actors speaking the dramatist's playful, angry, incisive thoughts. "Very little ambient light," said Frankel. "Later on it became more sophisticated—there was a fol-

CLOCKWISE FROM TOP LEFT:

Lucille's father, Harry Wadler, as an aspiring businessman.

Lucille's imposing mother, Anny Wadler, when she was in her seventies and calling herself Anna Mayo.

Lucille, the young dancer.

Toddlers Mayo, Ruth and Lucille.

LEFT: Mayo Wadler around the age of eighteen.

BELOW: Lucille and her sister Ruth could almost have been mistaken for twins when they were in their twenties.

BOTTOM LEFT: Leopold Godowsky, Jr., when in his forties.

A still of Lucille from the silent short film *Freddys Liebstod*, which she probably made in 1922.

Lucille at twenty in 1921 in her costume as The Swallow at the American Academy of Dramatic Arts.

Achille Volpé's publicity photograph from the 1920s has Lucille looking demure . . .

. . as does this production shot from *One Man's Woman* in 1926.

LEFT: Lucille strikes a pose as the seductive dancer with whom Sessue Hayakawa has a torrid romance in the film *The Man Who Laughed Last*.

BELOW LEFT: A still from a Warner Bros. short filmed during the early 1930s. Lucille hooks arms with actors Charles Judels and George Givot, who was known as the "Greek Ambassador."

BELOW RIGHT: G. Maillard Kesslere's sensual publicity photograph of Lucille, taken in 1930 when Lucille was twenty-nine.

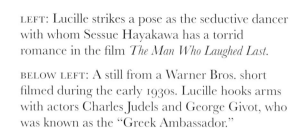

BELOW: Lucille and Louis Schweitzer, third and second from right, on March 23, 1931 after their wedding on the S. S. *Leviathan*.

LEFT: The white barn that Lou and Lucille transported to their Westport property shortly before the United States entered World War II.

ABOVE: The barn's second story before its transformation into a theatre.

LEFT: The White Barn Theatre in its earliest incarnation.

The first performance: a staged reading of *Painted Wagon* in 1947.

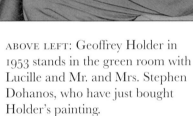

ABOVE LEFT: Geoffrey Holder in 1953 stands in the green room with Lucille and Mr. and Mrs. Stephen Dohanos, who have just bought Holder's painting.

ABOVE RIGHT: Sean O'Casey's *Red Roses for Me* with Kim Hunter in 1948.

LEFT: Sada Thompson, Helen Bonstelle and Robert Fitzsimmons in *U.S.A.* in 1953.

RIGHT: Ruth Chatterton and Anne Meacham in *Sign of Winter* at the White Barn in 1955.

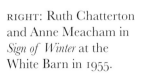

A trio of White Barn supporters: Ralph Alswang, Clarence Derwent and Eva Le Gallienne, with Lucille.

LEFT: Ralph Alswang's redesign
of the White Barn's stage allowed the rear to open for a
view of the trees beyond.

RIGHT: A 1992 view of
Fairweather, the house
in Westport that Louis
Schweitzer bought for
Lucille and himself in
1938.

RIGHT: Ever publiciz-
ing her productions,
Lucille grabs a micro-
phone and trades re-
marks with radio host
Barry Gray.

LEFT: The interior of
the Hudson Playhouse
is destroyed to create
the Theatre de Lys.

BELOW: William de
Lys, the Theatre
de Lys' provocative
founder, is second
from the left.

Stanley Chase, Lotte Lenya,
Marc Blitzstein, Lucille, and
Carmen Capalbo

The marquee of the Theatre de
Lys omits the name of Brecht
from *The Threepenny Opera*.

The ANTA Matinee Series made its debut at the Theatre de Lys in 1956 with
Cry, the Beloved Country. Earle Hyman is second from the left.

For 19 years, Lucille, as artistic director for the ANTA Matinee Series, would present some of Off Broadway's most innovative plays and performances. ABOVE LEFT: *Notes from the Underground* with Kathleen Widdoes and Michael Kane; ABOVE RIGHT: *Come Slowly, Eden* with Kim Hunter and John Beal; LEFT TOP: Eugene O'Neill's *Before Breakfast* with Eileen Heckart; LEFT BOTTOM: *The Lady Akane* by Mishima with Anne Meacham, Michael Karlan and Dona Marans; BELOW LEFT: *Pale Horse, Pale Rider* with Margaret Linn and Douglass Watson; BELOW RIGHT: James T. Pritchett in Samuel Beckett's *Embers*.

D'Arlene Studios, Inc.

Martha Swope

CLOCKWISE FROM ABOVE:

Lucille and Virginia Inness-Brown in 1954.

Salome Jens and John S. Dodson in *The Balcony* in 1960.

Fam and Yam by Edward Albee at the White Barn with James T. Pritchett and Eugene van Heckle.

Shakespeare in Harlem by Robert Glenn with Godfrey Cambridge and Isabel Sanford.

LL Collection

Avery Willard

Moss Photos

LEFT: Lucille's nemesis, Felix Munso.

LL Collection

Eileen O'Casey with Lucille around 1980.

Henry Grossman

BELOW: Athol Fugard's *The Blood Knot* with James Earl Jones (standing) and J. D. Cannon.

Lotte Lenya with the portrait of Bertolt Brecht behind her in *Brecht on Brecht*.

LL Collection

Ruth Wadler (Mrs. Francis Coradal-Cugat) in the 1960s.

Louis Schweitzer, Lucille and cat.

Carl Schaeffer and Lucille.

Ben Sprecher, Lucille's general manager on Christopher Street from 1981 until after her death.

COUNTERCLOCKWISE FROM ABOVE:

At the Sherry Netherland, a forest of paintings, photographs and mementos honors Lucille's career.

In 1982, Lucille finally saw her portrait go on the wall at Sardi's.

Gertrude Stein and a Companion with Jan Miner and Marian Seldes.

Lucille with the South African playwright Athol Fugard, whose work she brought to the United States.

ABOVE: Sam Waterston and Robert Prosky in a scene from the Broadway production of *A Walk in the Woods*.

ABOVE RIGHT: Lucille and Sir Alec Guinness backstage at the Comedy Theatre in London.

Lucille with one of her oldest friends, Mimi Bochco (BELOW) and with close friend Anna Strasberg (RIGHT).

TOP: Helen Hayes and Lucille sat side-by-side in 1988 at the dedication of Lucille's theatre at the Actor's Fund Home in New Jersey.

CENTER: In 1996, Lucille paid a visit to Brown University, where she and playwright Paula Vogel talked with the playwriting students.

BOTTOM: At the 50th anniversary of the White Barn Theatre in 1997, Lucille danced with Donald Saddler, while Vincent Curcio looked on.

low spot. But not vaudeville style; just to light the actor." Sandra Schmidt wrote in the *Village Voice:*

> Eight people on stools on a stage. A stagehand holds up a sign: "Brecht Sings." Another stagehand switches on a tape recorder and Brecht sings. "Lights!" and the lights go up—not, as Michael Wager quotes Brecht, the lights of twilight or make-believe, but the glaring lights of full day, of reality.

The audience was enthralled. "Everything brought the house down," Jackson remembered. "Lots of standing and applauding. Lenya brought the house down singing 'Pirate Jenny.' " The critics applauded in print, and the demand for tickets was so great that Lucille scheduled another performance the following Monday evening. It, too, sold out.

The magical ingredient, as Tabori and Frankel understood from the beginning, was simply Brecht—his words, theatrical instinct and underlying humanism. "There is a cult about Brecht," Tabori told a writer from the *New Yorker* magazine in June 1962. "Eric Bentley is the Pope—the first man to write extensively in this country about Brecht and his work—and there are Martin Esslin and various other Cardinals. They are all very scholarly, but I wouldn't want to write an essay on Brecht myself. The point is that Brecht wrote more about the theatre than any other dramatist. If he wanted to say something about props, he would write a poem about them. He was never pompous or solemn. He always gave the theatre superb and gracious treatment. He deserves the same."

Lucille had finally found the production that could replace *Threepenny Opera* at the Theatre de Lys.

Since the summer there had been rumors that *Threepenny* was in its last months. Early in September Capalbo, Chase and Lortel had allowed a two-week stock presentation at New Jersey's Paper Mill Playhouse, always a sign that the original production is faltering. Also that month, the three producers launched a thirty-five-week national tour starring Gypsy Rose Lee. But the burlesque queen and Bertolt Brecht were a bad match, and the producers shut the tour down in Toronto after two weeks of poor ticket sales. Finally, Lucille told Corinne Jacker, she closed the New York production. "Actually, I said, 'Look, boys, that's enough. Seven years—let's do something else.' "

On December 17, 1961, the day after Lucille's sixty-first birthday, Mack the Knife's sardonic words, sung by Virgil Curry, the production's last Macheath, drifted from the de Lys stage for the last time. During seven years, 709 actors had played the 22 roles. And 750,000 customers had paid nearly three million dollars to see them.

The farewell performance brought tears to everybody except Lucille, who watched the show for the final time from her aisle seat in the third row. "Everyone has long faces, but I don't see why," she said within earshot of a reporter; however, later she whispered, "Oh, but I'm going to miss it." Afterward everybody drank champagne, served in blue paper cups in true Off-Broadway style. And then it was over.

There would be a new tenant at the de Lys, but Lucille would not be its producer. Lou wanted his wife with him in Florida during the winter, and so Lucille asked Cheryl Crawford if she would produce *Brecht on Brecht* for the Greater New York Chapter of ANTA, which would receive a share of the profits. Crawford agreed. When the production reopened at the de Lys on January 3, 1962, Lucille was resting on her houseboat, recuperating from the tensions of the Equity investigation and the fall season, and wishing she were up in New York. Crawford wrote her on January 9, "Business continues hot as Milton's Hell..."

Margo Jones, the dedicated producer and director who had founded a theatre for new plays in Dallas, Texas, had died in 1955 at the age of forty-two. In 1961, the playwrights Jerome Lawrence and Robert E.

Lee established an annual award in her name for a producing manager of an American or Canadian theatre whose presentation of new work "continues most faithfully the tradition and vision of Margo Jones." Lucille decided to campaign for the award. In part she wanted to counter pressure from Lou, as she wrote to her friend Audrey Wood on October 5, 1961.

> Dear Audrey,
>
> Considering the record of the White Barn Theatre and the ANTA matinees, do you think that I would be eligible for the Margo Jones Award?
>
> When Margo Jones visited the White Barn, we both felt that we were the only ones interested in doing the plays of new writers and before she died we agreed to exchange new plays for our respective theatres.
>
> Since you can see by the enclosed that two of your authors are on the Committee, it would be especially valuable for me to have your opinion. I would be especially thrilled to get it so that Lou would think I was important enough to continue with the theatre.

The authors were William Inge and Tennessee Williams, who, with Lawrence and Lee, theatre curator and critic George Freedley, Dallas drama critic John Rosenfield, and actor Howard Lindsay, comprised the judging committee. Wood wrote back three days later, "I certainly think you should be eligible for the Margo Jones Award. Therefore I will send in the form and fill in your name."

Within the next week, Lucille sent almost the same letter to Henry Hewes, Joseph T. Shipley of the *New Leader*, Emory Lewis, Harold Clurman, Robert Glenn, and Robert Brustein. Shipley immediately dropped a note to George Freedley, strongly supporting Lucille, and on October 31 Freedley responded very encouragingly: "I shall make sure that her name is given proper consideration at the meeting of the Committee." Glenn wrote her, "I will submit your name to the Judging Committee ... and I will write directly to John Rosenfield, since I know him personally."

Lucille continued her campaign with thank-you notes and in November sent copies of a book about the White Barn that Lou had arranged to be published as an anniversary gift. Wood wrote Lucille that she could not secure promises from Williams or Inge, and on November 17 Robert Brustein wrote her, "I have always had a peculiar reluctance to nominate people for mere 'honors,' no matter how richly deserved. My recommendations are reserved for the kind of people you and your husband have always helped along so unremittingly: those needy artists who must have financial help in order to let them continue their careers." Somewhat insistently she wrote back that this was "a producer's award—not a writer's, not an actor's not a director's." But Brustein did not change his mind.

In the new year, she wrote the judging committee on January 4, "It is my understanding that my name has been submitted to your Committee for consideration for the Margo Jones Award for my work in the theatre during 1961" and she sent along support material for them to read and look at.

Early in February Jerome Lawrence, for the Committee, wired Lucille at Harbor Island: "We are delighted to announce you have been selected winner of first Margo Jones Award...."

She was enormously proud. That she had campaigned for the honor did not matter. She felt she deserved it. She had learned to pursue what she wanted and she made sure that news of the honor got around. She asked the press agent Sol Jacobson, who had handled publicity for *I Knock at the Door* on Broadway, to send clippings to the Miami newspapers and other news outlets around the country, and Leo Miller in Westport passed the announcement to local papers there.

On February 18 the Actors' Fund held a benefit at *A Man for All Seasons*, which was playing at the ANTA Theatre. Before the curtain went up, Jerome Lawrence presented Lucille with her award—a commemorative medal designed by Professor Edward Bearden of Southern Methodist University and a check for $250. Lawrence stated that the Committee selected Lucille Lortel because in their opinion her 117 premieres of new works at the White Barn Theatre, the ANTA Matinee Series and Off Broadway qualified her as "the theatre executive" who made "the most significant contribution to the dramatic art with hitherto unproduced plays, that having been the ardent spirit and unremitting purpose of Margo Jones."

Congratulations streamed in. Virginia Inness-Brown sent a telegram on behalf of the Greater New York Chapter of ANTA. Abner W. Sibal, who represented Lucille's Connecticut district in Congress, praised "the White Barn Theatre in Westport, one of Fairfield County's leading cultural centers..." Nina Vance, founder and managing director of the Alley Theatre in Houston, and conceivably Lucille's competition for the Award, graciously wrote her, "I worked for Margo, and it is gratifying to know that this award has been given to one who is carrying on so successfully the traditions in American theatre in which she so deeply believed." On the afternoon of March 16, at a cocktail party on the stage of the Shubert Theatre, Lucille presented her $250 check to New Dramatists.

"It seems to be my year for awards," she wrote to Jerome Lawrence in March, for to her surprise and pleasure, on March 6 the officers and board of directors of national ANTA cited her for "pioneering work in the fostering of promising new playwrights, directors and actors, and for her invaluable aid to theatrical experimentation..."

On April 2, she took the train to Washington for two nights of performances of *Fam and Yam* and *The Shepherd's Chameleon* at the Library of Congress. David Brooks again staged the Ionesco, but Albee directed his play himself. After each performance there was a symposium with the unfortunate title "Avant-Garde Theatre—Real or Far Out?" The first night, the symposium included Albee, Brooks, the playwrights Jack Richardson and Arthur Kopit, Henry Hewes, and Richard L. Coe, drama editor for *The Washington Post,* who invited Lucille to his home afterward. On the second night, Hewes and Albee did not reappear, Hewes possibly because he had laryngitis, Albee probably because the night before the first question he received from the audience was "Did Mr. Albee know Tennessee Williams?" followed by "What is this theatre of the absurd?" Rosamund Gilder took their places.

Lucille handled this with equanimity. No disgruntled playwright could squelch the pleasure with which she read Richard Coe's column in the *Washington Post* when she woke up on April 3:

> Lucille Lortel, who recently received the first Margo Jones award for her "significant contribution in presenting new plays," is in town for the third of her New York ANTA Chapter productions to be presented at the Library of Congress.
>
> A former actress whose White Barn Theater offerings at Westport, Conn., put her on the producing map, Miss Lortel might be called The Queen of Off-Broadway...

Coe crowned her, and ever after the press referred to her as the Queen of Off Broadway. Of all the public praises sung of her, this was the one she embraced most tightly.

She returned to New York knowing that soon she would have to face the recommendations of Equity's Stock and Off-Broadway Committee regarding her operation of the White Barn. On April 12, before leaving for Florida for a month, she wrote her own suggestions to Angus Duncan, Equity's executive secretary. She was angry, hurt and tired by the conflict, and her recommendations sound almost like a dare, as though she anticipated Equity's ruling would be harsh and she was not prepared to be conciliatory. She was already telling friends that there might not be a White Barn season, because she was going to Europe with Lou.

She proposed to Duncan that the White Barn use Equity actors for unspecified rehearsal periods and no more than two performances; that the actors receive no remuneration at all; that there be no written contract; that other than those changes, the White Barn's policy remain the same. "Aside from the above," she wrote, "we would like to continue working under the same general conditions and arrangements as we have in the past, including our contribution to ELT."

The committee disagreed. On May 8, it recommended to the Council that rehearsals and one performance be limited to one week; that there be a letter form of contract; that an actor be paid $50 for rehearsals and performance; that overtime rehearsal be at the rate of $1.25 an hour; that any charitable donations Lucille made would "in no way be considered to have any bearing on her obligation for payment to actors who may appear at the White Barn Theatre..."

At the end of May, Lucille returned from Florida to find a letter dated May 23 from William Gibberson, Equity's assistant executive secretary, who conveyed the Council's decision. She sent a response to Angus Duncan on June 27, the day before she and Lou sailed:

> This will acknowledge receipt of the letter of May 23rd from Actors Equity Assn. setting forth the conditions under which the White Barn Theatre in Westport, Conn. can work in the future and employ Equity actors. The contents have been thoroughly considered by me and I must reluctantly conclude that I cannot function under the new conditions imposed. Perhaps, therefore, it might be practical to reconsider the conditions which make it possible for the White Barn Theatre to operate.

The letter, to which lawyers and Lou undoubtedly contributed, outlined the White Barn's not-for-profit nature and that she herself had
never been compensated financially. "The White Barn, therefore, cannot
be viewed by actors or anyone else as a means of making money but
rather as a 'showcase' which exists by a subsidy from the Foundation."
The letter concluded:

> I find myself in the uncomfortable and dual role of being a former
> actress and understanding and sympathizing with the necessity of
> the Union's protecting its members to the fullest extent; however,
> as President of the White Barn Foundation I must seriously con-
> sider the extent to which I can expect it to make funds available for
> the operation of the theatre. It is in the second role that I regret to
> state that the new ruling puts the question of the finances out of all
> proportion to the reality.

The following day, she and Lou sailed on the S.S. *Caronia* for a cruise
to the North Cape of Norway. When the excursion was over, they
planned to disembark at Southampton and stay in London, not returning to the United States until the end of August. For the first summer
since Lucille founded it in 1947, the White Barn Theatre was dark.

CHAPTER 7

·*Passages*·

*L*ucille spent part of her 1962 trip to Europe visiting friends she had not seen in a long time. The *Caronia* stopped in Glengarrif, Ireland, and Lou and Lucille hied to Dublin for one night. Maureen Halligan, who had acted at the White Barn with the Dublin Players in the early 1950s, organized a press reception at Lucille's request and invited Milo O'Shea, Alex Dignam, James Neylin, and other former Dublin Players. Then Lucille and Lou took in Denis Johnston's *Strange Occurrence on Ireland's Eye* at the Abbey Theatre.

Moving on to London, they settled into the Berkeley Hotel, and Lucille contacted theatre people with whom she hoped to do business: actor and director George Devine, who had established the English Stage Company at the Royal Court, where John Osborne's revolutionary *Look Back in Anger* had been produced; Harold Pinter's agent, Emanuel Wax. To her disappointment, she was unable to go to Devon to see Sean and Eileen O'Casey. Sean was ill, Eileen wrote her, and it would not be a good idea. Sean did write her himself on August 23, a letter she treasured:

My dear Lucille,
    It was rotten luck . . . that prevented us from meeting this

summer in the sun or the shadow of Torquay; but we old ones cannot forsee what a day—or an hour—may bring forth. Often, when we think we'll be up, we go down; &, at times, when we're afraid we'll go down, we find ourselves sitting on top of the world for a minute or two.

After a bout of influenza, as you may know, there is often a time spent in a bit of depression, when the usual O'Casey quick-step in life has to become a crawl, within a mood that wants to smash the window on the world, or even send a good-sized stone flying each through Shelley's "magic casements."

Come again, my dear, and I'll see you, unless I'm in "extremis mortuis"—which I'm told is Latin for someone bidding goodbye to time; I can chat, talk, and argue, from my bed . . . if the infection be gone, I'm no danger to you—O'Casey "Bedside Talks" are becoming quite common now!

It would have been fine to see Louis and you, but the invisible voices stood in the way, & kept us apart.

I hope, my dear Lucille, that you may be able to understand this writing. I am writing, not by sight, but rather by touch & by the feel of the pen, while hoping for the best.

My love to Louis and to you, with a kiss for you carried to the usa on the wings of—Picasso's Dove of Peace.

As ever,
Sean.

Back in the United States, she would gradually find that her personal theatre world was changing. But for the time being it looked and felt the same. Revitalized by two months away, she eagerly launched into the 1962–63 season, opening the ANTA Matinees on October 30 with two of O'Casey's satiric one-acts, *Figuro in the Night* and *The Moon Shines on Kyle-namoe*. Amid all the activity, Lou suddenly became ill and went into New

York Presbyterian Hospital. "I go there daily," she wrote Eileen O'Casey on October 12, "and while he is better now, I have no idea of how long he will be in." But she pressed on with the one-acts, and on November 2 she proudly wrote Eileen that "the plays came off very well last Tuesday. We had a full house and the audience, as well as the actors, enjoyed both plays a great deal. Brooks Atkinson was there, and Peggy Wood made an opening address; a splendid beginning for the ANTA Series this season."

The first change Lucille encountered was that *Brecht on Brecht* planned to close at the de Lys on January 6, 1963, after 424 performances and would move to the smaller Sheridan Square Playhouse.

She had been frustrated by the lengthy run of *Threepenny Opera,* but she had also been spoiled by it and by the smooth transition to another success. Now she needed to find bookings as other theatre owners did. And while she was not financially dependent on hits the way most producers were—she was more interested in a play she liked than one which would run seven years—she still wanted the gratification and the reputation of hosting well-received productions that also thrived at the box office.

The first customer after *Brecht on Brecht* was a comedy by Arthur Kopit called *Asylum, or What the Gentlemen Are Up To, Not To Mention the Ladies,* produced by Roger L. Stevens; it previewed then closed the night before its official opening. There followed a string of plays by up-and-coming writers such as Lewis John Carlino and the television dramatist Roger O. Hirson, even a musical revue called *Put It in Writing,* which had been popular at the Happy Medium Club Theatre in Chicago and which Lucille produced at the de Lys with Arthur Cantor. Some of these received favorable notices, but none toted up respectable runs.

One of the difficulties was that productions frequently sought to rent the de Lys after garnering glowing reviews at small theatres, only to find that they could not fill the 299-seat house and so could barely break even, let alone make a profit. In the 1960s, Lucille usually charged $1,000 to $1,250 a week for rent, and while she often forgave part of the rental to help a producer and keep her theatre lit, a number of productions struggled. Toward the end of the decade, in 1969, Harlan P. Kleiman rented the de Lys to produce Rochelle Owens' raucous comedy *Futz!*, which had played Off Off Broadway at Cafe La Mama. He eventually moved it to the Actors Playhouse, where, he wrote investors, he could "decrease our Operating Cost by $1,200 a week."

Actors' Equity posed the second major change for Lucille. She had felt guilty about canceling the 1962 season at the White Barn, she wrote to playwright Harry Tierney in England, and he had written back reassuringly, "You've done more for the theatre than any ten women I can think of." Now she realized she had to confront the situation in order to have a 1963 season and she sent a letter to Angus Duncan on July 1, 1963. The letter reaffirmed the points she had made to Duncan the previous year about the White Barn's nonprofit status and suggested a few adjustments, including that "each actor will receive $50.00 as total compensation, less room and board to be charged at the current rates in Westport. He will also receive round trip transportation from New York." She argued for a more flexible rehearsal time than six straight days: "... it could at least be divided over a two week period for the convenience of the actor.... Many actors coming to the Barn are working in the daytime or evening and they should determine their schedule with the director." Equity compromised on a $40 actor fee and rehearsals spread over two weeks, and stipulated that Lucille would have to reapply to Equity every spring to reinstate the terms of this special agreement. What was to be the White Barn's brief fifteenth season opened on July 23 with *Brecht on Brecht*, for which Lucille imported Viveca Lindfors, Luther Adler, Lou Antonio and Diana Sands, of the New York production.

But Lucille was encountering a deeper challenge than booking the Theatre de Lys or even dueling with Actors' Equity. Off Broadway itself was changing. The European playwrights whom she had pioneered—Brecht, Beckett, Ionesco, Genet—were no longer rarities Off Broadway, or even outside of New York. Producing them was no longer a unique exercise. In addition, with more competition for their work, Genet, Ionesco and Beckett had become particular about cultivating the United States market, which they wanted but about which, with the European intellectual's arrogance toward supposedly untutored Americans, they felt superior. Lucille needed an emotional connection with a playwright as well as with a play, and Genet and Ionesco, the two avant-garde dramatists with whom she had had the most contact, were uninterested in giving that.

Indeed her enthusiasm for the avant-garde Europeans had temporarily wilted, and she had let producing possibilities fall through. Since first presenting *The Shepherd's Chameleon* for the Matinee Series in November 1960, she had held the option, hoping to find a suitable companion piece. She had thought of putting it on a bill with *Victims of Duty*, but Genet did not consider the Ionesco play an appropriate companion piece. As Bernard Frechtman explained pedantically to Lucille, "The SHEPHERD would not have meaning outside a limited circle. I told this to Ionesco as well, and he quite agreed. In fact, he went on to say that although the SHEPHERD was favorably received in America, it was not understood."

In May 1962 Ionesco's agent became annoyed that she had done nothing with the script, and she let her option go. Before leaving for the North Cape cruise, she wrote Sol Jacobson, "I decided not to do THE SHEPHERD'S CHAMELEON since it became too involved in casting and finding the right companion piece." Perhaps also she instinctively knew that *Chameleon*, while intriguing for a Matinee or the Library of Congress, was not strong or accessible enough for Off Broadway.

As for British dramas, the commercial ones had largely become the territory of two Broadway producers, Alexander Cohen and David Merrick. Playwright Harold Pinter had also avoided her reach. When Lucille approached Emanuel Wax about doing one of Pinter's plays in the

Matinee Series, Wax turned her down, telling her that Pinter wanted only
Alan Schneider to direct his American premieres and that he needed to
know and approve all the actors. Wax did offer Lucille the Off-Broadway
rights to *The Caretaker,* but she was too smart to produce a play that had
been staged on Broadway as recently as 1962. She wrote to Mary Grew
in London in 1963 and asked her to research the availability of Joan Littlewood's satire *Oh, What a Lovely War!*—but nothing came of it.

She wanted to produce a writer nobody else had produced in America, someone few people had perhaps even heard of in America. With a
kind of sixth sense, in November 1963 she wrote to her friend Michael
White in London, that "...when Leonard White was here he said he
would try to check on 'The Blood Knot', although I still do not understand who has the rights to it....Do you have another play by Atholl
[*sic*] Fugard? If you do, and there's no trouble about getting the rights,
send it to me right away."

In 1963, Athol Fugard was a poor thirty-one-year-old white South
African playwright, actor and director, dedicated to theatre and to revealing the racial injustice of his country's policy of apartheid. He had
completed *The Blood Knot* in 1961, when he was living in Port Elizabeth
with his wife and new-born daughter.

The play, which consists of seven lengthy scenes, takes place during
the 1950s in Korsten, a designated black location near Port Elizabeth. In
a notebook from the early 1960s, Fugard described the area as a "dumping ground for waste products from the factories. Terrible smell....A
collection of shanties, pondoks, lean-to's." In one of these shanties lives
a dark-skinned, somewhat slow-witted man named Zachariah. His
lighter-skinned half-brother, Morris, who has at times passed for white,
has returned to stay with him. But bitterness erupts after Morris tries to
find Zach a female pen pal and they discover, when she sends a photograph, that she is white. All of Morris's conflicts and anxieties about his
identity surface, as does Zach's resentment. Zach asks Morris to stand in

for him and meet the girl, and they spend their energy and the last of their money preparing Morris for a rendevous that never takes place.

The Blood Knot opened in September 1961 at the Rehearsal Room, a private theatre on the third floor of an abandoned clothing factory in Johannesburg. Then a commercial production company toured the play for six months, with Fugard directing and playing Morris, and Zakes Mokae playing Zach. "It was still possible," Fugard wrote in his notebook, "for a black man and a white man to appear on the same stage before a mixed audience." After this production, it would not be. In 1963 John Berry, an American film director who had moved to Paris after being named a Communist during the House Un-American Activities Committee hearings, staged the first British production at Hampstead's New Arts Theatre; Mokae again played Zach, and Ian Bannen acted Morris, with Fugard occasionally covering the role. Kenneth Tynan, the most influential London critic and self-anointed kingmaker of new British drama, wrote a negative, racist review, and the production did not do well as a result. But word-of-mouth extolled this excruciating dissection of two men's existence in racist South Africa, and Fugard began to make his international reputation.

"John Berry's faith in the play remained strong," the playwright recalled years later, "and he decided to give it a chance in America. So he went over to New York with the script." According to Fugard, Berry gave the script to Sidney Bernstein, who had produced Genet's *The Blacks* Off Broadway, and Bernstein took it to Lucille. In the meantime, Lucille had heard about the play through Leonard White, a British actor who had performed in her production of *A Sleep of Prisoners* and who had undoubtedly seen the drama in London.

Here was the sort of play for which Lucille had been searching: novel, in that its setting and the characters' backgrounds were foreign to American audiences, but at the same time undeniably sympathetic. What American would not find a parallel between South Africa's apartheid and America's own history of racial prejudice? Who among New York City's largely Jewish theatregoers would not respond to characters deprived of self-respect because of a prejudicial political system? Who, no matter what their background, could help empathizing with the brothers' fear and anger, and love for each other?

Here, too, was a dramatist who had never been produced in the United States, one whom Lucille could legitimately feel she had discovered.

Bernstein and Lucille joined forces to produce the play in the spring of 1964, with Bernstein, who would manage the production, putting up $6,500 and Lucille Lortel Productions $6,000. Because the de Lys already had an occupant—a tepid vehicle called *Riverside Drive* with Sylvia Sidney and Donald Woods—Lucille and Bernstein decided to open *The Blood Knot* at the Cricket Theater, a 144-seat house at Second Avenue and 10th Street. Run by Lucille's friend Blanche Marvin, it had a reputation for presenting adventuresome new plays. John Bury designed the set—a spare, corrugated tin shack. Once again John Berry directed. He cast the gravelly-voiced J.D. Cannon to play Morris and the imposing James Earl Jones to play Zacharias.

Jones, who was then thirty-three, remembered his reaction after reading the play for the first time: "I can do this. I want to do this." He loved the play, and he and Cannon worked together intensely. But they both had difficulty understanding their characters, Jones recalled. "J.D., not being a black person, could not understand the African aspect of his character, and I had no reference to the South African nature either, so I was as lost as he was." Fugard was not there to help, for he was in Northern Rhodesia directing a production of Brecht's *Caucasian Chalk Circle*. "I over-shot and made the character even more universal than Athol wrote him," said Jones. "I played him as viscerally as I knew how." A friend had told Jones that it was difficult to believe a character who was less intelligent than the actor playing him, and in response, Jones said, "I felt I had an obligation to lift the character above that level." In 1980, when Fugard was directing Jones in the first American production of *A Lesson from Aloes* at Yale Repertory Theatre, Jones finally understood what he thought he had done wrong. "Fugard was adamant about not playing the character with the same kind of psychic freedom that one played American characters. These characters had accepted being 'niggers,' Athol said, because apartheid had affected the life force in them."

Jones may have felt anxious, but when *The Blood Knot* opened on March 1, 1964, the New York critics had few complaints. "No play in town is simpler and more penetrating, tenderer and more bruising," wrote Howard Taubman in the *New York Times*. Jones and Cannon, wrote Taubman, "are giving 'The Blood Knot' the brilliant performance it deserves. Mr. Jones plays Zachariah with a rare grasp of his slow simplicity with its warmth and slyness, and he brings tension and fury to the bitter, explosive scenes. Mr. Cannon is patient and artful with this difficult brother, and he summons a searing intensity for his passages of terror." *Newsweek, Time, The Nation*—their critics entered the tiny theatre on Second Avenue uncertain what to expect and exited tossing verbal bouquets.

Fugard had not planned to come to New York. But during the first week in May the government of Northern Rhodesia threatened him with deportation for being at a bar in Lusaka, the capital, with two nonwhite actresses from the *Chalk Circle* company. He had also stated publicly that Northern Rhodesia was even more repressive than South Africa. So he left quickly—"I had to run for it," he said—and his agent wired him the money to come to New York. A thin, intense man with shaggy brown hair and an unkempt brown beard, he arrived, Lucille recalled, carrying his belongings in a box. He stayed in John Berry's apartment for a bit, and when that did not work out, Lucille offered him the office above the Theatre de Lys.

Fugard said of Lucille, "My first impression was of a very strong woman. Although Lucille and I never became close friends, we shared an absolute passion for theatre, and for a specific kind of theatre, which was the kind of theatre I wrote. Theatre of content, theatre of language, ideas, and rich and deep emotion. We never sat down and talked about what we liked in the play, or what it was about. It was an intuitive sympathy."

New York intimidated him, especially the world in which Lucille moved. "I can remember having a meal with her in the Plaza Hotel," he said. "I didn't know how to order. I said, 'Oh, steak.' The next thing I knew there was this colossal steak, and I couldn't send it back. I took as much as I could, and then I put my fork down and pushed my plate back, and the waiter asked, 'Was there something wrong with it?' So then she asked for a 'doggy bag,' and I didn't know if she had a dog or what, but she rescued me from a very difficult situation."

Lucille warmed to Fugard's awkward grace and his way of talking to her about theatre which recognized her as an equally serious theatre person. She found him supportive when Sidney Bernstein suddenly fell ill and she had to manage the production, a task she rarely undertook. The original cast had given notice that they were going to leave May 17, but Lucille had not been able to find replacements, nor could she locate Berry to help her out. The cast agreed to stay until May 24, and occasionally Fugard himself went on in the role of Morris. Eventually Berry turned up, and Louis Gossett, Jr., and Nicholas Coster were cast, although Fugard, who thought Jones and Cannon had been "electrifying," felt uncertain about the new duo. Perhaps because of the change, by June 8 the production was doing only modest business, and Lucille, who wanted to keep it running during the summer, asked Fugard, Berry and John Bury, the set designer, to forfeit their royalties, which they agreed to do.

Three weeks after he arrived, Fugard suddenly departed, leaving only a note for Lucille in her apartment. "Dear Miss Lortel," he wrote, "A long-distance call to S.A. has established the need for my return. What more can I say?—except to apologize for seeming to be difficult and unco-operative, which certainly I am not....Goodbye and my humble thanks for your many kindnesses. Athol Fugard."

From anyone else, such an abrupt exit would have infuriated Lucille. But she forgave him. "I'm just getting over the shock of your leaving," she wrote him in Port Elizabeth on June 15. "I can't tell you how much I miss you. Your just being here gave me the moral support I needed for the show....I believe in the play and feel almost positive that if we could keep it running during the summer, we can get a long run out of it. Maybe then you can return, as we all enjoyed seeing you play in it." Fugard wrote and thanked her for "your warm, generous and forgiving letter," and they corresponded for the rest of 1964, with Fugard always addressing her as "Miss Lortel"; he was trying to untangle agent and royalty problems, and Lucille endeavored to help him. "On my side," he wrote, "all I want to say is to repeat my hope that when my next play is finished you will read it. Needless to say there will be a next one, it is already taking shape on paper. It is too late for me to change. All I will ever be able to do is write..."

Lucille brought Gossett and Coster up to the White Barn on July 19 and 26, to give benefit performances of *The Blood Knot* for the Free Southern Theatre of Tougaloo, Mississippi. Following the first performance, Gossett, the playwright Lorraine Hansberry, the *Tulane Drama Review*'s editor Richard Schechner, and Joy Manhoff, coordinator of the Free Southern Theatre, participated in a discussion with the audience, and on Sunday, July 26, Paul Newman and his wife, the actress Joanne Woodward, joined the post-performance talk.

The Blood Knot closed on September 27, having played 239 performances, a run in which Lucille, as well as Fugard, could take satisfaction. Over the years the play would be produced by amateur and regional theatres all over the country. It was one of the few she produced that recouped many times her original investment.

In 1985, on the twenty-fifth anniversary of the play's birth, Yale
Repertory Theatre revived it in a cut version entitled *Blood Knot*, with Fugard and Zakes Mokae playing the roles they had created in South
Africa. When James B. Freydberg transferred the production to Broadway, Lucille put up one third of the $350,000 capitalization. But this was
the politically conservative 1980s, and this was a Broadway that hardly
sustained serious drama anymore. The production ran for thirteen previews and only eighty-three performances.

Sean O'Casey died on September 18, 1964. Eileen was devastated, both
financially and emotionally. She wrote to Lou, asking if he could put her
in touch with someone who might be able to rent her a flat in London,
preferably with a big room for her books and a tiny garden, for she was
having to move out of Torquay in the spring. Lou wrote back that he
would definitely arrange something, which he did.

   For her part, Lucille quickly set about organizing a tribute to O'Casey
by producing consecutive revivals of *I Knock at the Door* and *Pictures in the
Hallway*, the adaptation of his second autobiographical novel, which The
Playhouse had produced in 1956. Each would run for three weeks at a
combined cost of $15,000. She asked Paul Shyre to direct the concert-
style presentations, which, as in the 1950s, were staged with the actors sitting on stools in front of music stands, while Eldon Elder's lighting
turned the cyclorama a peaceful blue behind them. Shyre and Lucille
assembled a vibrant cast, with Lucille asking Jessie Royce Landis to play
O'Casey's mother and Staats Cotsworth to read the narrator in *Knock*,
Peggy Wood to play the mother and Cotsworth again to narrate for *Pictures*. The supporting casts consisted of Rae Allen, Stephen Elliott,
Robert Walker (making his New York debut playing the young O'Casey),
and Shyre himself. To keep expenses down and gain more money for
Eileen, to whom Lucille intended to send any profits, Lucille asked the

actors to take identical salaries, and they agreed. "I do hope that these two readings will be a great success financially for you," she wrote Eileen on November 6, "as the main purpose in doing this is to create an interest here for O'Casey and for you to gain some benefits from it." Feeling as though she was not doing enough, at one point Lucille asked Eileen's permission to rename the de Lys after the great Irish playwright. But Eileen, with her innate modesty—and understanding of Lucille—declined. "My dearest Lucille," she wrote in October, "I thank you with all my heart for your kindness. I realize only too well how kind you are, and all you want to do. The naming of your theatre, which is so much part of you—you will understand my refusal."

The opening night of *I Knock at the Door,* November 26, Lucille watched Peggy Wood stand on the apron of the de Lys and in her clear, strong voice read a letter in which Eileen described Sean's last weeks and last words to her: "Darling, Eileen, I am so very, very tired but I don't want to leave you." After the performance the cast and special guests repaired to an Irish coffee party in the mezzanine, catered by Jim Downey's restaurant, which had been serving Irish coffee and stronger spirits to theatre folk for years.

Reviews were generally favorable. Richard F. Shepard at the *New York Times* wrote that the actors' voices "took the warm poetic words and, with the barest of gestures, re-created an old Ireland—its people, its flavor, its great occasions and its perennial troubles." He especially praised Landis for her interpretation of O'Casey's mother. "She has magnificent force and emotion, which is in keeping with the simplicity of the script."

At the *New York Herald Tribune,* John Molleson wrote that the actors "made their characters live in lines that were the very breath of childhood—a poet's childhood....At the heart of the drama is the wonderful portrait of O'Casey's mother movingly played by Jessie Royce Landis."

But these opinions were more quietly appreciative than effusive, and there were negative ones from Jerry Tallmer, then at the *New York Post,* and from a surly Martin Gottfried in the *News Record.* To Lucille's deep disappointment the plays did not do the business she had hoped; there was no windfall for Eileen, although Lucille sent her a check anyway. She and Lou would always see to Eileen's welfare and provide for her, a practice that Lucille continued after Lou's death.

In 1964 Lucille hired thirty-two-year-old Paul B. Berkowsky to manage the Theatre de Lys. A smiling, balding, good-humored man, with as much energy and obsession for detail as Lucille, and the same devotion to theatre, he was generally an excellent choice for the de Lys and for hypercritical employers like Lucille and Lou. He had managed productions for the nonprofit Phoenix Theatre and for commercial Off-Broadway producers and was well-versed in Off-Broadway's regulations and practices, knowledge that Lucille sorely needed at the de Lys. Lucille did not pay Berkowsky well: during the twelve years he worked for her, his base salary never exceeded $100 a week. But they arranged to split money that came into the de Lys above the $1,250 a week that Lucille usually charged for rent, undoubtedly a stimulus for Berkowsky to keep the theatre booked. Berkowsky also hired himself out as manager for the shows that came in. One of his drawbacks as a general manager was that by 1969 he was writing prospective renters that they were expected to employ him, a situation which presented an obvious conflict of interest and which producers did not always appreciate.

Berkowsky liked Lucille and knew that managing the de Lys was a visible position through which he met everyone in Off-Broadway theatre. So he acclimated himself to her professional needs. He read scripts, attended readings, arranged readings for Lucille to hear, rented out the theatre for backers' auditions, and kept the theatre booked. Toward the end of the 1960s he also began coordinating the Matinee Series. And no matter where Lucille was, he sent her status reports. "Paul didn't make a hell of a lot of decisions," recalled his widow, Sheala Berkowsky. "He ran everything by Lucille. She said 'no'—it was out."

In addition Berkowsky possessed bottomless patience for Lucille's personal needs. He often drove Lucille and Lou home to the Plaza after a performance, and he and Sheala would see them off when they sailed to Europe or went to Florida. Sheala recalled that Lucille, ever the insomniac, would summon Paul late at night, even after he and Sheala bought a home in New Jersey and moved there with their two daughters. "If Lucille called, he was in the car on his way," said Sheala. "To talk to her if she wanted to talk. He was just there for her."

During the 1960s Lucille was fortunate that Berkowsky was on hand, for as the decade went along, her family required more and more of her time. In 1963 Lou suffered heart failure, and two years later he developed a blood clot in his right arm. He seemed to improve and, even though he had retired from the Schweitzer division of Kimberly-Clark, continued to go to his office, where he was still observed to fill ashtrays and inadvertently set the butts alight by smoking yet more cigarettes. But he wanted to spend more time in Florida during the winter, and so Lucille spent longer periods there too, leaving Berkowsky to handle business in New York.

By the mid-1960s, Lucille's sister began to show signs of the dementia which eventually would require the family to put her in a facility in Fairfield, Connecticut, where she could receive care twenty-four hours a day. "As time went on," said Robert Glenn, "her skin became whiter, her hair became whiter, her hats became blacker. Ruth was, in her whiteness and her hair and her demeanor, lovely. But I began to notice that she was a little more vague. There would be receptions in the balcony after the Matinees, and she'd be sort of wandering." Watching Ruth slip away from her was one of the hardest trials of Lucille's life.

When Lucille was in New York, she defiantly kept to her hectic schedule, as though determined not to give in to the ills undermining people close to her. Still, even with Berkowsky's help, it was difficult to keep her eye on the de Lys, the Matinee Series and the White Barn. To reduce costs in Westport, she now regularly began the season after the middle of July and ended it before Labor Day. She began searching for small-cast plays and one-person shows, which not only were less expensive to produce but also were easy to present, for they usually required little scenery.

Die-hard subscribers from the 1950s could not help but notice that the seasons were sparse and that critics from New York came less regularly than in the past. But Lucille still treated audiences to the unusual. In 1964, Robert Glenn staged *The Legend of Charlie Parker,* a play with music based on Robert Reisner's book about the great jazz musician, with a cast that included a loose, inventive nightclub comic named Clerow "Flip" Wilson. The following year she presented Adrienne Kennedy's *The Owl Answers* and in 1966 *Come Slowly, Eden,* a drama by Norman Rosten about the poet Emily Dickinson. "I never knew much about Emily Dickinson until that play was sent to me," said Kim Hunter, who played Emily, "and I fell apart. I just absolutely fell in love with it." That summer Lucille also brought a touching blend of comedy and drama called *The Effect of Gamma Rays on Man-in-the-Moon Marigolds* by a chemistry teacher named Paul Zindel. Eventually produced Off Broadway, although not at the de Lys, it would win the Pulitzer Prize for drama at the end of the 1970–71 season.

Lucille felt frustrated by the adjustments she was making to comply with Equity's regulations. At one point she even asked Leo Nevas to investigate if the White Barn could become a commercial enterprise, perhaps thinking that, if Equity was going to treat her like a regular stock company, she might as well become one. The zoning laws, Nevas informed her, prohibited such a change.

But if she was troubled by the leaner seasons and slackening attention from the New York press, she did not talk about it publicly. Westport was her retreat. Her mother and Lou were there. Friends lived nearby: the actress and producer Haila Stoddard and her husband Whit Conner; Ralph Alswang; the publicist and producer Jean Dalrymple, who threw a gigantic picnic at Pinafore Farm, her bucolic home in Danbury, every Labor Day weekend. On sunny days, Lucille sat in a patio chair outside the White Barn and tried with little success to read scripts, while actors went in and out of the theatre and apprentices painted sets behind the barn. Lou would occasionally trudge by, on his way to the house, theatre or radio shack. For Lucille, to be at the White Barn was to be among the people and things she loved most.

Equity once again shattered her idyll, in 1967, the year she and her board members Ralph Alswang and Eva Le Gallienne planned to celebrate the White Barn's twentieth anniversary. When Lucille reapplied for her special contract in the late spring, Equity informed her they were raising the minimum salary to $65, that she had to pay 5 percent of the actors' salaries into the Pension Trust Fund and also cover actors for unemployment insurance—reasonable requests from Equity's point of view but intolerable to Lucille. Furious, on June 1 she wrote to Marvin Poons, Equity's new assistant executive secretary, threatening to cancel the season. But after further negotiating, Equity reduced the minimum salary to $55, and she agreed to the pension and insurance payments.

The twentieth anniversary season turned out to be one of the strongest in several years. A preseason backers' audition of *Now Is the Time for All Good Men,* a musical about civil disobedience by the new lyricist-composer team of Gretchen Cryer and Nancy Ford, jolted the summer into action; in September, it would go into the de Lys for a brief run. Then the season swung into a well-conceived balance of conventional and innovative entries. In *Madrigal,* Peggy Wood and Ethel Barrymore Colt pleased White Barn regulars with scenes from Shakespeare and songs from musicals like *The Boys from Syracuse* and *Kiss Me Kate.* Anna Marie Barlow contributed realistic, well-crafted one-acts. Just as local critics were settling into what they thought would be a string of reassuringly straightforward plays, Lucille surprised them with Terrence McNally's *Next*, an anti-war satire about a draftee who shows up for his physical and, as Don Rubin wrote in the *New Haven Register*, desperately tries to convince an absurd female doctor that he is "too old, too fat, too stupid, too queer..." to go to war. Playing the reluctant draftee, James Coco was alternately hilarious and piteous, as only James Coco could be.

The season wound to an end with one-act dramas about the insensitivity of capitalism, *Our Man in Madras* and *Vacation in Miami*, by a German-born playwright named Gert Hofmann. Ironically the only weak entry was the final one, an unformed drama called *Animal Keepers* involving lonely people who meet in a veterinarian's office, a first play by an actress named Marian Winters.

This would be the last full season of the White Barn until 1974. Later in 1967 Lou and Lucille bought a four-room apartment on the eighteenth floor of the Sherry-Netherland, a residential hotel diagonally across from the Plaza at Fifth Avenue and 59th Street, and the move and the renovations disrupted their schedule. But Lucille really cancelled the 1968 summer lineup to spend time with Lou and Anny, who was also ailing. "Lou didn't seem actively ill," Haila Stoddard recalled years later. "He just seemed weak. He wanted to go back to Paris and he wanted her to go with him. They had been through a lot in the relationship by that time." In 1969, Lucille asked Stoddard, who lived in Weston, to run the theatre. Over three September weekends Stoddard produced experimental workshops, including two rock musicals by Gretchen Cryer and Nancy Ford with the umbrella title *The Last Sweet Days of Isaac*, which would go to Off Broadway and win an Obie. There was no White Barn season in 1970.

Lucille also faced changes at ANTA. The national organization, burdened by an overabundance of projects and an undersupply of money, was sliding sadly and uncontrollably into oblivion, and the Greater New York Chapter had not prospered either. On April 30, 1966, the latter's balance sheet showed a deficit of $95,862.07. The Chapter's income could never erase that shortfall: membership dues only brought in around $20,000 annually, of which a portion went to national ANTA, and that season the Matinee Series only took in about $1,128. The national organization certainly could not afford to wipe out the debt. So in 1966 the New York Chapter was dissolved.

National ANTA promised to continue to lend its name to the Matinee Series, but Lucille, now sole producer, lost no time moving the bookkeeping and membership records to the de Lys, where she handed their oversight to Paul Berkowsky, and she began campaigning to transfer whatever money was left in ANTA's Matinee Series account. She knew that ANTA's situation was dire. In 1969 a new board of directors announced enthusiastically (and overoptimistically) that ANTA would become an arm of the recently formed National Endowment for the Arts. The outgoing directors discontinued ANTA's programs, except for the Matinee Series, and, in a sad indication of how far ANTA had declined, stated that the organization was to be referred to by its full title, "American National Theatre and Academy," because no one knew what "ANTA" stood for anymore. This first attempt at a national theatre never exactly died—it simply faded into impotence.

Nevertheless the Matinee Series thrived during the middle and late 1960s. At the start of the 1966–67 season, Lucille added a Monday night performance. But the profile changed with the shifting contours of Off Broadway and a shift in Lucille's own taste.

Lucille's Matinee Series was now competing with new, not-for-profit institutions like the American Place Theatre and the Chelsea Theatre Center, which could afford to present plays that were noncommercial in nature. "Theaters . . . subsidized by the government or by grants—will be where the future of the theater will be," Lucille told the reporter Larry DeVine.

The Series was also contending with a host of Off-Off-Broadway venues, all of which pursued a crop of emerging American dramatists.

Lucille's pioneering efforts were, in effect, being echoed in churches, cafes and cubbyholes in Greenwich Village and beyond. Caffe Cino, Cafe La Mama, Theatre Genesis, the Old Reliable—they drew young writers who, for the time being at least, scorned any semblance of established theatre. Even though Lucille's base was Greenwich Village, to this new wave she represented an older, conventional generation.

In truth Lucille herself was changing. For one thing, her Puritan side was emerging. The producer who had been fascinated to watch *The Balcony,* unfazed by Genet's sexual imagery, organized the symposium "Four Letter Words: Pro and Con," to take place on December 14, 1965, after Vinie Burrows' *Dark Fire* and Adrienne Kennedy's *The Owl Answers.*

Initially, Lanford Wilson's *Ludlow Fair* was supposed to be on the bill with Kennedy's play, both to be directed by Michael Kahn. Lucille and Kahn had asked Wilson, through his agent, for permission to change a four-letter word, and Wilson had agreed. However, when Lucille wrote to the agent asking to change the expression "pissed off," and when she added, "Throughout I feel there are entirely too many 'Christs.' I feel it is possible to make a true and telling point without undue vulgarity, as Miss Kennedy's play proves,"—Wilson rebelled.

The question of a dramatist's right to use so-called bad language on stage was a hot topic, because it went to the heart of the difference between downtown and uptown theatre. Several weeks before Lucille's symposium, Peggy Wood had walked out of a conference organized by *Tulane Drama Review,* because she opposed what she termed "the vulgarity, brashness, gobbledygook and verbal diarrhea" at the conference. That exit had prompted an article in the *New York Times* and many letters to the editor. Offering Wood a chance to have her day in court, Lucille invited her to be on the panel, along with the *Village Voice* theatre critic Michael Smith and Douglas Turner Ward, artistic director of the Negro Ensemble Company. But it was Lucille who ended up drawing fire. Admitting that she had turned down a play by Rosalyn Drexler, because she worried that its language might endanger ANTA's charter and funding, she found herself criticized by her usually loyal cadre of female subscribers, who told her emphatically that they wanted the opportunity to experience everything and decide for themselves.

Lucille calmed down a bit on this issue, for she did accept Rochelle Owens' *Futz!* for the de Lys in 1968 and even invested in it. A touching comedy about a man who loves a pig and is brutally set upon by his neighbors for this passion, *Futz!* exemplified Off Off Broadway's affinity for ribald action, although the language was poetic, almost Elizabethan in style. Tom O'Horgan had directed it, and in typical O'Horgan fashion there was nudity, and actors writhed all over each other. Albert Poland, one of the producers, remembered that, when the show actually came into the de Lys, Lucille was in Florida and "everyone was hysterical about what she would think of it" when she returned to New York. Poland was designated to take her to see it. "We sat there," he recalled, "and watched people writhing and licking, and she was very quiet but attentive throughout the whole thing. After it was over, she turned to me, patted me on the hand and said, 'It's Biblical, dear.' " And so it was.

Still, for the rest of the 1960s, the Matinee Series largely reflected Lucille's accelerating taste for plays that explored human relationships and did not use four-letter words or what she considered crude sexual terms. The worst of these were ponderous, like Conrad Bromberg's *Dream of a Blacklisted Actor*, or Walter J. Fairservis, Jr.'s *Drums at Yale*, about Nathan Hale. The best told deeply affecting stories. In February 1967, Gert Hofmann's *Willie Doesn't Live Here Anymore* starred Mildred Dunnock as an elderly, mentally unstable mother who has lost her son in a war and takes into her home an exhausted soldier, played by Walter McGinn, who reminds her of the boy. The relationship ends so brutally that when her real son appears, she rejects him. Earle Hyman starred in December 1970 in *The Life and Times of J. Walter Smintheus*, Edgar White's complex drama about a scholarly, well-to-do African American, who disintegrates when he cannot confront or understand the passions of African Americans who do not inhabit his rarefied world.

Lucille also returned to writers toward whom she felt most loyal. In the fall of 1968, she paired two plays about revolution: Terrence McNally's *¡Cuba Si!* and Brecht's *Guns of Carrar,* with Viveca Lindfors playing the leads in both. "The ANTA Matinee Series," wrote Clive Barnes, who the year before had taken over the top drama post at the *New York Times,* "is often of surprising interest—surprising because elsewhere so much rubbish is put on for a run of eternity, and this series, planned for only two performances, is on occasion so much more rewarding." McNally's one-act, which Barnes dubbed "a strange symbolic fantasy," was about a girl called Cuba, a supporter of Fidel Castro, who camps out in Central Park while waiting for the revolution to break forth, and becomes a tourist attraction. Brecht's heroine Teresa Carrar, a dramatic forerunner of his Mother Courage, has lost her husband in the battle against the Spanish Fascists and hides his guns to prevent her two sons from joining the fray. But when the Fascists kill one son, she changes her mind. "Brecht's little play," wrote Barnes, "as subtle as a recruiting poster and as balanced as a pistol, is still oddly moving in its simple naturalistic writing and the depth of its feeling....Miss Lindfors played it beautifully, never overstressing the sentimentality, always giving a proper peasant weight to the words."

That same fall Lucille also produced *Hello and Goodbye,* Athol Fugard's disturbing, deceptively simple drama involving a brother and sister who have not seen each other in years and meet again when their father lies dying in the next room. Writing to Lucille from South Africa in the spring of 1968, Fugard's director and friend Barney Simon had announced:

> I hope that your Sabbatical is beginning to pall just a little, because
> I have some splendid news. Athol has been up in Johannesburg for

the past week. We've been discussing, arranging and auditioning for the plays we'll be doing next year.

It is at his suggestion—no, insistence—that I am writing to you. He says that the rights for 'Hello and Goodbye' have lapsed and that he wants me to have them for America and Britain. Having read it, would you be interested in presenting it—at the White Barn or elsewhere? I promise you that presented as we did it here, it is very, very exciting—funny, terrifying, warm full of reverberations and actually more perfect than 'The Blood-knot.' It needs next to no set—a table, chairs, boxes of junk. We played it against black tabs, and nobody, remembering, has realized that there wasn't a full set! The cast is just two. Both parts fantastically rewarding challenges—star-making! . . .

Lucille had glowed when she received this letter and immediately arranged to present *Hello and Goodbye* in the Matinee Series, hoping to move it Off Broadway herself or at least interest another producer. Barney Simon came from South Africa and staged it in November with Nicholas Coster and Kim Hunter, whom the critics praised for their textured characterizations. But Hunter could not stand the role. "I hated it. Just getting into this woman who was so goddamned mean. It just drove me nuts," she said. "They talked about doing it again someplace; I said, 'No thank you.'" In 1969 Kermit Bloomgarden produced *Hello and Goodbye* Off Broadway at the Sheridan Square Playhouse, with Simon directing Martin Sheen and Colleen Dewhurst.

But Lucille's sabbatical, as Simon called it, was nowhere near ending. Mimi Bochco visited Lucille in Westport one summer toward the end of the 1960s. Ruth was already living at the care facility in Fairfield, and Bochco, Lucille and Cugat had picked her up there and driven her to Fairweather for dinner. "While dinner was being prepared, I was sitting with Ruth in the living room," Bochco remembered, "and Lou was

coming down from upstairs with a nurse, and Lucille's mother was coming out from the downstairs bedroom with a nurse, and I felt as though
I was in a Chekhov play. I'll never forget it. And to Lucille it was a perfectly natural situation. There it was; you have to deal with it."

Her friends recognized the burden she was shouldering. To show
support and affection, and because they realized Lou was increasingly
ill, in November 1969 Audrey Wood and Bill Liebling wrote her and
Lou a letter. "I've been thinking about you both and am remembering
all the thoughtful things you both have been doing for so many people—including Liebling and Wood. And it is again time to say—you are
both outstanding in your treatment of others....So we bow to both of
you—salute you for all your virtues—and again rejoice in the warmth
of your friendship."

"You both live and work as if 'the world were truly all yours'—all the
bad as well as all the good," wrote Herbert Biberman in January 1970.
"I think of Lou—never concerned with the occasional battle he may
lose, never soured—always looking at life as though it were manageable
and *never turning his back* upon any part of it. I think of Lucille...pro-
ducing more works every year than Merrick, and doing so with her left
hand—her right so occupied in loving care of her loved ones."

Then on February 5, 1970, Anny died in Florida at the age of ninety-
three. She had lived to see one of her children attain wealth and
celebrity, to a great extent because of the determination and spirit that
she herself had communicated. Anny had lived more comfortably than
even she could have imagined, thanks to Lucille's care and Lou's generosity. "You and Lou did everything to make her life a long and happy
one," wrote Albert Dickason. Lucille had fulfilled the ambition on which
Anny and Harry had subsisted during those years of the Lower East
Side, the Bronx and Riverside Drive, although it is unlikely that Anny
ever acknowledged that to her daughter.

Lucille did not talk about her mother's death. "She was very much in control of these things," said Mimi Bochco. "You never really knew what was going on inside. She veiled it. I think she feared death, and I think she had a way of escaping it. She hated to go to funerals. It was a reminder of her own mortality. I remember when Cugat died in 1981, she just didn't want to go to the funeral, the burial. She would do whatever had to be done afterward, but try to avoid that." Lou joined her the Sunday after Anny died, and they remained in Florida until the second week of April.

Back in New York, Lou went into Presbyterian Hospital for three weeks, and the following September he was admitted to Gaylord Hospital in Wallingford, Connecticut. Regretfully they gave up their Florida houseboat in Harbor Island Spa, turning it over to Seymour, and early in 1971 rented an apartment at the Sun and Surf complex in Palm Beach. Lou was having difficulty walking, and they decided an apartment would be easier for him to manage.

In defiance of Lou's infirmities, on Sunday, March 21, 1971, they gave a black-tie party to celebrate their fortieth wedding anniversary. "In 1931," read the printed invitation, "Lucille Lortel and Louis Schweitzer merged to form an unlimited partnership. This 'affair' is now celebrating its 40th Anniversary... 'Life Begins at 40.'" They invited friends for cocktails at the apartment and dinner at the Voisin, close by in the Sun and Surf so that Lou would not have to go far. Copies of the marriage certificate from the S.S. *Leviathan* went to seventy guests, and an ice carving of that never-to-be-forgotten ship rested on a table behind a two-tiered cake. Lucille proudly adorned herself with the spectacular diamond and cabochon ruby necklace that Lou had given her several years earlier and with matching ring and earrings.

It was, in a way, a family reunion. Lou's two sisters and brothers-in-law were there, as were Mayo and Laura, and Seymour—by himself, for his wife had divorced him two years earlier. Lou's face looked drawn, but he seemed pleased, and Lucille smiled broadly when they posed on either side of the ice-*Leviathan*.

Three months before, Lou had made up a silly and serious poem for Lucille's sixty-ninth birthday, as he had used to do early in their marriage:

When I asked you yesterday what you wanted for your birthday, you said that all you wanted was one sweet letter from me.

As a diabetic, I can't give you such a letter. So, please excuse me if you find it sugar free!

Although I am dictating this letter to my secretary, let me assure you that not one idea expressed herein comes from her. It's all my own thoughts.

I really wanted to give you a birthday present, which would have been a lot more easy to do than to write this letter. So, if you change your mind and get an inspiration, please let me know.

In the meantime, I just want you to know that I LOVE YOU very much and shall continue to do so.

· CHAPTER 8 ·

On Her Own

A nyone looking at Lou Schweitzer in 1971 could see he was a sick man. At a reception in Westport that June to honor Democratic Senator Eugene McCarthy, Lou's face appeared thin and shrunken behind his glasses. Sheala Berkowsky recalled that Lou shuffled now, unable to pick up his feet when he walked, and Paul Berkowsky had to help him up and down stairs.

Still, he and Lucille made plans to sail to Europe in August, to visit Lou's younger brother, M. Peter Schweitzer, in the South of France. William Schweitzer had died in May, and for the two remaining brothers this was to be a special visit. Perhaps, too, Lou wanted to see Peter while he was still able. Lou signed a final draft of his will on August 11, and on the night of the twelfth he and Lucille sailed on the S.S. *France*, armed with a drugstore's worth of pharmaceuticals and the names of doctors to call in an emergency. They disembarked at Le Havre on August 17 and went on to Paris, where they stayed at the Ritz before taking the Train Bleu to the Riviera on the twentieth. The next day they arrived in Cannes, where Peter, who was fast spending his portion of the Schweitzer fortune, was keeping a yacht. Lucille sent a postcard to

Mimi Bochco telling her that they had gone with the boat to St. Tropez and were planning to visit Monte Carlo. "It has been a glorious trip," she wrote.

They returned to Paris and on September 8 flew across the Channel to London. There Lucille learned to her distress that her friend and theatrical mentor Mary Grew had died the previous March. But she was able to visit with Eileen O'Casey and with Kitty Black, who observed that Lou "was looking very frail." When Lucille went to the theatre, she engaged someone to stay with her husband.

On Friday, September 17, Lou and Lucille took the boat train to Southampton and boarded the S.S. *France* for the voyage home. Many years later Lucille told her general manager Ben Sprecher that on Sunday night she and Lou ate supper in the dining room; they ordered chateaubriand for two, petit pois and the chef's special potatoes. Lou was gulping his food, and she admonished him to eat more slowly. Back in their staterooms Lou experienced severe indigestion, and Lucille called the ship's doctor. But there was little the physician could do: Lou was having a massive heart attack. Lucille later scribbled in her travel diary, in an almost illegible hand, that at 1:15 Monday morning, September 20, "Lou passed away." He was seventy-two years old.

Among the passengers who soon learned of Lou's death, were sixty-six-year-old Lilian K. Swartburg and her husband, Robert, an architect from Miami Beach, both of whom had met Lou and Lucille in Florida and been guests on their houseboat. More than thirty years later Lilian clearly recalled that they immediately went to the Schweitzers' suite, where they found Lucille lying on her bed crying, a moistened white napkin on her forehead. Lucille asked Robert if Lilian could keep her company that night, and she did. "I fixed her tea and toast, and she slept on and off," said Lilian, who remained with Lucille until the ship docked in New York on Wednesday, September 22. "This is so uncanny,

Lou's dying," Lilian remembered Lucille saying. "Forty years ago we were married on a ship. He loved the sea." Robert gathered about twenty Jewish passengers and arranged a small shipboard service, which Lucille attended.

In New York, Genevieve and Art Murray met Lucille at the pier and took her back to the Sherry-Netherland, where Lou's bedroom-study gaped emptily. The next morning a limousine took Lucille to Frank E. Campbell, the elite funeral home at Madison Avenue and 81st Street, for the service.

"The place was black with people trying to get in," said Lilian Swartburg. The guests' names filled two registers. Nicholas deB. Katzenbach, who had been attorney general under President Lyndon B. Johnson, delivered a brief eulogy that particularly praised Lou's challenge to an unfair bail system and his establishment of the Vera Foundation:

> Louis Schweitzer believed passionately in the ability and obligation of ordinary men to make the Constitution work. He would not leave the law to lawyers and he was right. He thought that the Constitution and the Bill of Rights should mean what they said .... He thought it was morally wrong to let men rot in jail before they were tried; their families left without support, their jobs forfeited....
>
> Louis Schweitzer enjoyed people and was tolerant of their failings. He was a generous man with a warm sense of humor. He was a modest man who, in his giving, always stayed in the background. There are no Lectures or Awards or Chairs or Buildings named for Louis Schweitzer. The legacy left is the thousands of human beings who have their liberty because he cared, as well as the administration of criminal justice which is more humane and has a more hopeful horizon, because he cared.

While Lou would have appreciated Katzenbach's words, his heart would have been with the memorials of fellow ham operators like Vincent J. Skee, who wrote affectionately about Lou for a ham radio journal:

> *Silent Key*—Mr. Louis J. Schweitzer, W1BE, Westport, Connecticut:
> ... Lou took his cues from his call letters—he was always looking for better ways *to be,* and was urgently opposed to outmoded traditions which were not in keeping with human aspiration and dignity.
> He lived the Amateur Code, and many groups, clubs, and individuals felt the warmth of his generous spirit....We shall deeply miss his friendly wisdom, good will, and savoir-faire, and the wonderful smile which always came through loud and clear.

He was buried in his family's plot at Mt. Carmel Cemetery in Queens.

Sympathetic letters poured in to Lucille from friends who extolled Lou and expressed concern for her. "My dearest you must feel so very lost after all the years with Louis," Eileen O'Casey wrote in October, "and the latter years in looking after him." Dictating to Lou's secretary, Lucille answered literally hundred of notes over the next two months.

Her friends were right to be worried, for she was anxious and depressed. Two days after the funeral she jotted in her appointment book that her weight, which she usually tried to keep in the mid-140s, if not lower, had ballooned to 157 1/2, although by October 3 she had squeezed it down to 156 1/4. In 1988, when Peter Cotes' wife died, Cotes wrote Lucille, "I simply cannot concentrate on anything....In fact when dear Lou died I was over in NY and recall how distressed you were for such a long time after *his* death."

Someone who did not know Lucille might have thought she was being callous in the aftermath of Lou's death, for her response to a condolence letter was often a thank-you followed by a rundown of the sixteenth season of the Matinee Series, which, she wrote Anne Jackson and Eli Wallach, was now being sponsored by the White Barn Theatre Foundation.

But careful observers and close friends saw that Lucille feared being alone and that Lou's death had deprived her of a vital mooring. The two had been companions and partners for forty years. They shared a liberal, nonjudgmental outlook on the world. Her lack of extravagance was in harmony with his, as was her feeling for the generous gesture. Lou had insisted that she give up acting, but he had ultimately encouraged her as a theatre producer and owner. Through financial support and shrewd business advice, he had enabled her to use her considerable organizational skills and theatrical instincts to build a new, stronger career. In the face of his womanizing, she asserted her own goals and in that way reaped the benefits of the marriage.

With Lou gone, Lucille felt bereft and she was filling herself and her time with work. "I am involving myself into the theatre as quickly as possible and keeping busy as much as I can," she said in a letter to Lyn Mosten, a friend of Lou's and Lucille's in London. To Marjorie Dycke she wrote, "My only salvation is work and work for me means THEATRE."

The Saturday after the funeral Lucille's steady, unassuming friend Margaret "Marge" Farwell drove her to Westport, and when Lucille returned to New York the following Monday, Marge stayed with her at the Sherry. In the afternoons Lucille usually went to her office, and in the evenings, if she was not listening to readings, she went to dinner with old friends like Frankie Godowsky and Mimi Bochco. But they could not assuage her anxiety. Tension fueled her insomnia, and late at night she often made lengthy telephone calls to Blanche Marvin, who was now living in London.

Friends tried to ensure that she was not alone. Grace and Daniel G. "Danny" Ross—Lou and Lucille's long-time lawyer—invited her to their home on her seventieth birthday, and others urged her to spend Christmas with them: Lou's sister Sarah Leffert asked her to go to La Costa Spa in San Diego; Gale Sondergaard invited her to California (Sondergaard's husband, Herbert Biberman, had recently died also). "I shall have to learn to get used to being alone," Lucille said in a letter to Sondergaard, "although I am invited out to different peoples' homes. It is still a little sad to go without Lou." She spent Christmas Day in Connecticut with Mayo, his wife, Laura, and their two sons, Michael and Rodney. She needed to be with someone who could give her a sense of family and to whom she could turn for advice.

Among Lucille's worries was the complexity of the estate Lou had left behind and the length of time it was taking to clear. There was also the burden of dealing with a battery of lawyers, accountants, brokers and bankers who were figuring the most financially advantageous ways to fulfill Lou's bequests and were making recommendations to the three executors and trustees: Lucille, M. Peter Schweitzer and Danny Ross.

Most of the $40 million about which Lou had boasted to Felix Munso must have been in real estate, for not counting the property he owned with Lucille in Connecticut, or the land and building which housed the Vera Institute of Justice and which he bequeathed to the Institute, Lou had left a taxable estate of roughly ten million dollars. He designated a few personal charitable donations, but the bulk of his wealth went either to Lucille directly or was to be for her use. An outright marital bequest gave Lucille $5,000,000. Lou had endowed a charitable trust with nearly $2,000,000 and empowered Lucille to be the sole judge of which organizations received the trust's annual net income or, if she deemed it necessary, part of the principal. Most of the rest was in trust for Lucille, to provide her with quarterly income. Not only was Lucille now a millionaire in her own right, she also possessed the tools for becoming a prominent philanthropist.

For the moment, however, Lucille could make little use of her inheritance. Lou's assets had been largely in stocks and bonds. Some had to be sold to fill immediate bequests, others had to be distributed and invested to ensure that they would provide the income Lou had intended. Over the next two years, Lucille signed a blizzard of documents, including a new will for herself.

On New Year's Eve 1971 she went to Lee and Anna Strasberg's, where she always enjoyed herself. Paula Strasberg had died, and in 1967 Lee had met and married Anna, an actress who had grown up in Caracas, Venezuela. She was a vivacious hostess, and their sprawling apartment on Central Park West was an oasis of tasty food and lively theatre people.

On January 11 and 12, Lucille attended the last performances of the season's Matinee Series: *A Place Without Mornings* by Robert Koesis, about a seriously dysfunctional family. Then on January 16 she boarded a train to Palm Beach accompanied by a young Norwegian woman whom she had hired to drive her around—Lucille sent a car down from the city— and who would stay at the Palm Beach apartment in Lou's old bedroom. Among other things, Lucille would have to decide whether or not to let her beautiful apartment go.

Florida seemed to act on her like a tonic. At least three days a week she went to the gym. She attended theatre with William Schweitzer's widow, Gertrude, who had a home in Palm Beach, and she went to dinner with Lou's sisters, who now lived year-round in Florida. Mayo came down from New York in February, and shortly afterward brother and sister traveled up to Washington, D.C., to see the Matinee Series production of Sam Dann's *Sally, George and Martha* at the Library of Congress. Then it was Fairfield to visit Ruth in the nursing home, New York to see Michael Weller's *Moonchildren*, which David Merrick was producing on Broadway, and back to Florida. She did not return to Manhattan until April 20.

But things were hardly back to normal. As in the years shortly before Lou died, there was barely a season at the White Barn in 1972. The Theatre of the Open Eye, an innovative company founded by the choreographer and director Jean Erdman, performed two plays and a program of dances on July 30—the summer's entire slate.

Lucille's Matinee Series schedule looked promising in the fall of 1972. The opening entry on October 30 and 31 was a remarkable play by Yukio Mishima called *Madame de Sade,* in which the Marquis de Sade is seen through the eyes of women who both lust for him and despise him (in 1989 the Swedish film and theatre director Ingmar Bergman would stage Mishima's imaginative drama for an international audience). Herbert Machiz directed the presentation at the de Lys, and a sterling cast included Florence Anglin, Ruth Ford, Cavada Humphrey, Lucille Patton and Avra Petrides.

But here, too, the length of the season was half what it had been in years past. In December Lucille produced Frederick Gaines' *Wilde!* and then early in January, with one-act plays by Ronnie Paris and Don Evans respectively, this seventeenth edition of the Matinee Series ended.

Part of the reason for these abbreviated seasons was that Lucille was supporting them out of her own bank accounts, pending the release of the money in Lou's will, and she did not want to spend too much. For the first time since the Matinee Series began in 1956, she raised the price of subscriptions, to $17.50 for Monday nights, $15.00 for Tuesday afternoons.

But other issues were tugging at her energy and enthusiasm, both of which were usually so high. For one thing, she was hurt and frustrated to see a series that meant so much to her dismissed by critics as never before, particularly at the *New York Times.* Clive Barnes had disliked *A Place Without Mornings* so intensely that he wrote merely four brief paragraphs and did not mention the cast—possibly he thought he was doing them a favor. "I cannot tell you how badly I feel about the review the *Times* gave regarding your play," Lucille wrote the author, Robert Koesis. "The audience loved it as you know, and I strongly feel that had your play had a chance to settle into a regular run, the reception from the other critics might have been quite different. Please do not feel discouraged."

Mel Gussow, who had become a *Times* theatre critic in 1969 and was carving a niche for himself by covering Off Broadway, seemed to have little respect for what, nearly two decades earlier, critics had regarded as a vital showcase for new work. Gussow compared Mishima's play to Peter Weiss's *Marat-Sade* and found it wanting. He chastised the "skimpy" scenery that of necessity had to share the stage with the de Lys' main production. Actors he frequently praised; plays, seldom. "As is often the case with the Matinee Series," he wrote on January 1, 1973, reviewing the one-acts by Paris and Evans, "the actors, not the playwrights, are the major contributors to the entertainment."

Finally, busy though Lucille tried to be, she had not gotten over Lou's death or the unfamiliarity of being on her own.

On December 9, 1972, she went to the ANTA Theatre to see *The Last of Mrs. Lincoln* with a rich businessman named Charles Heidt, his wife, Eidell, and a sixty-four-year-old theatrical lawyer and widower named Carl Schaeffer.

She had known Carl Schaeffer at least since the 1950s. He had been Clarence Derwent's attorney and later the executor of the Derwent Awards after the actor died; he had been active in the New York Chapter of ANTA—he and Lucille had attended many meetings together—and was also on the board of the Actors Studio. Whether this foursome was Schaeffer's idea or the Heidts' or Lucille's is not known. But apparently the chemistry between the two was pleasant enough that on December 12 they saw each other again, and a third time on New Year's

Eve. Lucille went to Palm Beach on January 16, 1973, and by January 21 Schaeffer was there, too. A romance was clearly blossoming. In her appointment book she began referring to him simply as "Carl" and she saw him sometimes three evenings in a row. He was with her when she threw a party in her apartment for Anne Jackson and Eli Wallach, and she went to a dinner party with him and met his friends. Soon, whether in Palm Beach or New York City, guest lists included Lucille and Carl. They were a couple.

Lucille's relatives and friends metaphorically shook their heads over her attraction to Schaeffer, an undistinguished man with gray hair and a short white beard, a toothy smile and, in their opinion, an oily manner. "A goat. That's what he reminded me of," said Lynne Mayocole years later.

"He was like a fox in the henhouse," said Hope Alswang. "He was really creepy-looking, and she was totally, completely smitten."

"I didn't like him," was Robert Glenn's blunt opinion.

But Lucille did not intend to join the cadre of widows who cling to other widows. She needed to walk into a theatre, a restaurant or a party on the arm of a man. The actress June Havoc, who lived nearby in Wilton, Connecticut, and came to know Lucille well after Lou died, believed that on some level Lucille lacked a sense of her own uniqueness. "Otherwise," said Havoc, "she would not have had the problem of being unable to really, in her own, very dear, beautiful skin, go wherever she wanted to alone. Lucille felt she just couldn't. She told a lot of people, 'I wish I could be like June is, because she doesn't think she has to have a man around every time she goes anywhere. She goes everywhere and doesn't give a hoot.' Lucille borrowed people's husbands and boyfriends. In a nice, delicate way you'd say, 'Well, I'm not going to be here, Harry will take you.' 'Oh,' she'd say, 'thank you.'"

Havoc was one of the few who thought that Carl "was wonderful for Lucille," at least at the beginning of the relationship. "She turned into a sixteen-year-old," the actress remembered fondly. "Lucille was completely happy that way for the first time since she lost Lou, and it was beautiful to behold." Photographs of the couple in Palm Beach show Lucille smiling gaily in a way that she rarely does in forty years of pictures taken with Lou. "Life has been pretty cruel these last few years," she had said in a letter to Betty Gardner, an acquaintance in Denver. It was as though, after three years during which she lost her mother, her husband, and her sister—Ruth, who had not recognized Lucille for years, had died mercifully in October 1973—she could relax and play.

Play she did. "They went everywhere," said Havoc, "and she bloomed." She and Carl took a West Indies Cruise on the S.S. *Michelangelo* in November 1973. The following spring they sailed to Europe on the *Queen Elizabeth II*, going to London and Paris, which Lucille had once said she would have difficulty visiting again without Lou (ironically, they returned to New York on the S.S. *France*). They kept separate cabins and hotel rooms, and Carl, like Lou, left her affectionate notes, calling her "Bubbie," "Lady Lortel," and "Snookie Girl" and on occasion signing them "Mr. Husband." The sexual relationship mostly consisted of kissing and fondling because, Lucille told Mimi Bochco, Carl had a prostate condition which hampered his sexual function. Bochco, who believed that Lucille never lost her prudishness where sex was concerned, thought that Lucille probably preferred a less intimate physical relationship anyway. Whatever the situation, Carl grew increasingly ardent. "To the sweetest sweetheart on her birthday," he wrote in December 1975, "may she stay as young & fresh for a long time—and may I have her love always & as fully as I love her."

Theatre largely took a back seat for Lucille during this second adolescence. The 1973 season at the White Barn consisted of three entries: a film; Ronald Rogers and Jan McArt performing an anthology of songs from American musicals; and a presentation involving the German-Jewish folk singer Martha Schlamme and Eva Le Gallienne's

students. Knowing that she would come back from Europe too late in
1974 to organize the White Barn's season, she turned the theatre over
to Ralph Alswang, who delightedly arranged an international festival
and rejuvenated both the subscribers and the local critics. He brought
in the Chicano company El Teatro Campesino performing their earthy
La Gran Carpa de los Rasquachis, or *Tent of the Underdogs.* From New York
came La Mama ETC (Experimental Theatre Club) presenting a Mo-
roccan fable, *The Night Before Thinking.* The Trinidad Theatre Company
offered two plays by Derek Walcott: *Ti-Jean and His Brothers* and *Dream
on Monkey Mountain.* Each gave five performances, unheard of at the
White Barn. "It was probably one of the most rewarding activities of
Ralph's career," said Hope Alswang. "This was just a fabulous summer
for him."

As for the de Lys, Paul Berkowsky kept booking the house, making
sure Lucille knew about prospective productions and heard readings,
or that she at least received scripts if she was relaxing in Florida. In
June 1971, J.E. Franklin's *Black Girl,* a gentle but tough drama involving a determined African-American woman and her relationships
with her mother and grandmother, had come to the de Lys from the
Henry Street Settlement's New Federal Theatre; it closed on January
16, 1972, after 247 performances. By October 1972, *Berlin to Broadway
with Kurt Weill* had ensconced itself for 153 performances, after which
Michael Weller's *Moonchildren,* a drama about the disenchanted hip-
pies of the 1960s, moved in on November 4, 1973, for nearly a year's
run. *Moonchildren* had closed in March 1972 at the Royale Theatre,
after twelve previews and thirteen performances, and in an unusual
Broadway-to-Off-Broadway journey found a more congenial home
on Christopher Street.

Outside of the White Barn, Lucille had not produced Off Broadway
since 1967, when she rescued the British comedian David Kossoff,
whose first American vehicle had closed out of town, and brought *A*

Funny Kind of Evening with David Kossoff to the de Lys for three performances. She had not put a show on Broadway since she coproduced *I
Knock at the Door* in 1957. But in 1973 she was an associate producer for a
major revival of Tennessee Williams' *A Streetcar Named Desire*. This, the
last entry of the ill-fated Repertory Theatre of Lincoln Center, where
she served on the board, had curiously been one of its most successful
at drawing audiences: Ellis Rabb had directed; Rosemary Harris glow-
ingly played sexually yearning Blanche DuBois; and James Farentino
acted brutish Stanley Kowalski. Lucille's money helped Jules Irving, the
Repertory Theatre's artistic director, move the production to the St.
James Theatre, a proscenium house that helped focus Williams' action
but was probably too large for the drama's subtle characterizations and
shifts of mood. Although he had preserved Rabb's staging, Irving himself was now directing, and a different cast included Lois Nettleton as
Blanche. The production lasted only fifty-three performances, despite a
number of warm reviews.

By the time of *Streetcar*, Lucille was involving Carl in her business affairs, a role that he willingly accepted. She sought his advice as she had
Lou's, and since Carl was a lawyer, the advice was initially about legal
matters. But by January 1974 he was assuming signature power on the
White Barn Manager's account, out of which Lucille supported the
Matinee Series as well as the summer theatre. Paul Berkowsky was writing him about repairs to the Theatre de Lys—the warped doors connecting Christopher Street to the alley behind the theatre were a
security risk; the mezzanine's carpeting was torn; the lighting board was
constantly failing and probably needed to be replaced—and also submitting bills for Carl's approval. Fall of 1974 had Berkowsky communi-
cating with Carl regarding Theatre de Lys license agreements and
informing him about the capitalization and running costs for *The Prodigal Sister*, a new musical by J. E. Franklin and Micki Grant which Woodie
King, Jr. was producing at the de Lys that November. Lucille, as she

often did when a production was tight for cash, had waived the theatre
bond of $6,000. If Berkowsky was concerned about Carl's increasing
participation, he kept it to himself. Lucille, after all, was his employer
and she was allowing it.

Friends would have been surprised at the amount of room this very
private woman gave Carl in her life. "Sweetheart," he wrote in a note
one Saturday in 1975, "Have already opened all our mail, assorted the
financial transactions, and am ready to dictate responses to letters..."
He went on to write that he had met with George Shaskan, her investment counselor, "and gone over every portfolio." He had spoken with
Michael Hecht, Lucille's accountant, "at great length"; received papers from an agency about hiring a maid; and visited Chemical Bank
regarding Lucille's certificates of deposit. Among other things, he and
Lucille shared a bank account. Carl was acting as though he were in
charge. He had even brought Lucille his secretary, Dina Kley, who now
worked for them both.

The last entry in Lucille's Matinee Series took place on January 6 and 7,
1975. Appropriately for a series that had always devoted itself to uncommon work, the play, called *The Long Valley*, was an adaptation of several stories by the American novelist John Steinbeck. Appropriately, too,
Robert Glenn, who had staged plays for the Series almost since its beginning, was the adapter and director.

The idea for *The Long Valley* had originated in Lucille's office in 1974.
Glenn believed that John Latham, one of Lucille's assistants at the time,
came from California's Salinas Valley, where Steinbeck set his tales, and
Lucille called Glenn in Dallas and asked him to read both *The Long Valley* and *The Pastures of Heaven* and decide if the stories could be adapted
to the stage. Immersing himself in Steinbeck's geography, characters and

language, Glenn edited and wrote intensely, creating a script of flexible scenes and soliloquies and using Woody Guthrie's songs to help suggest Steinbeck's hardscrabble 1930s. Actors would set the stage by shifting simple props and scenery. In October he sent a first draft to Lucille in Palm Beach, where she had gone finally to close out the lease on her apartment—in the future she intended to stay with friends or with Mayo, who had moved there in the early seventies.

Her initial response was not what Glenn had wished. Lucille, writing a joint letter with Latham, said that they found the episodic structure plodding and the piece lacking in thematic coherence. So Glenn cut and rearranged and invented a sort of Steinbeck figure as narrator, eventually played by Will Hare, to unify the play.

Lucille had hoped for a commercial production, but there never was one, possibly because there were no New York reviews. The day of the first Matinee, January 6, 1975, one of the actors, Alan Marlowe, died in a plane crash en route to New York, another actor went on script-in-hand, and the critics were disinvited. But Lucille, who never gave up, engineered two performances in April 1975 at the Library of Congress and also produced it at the White Barn that summer, with Mason Adams playing the Narrator.

Almost a year later, on December 1, 1975, this exuberant experiment in presenting new plays and fresh talent took its final curtsy, when a gala performance at the Theatre de Lys celebrated twenty years of the Matinee Series. ANTA's money difficulties had initiated the demise, but a plethora of Off-Off-Broadway showcases, nonprofit theatres and reading series had completed it. They had, in effect, borrowed Lucille's original impulse and supplanted it.

Lucille was not one to go quietly. Twenty years of innovation required a party. Jean Dalrymple produced the Series' last hoorah, with Carl as executive producer and Stuart Little, who always thought the Matinee

Series the most original and influential of Lucille's ventures, writing a booklet detailing its history and high points. Lucille guided from behind the scenes and was the object of the evening's applause.

By 7:30 that night, actors, producers, journalists, and longtime subscribers filled the de Lys, when at the last moment Lucille entered with Carl and took her customary seats, C101 and C102 on the aisle. The audience reexperienced plays and performances of the previous two decades. Earle Hyman and Vinie Burrows acted a scene from *Cry, the Beloved Country*. Eileen Heckart gave a taste of her startling portrayal from Eugene O'Neill's *Before Breakfast*. Cathleen Nesbitt and Walter Abel spoke poetry, as they had in 1961 when they and Richard Burton awed a standing-room-only crowd. There were selections from *Pale Horse, Pale Rider; Shakespeare in Harlem;* Sean O'Casey's *Time to Go; Come Slowly, Eden; U.S.A.;* and finally *Brecht on Brecht,* for which Gene Frankel reassembled Anne Jackson, Viveca Lindfors and George Voskovec. The League of Off Broadway Theatres and Producers gave Lucille a plaque for distinguished achievement. Stars like Helen Hayes, Eva Le Gallienne and Mildred Dunnock, whose engagements out of town prevented them from praising the Series and its doyenne in person, sent letters and mailgrams, which were read from the stage. Lucille had a role in this, having written Hazel Vincent Wallace in England for a few complimentary words from Dame Sybil Thorndike. New York City Council president Paul O'Dwyer, invited by Carl, could not be there but had arranged for something better: a Proclamation "on behalf of the City and its seven and a half million citizens" honoring Lucille Lortel "for her contribution to the cultural level of the City of New York." And a certificate of appreciation was sent from Mayor Abraham D. Beame.

Afterward people found taxis or gaily walked through the chilly night to the Fifth Avenue Hotel at 9th Street, to eat supper and dance. Lucille entered the softly lit rooms on Carl's arm. She had given industry and dedication to the Matinee Series, but now she felt it was time to let it go. For the moment she basked in an outpouring of praise.

Maybe the image of Ralph Alswang's 1974 success at the White Barn roused her to action, for Lucille produced a complete summer season in 1975 and she would continue to do so for the next twelve years. Plays, dance, cabaret, film—once again the White Barn proffered theatrical nourishment from shortly after the Fourth of July until right after Labor Day; what is more, for the first time shows played Friday through Sunday. Lucille's wish to avoid Equity salaries undoubtedly drove some of her choices, especially the increasing number of one-person perform- ances. But as always, she opened her theatre to projects she found al- luring—or to people who simply needed her. She enabled Eva Le Gallienne to perform in Barbara Wersba's *The Dream Watcher,* a drama about an aging actress that Le Gallienne had been unsuccessful in plac- ing elsewhere. She enticed seventy-eight-year-old Molly Picon, an adored star of the Yiddish theatre, to leave mourning her husband and perform in a tender one-act called *Love's Old Sweet Song.* "I said, 'Molly, read this and come.' " Lucille told Corinne Jacker. "She said, 'Oh, no. I'm through, I'm through.' But she fell in love with the play, and the au- dience loved her."

Fairweather continued to provide a refuge. During the day Lucille could stroll about without makeup, in shorts and sandals with white socks—an outfit she never would have allowed the press or her audi- ences to see. It was a safe place to recover her eyesight, after she under- went an operation to remove a cataract from her right eye in the spring of 1977. Gavin Choi, a Chinese student from Hong Kong who was at- tending Oberlin College, remembered her eyes were bandaged when she interviewed him for a job that spring. "Later on," he said, "I found out that she never saw my face, even after the summer. She could only hear my voice."

Lucille could no longer see objects with clarity, but as far as the staff were concerned, the problem did not impair her attention to the minutiae of running the White Barn. To her face the staff called her Miss Lortel, but privately they referred to her as "Big Mama" because, said Gavin Choi, "she was so controlling." By this time, Derwent House had been sold, and Lucille was putting the actors up in a former carriage house on her beachside property. Gavin's task was to see that the actors were fed and housed comfortably. "My first summer," he said, "we had a barbecue in front of the garage at Fairweather. I said to myself, 'Gee, it doesn't make sense to make each hamburger by hand; why don't we spread out all the meat and cut out each hamburger with the bottom of a glass or something.' The first time she saw it, she said, 'No, no, no, that's not how you do it. How can you be so sure it's a quarter of a pound?' She wanted each hamburger to be exactly a quarter pound, and we had to put them on a scale. She was very mad at me. I thought, 'I'm going to get fired.' But I had cut my finger on a slicer and it was bleeding—I was holding my hand behind me and she didn't see—and the next day she came to me and apologized; she'd heard that I had to go to the emergency room. So after that first experience, we made up: 'Okay, you can do what you want.' But she still made a point to check on everything."

Unfortunately Lucille's diminished eyesight accentuated her frequent perception that the productions were not lit brightly enough. Eloise Armen, who was publicity director in 1977 and general manager in '78, recalled that Lucille would come to dress rehearsals on Friday night and tell Ralph Alswang, " 'Ralph, that's too dark.' You could hear her during the show, after it had been restaged and relit and had gone back to dark, 'I told him . . . ' " In the middle of performances she could also be heard admonishing actors to "speak louder, dear."

"She was maddening," said Armen, "but endearing."

Armen was being a touch condescending; she did not really respect Lucille. But Gavin Choi did, finding that Lucille's endearing qualities surpassed her overbearing ones. For instance, Carl used to call Lucille's employees by their first names, but he always called Gavin "Choi." Lucille asked Carl one day, as Gavin remembered, "Why do you call him 'Choi'?" "Well," Carl said, "his last name is 'Choi.' " "Well, maybe he doesn't like it."

"So then, in front of me, Miss Lortel said, 'Do you mind being called Choi?' I said, 'I don't mind.' I was joking and I said, 'As long as you call me when dinner time comes, I don't care.' From then on he called me Gavin."

Gavin Choi worked for Lucille well into the 1980s, although he was not sure why Lucille liked him so much; he attributed it in part to his loyalty. "I asked for her autograph one time on a photograph, and she wrote that I was the son she would have loved to have. She would say, 'I love you, but don't tell anybody, okay?' "

When Gavin graduated from Oberlin, Lucille asked him what he planned to do next, and since he did not know, she suggested that he go to school near Westport. Wielding her influence as a substantial donor to the University of Bridgeport, and as a member of the Sponsors' Council for the University's newly established College of Fine Arts, Lucille arranged for Gavin to receive a scholarship to the graduate program in urban planning and administration and then to the School of Law. He began living at Fairweather year-round. Sometimes, when Lucille was not busy, they would go to a movie in Westport. To Gavin's amusement, Lucille, who was particular about so many things, did not care what sort of car got her where she wanted to go and would eagerly squeeze into

Gavin's two-seater Honda CRX, leaving her ungainly Lincoln Continental behind. She liked to advise Gavin about dating girls. "One time we went to the Westport Country Playhouse, and she kept saying, 'That girl is interested in you.' She has, like, the instinct. When I was dating, she would say, 'You need more money.' But when I was serious—when I introduced her to Felicia, who became my wife—then she realized she was losing me. She was like a mother," he said.

Mayo, Lucille's older brother, had gone into the Good Samaritan Hospital in Palm Beach in late June, 1976, and died there of heart failure on July 8. In October he would have been eighty-one. He had been in and out of hospitals so frequently in recent years that Lynne Mayocole did not realize the severity of this latest attack, and possibly Lucille did not either. She flew to Palm Beach. Mayo was cremated, and his ashes scattered. In September Lucille would organize a memorial in New York.

"Now," said Mayocole, "Lucille was all alone." To be sure, Seymour was still alive, but she had never felt close to her younger brother; they had little in common, and in recent years he was becoming reclusive and disoriented, states which continued until he died in 1980. Mayo had been the first star in her life. He had been the link to her family, her youth and theatrical ambitions, her history. "She was very, very distraught," said Mayocole.

Lucille returned to Westport and Carl. He continued to come up from New York every weekend, perhaps because she needed his presence even more now that Mayo was gone. But he increasingly annoyed the staff. "Her gentleman friend would help himself to cash from the box office," said Eloise Armen with a combination of tact and distaste. His raids on the cash drawer meant that Armen could not reconcile the take with the number of tickets sold. Because Armen disliked dealing with money and did not like Carl, at the end of the 1978 season she told Lucille that she would not be back.

Carl used his relationship with Lucille as a sort of license, whether it was to take money from the box office or to inflate his influence with Lucille in others' eyes. Leland Miles, the president of the University of Bridgeport, met with Lucille and Carl in September 1977 to discuss bringing White Barn productions to the University on a regular basis. But a year earlier Carl had told Miles privately that Lucille might be interested in turning over the White Barn property to the University, either during her lifetime or as a bequest after her death. Writing Carl confidentially in September 1977, Miles indicated that the University would be happy to accept such a bequest pending certain arrangements. Now Carl had to backpedal; he waited until December to respond and then wrote that the idea of Lucille's bequest was "my personal thought of having the University of Bridgeport succeed to the Westport property owned by Lucille, so that the White Barn Theatre could be continued after her demise. I had not yet mentioned this to Lucille."

Miles, who had known Lucille since the 1960s when he was Dean of the College of Arts and Sciences, was apparently mystified by Carl's contradictory stories. At the suggestion of theatre director Marcella Cisney and her husband Robert Schnitzler, both of whom knew Lucille from Westport, he sent Lucille all of Carl's private correspondence on the subject. One can only imagine Lucille's anger.

Lucille's friends trusted that eventually she would extricate herself from the relationship. June Havoc believed that Lou had taught Lucille self-preservation: "Just be careful. Just test everyone not once, twice, but dozens of times. Is it you or what you represent? Be sure it's you." Mimi Bochco thought that Lucille's unerring instincts about people would lead her straight. And Anna Strasberg, who knew Carl from the Actors Studio, asserted that Lucille "only let Carl get away with things about which she thought, 'That's okay.' " Strasberg observed, "He would walk around the Theatre de Lys and say, 'Oh, we're going to change our theatre.' *Our* theatre. But he only did what she wanted."

All these friends were partially right. In April 1978 Lucille was recovering from cosmetic surgery and assiduously kept track in her appointment book of when Carl came to visit her in the hospital: "After 4 P.M.; 4 P.M.–8." In penciled notes that call to mind her anxiety when Lou was drifting away from her during the 1940s, Lucille recorded that on Saturday, April 15, when she was back home, "Carl didn't call me. I phoned him & he was very indifferent." Then on Sunday, she went to a party at the Strasbergs and "Told Carl off." In a note to herself on Saturday, April 22, she wrote, "Told Carl I will be going out with others..." Most likely she had discovered that Carl was seeing other, younger women, a humiliation for her and a deep betrayal.

But the relationship did not end immediately. She jotted in her appointment book on June 3 that Carl came to the Sherry and stayed with her because she was sick. They occasionally went to the theatre and to dinner. If friends thought she was well rid of him, Lucille perhaps was not so sure, for she was obviously despondent. Philip Huston wrote her warmly six months later, on December 3:

> I am worried about you. Mind you—I've been worried sometimes about your health—your eye trouble—etc.—but never before have I been troubled about your spirit. I am now.
>
> You have come far—done extremely—miraculously—well. Your power should be crescent.
>
> But I find you depressed to the point of spiritual surrender—
> I'm vaguely aware of what is contributing to this—
> Let me talk with you at your earliest convenience.

Possibly because of some advice from Huston, or because of her own need, the affair with Carl resumed for a time. From December 1978 through March 1979 they saw a good deal of each other; they went for long walks, and he took her dining and dancing in Florida, where, in February, she received the shocking news that Ralph Alswang had had a heart attack and died. She actively involved herself in producing that spring: she, Lester Osterman and Marc Howard picked up *Getting Out,* Marsha Norman's riveting drama about an ex-convict's battle to turn her life around, and put it into the de Lys. Even so, Vincent Curcio remembered that Carl was around the White Barn during the summer of 1979. But finally it ended. According to Anna Strasberg, Lucille would only marry him if he signed a pre-nuptial agreement, and Carl refused. "He said it was insulting. Wouldn't sign it. She said, 'No wedding.' "

"I was staying with Lucille at the Sherry in that little room off the living room," Havoc recalled, "and I was lying down in the afternoon having a nap, when a covey of lawyers arrived, and they were talking estate. And she said, 'I just want to be certain there is no one, ever, benefiting from anything of mine unless I designate it. I don't want anybody to have any claims on me.' And I lay there and I thought, 'Gee, he's gone.' "

Within a year Carl married an actress named Gayle Greene who was studying at the Actors Studio. Even so he was not completely out of Lucille's thoughts. She tried talking about it with a therapist, but that lasted about two weeks. "She just couldn't stand it," said the producer Evangeline Morphos. "Because she wasn't getting results."

In the summer of 1981 Carl and his wife traveled to London and, with the obsession and curiosity of someone who has not completely recovered from a past romance, Lucille asked Blanche Marvin to see them and report back. But as often happened, Marvin went overboard: she saw Carl and his wife more than once, gave him a couple of scripts and generally acted in a way that Lucille felt betrayed her. Trying to soothe her friend, Marvin stressed her impression that Carl's marriage was an arrangement of convenience; Carl's prostate cancer had progressed, and

Gayle was essentially nursing him. Marvin drew a portrait of a man who was trying desperately to keep in touch with theatre and maintain an image of his own importance. He died in December 1982.

Many years later Robert Glenn was having dinner with Lucille at the Sherry and, feeling that they were talking on a personal level, said, "Now that it's over for a long time, what is your bottom line thought about Carl Schaeffer?" "The biggest mistake I ever made in my life," she said.

CHAPTER 9

Of Renewal, Honors and Gifts

A slightly built, open-faced man with the energy of a cyclone and the edginess of a buzz saw had walked into Lucille's office in the fall of 1980. Lucille needed a new general manager for the Theatre de Lys, and twenty-five-year-old Ben Sprecher was applying for the job.

Lucille had parted company with Paul Berkowsky in 1976. To an extent, Carl was the cause; as Sheala Berkowsky told it, "Carl thought he could move in and take over Lou's role, but Paul and he did not see eye to eye."

Berkowsky had also grown restless. He had worked for Lucille for more than ten years and needed more money and authority. Perhaps he knew, too, that Lucille and Carl had considered firing him. She often rummaged about noisily for replacements when she began to be dissatisfied with employees.

The last show that Berkowsky booked into the de Lys was also the first one he produced: Tom Cole's *Medal of Honor Rag*, a stimulating if flawed drama about an African-American Vietnam veteran and the psychiatrist who treats his guilt and depression. Lucille put up half the $60,000 capitalization, both as a gesture of support for Berkowsky and because she gravitated toward the drama's raw human tale. New York audiences, however, did not follow suit, and after forty-eight performances *Medal of Honor Rag* closed on May 2, 1976. By the fall Berkowsky had moved to his own office. He continued to produce and established the highly success-ful School Theatre Ticket Program, which made low-priced tickets avail-able to students and teachers in the New York area.

Carl immediately stepped in to book the de Lys, a job at which he proved surprisingly adept. In November 1976, the Negro Ensemble Company took over the theatre for their tenth anniversary season, which they inaugurated with Charles Fuller's devastating indictment of Amer-ican racism, *The Brownsville Raid*. The next year, in October, David Mamet's poignant theatrical valentine, *A Life in the Theatre*, rented the the-atre for 288 performances.

But nobody was standing at the general manager's helm, not even during the rental of Sam Shepard's *Buried Child*, which the producer Burry Fredrik brought to the de Lys on December 1, 1978. It was one of the few productions in which Lucille tried to invest and discovered her money was not needed. "I delivered the script to Lucille," Fredrik re-called, "she had it read to her, came back next morning to my office: 'How much do you need?' 'We have it all,' I said. She was a little non-plussed. To her great chagrin, she did not put money in *Buried Child*."

Finally in 1979, at Mimi Bochco's suggestion, Lucille hired Danny Banks, who had assisted Rudolf Bing at the Metropolitan Opera. But Banks gave his notice in June 1980. "What killed it was when Lucille asked him to pick up a quart of milk at the grocery store," said Vincent Curcio.

Ben Sprecher, born in California, had come to New York as a produc-tion stage manager for a Broadway revival of *She Loves Me* with Madeline Kahn. His experience was largely with touring vehicles for stars who had passed their prime: production stage manager for a Broadway produc-tion of *Knickerbocker Holiday* headlining Richard Kiley; company manager for Lee Guber's tours, among them *The King and I* with Yul Brynner and

The Merry Widow with former opera star Roberta Peters. He worked for the actress and dancer Mitzi Gaynor, who toured her own show after her film career fell apart in the 1960s. Sprecher knew commercial theatre; he had little familiarity with the avant-garde theatre Lucille favored.

"I don't think Lucille was particularly impressed," Sprecher recalled about their interview, which took place in her office at 60 West 57th Street. "I think she was looking for somebody a little more seasoned. But in hindsight I think I presented well, and that was important to Lucille." A month went by before Sprecher received a call; he believed that Lucille had first offered the job to somebody else. He negotiated a salary of $500 a week and began working for her on New Year's Day, 1981.

When he first walked into his office above the de Lys, the show playing downstairs was an item called *Trixie True, Teen Detective,* a frivolous musical for which Lucille did not care much. When it exited about a month and a half later, Lucille rented the space to the Roundabout Theatre, which installed Terence Rattigan's drama *The Winslow Boy* for a limited run. Then Sprecher and Lucille faced renting to Caryl Churchill's rowdy, challenging farce about sexual role-playing, *Cloud 9.*

Cloud 9 was like nothing that either Lucille or certainly Ben Sprecher had experienced before. The comical first act takes place in the nineteenth century in Victorian colonial Africa, where British imperialism rules sexual inclinations as stringently as servants and insists on heterosexuality no matter what the personal price. The affecting second act takes place in England during the 1970s, when the same characters explore any sexual inclination they please. In the first act, men play women and vice-versa, in a farcical presentation of how sexual preference often bears no relation to gender. One hundred years later these same men and women seize the freedom to determine their sexuality for themselves, although not always happily. The two acts differ in tone and style, but they play off each other—just not in a conventional way.

In London *Cloud 9* had received mixed reviews. But an American dancer turned costume designer named Michel Stuart had fallen in love with the play and wanted to produce it. He brought the script to Sprecher, who told Lucille that Tommy Tune, the lanky six-foot-six-inch dancer and choreographer from Texas, was set to direct. Lucille said to Sprecher, "Darling, I think we should have a reading," and so it was that Tune and an ensemble of playwrights and actors trooped to the Sherry, sat in Lucille's living room and read the British playwright's sometimes hilarious, sometimes sad comedy.

As Sprecher tells it, he did not understand the play and neither did Lucille. "Never," he said. She talked with Blanche Marvin; she called people at the Royal Court Theatre, which had presented *Cloud 9* in London. They told her she had to see the play on its feet to understand it. "It became apparent," said Sprecher, "that there was very interesting stuff going on in this play, and so we talked about it. She was very clear in her desire to champion avant-garde material. There were a lot of good people around this, and her instincts about people artistically were often correct. She said, 'Okay, let's do this.' It ran over 900 performances."

But if Sprecher had difficulty deciphering Churchill's postmodern dramaturgy, he had, by his own account, no trouble figuring out his job. Aside from renting the de Lys, he realized that the essence of his work was relating to Lucille. He established right away that he would tell Lucille about every play available to the de Lys at any given moment. "I made a habit," he said, "which I learned in the past from dealing with other stars—because I dealt with Lucille as if she was a star, as if she were Lauren Bacall or anybody else—of making my information system consistent and dependable. I set up a pattern on January 1, 1981, that I would call Lucille every morning at eleven o'clock as soon as she got up, whether or not there was something to say to her. I gave her an eleven o'clock phone call every day for eighteen years. Monday through Friday. Never on Saturday or Sunday; she had to call me. I gave her a state-of-the-theatre address. Wherever she was in the world."

Although private play-readings for Lucille were customary long before Sprecher came on board, he made them, he said, "an iron rule" for
doing business at the de Lys. With the self-importance that often characterized him, he said, "Everyone in the American theatre knew that if
you wanted this theatre, forget the deal, you had to read for Lucille."

Ever since *Threepenny Opera*, she had always insisted on "in association
with" or "by special arrangement with" billing on her theatre's programs
and advertising. But that usually ran below the other credits. Under
Sprecher's regime, "Every play that went into that theatre gave billing to
Lucille Lortel above the title. And toward the end of her life, in the last five
or ten years, I just stuck her in as a producer, and every producer accepted
it. It was just the cost of going into the theatre." He convinced her to "gut-
renovate" the theatre, and during their first ten years together, they spent
from $300,000 to $400,000 to refurbish the interior and upgrade equipment. "We redid the marquee, the box office, the outer lobbies," said
Sprecher. "We stepped that theatre into the twenty-first century, and I
think Lucille took great pride in having a pristine, elegant place to go to."

But Sprecher's intentions were more than cosmetic. He saw himself as
a protector, someone who, as he put it, could "translate the world" for
Lucille when it came to her theatre business, a realm whose details he
knew she did not grasp except in an intuitive way. Sprecher had not
known Lou, but he understood that "Lou, to a great extent, really prepared the field so Lucille could walk gracefully through it. And I did that
in our professional life. I took care of the practical side of Lucille Lortel,
the business side that she didn't really want to worry about."

Sprecher knew how Lucille viewed his role. "There were two cate-
gories of people in Lucille's life," he said. "There were stars and there
were slaves. I was definitely a slave." But rather than resent this casting
or, like many people around Lucille, be fawning, he tried directness.
"People had a tendency to become sycophantic in her presence, because
of the amount of wealth there. And she liked that. I never did that. She

and I had some pretty good screaming matches, but she also knew that if I told her this was what was going to happen and how, then that's the way it would go. Through this process we built up trust."

Sprecher also possessed the ability to distinguish between Lucille's foibles and her good intentions, to recognize her weaknesses but defend her strengths. "There are many wealthy people who get up in the morning and think, 'Where am I going to go shopping, where am I going to have lunch?' Lucille got up in the morning and said, 'What are we going to produce today?' Almost obsessively. Her goal was to do important stuff. Not necessarily stuff people wanted to see, but stuff people should see. Which is why we had few commercial successes."

More astutely than Berkowsky, Sprecher found a way to work for Lucille and also nourish his own career. According to producer Daryl Roth, everyone knew that to get into her theatre, Lucille had to like your play—but you made the deal with Sprecher. He acquired a reputation as a tough—some said abrasive—negotiator.

During the long run of *Cloud 9* he realized that he needed to expand professionally but that there was no way to do so at the de Lys. Once a production came in, there was little work for him on a daily basis. So during the summer of 1982 Sprecher broached to Lucille that he was thinking of building a theatre called the Promenade at Broadway and 76th Street, and he asked if she would give him permission to do that and work for her at the same time. "The act of asking Lucille's permission was in and of itself often enough," he said. "Giving her the ability to say 'no,' and her believing that if she said 'no' I would not do it, and that's true, made her feel comfortable enough to allow me to do it."

"We were up in Connecticut, sitting at Cranbury Farm," Sprecher recalled, "and I said, 'Lucille, I really want to do this. Can I do this?' And she said, 'Well, darling, if you really want to, go ahead.' "

Lucille would not always be so amenable to Sprecher's personal projects. The general manager Dorothy Olim, who knew both of them, once described their relationship as a kind of marriage, with all of a marriage's jealousies, fights and reconciliations. But in the beginning Sprecher pleased Lucille enormously. On April 10 of his first year with her, she said in a letter to Blanche Marvin, "I'm very happy with my new manager. We see eye to eye on most plays and it is a great relationship."

Slowly Lucille's life returned to the stability she had enjoyed before Lou became ill and Carl disrupted her emotional balance. She would wake up around ten in the morning. Olive Wright, who had replaced Rosamund in 1977, would make her a light breakfast—coffee, a bran muffin, cold cereal—which Lucille would eat in bed. Sandra "Sandy" Starr, a plain, eager-to-please woman in her forties, whom Lucille had hired in 1983 as her personal secretary, would come down from the nineteenth floor, where she lived in a maid's room, and they would go through the mail if it had arrived. Lucille would dictate letters and map out her day's schedule, then she would take and make telephone calls. Wright helped her dress, put up her hair and applied her makeup. Before sallying forth Lucille would choose from among her many stylish hats, a fedora tipped over one eye usually the favorite. "That was her look," said milliner Suzanne Daché, who owned a hat store in Westport where Lucille often shopped.

Wright or Starr would accompany Lucille everywhere, for claustrophobia made her fearful of being alone in elevators, and her sight was still poor, although she covered the condition well in public. Macular degeneration in her right eye had left her with only peripheral vision there, and a cataract in her left eye impaired vision further. Finally in 1986 a permanent lens was inserted in her left eye, which enabled her to see quite well.

There was no Carl in her life, but there was a raft of escorts, many of them gay, each thinking he was dearer or more esteemed than the other. "I have a lot of escorts, darling," she told an interviewer for *Playbill* in 1986. "I like to lean on a man. If there's dancing after an opening, I go with Donald Saddler. When I'm invited to Joe Papp's shows, Franklyn Lenthall is my escort. There's Drew Eliot, Willoughby Newton, Robert Buzell. All of them are charming and gallant."

Robert Taylor, the curator of the Billy Rose Theatre Collection at the New York Public Library for the Performing Arts, fondly remembered attending theatre and parties with Lucille on his arm. " 'Darling, I always have such a good time with you,' she would say. She would tell me her theatre stories and talk about herself, and we would laugh. I know people said she never talked about anything but theatre, but I found her charming. Childlike. When we were out, I couldn't keep my hands off of her—I always wanted to touch her and protect her."

Certainly she was not alone. She went to Beatrice Milwe's home in Westport for Passover; to Anna Strasberg's at Thanksgiving; and on Christmas Day, Hope Alswang and Henry Joyce invited Lucille to their apartment for dinner with Hope's sister, Frances, and Ralph, Jr.,—whom Lucille adored—and later with Hope and Henry's two children. Every December Lucille attended a string of parties. During most of the 1980s, David Hays, the set designer who had founded the National Theatre of the Deaf, and his wife Leonora threw a December brunch for Lucille at their Upper East Side town house, as a sort of birthday party for which Lucille made up the guest list and paid the expenses. On Christmas Eve she went to the Fifth Avenue apartment of John Stevenson and his wife Isabelle, who was president of the American Theatre Wing. Lucille would arrive with a box of caramel popcorn, which she and John Stevenson would sneak off to a corner and devour, while everyone else listened to the Salvation Army sing Christmas carols and yearned hungrily for food.

New Year's Eve might find her at the home of David and Lois Berman; Lois was a dramatic agent whose star client was Sam Shepard. On New Year's Day Lucille often gave her own party at the Sherry. A Christmas tree glittered in the living room, flowers from admirers decorated every table, and she piled the white grand piano high with the presents she had received. Her gifts to friends were amusingly legendary: each received a carton of Kleenex, paper towels, paper napkins, and toilet tissue directly from Kimberly-Clark, in which she still owned a sizable amount of stock. At one point Kimberly-Clark discontinued this perquisite, and Lucille called the CEO to protest. For her, he reinstated the present.

But of all the parties Lucille attended, she relished most the one Anna Strasberg regularly gave in December in her honor.

According to Anna, Lucille had really been Lee Strasberg's friend, until Lee died in 1982 and Anna fell into a depression, as Lucille had when Lou died. "I was in the twilight zone," Anna recalled. "I wouldn't leave the house, I wouldn't go to the theatre, I wasn't taking care of the children."

One evening at around seven o'clock, Anna received a call from Lucille.

" 'Darling, I'm waiting for you on the street. How can you keep me waiting?' " She and Sidney Kingsley were waiting for Anna at the theatre; the only trouble was, Anna did not remember promising to be there. "My mind started racing: 'When did I say I was going to meet you? I'll be right there.' She and Sidney were betting on my good manners not to leave them standing in front of the theatre. So into the car, rush downtown. I was having such an anxiety attack going out into the world that I had shared with Lee. I get out of the car, Lucille grabs one hand, Sidney grabs the other, and we go inside. I don't even remember the play; I thought, 'I can't show how panicked I am.' I sit between Lucille and Sidney, which is very unusual, because she likes to sit with the men. They're still holding my hands, and the lights go down, and she leans over and says, 'Darling, this is Lee's gift to you. Don't throw it away.' And I started to cry. The tears just kept rolling down my face. And I thought, 'No, Lucille, this is your gift to me. Because you're giving me something that I would never have come back to.' "

Some observers believed Anna was softening Lucille for large contributions to the Lee Strasberg Institute of the Theatre, especially after

Lucille was given the first Lee Strasberg Lifetime Achievement in Theatre Award in 1985. But Lucille had made significant contributions to the Actors Studio long before she and Anna became friends—long before Anna had married Strasberg. Those who saw the attachment to Lucille in a financial light forgot that Anna's own resources were considerable.

Ben Sprecher and others saw a warm relationship much like that between a mother and daughter who trusted and truly liked each other, with Anna often functioning as the mother. Unlike the relationship between Lucille and Blanche Marvin, which was intense, Anna and Lucille's friendship was relaxed. Anna liked being Anna: emotional, demonstrative, excessive. Most people wanted something tangible from Lucille—money, the use of her theatres, the shared light of her celebrity. Anna already possessed those things. She liked to give to her friend: food, earrings, a splendid red Valentino coat. "I was wearing it. She loved it. I said, 'Lucille, you can have it.' Of course, she was shorter than I. 'Oh, no, no, no.' But she took it."

Anna gave physical affection, which Lucille, who usually did not like to be touched let alone embraced tightly, accepted, pleased in spite of herself. Anna and her young sons, David Lee and Adam Lee, provided Lucille with a second family. And finally Anna easily gave the things Lucille wanted most: lavish praise and a roomful of people to admire her.

After Lee died in 1982, Lucille began taking Anna out on his birthday, November 17. To reciprocate, Anna gave her a champagne supper on December 16, 1984—a bash that became a yearly tradition. These were not so much birthday parties as opportunities for Anna and Lucille to celebrate an event in Lucille's life: the Lucille Lortel Room at the New York Public Library for the Performing Arts; producing Larry Kramer's *The Destiny of Me*. "She was very funny about those parties," said Anna. "Who was invited was very important. She micro-managed that party. All I did was give it; the guest list was hers."

The draw for Lucille as much as her friends was the chance perhaps to see Al Pacino cutting himself a slice of turkey in the kitchen, or to overhear former film star Luise Rainer quiz Pacino in her Viennese accent, "What do you do young man? What movies have you been in? Let's take a photograph." People milled about, ogling Lee Strasberg's collection of Russian books and his theatrical memorabilia. Anna always ordered an enormous cake exquisitely decorated with an elaborate message: "Queen of the Theatre, Queen of Our Hearts"; "To Our Living Legend Lucille Lortel for Her Genius and Her Humanity." And the object of the party sat through it all, smiling and nodding, greeting friends and holding court. When the evening was over, she would take the entire cake home, usually to store it in her freezer.

With the return of stability gradually came renewed enthusiasm for bringing plays from the White Barn to New York. In 1981 Vincent Curcio had brought Lucille Casey Kurtii's *Catholic School Girls*, a well-crafted, atmospheric satire of Catholic school life in the 1960s. Lucille liked it, Burry Fredrik directed it at the White Barn, and in March 1982, Lortel, Fredrik, Haila Stoddard, and an investor named Mortimer Levitt produced it, inaugurating the Douglas Fairbanks Theatre on West 42nd Street. "Lucille had an uncanny sense of what was good in the theatre," said Fredrik. But Lucille also had a stubborn streak that ignored warnings of commercial failure. "We were the third Catholic play that year," Fredrik remembered.

"The problem we had," said Curcio, "was that Christopher Durang's *Sister Mary Ignatius Explains It All for You* had already happened. *Catholic School Girls* became the also-ran." To drum up business, Lortel and Stoddard took to the radio talk-show circuit the day the reviews came out, even though Lucille was nervous and had difficulty being spontaneous during such interviews; she usually brought pre-written comments with her on easy-to-read cards, a copy of Markland Taylor's history of the White Barn or a colleague who could back her up. Despite her efforts, *Catholic School Girls* closed after fifteen previews and thirty performances.

But with long-term rentals like *Cloud 9* and, in 1984, Wendy Wasserstein's *Isn't It Romantic,* Lucille had little opportunity to transfer from the White Barn anyway. She concentrated instead on solidifying her professional reputation, on making financial contributions, and the future of her theatres.

Following the advice of her lawyers, in 1980 she had established the not-for-profit Lucille Lortel Foundation, which was intended to support playwrights, directors, actors and designers; the arts in general; theatrical productions in particular; public interest in the arts, specifically drama; and an institution of learning for the theatre.

But the Foundation left unanswered the question of what would happen to Lucille's theatres after her death. Deeply worried on that score, she explored leaving them to several established, not-for-profit theatres, among them Circle Repertory Company, or Circle Rep as it was called. Founded in 1969 by Marshall W. Mason, Robert Thirkield, Tanya Berezin, and Lanford Wilson, Circle Rep defined its mission as the rediscovery of "lyric realism" in the American theatre, a style embodied in Wilson's plays. Largely because of his dramas—plays such as *Hot l Baltimore, 5th of July* and *Talley's Folly*—and fine acting, the company's reputation had climbed. Mason was artistic director.

Sprecher, who had a nose for sycophancy, believed that Mason was "working" Lucille. By Mason's account, he was flattered that Lucille introduced him in public as "my favorite director" and he claimed that "our friendship was genuine, with no strings attached. I admired her for all the things she had done in the theatre, and she admired me. We loved each other. I think she trusted me absolutely."

Undoubtedly she realized that Circle Rep was "working" her, as Sprecher put it; she may have liked flattery, but she usually recognized it. Still, she genuinely seemed to appreciate Mason and she responded to the plays Circle Rep produced. According to Mason, "she loved Lanford's work." When a professional fund-raiser named Charles D. Webb became Circle Rep's board chairman in the late seventies, someone told him that Lucille usually gave the theatre $25,000 a year, and he set out for the Sherry-Netherland to meet her.

The result, as Webb described it years later, was a friendship and Lucille's increasing belief that she should leave her theatres to Circle Rep, a possibility that some at Circle Rep thought she was dangling before other theatres as well. "I kept very close to her," said Webb, who sincerely believed in his mission. He owned a home in Florida about forty miles from the Pritikin Institute, where Lucille had taken to enrolling herself for a week of dieting. Webb would drive over, and they would go for walks on the beach at night.

Circle Rep asked Lucille to join its board in the spring of 1981, and she agreed. With a fund-raiser's instinct for pursuing his cause, Webb wrote Lucille on June 25, "The two dominant forces in Off-Broadway Theater in Greenwich Village have been Lucille Lortel/Theater de Lys and the Circle Rep. The possibility of an arrangement which would combine them into a lasting institution is, in my opinion, the best of marriages."

Cugat died on July 13, in the same Connecticut nursing home where Ruth had spent her last years. His death heightened Lucille's anxiety about her estate and that very day she wrote her accountant and advisor Michael Hecht, "I feel I should put my house in order." She added, "I do feel that the present people that are with me now would not answer the purpose as much as an organization like the Circle Repertory Theatre [*sic*].Their [*sic*] not a group that could work together and too much ego is involved with it." She enclosed a copy of a letter that she was thinking of sending to Circle Rep's board president, Porter Van Zandt, in which she had written, "I do feel that the Circle Repertory Theatre is the best one I would like to leave the White Barn property to. Your aims seem to fit into the same category as I do at the White Barn Theatre."

Most likely Hecht counseled against sending that badly phrased letter to Van Zandt, for on July 28 Charles Webb responded to her "request" for "some ideas which would suggest how we might cooperate in guaranteeing the continuance of our commonly shared aspirations and goals in the theater." In a lengthy letter, Webb outlined seven points, notably that Circle Rep would operate the Theater de Lys as the Lucille Lortel Theatre; operate the White Barn during the summer season; and use the White Barn the rest of the year as a center for playwright's conferences, residencies and workshops. To soothe Lucille's desire that systems be in place to memorialize her, Webb proposed a Lucille Lortel Award; an ongoing exhibit in the lobby of the Lucille Lortel Theatre, as well as commemorative pages in every program; an annual gala; and a Lucille Lortel Gallery at the White Barn. It was not clear from Webb's outline when all of this would start.

Lucille passed Webb's letter on to her lawyers, and meetings followed. One can practically feel the elation rising from the pages of Webb's correspondence as Lucille and Circle Rep seemed near an agreement. Lucille attended a board meeting in November and pledged $5,000, and she apparently appeared at play-readings and other Circle Rep events. During the summer of 1982 Marshall Mason directed a workshop of a new Lanford Wilson play, *Angels Fall*, at the White Barn, and Lucille put up $75,000 to help take the play to Broadway in January 1983.

But whether uncertain about her own decision, or responding to some coolness on the part of her lawyers, she did not sign a memorandum regarding the dispersal of her property to Circle Rep until June 30, 1983. The memorandum noted that she intended to leave her theatres to the Lucille Lortel Foundation and asked that the Foundation lease both theatres to Circle Repertory Company "free of basic rent" and with "annual grants ... to assist the Company." Webb's seven-point letter was attached, "which sets forth proposals by the Company which have induced me to make the provisions in my last will and testament." For the time being, she had arrived at a resolution.

While Lucille was finalizing arrangements with Circle Rep, Jack Garfein, artistic director of the Harold Clurman Theatre, asked her for money, which she gave, to coproduce three brief plays by Samuel Beckett—*Ohio Impromptu, Catastrophe* and *What Where*—all directed by Alan Schneider. They opened on June 15, 1983.

Sprecher, employing an esteemed Yiddish expression for a sponger, called Garfein "a schnorrer of world-class proportions." To Lucille the project sounded valuable artistically, and she had always supported the European absurdist playwrights. Garfein probably discerned that Lucille would relish the opportunity to associate her name with Beckett and he hinted that she might meet the renowned Irish dramatist. "Garfein took advantage of Lucille at every opportunity," said Sprecher. " 'Money. Give us money. We'll do this, we'll do that.' " Rewarded with ecstatic reviews—the production played 344 performances and eventually went to the Edinburgh Festival—Garfein soon asked Lucille to support another trio of Beckett plays in February 1984: *Enough, Footfalls* and *Rockaby*. These starred British actress Billie Whitelaw, an extraordinary Beckett interpreter. Whitelaw, too, was astounded by Garfein's nerve. In her memoir *Billie Whitelaw . . . Who He?* she recounts arriving in New York to discover that the new Samuel Beckett Theatre on West 42nd Street, where Garfein had told her she was to perform, was still under construction: no dressing room, no bathroom and barely an auditorium (amazingly, the theatre was more or less ready for opening night). Lucille, by Sprecher's estimate, put up at least $75,000 all together. And she never met Samuel Beckett.

At the opening night of the first round of Beckett plays, in 1983, Albert Poland saw Lucille standing on the sidewalk outside the theatre and he approached her with an enticing idea.

It all started, he recalled, when he was general manager for *Little Shop of Horrors*, which had won the New York Drama Critics Circle Award for Best Musical that year. At the awards party, Poland remembered, "I had had a drink or two, and Michael Feingold was there from the *Village Voice*, and I said, 'One thing's for sure, we'll never win an Obie, because we're not in a basement, more than three people have seen us and nobody at the *Voice* has slept with anyone involved in the show.' " Tired of what he and others believed was the Obie Awards' preference for nonprofit theatre, Poland thought there should be an award for Off Broadway's commercial productions. " 'You know what,' I told Feingold, 'We'll start our own award.' And the minute I said that, I thought: Lucille." The next day, at a meeting of the League of Off-Broadway Theatres and Producers, Poland suggested awards called "The Lucys." And on June 15, 1983, he walked over to Lucille at the Beckett plays and said, "Lucille, what would you think of establishing some new awards for Off Broadway in your name?" "How much would it cost?" she asked.

They would not be called "The Lucys"—Lucille hated that nickname. They would be called the Lucille Lortel Awards, and in 1986 she herself would select and present the first one for Lincoln Center Theater's *Woza Afrika!* Festival.

The apartment at the Sherry-Netherland had always felt more Lucille's than Lou's. During the 1980s it became a shrine to her and her life in the theatre.

One entered the apartment through a foyer lined with colorful posters of plays Lucille had produced and black-and-white photographs of their stars. Turning left one stepped into the living room, and Lucille was everywhere. Portraits blanketed the walls and filled the tops of tables, an easel, the top of the grand piano. Over a curved couch against the left wall, dominating the other likenesses, was Ruth's oil portrait of Lucille wearing a diaphanous white gown. Other, smaller portraits surrounded it, as though radiating from that central dark-haired beauty. Where there were no portraits and no photographs, there were honorary plaques, award certificates and congratulatory letters. A bathroom off the study that had once been Lou's bedroom displayed wall-to-wall theatrical posters of Lucille's productions.

There were also mementos of her personal life: a few of Ruth's landscapes, several of Cugat's paintings, Sidney Kingsley's self-portrait as an Adonis of a young man and his bronze sculpture of a dancing figure, a framed sheet of the first three bars of "O give me something to remember you by" in Arthur Schwartz's own hand. Lucille spoofed her self-importance with touches of humor, too. Numerous miniature pillows embroidered with phrases like "The Queen is out" and "It's not easy being a Queen"—presents from friends—decorated one small couch.

But the overall effect was of someone memorializing herself, encircling herself with visual and verbal testimonies to her career. Insecure about her standing in the profession, she tried to ensure that she be honored and remembered, at home and in the theatre community.

In a sense the memorializing had begun when Lucille started collecting photographs of herself with visiting celebrities at the White Barn. But the public memorializing really began in 1980, the year which marked a quarter of a century since Lou had bought the Theatre de Lys as an anniversary present. As with her grand finale to the ANTA Matinee Series, Lucille believed a celebration was in order. Thus it was that on Monday, September 29, "Broadway Salutes Off-Broadway" took place at what, beginning that night, would be called Lucille Lortel's Theatre de Lys. The event, produced by Jean Dalrymple, coordinated by a publicist and friend of Lucille's named Raymond R. Rebhann and directed by Haila Stoddard, was technically a benefit for the Actors' Fund of America. But it was organized so that the theatre community could honor Lucille, who underwrote the evening for $60,000. Nedda Harrigan Logan, the tall, gracious president of the Actors' Fund, told the audience, "We're paying tribute to one woman. More than anyone else, she stands for Off Broadway. Without her, Off Broadway could not have attained the importance and prestige it now enjoys."

Fourteen months later, at another Actors' Fund benefit and during *Cloud 9*'s run, Lucille changed her theatre's name to the Lucille Lortel. Needless to say, the producers of *Cloud 9* were not happy about the expense of reprinting programs and advertising that already read "Lucille Lortel's Theatre de Lys." Sprecher recalled Michel Stuart saying, "You can't do that. We're in the middle of a run." But Sprecher, who understood Lucille by now, said, "Michel, I think we're changing the name of the theatre." Stuart said, "Well, I'm calling my lawyer." "Call anybody you like," Sprecher said.

Actually first Stuart wrote Lucille a gentlemanly letter, cogently stating his objections and flattering her that the name Lucille Lortel's Theatre de Lys combined two great theatrical traditions. It did not work. As Sprecher remembered it, "Lucille got on the phone with her theatrical attorneys at Cohn, Glickstein and Lurie, and Sidney Cohn said, 'Lucille, you change the name of your theatre to anything you like.' She hung up the phone and said, 'Ben, we're changing the name.' I said, 'Okay. Done.'" Sprecher arranged a meeting with *Cloud 9*'s producers, brought a lawyer to the meeting and never heard anymore about it. On November 16, 1981, the theatre that William de Lys had built on Christopher Street officially became the Lucille Lortel Theatre. The producers of *Cloud 9* changed their advertising.

Celebrations of Lucille seemed to be everywhere—often spontaneous, just as often hand-in-hand with her philanthropy. She was an active board member of the Friends of the Theatre and Music Collection of the Museum of the City of New York; L. Arnold Weissberger, a noted theatrical attorney who was the board's chairman and Lucille's friend, suggested the establishment of a Lucille Lortel Archival Collection at the Museum. She gave $25,000 for the purpose, only to discover that the Museum had needed the money for something else and used it. So in 1980 she contributed another $25,000, and in April 1981, the Lucille Lortel Theatre Gallery at the Museum of the City of New York opened with the exhibition "The Queen of Off-Broadway," curated by the theatre collection's director, Dr. Mary C. Henderson.

But philanthropy had its limits. Lucille hated for anyone to take her donations for granted. In 1982 the Museum's director, Joseph Veach Noble, asked Lucille for money to keep the Gallery's exhibits in top condition, apparently assuming on the basis of a previous conversation that money would be forthcoming regularly. Lucille responded in an irate letter, "I have no recollection . . . of agreeing to a grant of $25,000 on an annual basis. I do, however, recall saying that if the gallery in the Minskoff Building were named after me, I would be inclined to give a larger contribution for that." Nevertheless she donated another $25,000.

In March 1982 Lucille received the Theatre Hall of Fame Arnold Weissberger Award, and that year John Willis, the longtime editor of *Theatre World*, dedicated the thirty-eighth volume to her. The Lucille Lortel Gallery and Museum opened at Cranbury Farm on July 12, and as part of that exhibit, Lucille proudly screened *The Man Who Laughed Last*. The original nitrate film had been located at the Library of Congress, which made a print for Lucille and also found a copy of the script; the sound disc was long gone, a new soundtrack was made using the filmscript. Anna Strasberg and others encouraged Lucille to find a publicist to take the story of her life and career to the media, and Lucille conceived the idea of a documentary film.

Titled *The Queen of Off-Broadway*, it was written by Evangeline Morphos, who at the time headed the Drama Department at New York University's Tisch School of the Arts; Harry Kafka produced, directed and edited it. The film was nearly an hour of truth, exaggeration and heartfelt testimonies to Lucille's greatness from playwrights and colleagues who appeared on camera.

Lucille used the film as her calling card. After its initial viewing on the stormy evening of March 29, 1984, in the MGM screening room on Sixth Avenue, she showed it at every opportunity. April 1984 saw it screened at the British Academy of Film and Television Artists, during a seven-day tour of British theatre billed as Lucille Lortel's Theatre World, on which she traveled as a theatre expert and star. Returning April 9 on the *Queen Elizabeth II,* she appeared as a guest lecturer, showing the film one day and taking questions about it the next, a format she repeated during two subsequent crossings. Well into the 1990s *The Queen of Off-Broadway* made an appearance at benefits, award ceremonies, museums, libraries, and universities. Whatever the film's merits, for Lucille, who felt uneasy talking to groups of people and making impromptu comments, it was an ingenious tool. After a screening, she could sit on stage with someone like Anna Strasberg or Vincent Curcio by her side, and they would repeat questions if she could not hear, prompt her or even answer questions themselves.

She was also occupied with finding a repository for the vast number of papers and photographs documenting her theatres' existence. Executives at the Museum of the City of New York were failing to treat her as she wished, so she and Mary Henderson, to whom Lucille looked now for archival advice, began seeking another permanent location. Ralph Sheffer, a well-to-do businessman who lived in Westport, was leading a capital campaign to build a new Westport Public Library. He approached Lucille for money and in 1983 she pledged $300,000 with the understanding that a portion of the building be a resting place for her collection. On the balmy evening of September 1, 1988, the collection's arrival was marked by a reception at which the Library's trustees surprised Lucille with a lithograph portrait by the famous caricaturist Al Hirshfeld. Few gifts could have pleased her more.

If one had asked Lucille during the 1980s which honor she liked the best, she probably would have answered, "The one I'm getting at the moment, darling." But no doubt she was proudest of the First Annual Lee Strasberg Lifetime Achievement in Theatre Award.

Lee, Anna Strasberg said, always wanted Lucille to receive the first one. On October 11, 1984, actress Sophia Loren and opera star Placido Domingo announced the award's establishment and its first recipient. Lucille accepted it on April 1, 1985, toward the end of a gala celebrating thirty years of what was now the Lucille Lortel Theatre.

Her friends were accustomed to being invited to exalt Lucille, and the theme for this latest jamboree was to the point: "The Stars Salute the Queen of Off-Broadway." Backed by Colin Romoff on the piano and by bass, guitar and drums, a full-voiced John Cullum sang Burton Lane and Alan Jay Lerner's stirring "On a clear day (you can see forever)." Jo Sullivan Loesser, dashing in a white and black gown, imitated a stern Lotte Lenya telling her how to sing Polly Peachum thirty years earlier in *The Threepenny Opera*. With delicious understatement, George Irving performed a salacious number from the failed 1976 musical *So Long, 174th Street*, and flame-haired Vivian Blaine sniffled delightfully through "Adelaide's Lament" from *Guys and Dolls*. Right before intermission, June Havoc called members of the audience onto the stage for a conga line.

Lucille watched the performances and smiled and laughed with the rest. During the evening's second half, when Joseph Papp was master of ceremonies, she felt gratified once again to watch *The Queen of Off-Broadway* and hear congratulatory missives from absent celebrities. The A-list of performers and presenters had been scoured by Jean Dalrymple, as producer, and Robert M. "Bobby" Zarem, whom Lucille had hired to handle publicity, when they planned the gala. Zarem, who found Lucille a trial, wrote her testily, "I am not in a position to ask Mikhail Baryshnikov, Gregory Hines or the like to perform." But Lucille could hardly have been disappointed when the esteemed television newsman Walter Cronkite read a letter from Governor Mario M. Cuomo and one from President Ronald Reagan, who wrote, "Nancy joins me in wishing you continued success and happiness."

Finally James Earl Jones walked on to present her with the award, which was a mask of Lee Strasberg's face and hands on a wooden base, where a brass plaque was engraved with his words, "We came into the theatre on the wings of a dream." Lucille felt fearful about going on stage to speak, but she looked exquisite. Her hair, dyed chestnut that day and impeccably arranged in a French twist, glinted under the stage lights. She wore a black Stavropolous gown with a ruffled, plunging neckline accented by a diamond brooch and a diamond necklace. A bouquet of flowers nestled in the bend of her right arm made for an awkward moment when she accepted the award from Jones with her left hand. But she gracefully thanked him for coming down from New Haven, where he was in rehearsal. She asked Anna Strasberg and "Lee's best friend" Sidney Kingsley to join her on stage, and Kingsley saluted Lee Strasberg as well as Lucille. "I feel that this theatre, tonight, is filled with Lee's starlight, and this fragment of Lee's starlight is appropriately given to Lucille, who is not only honored by it, but who honors it."

Anna and Kingsley returned to their seats, which left Lucille momentarily alone and uncertain what to do next. But Papp and Jones went to her side. The orchestra swung into "O give me something to remember you by," and Papp, a cabaret performer on occasion, chimed in and encouraged Lucille to sing a few bars, which she did, in a thin voice and off-key but game anyway. With that trio on stage, the event ended and guests were ferried across town for supper at The Players, the famous and at that time all-male theatrical club on Gramercy Park.

The following month, Kingsley wrote Lucille the sort of note she cherished, "If Lee were present that night, he would have insisted upon giving the award to you personally because he knew, loved and admired your lifetime record."

Lucille accumulated so many awards and honors that only Sandy Starr could keep track of them. In May 1985, the University of Bridgeport dubbed her an honorary Doctor of Fine Arts, a degree that would have overjoyed her long-ago teachers at the Clark School for Concentration. She was saluted in November by The Players as "The First Lady of Off-Broadway." The Women's Project, an Off-Broadway company, held a reception at the American Place Theatre on March 24, 1986, to recognize the exceptional achievements of six women: actress Colleen Dewhurst, playwright María Irene Fornés, tennis champion Billie Jean King, Ruth Mayleas of the Ford Foundation, Rachel Robinson, widow of baseball player Jackie Robinson, and Lucille. Accepting her award, Lucille said, "This is the first time I've received an award with other people." To her surprise, the audience roared.

Behind the laughter was affection but also perplexity about Lucille's obsessive need for recognition. "I was general manager for *As Is* on Broadway," said Albert Poland, "and she asked me if I would take her to the Drama Desk Awards, which were at the Rainbow Room. I loved the idea, and we had a lovely time. Until it came time for the award for best play. The playwright, William M. Hoffman, rightfully went up to receive it, and she just fell into the abyss. 'Why didn't they ask me to come up to receive it?' We got on the elevator, and she continued to rant and rave, and as we got out of the car, I said, 'You know, Lucille, this aspect of you hurts me. It's disappointing. You are a bigger person than to collapse like a house of cards if you are not constantly acknowledged.' It was something that engaged my sympathy more than my scorn. But when you sat through those four-hour evenings…"

"She did not realize that she had a name, too," said Mimi Bochco. Visiting New York one time from California, Bochco accompanied Lucille to a reception for the French ambassador. Going through the receiving line, Lucille began handing out flyers for her current play. "I pulled her away," said Bochco, "and I said, 'Lucille, darling, it's a receiving line. You don't have to do that. You don't have to prove who you are. Everyone knows who you are.' She said, 'Do I do that?' I said, 'Yes. You do.' She said, 'I feel terrible. That's why I love you, darling, because you tell me the truth.' A lady comes over and says, 'Lucille, you look wonderful, I haven't seen you in some time,' and Lucille says, 'By the way . . .' and starts taking flyers out of her pocketbook. I knew then that it was built in."

"Lucille was terribly insecure that she wouldn't be taken seriously," said Ben Sprecher. "Her need was very personal."

More personal than many realized. At The Players salute in 1985, she got up at the end of the evening and gave an unusually long and emotional thank-you, which was recorded by a member of the audience. "I just can't tell you how important the theatre means to me," she said. "I lost my parents . . . , my husband in '71, my sister followed shortly after that. My brothers. And if it weren't for the theatre, I just don't know what I would have done. I—the theatre became my family, and—" her voice broke so that she had to stop—"and the actors and playwrights my children, and thank God for the living theatre, and thank you all for coming here to share this salute with me."

Ironically for someone who made her reputation Off Broadway, she always wanted Broadway's highest honor, the American Theatre Wing's Antoinette Perry Award, or Tony. As a producer of a Tony-nominated best play or musical, she came close: *Angels Fall, As Is,* the revival of *Blood Knot, Sarafina!* and *A Walk in the Woods.* She particularly yearned for a Special Award that the nominating committee sometimes gave to exceptional people who fit no category, like caricaturist Al Hirshfeld, or the award given on the recommendation of the American Theatre Critics Association (ATCA) to an outstanding regional theatre.

Friends campaigned for her. When gossip columnist Liz Smith announced in May 1981 that the Tony awards would salute women in the theatre, publicist Raymond R. Rebhann wrote to Alexander Cohen and his wife Hildy Parks, who were producing the Awards, and asked, "Is there any one more deserving than Lucille Lortel? . . . If she could be included some how in the Tony Award Program it would be an exciting climax to a year of tribute." Cohen, in fact, did mention Lucille during the event. But no award was forthcoming.

Richard Coe of the *Washington Post* and Mary Henderson, who for a time was on the Tony nominating committee, tried to secure this prize for their friend. In an October 13, 1981 letter to Coe, Lucille wrote that she had had lunch with Isabelle Stevenson, president of the American Theatre Wing, and Stevenson "felt that I should be getting a Tony Award as a private person for my contribution to the theatre." Coe investigated from the American Theatre Critics angle, but Henry Hewes, ATCA's executive secretary, said the White Barn was not eligible.

Not one to give up, four years later, in January 1985, Lucille put the request straightforwardly to Stevenson in a letter. "Since I've had two shows on Broadway this year, AS IS and BLOOD KNOT, feel this is probably the last chance for me to get a special. How about it? It's the one award I'd really like to have before my light goes out." Again the word was no. Richard Barr, president of the League of New York Theatres and Producers and administrator of the Tony Committee, wrote Mary Henderson on April 8, "All of us are fully appreciative of Lucille's enormous contributions to the theatre but the Committee did not approve the recommendation as being consistent with the requirements of this award." Stevenson, who possibly had her own issues, said bluntly years later, "I guess she wasn't that much of a legend to be given a special honor, like Robert Whitehead or Julie Harris. Somehow or other she got lost in that group."

Said Sprecher: "I think the theatre community was a little jealous that, given how hard it is to create a nonprofit theatre funded by grants and federal money, Lucille just was doing it. There was a subtle jealousy that permeated the professional community and kind of pooh-poohed what Lucille was doing—that it was important to Lucille but it really wasn't all that important."

She acquired honors, but she also gave. As Lou had intended, she became in her own way a philanthropic force.

Proceeding slowly at first, she contributed where those closest to her had given. When Mayo died in 1976, he had been researching the music of children in the Czechoslovakian concentration camp Theresienstadt and preparing a concert; he intended that the proceeds go to Israel's Ben-Gurion University of the Negev. Lucille set up a perpetual scholarship at the University in his name and in 1984 flew to Israel with Mimi Bochco to unveil a plaque in her brother's honor.

The year after Mayo died, she sponsored a memorial concert by the Senior Citizens Orchestra at Carnegie Hall and every year thereafter donated funds for a spring concert and reception. In 1979 she also established the annual Waldo Mayo Memorial Violin Competition, and the youthful winner received $1,000 and the chance to play at Carnegie Hall with the senior musicians.

During the 1980s it must have seemed to Lucille that requests for donations arrived by the truckload. At some point she gave money to almost every not-for-profit theatre of worth: Playwrights Horizons, Manhattan Theatre Club, the Negro Ensemble Company, the New York Shakespeare Festival—the list went on. Right behind requests for money came invitations to join boards of directors. She often accepted, although she rarely attended meetings. She knew that she was there to write an annual check, buy a table at the yearly fund-raiser and give the development department her rich friends' names and addresses. If she enjoyed the blandishment, she had few illusions that it was a seduction. "She would call me," said Anna Strasberg, "and she'd say, 'I have to go to lunch. So-and-so asked me to lunch.' I would say, 'Well, that's nice.' 'Darling, they're going to ask me for money.' I'd say, 'You know and you're still going?' 'Yes,' she would say, 'why not? I'll get lunch.' "

She selected the people and institutions to which she wished to contribute carefully. Lawyers and accountants advised her on how to make the donations, but she decided who would receive them. She had fun doing it. She gave substantially to the medical institutes and departments of her personal physician, Dr. Theodore Tyberg, and her eye surgeon, Jackson Coleman. Sometimes she gave personal gifts of money to Dr.

Tyberg's family as well. But mostly she contributed to theatre organizations: the American Theatre Wing, which she had supported since the Second World War; the National Theatre of the Deaf; the Eugene O'Neill Memorial Theatre Center, which she and Lou had endorsed when George C. White founded it in 1964.

Since the 1960s, she had been giving to the Actors' Fund, but she had never been to Englewood, New Jersey, to see the Actors' Fund Home, a long-term care facility for people in the business. One day in January 1982, Wallace Monroe, the Fund's director of public relations, sent a limousine to bring Lucille and the singer Frances Koll to the Home, where the tall, red-headed Koll was to perform that afternoon for the residents. "After luncheon," Koll recalled, "Wally took us around to see the accommodations. 'When can I move in?' Lucille said. 'This looks great.' Wally said, 'Lucille, you have too much money. But we would love a donation.' "

For years afterward the Fund's president Nedda Logan gently pursued Lucille for a sizable gift, inviting her to the home's convivial Christmas party and suggesting at one point that Lucille underwrite the cost of a lounge in a new building going up at the Englewood site. Lucille responded in December 1986 that "in my will (as I will be richer when I am no longer here than I am now as all my property, my apartment and everything will be sold and given to the Lucille Lortel Foundation) I have stipulated that the Actors' Fund will receive an equivalent of more than the required amount." But Logan persisted, writing in September 1987, "A beautiful little theater is under construction at the Home. It's bound to be a place of much joy where our guests can entertain and be entertained. We would like to memorialize it in your name, Lucille."

She could not have hit on a better item for Lucille to support. That December Lucille saw the room for the proposed theatre with Vincent Curcio and the Fund's director of development, Joseph P. Benincasa, and soon after she pledged $100,000. The Fund sent a car on April 5, 1988 to bring her to the Home for a luncheon and the formal dedication, at which Alexander Cohen spoke and Lucille was photographed with Helen Hayes. The "theatre" was really an all-purpose room with a low, shallow platform along one wall, but there was a plaque which read "Lucille Lortel Theatre." This was the sort of contribution she liked to make, one that brought tangible benefits and could also be visibly identified as having been provided by her, whether with a plaque, a program note or, best of all, a room named after her.

Just as she gravitated toward plays which were unusual and put her ahead of the pack artistically, so in her giving she often elected to support an item that stamped her as an innovative philanthropist. Jane M. Gulong, the director of development at the New York Shakespeare Festival, asked Lucille in 1984 if she would consider helping the Festival install infrared listening systems, the first such systems at an Off-Broadway theatre. That December Lucille sent checks for a total of $24,850 and a note: "As soon as you have the system in place, please let me know as I might like to put it into the Lucille Lortel Theatre, as well." Subsequently she provided money for infrared systems in the Roundabout Theatre and the Vivian Beaumont Theater at Lincoln Center, prompting Bernard Gersten, Lincoln Center Theater's executive producer, to thank her "in the name of the literally thousands of theatergoers who, during the next number of years, will hear the spoken words at the Beaumont as they perhaps never have before."

As a philanthropist, Lucille had unspoken rules for how she wanted to be approached. She liked being feted and to hear that her contribution would be unique and of long-lasting benefit. She liked to receive roses from presidents of universities and to feel that she was the most important donor an institution had ever encountered. Despite some grumbling, she usually could be good-humored when people beat a path to her door, hat in hand. An old friend, writer Max Wilk, asked her to attend a Lincoln Center Theater benefit in May 1987, which of course meant laying out money. Her response began with a summary of how much she had given the company in the past and then she jokingly explained why she did not want to give anymore in the present:

> And, I'm really tired of going to affairs and seeing a bunch of artists perform that I've seen over and over again.
>
> And, I have no desire to sit with a couple of yentas who want to dance with my date because they won't spend the money to take one.
>
> And, I am also tired of inviting the same escorts over and over again. Unless you can get me someone as charming and delightful as yourself, I'd rather not go.

But finally she agreed. "If you feel I haven't done enough for Lincoln Center I'll give you what you want."

In some respect the way she wished to be treated was so obvious that it was surprising when an organization tripped up, as had the Museum of the City of New York in the 1980s and as New Dramatists would do in December 1991. Isobel Robins Konecky, president of New Dramatists' board of directors, wrote first asking Lucille to serve as honorary chair for their 1992 luncheon and in the next sentence, "As honorary chairman we ask that you contribute $10,000 towards the support of New Dramatists."

"If there's anything that riles me or gets me upset," Lucille shot back, "it is someone offering me an honor and then telling me how much I have to pay for it....I've never asked to be honored because I love what I do in theatre. But, if I am honored, I do not like to feel I'm being honored because of the financial support I give my love of theatre. It should be for what I represent and my life's work in the theatre." Profuse apologies followed from both Konecky and the director of development, but Lucille did not serve as honorary chair.

She could also change her mind where gifts were concerned, as she did in April 1986 about her bequest to Circle Repertory Company.

Perhaps Circle Rep had ignored Lucille's need to be thanked and praised. Just as likely she had begun to feel uneasy about Circle Rep's leadership and financial stability. Over the years the company had racked up a sizable deficit, and although tighter management and the success of *As Is* in 1985 had whittled away at it, the deficit began to rise again. Board member Charles Webb, citing artistic plans that he thought were impractical, resigned. Like other philanthropists, Lucille never felt comfortable supporting organizations that could not manage their fiscal affairs.

But most important, around 1985 Marshall Mason had decided to resign as artistic director. In recent years his tenure had been expensive for Circle Rep, and since he had always wanted to direct movies and was now forty-five-years old, he decided to move to Los Angeles and try. His departure probably alarmed Lucille, who, he believed, "liked me a lot better than she liked Circle Rep."

After meeting with her accountant Michael Hecht and her investment counselor George Shaskan, Jr., on April 28, 1986, Lucille signed a memorandum canceling the June 30, 1983, letter in which she had instructed the Lucille Lortel Foundation to lease her theatres to Circle Rep after her death. She did not tell Mason or Circle Rep about her change of heart. Webb, who was off the board by that time anyway, never knew. As late as 1988, Ciro A.Gamboni, a lawyer who at one point was also Circle Rep's board chairman, was still assuming in correspondence that the bequest was in place. "I did not know until after her death, in 1999," said Gamboni, "when I sent the original document to her accountant, and he called back and said it had been changed." In any case Circle Rep had folded in 1996, owing the Internal Revenue Service $700,000. The company became one of several possibilities that Lucille took up and discarded as, during the last two decades of her life, she tried to control the fate of her theatres.

. . .

During a window of opportunity when the Lortel was dark, in the fall of 1983, Lucille rented it to *The Lady and the Clarinet*, a comedy by Michael Christofer, who had won a Pulitzer Prize in 1977 for *The Shadow Box*. His new play involved a young woman, played by sexy Stockard Channing, who describes three love affairs to a clarinetist and reenacts them with the men in question. Elizabeth I. McCann and Nelle Nugent were the producers, Lucille was a name producer and she committed $100,000.

The production opened on November 28, and to Lucille's surprise, the majority of critics, including Frank Rich at the *New York Times*, dismissed the play. "If ever I thought I had a hit, it was this one!" she wrote Blanche Marvin after the notices came out. Nugent opined years later that the independent-minded central character was perhaps threatening to the mostly male New York reviewers. "Clearly we hit a nerve," she said. McCann and Nugent wanted to close the show, which was doing no business and racking up losses. "We did not want to run out the investment," Nugent said. Lucille did not want to put the actors out of work before Christmas. "I've never seen her so furious," said Anna Strasberg. As Sprecher remembered it, Lucille said, " 'Let's take it over.' And I said, 'Well, Lucille, what would you like me to do? Would you like me to negotiate this as a loan? Do you want me to take equity for this?' (which she didn't understand). She said, 'No, darling, I don't want it to close until after Christmas. Please don't make it complicated.' " Once more Lucille's personal value system overrode Sprecher's sense of good business. Spending an additional $37,000, she kept the show open until December 31.

"I recognized very early on," Sprecher said, "that sometimes Lucille did things that made no financial sense. That sometimes she just chose to make gifts to things and shows and there was no quid pro quo. It was just an act of charity, even though the recipient of it was really not in my mind a suitable charitable cause. But that was not up to me to determine.

So what I tried to do was create a situation where there was consideration—quid pro quo—and at least allow her to make the decision of not
requiring it." Whether Lucille realized it or even cared, Sprecher was
trying to keep her—and himself—from looking foolish.

Foolish or not, Lucille continued to back plays that stirred her, notably
William M. Hoffman's *As Is*, the first drama about people suffering the
ravages of AIDS to reach Broadway. Developed by Circle Rep in a playwriting and directing workshop, *As Is* was staged by Marshall Mason and
presented initially Off Broadway in March 1985 by Circle Rep and The
Glines, a company dedicated to plays about gay issues. Mason brought
in Lucille to help take it to Broadway, and according to him she was in-
strumental in getting the Shubert Organization to ante up a considerable investment. She herself put $150,000 into the production, which
opened at the Lyceum two months later on May 1.

In 1985, for the first time in years, Lucille discovered a play for which
she wanted to be the sole producer, *Gertrude Stein and a Companion*. "She
was fanatical about it," said Sprecher.

Written by the British dramatist Win Wells, who had died in 1984,
Gertrude Stein and a Companion was a memory play about the relationship
between the iconoclastic expatriate American writer and her lover Alice
B. Toklas; Wells took his title from Ernest Hemingway's description of
the couple in *A Moveable Feast*. Blanche Marvin, who was working for the
Cochrane Agency in London, had had Wells for a client and perhaps
had mentioned the play to Lucille as early as 1983. A letter dated September 8, 1983, had Marvin reminiscing about how she and Lucille sat
in the living room at the Sherry and, she supposed, each had privately
considered the similarities between their friendship and that of Stein and
Toklas, minus, one assumes, the sexual component.

The play's world premiere at the Edinburgh Festival in 1984 had won
it an award, and a successful run was produced in January 1985 at London's Bush Theatre with Miriam Margolys acting Stein and Natasha

Morgan playing Alice. By early May Marvin sent Lucille the press coverage, a photograph and a copy of the script, all of which, Lucille wrote back, "looks extremely interesting." Most likely she was drawn to the play's European ambience and to the dramatization of the women's lives; she liked biographical plays. The drama begins in 1946 right after Stein dies, and as her ghost visits Toklas, one sees the origin and growth of their companionship. The two actresses who play Gertrude and Alice also portray the artists who frequented their Paris home, so the play offers cameos of Hemingway and Pablo Picasso, as well as Gertrude's older brother, Leo.

Lucille decided to put it on at the White Barn that August, and she and Vincent Curcio set about casting. She dismissed the idea of importing Miriam Margolys, even though Margolys asserted that she held the performance rights and threatened a lawsuit. Curcio did not remember who thought of Jan Miner to play Stein, but it was he who suggested either Anne Meacham or Marian Seldes for Alice B. Toklas. Lucille chose Seldes.

When Lucille telephoned to ask her to play the role, Seldes thought Lucille had made a mistake. Physically Toklas had been slight—barely taller than the stocky, squat Gertrude—and Seldes was tall and willowy. "Lucille said she had this marvelous play, and I said, 'Oh, I know about that play.' And I did. But I was sure she meant Gertrude. I didn't think I was exactly right for Gertrude, but I was sure I could do. And she said, 'I think you should play Alice Toklas.' I didn't want to say, 'It's a mistake.' I accepted instantly, because I had read about the play. And it's a very odd thing, but it was one of the best parts I ever had in my life."

For a director and on Marvin's recommendation, Lucille hired Ira Cirker, a television and theatre director who had once staged two plays for the ANTA Matinee Series. "I read the script and loved it," Cirker said. "It had a lot of problems, but I loved the material. So I called Jan and I called Marian—reluctantly, because Marian was Lucille's suggestion and the reason I didn't think of her for the part was that she's so tall. In reality, Gertrude and Alice were midgets." To deal with the height disparity, as much as possible Cirker staged Miner on a platform in a large chair and Seldes on a lower platform in a tiny chair. "Marian played small," he said. "I swear to God. She's an incredible actress."

They rehearsed for ten days, mostly in the living room of Cirker's penthouse apartment in New York City. "They started on a sofa," Cirker remembered, "Marian sitting in one corner, and Jan in the other. And as we progressed in rehearsal they got closer and closer. Jan would bring in gifts for Marian, Marian would bring in gifts for Jan. They took care of each other." At the White Barn, Bob Phillips designed a set in which portraits and easels decorated the stage, along with louvered screens and the occasional antique desk and chair. Costume designers Susan Hum and Amanda J. Klein dressed the sizable Miner in a maroon velvet robe and put Seldes in black. The two actresses moved little but talked expressively. Alice and Gertrude recall surviving as Jews in Paris during World War II; easily jealous, Alice speaks bitingly of Hemingway; they speak lovingly to each other.

The Connecticut critics appreciated the writing but swooned over the acting, and Lucille returned to New York after Labor Day 1985 determined to bring the production to the Lortel. The show was capitalized at $175,000, and she set about raising money. In a letter to Lawrence A. Wien, a lawyer, entrepreneur and philanthropist with whom Lou had been friendly, she said, "This is the first time that I have felt strong enough to produce alone, as I did while Lou was still alive. I believe deeply in this play and to have a close friend of Lou by my side in this venture would mean a great deal to me." Wien invested $10,500 for a limited partnership, as did a few others. But Lucille, more accustomed to writing her own checks than enticing others to fill out theirs, ended up supplying $125,000 and later spent an additional $55,000 to keep the production afloat.

New York jitters somewhat chastened Connecticut enthusiasm. Blanche Marvin insisted on changes in the look of the production, an instance where Lucille's habit of keeping in the background may have allowed others to take control. In addition, as *Gertrude Stein and a Companion* approached its first preview on December 27, Seldes felt dissatisfied with her performance. "I felt absolutely free in Westport, and I thought that my performance, for whatever it was, was what I wanted it to be. The audience at Westport was so receptive. They got Alice's humor. What made Alice wonderful was her insightful humor." For New York, Seldes believed that Cirker tried to pull her performance down, make it smaller. Then, said Seldes, "as we got closer to the opening, they began to tell me, 'Oh, you should do what you did in Westport.'"

Cirker for his part was dismayed that they were going to open in January, a notoriously poor time of year to bring in a new show. Indeed several artists connected with the production felt that the marketing was not receiving Lucille's customary personal attention and that Sprecher, behind her back, was impeding the production.

Despite these qualms, the New York critics generally echoed the opinions of their Westport cousins. Most found Wells' play more an intriguing lecture than a drama. Most admired the acting. "Miner is all hearty assurance," wrote Douglas Watt on January 10 in the *Daily News*, "while Seldes, in a remarkable performance for this tall actress, is kittenishly wayward portraying the small Toklas." But other critics were less charitable in tone. Clive Barnes, who still wielded influence even at the second-class *New York Post*, wrote sarcastically that "we learn more about Stein...from one glance at Picasso's celebrated portrait." At the *New York Times* Mel Gussow wrote that the play was "largely a stilted colloquy between the two women" and "does not adequately characterize Miss Stein's art or her effect on others." That killed it.

Lucille strove to bring in audiences. She sent her friends the positive reviews and asked them "to talk it up." Tickets were discounted, flyers distributed to schools; the actresses did every interview the publicist Jeffrey Richards drummed up. As a publicity stunt, Richards even organized a séance after one performance, with psychics who vowed to reach Gertrude and Alice in the great beyond.

After fourteen previews and fifty-four performances, Lucille closed the show on February 23, 1986. At least she had arranged for the production at the White Barn to be videotaped for the performing arts library at Lincoln Center. She also put up $25,000 for a professional videotaping that Cirker directed, and she had the satisfaction of seeing the result cable-cast on Bravo and, as an executive producer, of receiving a New York Area Emmy Award from the National Academy of Television Arts and Sciences. Like many plays Lucille embraced, *Gertrude Stein and a Companion* found an audience outside of New York. For years she received royalties as the play was performed in regional theatres and around the world.

The day after the production closed, she and Sandy Starr picked Seldes up in a car and drove to the University of Bridgeport, where Lucille had arranged for the actress to give a lecture to the theatre students—two years ago she had donated $10,000 to establish the Lucille Lortel Distinguished Lecture Series. Back in New York later that day she sent Seldes a note, "Thank you for being 'Alice' for me..."

· · · CHAPTER 10 · · ·

A Walk on Broadway

O n the stage at the Yale Repertory Theatre in New Haven, two actors sat talking on a slatted outdoor bench. One, playing an American negotiator, looked serious and spoke intensely, while the other, playing a Soviet diplomat, smiled, gestured broadly and joked. Behind them, huge tree trunks rose into the flies, dwarfing the actors and suggesting that, whatever the men were discussing, they were, finally, only two small human beings attempting to untie the knots in an immense and complex world.

It was February 20, 1987, and Lucille, Ben Sprecher and Sandy Starr had driven up from New York to watch the opening night performance of Lee Blessing's new drama, *A Walk in the Woods*. Des McAnuff, the artistic director of the La Jolla Playhouse in California, was the director. The two actors were Kenneth Welsh and Josef Sommer.

The play had been inspired by the 1982 disarmament talks between the United States negotiator Paul H. Nitze and his Soviet counterpart Yuli A. Kvitsinsky. Transformed by Blessing into John Honeyman and Andrey Botvinnik, the men escape the pressures and publicity of the negotiating table in Geneva to stroll in a forest and possibly reach the basis for an agreement in private. Honeyman, who is new to the peace

277

process, is an ardent moralist. Botvinnik, who has seen peace conferences come and go, believes that change is impossible and is amused by the American's energy and persistence. Time goes by, the seasons change, and the men amble, sit, talk and get to know each other better, but disarmament remains elusive. If, as Blessing intimates, peace between nations is unattainable, at least two human beings can communicate and save themselves.

Lloyd Richards, who was artistic director of Yale Repertory Theatre and Dean of the Yale School of Drama, had invited Lucille as well as a number of other New York producers to the opening. But he knew that Lucille's relationship to Yale differed considerably from that of her colleagues. As far back as 1965, on the fortieth anniversary of its School of Drama, Yale University had honored her for her own forty years in theatre. In 1983 she had given $5,000 to Yale for the first Audrey Wood Scholarship; Wood, a stalwart, protective agent for numerous playwrights, including Tennessee Williams, had suffered a crippling stroke in 1981 and never worked again. To foster the work of new dramatists, in 1985 Lucille pledged $300,000 to Yale, and that year August Wilson's *Fences* became the first beneficiary.

Cunning and stubborn about supporting his favorite playwrights and transferring productions to New York, Lloyd Richards thought Lucille might like *A Walk in the Woods*. "It was her kind of thing," he said years later. "It wasn't directly commercial. It was intellectually interesting. I thought it was the sort of play she might be interested in."

She was more than interested. "Lucille loved the play," said Ben Sprecher, remembering her reaction on opening night. "She was fixated on it. It was one of those moments when someone was falling in love with a project."

Sprecher always wondered what might have been going on in Lucille's life that she was so open to Blessing's drama. Earlier that month she had returned from Tuscaloosa, Alabama; the University of Alabama's theatre department, run by her old colleague Stuart Vaughan, had staged Marcel Aymé's *Lucienne and the Butcher*, which she and Lou had seen in Paris in 1949 and Lou, unknown to his wife, had translated. One day Vincent Curcio discovered the script stuffed at the back of a kitchen cabinet in the office, and with Lucille's money behind the project, the play went to Tuscaloosa.

Perhaps some memory of Lou and their spring trips to Europe made her want to produce *A Walk in the Woods*, especially since she had no plan to go abroad that year. But the play also contained elements to which Lucille had always responded emotionally: characters with intriguing personal histories; stimulating human interaction; a humane message. "It is so rarely that I find a play that moves me as much as this one," Lucille would write in April to Lee Blessing's agent, Lois Berman.

Lucille's instincts were corroborated on March 4 when the *Variety* critic called it "an exhilarating play that could be said to be profoundly pessimistic if it weren't shot through with lashings of humanity and roaring good humor" and predicted that it would go "well beyond New Haven." Mel Gussow, reviewing for the *New York Times* on March 8, praised the writing, the directing and the acting. "Because of its compactness and its timeliness, 'A Walk in the Woods' should have an extended life in the theater." Perhaps people were reminded that only five months earlier, President Ronald Reagan and Soviet President Mikhail Gorbachev had met in Reykjavik, Iceland, to discuss reducing nuclear weapons. But the talks had fallen apart over the issue of the United States' space-based missile defense program, or Star Wars.

Initially Lucille tried to tempt somebody else into being the front-line producer, expecting that then, as was usually the case, she would put up money and coproduce. "She had never thought of herself at that point of being the motor," said Sprecher. "But we were sitting at the Sherry-

Netherland, and she would talk about the play—and she would obsess about things—and I said, 'Lucille, why don't *you* do it?' And at that moment she said, 'Well, why don't I do it?' "

Spurred by Sprecher's encouragement and by her immediate connection to the play, on February 24 she had written Lloyd Richards a letter that brims with excitement:

> I cannot get "A WALK IN THE WOODS" out of my mind. I'd like very much to do it.
>
> I told Jerry Schoenfeld and Jim Freydberg to go see it, and then I thought "What am I doing? This is one I would like to do myself."

The La Jolla Playhouse in California was planning a production of the drama during the summer, so that Blessing and Des McAnuff, La Jolla's artistic director, could continue working on the script. But Lucille assured Richards that her current resident at the Lortel, a musical called *Groucho*, would end its run around then. "I'd love to put [*A Walk in the Woods*] on at the Lucille Lortel. Then if it warrants, it can move to Broadway."

Lucille became so impatient waiting for Richards' answer that on March 2 she asked Sprecher to call Benjamin Mordecai, Yale Repertory Theatre's general manager, to confirm her excitement. Perhaps as a result of this call, Richards wrote her on March 2. But his reply was cool, considering that a well-known commercial producer with ample resources had just offered to put the play on in New York. "Dear Lucille," Richards wrote,

> Thank you for your note and for being haunted by *A Walk in the Woods*. I am delighted that you are interested in producing the project. Please know that this desire will be given serious attention when we evaluate the future for Lee's play.

Mordecai, too, wrote Lucille a letter on March 2, and it also seemed intended to put her off: "I believe you are aware that the play will be presented at the La Jolla Playhouse this summer....It is following the La Jolla production that other opportunities for the presentation of the play will be considered. Obviously, we will urge the playwright to consider your proposal most seriously."

"They were fishing," was Sprecher's opinion of the Yale reaction. "Looking for the best offer." What they really wanted, Lucille soon learned, was a producer who would take the play directly to Broadway, something that all of her instincts and experience told her would be a mistake. The play demanded an intimate house; most Broadway houses were huge. Broadway productions were expensive, and the audiences who could afford the tickets cared little about serious drama. She was not alone. When Robert G. Donnalley, Jr., learned that Lucille was casting about for a coproducer, he wrote her that "I think this would be a wonderful production for your theatre and if capitalized at $300,000 it would be quite successful. I wouldn't however have the same enthusiasm (or commitment) for a Broadway production."

By the beginning of April, no word had come from Yale, and Lucille felt that she really could not wait longer for an answer; she had a theatre to fill come September. She also wanted to formalize her relationship with the play as soon as possible, although Richards admitted years afterward that "there weren't a great many offers for it." On April 2 she wrote to Lois Berman to ask the agent, "How can you help me move forward on this?" That same day she wrote Richards:

> It is possible at this time for me to hold the Lortel Theatre available for the Fall production. From a practical standpoint it would be very helpful to start Off Broadway and then move to Broadway with the Play. However if you would prefer beginning directly on Broadway, so be it, and I will book the Lortel accordingly.

Either way I want to proceed with this Play with the understanding that the Yale Repertory Theatre will maintain artistic control of the production. Finally, I want you to know that it will be my intention to assign my share of any net profit back to the Yale Repertory Theatre, earmarked for the "Lucille Lortel Fund for New Drama at Yale" in order that you may hopefully present more than one show a year under the auspices of the fund.

"That clinched it," said Sprecher. "The money to Yale Rep. She basically said she was going to put up all the money, and all the profits would go to Yale Rep. Then Ben Mordecai and Lloyd Richards got on board right away."

Indeed when Richards finally wrote her a formal response on June 29, the tone of his letter was markedly warmer, almost unctuous:

I wanted to take this opportunity to formally respond to your most generous letter of April 2, 1987. Not only is Yale fortunate to have a benefactor of your stature, the American Theatre is truly blessed that you are the major patron of the art. Your proposal is wonderful, flattering and—in short—we accept."

As for the question of Broadway or Off Broadway, Richards made a verbal show of leaving that open. "After consultation with you, I will recommend the specific venue, Broadway or Off Broadway, for the production. I will accept that responsibility." Although Lucille's office would retain final management authority, she wanted Yale's active involvement, and Richards and Mordecai selected Emanuel "Manny" Azenberg to be the general manager. Lucille chose Jeffrey Richards to be in charge of press. Meg Simon and Fran Kumin, who had cast the Yale production, were retained for Broadway.

Early in the afternoon on Monday, July 20, Lucille, Vincent Curcio and Sandy Starr took a flight to San Diego and drove to La Jolla. On Tuesday evening, Lucille and Curcio went to see *A Walk in the Woods.* McAnuff had recast the play with Michael Constantine as Botvinnik and Lawrence Pressman playing John Honeyman. On Bill Clarke's new, technologically deluxe set, hydraulic tubes built into the trees sprouted buds, leaves fell—all to mark the changing seasons. The trees themselves looked stark and ram-rod straight, and white walls enveloped the set on three sides. "These trees were not trees," Curcio recounted sarcastically. "They were missiles in a missile silo, and every now and then you'd hear rumble rumble rumble. That was supposed to be the rumble of the nuclear bomb." McAnuff explained that the design concept was postmodern but Lucille was dubious. Although producing *A Walk in the Woods* was energizing her more than any project in years, she began to feel that some of the artists involved had a stronger sense of self-worth than good theatre.

Around the time that Lucille was visiting California, the British producer Duncan Weldon happened to be driving from San Diego to Los Angeles. Going through La Jolla, he noticed that a new drama was at the Playhouse. He stopped to see it, liked it and acquired a copy of the script. "I saw the play by mistake as it were," he quipped years later. He began inquiring about the London rights and considering possible actors. "I thought of Alec Guinness and Paul Scofield," he said. Returning to London, Weldon, "took it 'round to Alec. He said 'yes' within twenty-four hours."

Back on the East Coast, Lucille and Vincent Curcio met with Richards and Mordecai in Westport on Tuesday, August 18.

Perhaps the outcome of the talk would have been different if Sprecher, not Curcio, had joined Lucille. Neither man actually had any formal involvement in the production, but Sprecher was a tougher negotiator and more willing than Curcio to take control. Sprecher had just gone on vacation, however, and in any case Lucille tended to look to Curcio for advice on artistic issues. She used Sprecher for hammering out the deals.

The four sat in the green room at the White Barn, surrounded by forty years of photographs. As Curcio remembered it, "Lucille said she thought the play should be done Off Broadway, and Lloyd said 'no.' She said, 'Okay, but if it is going to be done on Broadway, it should be done with stars.' She mentioned that Sir Alec Guinness and Sir Peter Ustinov were reportedly both interested in the role of Botvinnik. If Guinness, one of the world's most esteemed actors, would agree to appear on Broadway, that would be an exceptional coup.

"Lloyd Richards wouldn't have it," Curcio recalled. "He said, 'No, the play is the star. We don't need a star.' " Curcio, who did most of the talking, remembered trying to persuade them that Guinness and Ustinov were great actors and could spell the difference between the production's success or failure. In Curcio's opinion, "[Richards and Mordecai] didn't want anything but Broadway, but they didn't want to play by the rules of how to do it on Broadway." But he was alone in this battle, or as he put it, "You'd get together with Lucille and make snowballs, and then she wouldn't throw them."

Perhaps Lucille gave way regarding Broadway because she, too, wanted it and believed that eventually she would persuade Richards to accept Guinness or a comparable name. When it came to discussing which Broadway theatre they wanted, Curcio remembered, "This is when Lucille went into action. They said they wanted to open it at the Lyceum Theatre, and she said, 'It's the wrong side of Broadway.' " In addition, she noted that a building was coming down next door, and they might have to cancel Wednesday matinees because of construction noise. Richards and Mordecai were thinking of opening in the late fall, but that, she pointed out, was when the new Stephen Sondheim musical

Into the Woods was bowing. "She took a *New York Times*," Curcio remembered, "and she opened it and, smacking one side of the paper and then the other, she said, 'So, up here it's going to say "Into the Woods," down here it's going to say "A Walk in the Woods." Now what is going to keep our production from being confused with the other production, particularly since that's a musical, Stephen Sondheim, and this is simply a play, without anybody in it that's any great name?' " The meeting was inconclusive, and Lucille wrote to Lois Berman two days later that she "Had a little talk with Lloyd Richards and I'm a bit disturbed about what I think they want to do with 'A Walk in the Woods' for Broadway."

But Lucille had more pressing concerns than stars or theatres on the wrong side of the street. The estimated budget capitalized the Broadway production from between $600,000 to $750,000—a considerable sum even for Lucille to handle—with about $450,000 needed to take the production to opening. She needed to raise money, a task at which she always said she was not adept. Several producers in addition to Donnalley had told her they would not finance a Broadway outing. She tried to entice Lawrence Wien, who had invested in *Gertrude Stein and a Companion*— sent him material and wrote him on August 25, "I feel this play might be my 'Last Hurrah.' " Wien, recovering from surgery, declined.

But there was also good news for Lucille. Through Manny Azenberg's connections, the Shubert Organization committed the 781-seat Booth Theatre, one of the smaller houses on Broadway and an excellent choice. A tentative schedule had the production beginning rehearsals in New York toward the end of December 1987, playing a two-week try-out at Duke University in January—another Azenberg contact, for he taught there—then possibly moving to the National Theatre in Washington, D.C., for a limited run in February and finally opening in New York on March 20, 1988.

For an instant it also seemed possible that Guinness might perform the play in New York, although how possible is unclear; Duncan

Weldon always asserted that Guinness "hated New York." The prospect seemed to arise of Guinness playing *A Walk in the Woods* in both London and New York, the British production to come first, the star to spend a limited time in both. According to a memo Richards sent on September 25, he was inclined to endorse this proposal, provided that the people involved—Guinness, Lee Blessing, Des McAnuff and himself—met "to affirm for ourselves the positive interactive artistry that I am certain exists." Provided, too, that such an arrangement did not delay the production inordinately. With Gorbachev's ongoing cultural and economic reform in the U.S.S.R., and with increasing détente between Gorbachev and Reagan, Blessing's play might soon lose its timeliness.

Then on October 6 a distressed Richards sent Lucille a polite but angry letter. He wrote of learning that Guinness' representatives had informed Lucille the British actor would only do *A Walk in the Woods* in England with a director who had not done it before, thus eliminating McAnuff. This was no disrespect to McAnuff, Duncan Weldon explained years afterward; Guinness simply did not want to work with either a director or an actor who had been involved with a previous production and would have artistic preconceptions. Richards, McAnuff and Lee Blessing, who felt loyal to McAnuff, would not hear of it. What's more, Richards had also been informed that, if Guinness were not permitted to do the play under those conditions, Lucille would not support the project any further. While stating that he was aware of the prestige and economic benefits of Guinness' involvement, he averred that this approach "discounts and discards the core artistic team who have thus far been responsible for bringing along this project at the most critical time . . . it requires that Lee and I break faith with Des and discard him. I consider this a serious matter both artistically and morally." He closed with words aimed at Lucille's pride in her worth as a producer:

> Lucille, when you first approached us regarding *A Walk in the Woods* you had no thought even of Broadway let alone England and Sir Alec Guinness. You responded to the work of theatre artists surrounding, supporting and developing a playwright's work. It was pure; it echoed my own intention. I have and will continue to support Lee and his work first. I hope that you are still with me.

Lucille scheduled a luncheon meeting with Richards, Mordecai and Curcio for one o'clock in the afternoon on Monday, October 19. This was the day that issues like Guinness or anything else hanging fire were supposed to be finalized. That morning the stock market crashed. Curcio remembered walking into Lucille's apartment at the Sherry and sensing an atmosphere similar to the aftermath of an explosion. Every few minutes, he said, Sandy Starr would rush into the living room with another news bulletin about falling stock prices (Starr denied doing this). But she did order delicatessen, and everybody ate lunch at the table in the corner of the living room and tried to concentrate. Every now and then Lucille, perhaps enjoying Richards' and Mordecai's discomfort, would say, "Have a deviled egg, dear." She brought up Guinness, but no, Richards did not want him. Finally Mordecai, alluding to the Wall Street disaster, asked, "What's going to happen now? With this situation?" Lucille, Curcio remembered, calmly said, "Oh, we'll do the play. We'll get it on. I'm determined. If things come to the worst, I know I can always go to the vault and sell my jewelry in order to pay for it." And with that, said Curcio, "They heaved a big sigh of relief and had dessert and coffee and off they went."

Later Curcio asked Lucille why she had not seized this opportunity to get what she wanted. "No, I couldn't do that," she said, "I gave them my word. I said in the beginning that I would do it the way they wanted."

"She would never insist," said Sprecher. "She would never force an artist to do something he never wanted to do. Once she was on board a project, she would make suggestions, she would make observations, she would do anything that she thought was helpful. But make somebody do something? Absolutely never happen. If Lloyd wanted something, she would argue, she would cajole, but she would never insist."

By the middle of November, casting was complete. While the chosen couple were not of Alec Guinness' stature, they were skilled and well known. Tall, dignified Sam Waterston, who had recently been nominated for an Academy Award as Best Actor in *The Killing Fields*, would be playing John Honeyman. Robert Prosky, familiar to television audiences as rotund Sergeant Stan Jablonski on *Hill Street Blues*, would act Andrey Botvinnik. Lucille had a particular affection for Prosky, who had appeared in the 1957 ANTA Matinee production of *Pale Horse, Pale Rider*.

The financing eventually came together. Before the La Jolla production, the Yale people had conferred with American Playhouse, a series on public television that was embarking upon coproducing theatrical productions in order to restage them for the small screen after their live runs had ended. That connection brought American Playhouse Theatre Productions to the table as a coproducer and in December they agreed to put up $300,000 in exchange for the motion picture and television rights.

Richards and Mordecai had no need to worry about Lucille's resources. In addition to financing *A Walk in the Woods*, in December she donated $100,000 to Lincoln Center Theater, to help move the South African musical *Sarafina!* from the Mitzi E. Newhouse to Broadway.

Months of negotiating had finally resulted in an agreement that satisfied everyone. Now it seemed only weeks before *A Walk in the Woods* would arrive on Broadway. The opening had been pushed up from March to February 28.

Lucille went to Duke University to see both the first performance on January 25, 1988, and to screen her film *The Queen of Off-Broadway*. Back in New York she embarked on her own public relations onslaught, sending articles about the production to colleagues and friends and inviting them to the opening night. Jeffrey Richards, who catered to Lucille's need for personal publicity better than other press agents, set up interviews for her with the Associated Press, public television and with Nan Robertson of the *New York Times*. She attended meetings at Serino, Coyne and Nappi, the New York theatre's advertising agency of choice; lunched at the Russian Tea Room with Edwin Wilson, theatre critic for the *Wall Street Journal;* saw the first preview on February 10 and several after that; met with Manny Azenberg to work out the seating for opening night. In between she met with her broker and personal attorneys, and saw productions at Circle Rep, the Public Theatre and Manhattan Theatre Club.

On opening night, at 6:30 Sunday, February 28, a sparkling crowd milled about in the orchestra of the Booth Theatre. As befitted the play's theme, Jeffrey Richards had wooed and won a bevy of diplomats from countries in the United Nations Security Council, including Ambassador Alexander Belonogov of the Soviet Union, First Secretary Bernd Fischer of Germany, and Ralph Earle, who had been the chief United States negotiator of the Strategic Arms Limitation Talks from 1978 to 1980. Lucille had invited a coterie of friends and colleagues: Geoffrey Holder; William F. Brown, who had written the book for the musical *The Wiz*, and his wife, Tina Tippit; Lanford Wilson; Isabelle Stevenson; Bobby Zarem; Howard Taubman and his wife, actress Lori March; Joseph Papp; Eli Wallach and Anne Jackson; Willard Swire; Sidney Kingsley; Anna Strasberg and many more. Wearing a black, V-necked dress, a diamond necklace and a black fur hat, Lucille walked into the Booth Theatre on lawyer John Silberman's arm.

If all goes reasonably well, a Broadway opening night is a happy ritual, rife with nerves, affection and enthusiasm. By 1987 critics no longer dashed up the aisle as the actors took their bows to file reviews in time for the morning edition. The first-string critics for the daily papers had already come and gone during press previews, and their reviews were in. At the Booth the performance flowed smoothly. Prosky, affecting a slight Russian accent, portrayed a self-satisfied diplomat who enjoyed slyly teasing his American counterpart, while Waterston eked variety from the role of the intelligent but unbending Honeyman. They played off each other lightly and easily, providing laughter as well as moments of seriousness. Bill Clarke's trees bloomed and shed leaves on cue. At the end, the audience stood and cheered.

Lucille took all three floors of Sardi's for her opening night party. She sat at her table in the center of the first floor dining room and greeted dozens of well-wishers who stopped to congratulate her. She posed for photographs with Waterston and Prosky and gave interviews, delighted about the way the evening had gone and hopeful about the up-coming run.

When the first edition of Monday's *New York Times* hit the street around midnight, she woke up to the reality that Frank Rich had written a devastating review. He killed the production with his opening sentence: "In one of several funny passages that threaten to quicken 'A Walk in the Woods' into nearly a trot..." He faulted the dramaturgy, the political thinking, the acting, the directing, the set, even the background music. "As a piece of theater," he wrote, wielding the sort of clever line that made him entertaining even while he butchered, " 'A Walk in the Woods' is the esthetic equivalent of Switzerland." Neutral. Boring.

Even without Rich's pan, the reviews were decidedly mixed. Only a few critics raved. William A. Henry III of *Time* magazine called Blessing's drama "a work of PASSION and power with the ring of political truth." Howard Kissel at the *Daily News* wrote that the actors "do spellbinding work," and at the Associated Press Michael Kuchwara called it "a wise and witty evening of theatre."

A larger group of critics were complimentary but hardly enthusiastic. In a dull essay, John Simon of *New York Magazine* praised the drama for being that rare item on the American stage, a political play, but he nit-picked at its credibility. Edith Oliver of the *New Yorker* described the work as "always satisfying," and Edwin Wilson, whom Lortel had wined and dined, resisted her blandishments. From where many critics sat, the play was already dated. Merely three months earlier, on December 8, 1987, President Reagan and Soviet leader Gorbachev had actually signed the sort of agreement that Honeyman and Botvinnik are trying to negotiate: an intermediate-range nuclear forces (INF) agreement, the first major arms control treaty signed by the superpowers since they negotiated to limit arms in 1979.

At 11:30 Monday morning, February 29, Lucille and Ben Sprecher, John Silberman, Lloyd Richards and Ben Mordecai, Lindsay Law, executive producer of American Playhouse, and Emanuel Azenberg walked glumly into the Serino, Coyne office. "I remember seeing the dismay on Lucille's face," said Law. They were supposed to participate in the morning-after ritual of plotting an advertising campaign and figuring how much to spend where. Instead they asked the advertising people to leave the room, they asked the press agent to leave. They closed the door and reviewed their options.

If it had been up to Sprecher, he would have shuttered the production. That would have been the sound business move. But the decision was Lucille's to make. After Rich's review came out, she had talked to her general manager on the phone, and he was not surprised that she wanted to keep the show going. She had invested emotion and effort as well as money. This was not simply a business deal for her. She could not bear to turn her back on a play about which she cared passionately. Nor did she want a London production to vanish because of a quick, humiliating closing in New York. "She was prepared to run it through the Tony Awards," said Sprecher. "She wanted to go to London and have a play—rightfully so—with Alec Guinness. And I said to her, 'Here's how we do it.'"

On behalf of Lucille, Sprecher took over the meeting and polled the group. Azenberg recommended folding. There was no advance, he pointed out, and nobody was buying tickets. Richards deferred to Lucille. Saying he did not have the heart to ask her to spend more money, he thanked her for all she had done; any further move, he said, was at her discretion. Mordecai agreed. Lindsay Law, on behalf of American Playhouse, offered to put up additional money if Lucille would.

"Here's what Lucille wants," Sprecher announced when every man had his say. "We'll float this thing through the Tonys. And we want Alec Guinness approved in London."

Nobody argued. "That's how it got done," said Sprecher. "We just leveraged our commitment to run it." Silberman and Sprecher "came up with a money deal (against their better judgment)," Lucille wrote Vincent Curcio, who was in Paris. Lucille put up an additional $200,000 to carry the production for the next two weeks, and the other coproducers were supposed to come up with $100,000 for a third week, although Lucille knew she would end up spending more by the Tony Awards on June 5. By the time the production closed on June 26, she would have spent $750,000 on her production of *A Walk in the Woods*.

She had no illusions about what had transpired. In response to an encouraging letter from Howard Taubman and Lori March, Lucille wrote them on March 3:

> My manager, my lawyer, and Manny Azenberg's whole crew all
> said I should close the show, but I'm making a fight for it. Even
> though doing a show today on Broadway is exorbitant. I'm solely
> responsible for it financially from here on out. Someday the story

of my experience of producing this play on Broadway will be a chapter in my biography entitled, "How To Get Taken On *A Walk In The Woods*."

Because I wanted to start it Off-Broadway, and, if demand warranted, move it later to the Great White Way. But, the combined egos of the people who had the rights before they were given to me insisted it had to be done on Broadway.

The silver lining in this cloud is that Alec Guinness, who wanted to do it in London earlier this year, is still interested to do it, possibly in May...

Despite Richards' and Mordecai's agreement to go along with the deal, McAnuff resisted. Weldon recalled finally telling McAnuff that if he insisted on staging the London production, the production "won't happen." Blessing, who returned home to Minneapolis after the opening, remembered receiving a call from Silberman on either Monday or Tuesday and realizing "there were no alternatives anymore." The record showed that Blessing took his time signing the agreement to allow the London production to proceed according to Guinness' wishes, but Blessing denied holding out to the last moment. Lucille wrote Curcio:

> I finally got Lee Blessing to agree that Alec Guinness could choose his own director without Lee insisting we wait for Des's availability....Told him flat out that I needed this right or I'd have to close the show.

To Julia Hansen, executive director of the Drama League of New York, Lucille wrote on April 23:

> Considering the cost of the Broadway production,...I might have been better off sending the money directly to Yale over an

extended period of years. But, I would have missed the excitement and the passion of being involved with doing the play. It's just very hard to comprehend having to light an atomic bomb under the theatre-going public to get them to come to Broadway and see this play. Once they're there, they love it!

The support for Lucille's effort from people who had seen the play and admired it was enormous. The same people were equally incensed about Frank Rich's review. Around the theatre community Lucille became something of a heroine that spring for rescuing a show which seemed, the morning after, to be doomed. More than with many productions she had sustained in the past, her need for self-aggrandizement diminished beside her determination to buoy up this foundering ship. "Although it didn't turn the corner financially," said Law, "it was perceived as a play that had a run on Broadway instead of as a one-week flop."

On May 9 her tenacity was rewarded when the American Theatre Wing announced that *A Walk in the Woods* had been nominated for the Tony Award for Best Play, and Robert Prosky nominated for Best Actor. In the meantime, the chief of staff of the Democratic caucus had seen the play and, upon returning to Washington, recommended that Waterston and Prosky perform it at the Library of Congress for a specially invited audience. At the invitation of Senators Claiborne Pell of Rhode Island, Sam Nunn of Georgia and David L. Boren of Oklahoma, Waterston and Prosky performed at the Coolidge Auditorium at 7:30 on Monday evening, May 23. Just before the performance, Lucille stood up in front of the stage and presented an autographed, inscribed copy of the script to the senators for the Library of Congress. Only two potted trees decorated the stage, the lighting was minimal, but there were two actors and a bench. An audience that included Paul Nitze himself, Secretary of State George Shultz, members of Congress, and numerous Soviet and American diplomats listened and watched intently. Lucille felt the pleasure of bringing theatre to people who rarely tasted it, of taking a drama about the world's uncertainties to persons who, like Honeyman and Botvinnik, were controlled by the levers of war and peace.

Lucille liked to trump naysayers. Everywhere she went that spring, snap, her big black pocketbook yawned open and out came flyers. She could not single-handedly fill the Booth—there were many empty seats—but she tried doggedly. Unable to buy expensive space in the *New York Times* on a daily basis, especially for the kind of advertising push that follows a Tony nomination, she tried to wangle corporations into sponsoring ads. She wrote prominent New Yorkers like Lawrence Wien, cajoling them to take out ads, or make tax-deductible contributions to American Playhouse and earmark them for *A Walk in the Woods*.

Nor did she allow her campaign to interfere with attending a daily round of events, which at the age of eighty-seven she kept as hectic as ever. On Tuesday, May 3, she went to the opening night of David Mamet's *Speed-the-Plow*, and at 1:30 the next afternoon she attended that year's Senior Concert in honor of Mayo. Blanche Marvin was in town, and on May 10 Lucille took her to the New Dramatists' annual luncheon at the Plaza. The following day, a former assistant, Ken Richards, escorted her to Lee Breuer's *Gospel at Colonnus* and on Sunday, May 22 she arrived at Sardi's for the yearly "Tony Time" party. That morning in the *New York Times*, Michael Kimmelman had praised David Henry Hwang's *M. Butterfly*, which had also been nominated for a Tony, and sneered at *A Walk in the Woods* and the musical *Chess*. They "speak directly to an affluent generation of young, politically unmotivated viewers," he wrote scathingly. "Painting a veneer of social concern, these shows mask a call to inaction."

For the Tony Awards on Sunday, June 5, she took her seat at the Minskoff Theatre at 7:30. Privately she was fuming about an article by Frank Rich on the season's best plays and playwrights, which had appeared that morning in the *New York Times*. Rich had only mentioned *A Walk in the Woods* once, deep into the feature and only as "another Best Play nominee" from Yale (he did not even name Blessing). Publicly she presented herself as a winner. In addition to the recognition for *A Walk in the Woods*, *Sarafina!* had been nominated for Best Musical and Best Original Score, Leleti Khumalo had received a nomination for Featured Actress in a musical, and Mbongeni Ngemi for Best Direction of a musical. For these occasions Lucille herself always dressed up—from her point of view she was making a statement—so that evening she announced her presence in a red chiffon Stavropoulos gown, worn with the ruby and diamond necklace which Lou had given her years before.

A Walk in the Woods was competing against an unusually strong roster that season: *Joe Turner's Come and Gone* by August Wilson, the other Yale export; *M. Butterfly;* and Mamet's *Speed-the-Plow.* For Leading Actor in a play, competition was also fierce. Prosky was up against Derek Jacobi, who had starred in *Breaking the Code, M. Butterfly's* John Lithgow, and Ron Silver in *Speed-the-Plow.* In another season *A Walk in the Woods* might have stood a chance. But *M. Butterfly* took the honor for Best Play, Silver for Leading Actor. *Sarafina!* lost out to *The Phantom of the Opera.* Once again, a Tony Award eluded Lucille.

She had known that if the play did not win she would have to close it, but before that happened, she felt compelled to respond to what she believed was a pattern of negativity and neglect at the *New York Times.* In a June 9 letter to Arthur Ochs Sulzberger, the newspaper's publisher, Lucille cited Kimmelman's feature criticizing *A Walk in the Woods'* "watered-down" political viewpoint and asked why the paper had ignored the performance at the Library of Congress, which, they must have been aware, was taking place before an audience of politicians and diplomats the day after the article appeared. She noted Frank Rich's feature about the Tony Awards which "conspicuously ignored" Blessing. "A producer cannot ask for special treatment," the letter said, "but, at the same time, a producer must expect fair treatment. Respect for serious drama creates an atmosphere in which producers can continue to take risks in a treacherous commercial world. Without that respect, it will become impossible for producers to continue to take chances with new plays."

Responding for the *Times*, Max Frankel, the executive editor, cited his own litany of interviews and articles which mentioned the production. He averred that there was no relationship between a negative review and "our handling of feature articles," a claim that would have raised a hearty laugh among theatrical press agents. He gave Lucille no quarter, but at least she had aired her feelings.

A Walk in the Woods played its final Broadway performance on June 26. Lucille would continue to believe that, if the production had opened at her theatre, it would have had a long and prosperous run and then possibly moved to Broadway. Years later Richards tried to explain his position by saying, "I'm not a fan of Off Broadway to Broadway. If you're going to Broadway, go to Broadway. If you're going Off Broadway, go to Off Broadway meaning to be there." With the wisdom of hindsight, he said, "The question is, was *A Walk in the Woods* a play for Off Broadway or Broadway. *A Walk in the Woods* got caught in the middle. Its thinking and its approach were possibly Off Broadway at the time but also possible for Broadway. But it was not the kind of play that was a hit play. You had to put some names over the title for it to get an advance. If you were looking at Ralph Richardson, Laurence Olivier—yes, you'd do it. But we weren't expecting that." Lucille, as she kept trying to tell them, was.

She moved on. On July 20, American Playhouse videotaped the production for television, directed by Kirk Browning, long-admired for taping live broadcasts from the Metropolitan Opera. Earlier in the year, Lucille had licensed exclusive stock production rights to James B. McKenzie at the Westport Country Playhouse. With Lawrence Pressman and Michael Constantine as the two diplomats, the production toured several summer theatres, winding up at the Playhouse in late

August and early September. Lucille had licensed James Freydberg to present a national tour, but he encountered difficulty lining up stars and advised her simply to release the play to regional theatres, where both it and she could draw income.

Meanwhile, she eagerly looked forward to two events: the London production and a tour of the Soviet Union.

By April Duncan Weldon and Jerome Minskoff had moved forward to produce *A Walk in the Woods* in Britain, and shortly afterward Sir Alec Guinness was signed to play the Soviet negotiator. Guinness' director of choice was Ronald Eyre, who cast the American Edward Herrmann to play John Honeyman. The opening night was scheduled for London's Comedy Theatre on November 3.

This was going to be the production she had wanted in New York and she intended to make a feast of it. She contacted theatre critic and reporter Sheridan Morley, to ask if he would consider videotaping an interview with Lee Blessing. She wrote to Anthony Branch, a founder of the British American Drama Academy (BADA), to see if he would screen *The Queen of Off-Broadway* for his students. Then she spent most of September in Westport storing up her energy.

Traveling with Marge Farwell and Sandy Starr, she flew to London on Friday, October 21. Leaving Starr on her own for a week, she and Farwell moved on to a luxurious spa at Tring in Hertfordshire called Champney's, famous for its neuromuscular therapy. But she was incapable of giving herself over to the cure entirely and went into London twice, first for Morley's interview with Blessing and to see a run-through without an audience, and again to see a preview. She finally returned to London on October 30, and she, Farwell and Starr settled into a roomy apartment that Lucille had rented at The Arlington House, a short taxi ride from the theatre.

As always, Lucille had invited an entourage of friends to join her and witness this event, and among those who made the trip were writer Max

Wilk and his wife Barbara, Rita Fredricks and her husband Herbert Salzman, Haila Stoddard, Anna Strasberg, and from England Eileen O'Casey, Kitty Black and the elderly but still vigorous Hazel Vincent Wallace. On November 2 Jeanne-Marie Dana, who owned beachfront property near Lucille's in Westport, threw an elegant cocktail party for her at the Ritz. And the next evening Lucille saw seventy-four-year-old Sir Alec Guinness, after a ten-year absence from the London stage, open in *A Walk in the Woods.*

"You never quite see how Guinness does it," wrote Michael Coveny in his November 4 review for the *Financial Times*. "His left shoulder twitches slightly, the eyelids droop and rest for ten seconds of silent disapproval, he leans with sudden nonchalance, facing upstage, against a tree. It is, save for a few First Night bumps, a seamless and masterly performance by a virtuoso of the tiniest physical and vocal inflection. The fine American actor Edward Herrmann . . . is a sympathetic foil."

In London, unlike New York, the critics still covered opening nights, but their on-the-spot responses differed little from those of their American cousins with more time to ponder. There were those who liked and those who loathed. The difference was Guinness. What drew him to the play as an actor, he told *New York Times* correspondent Herbert Mitgang, was the character of Andrey Botvinnik and the relationship between the two men. These he played as subtly as he knew how, to the quiet satisfaction of audiences who had not seen him, except in films and on television, in years. Despite what critics said about the play, the London producers and Lucille had brought to light a performance that theatregoing Londoners wanted to see. The production ran twenty weeks, which was as long as Guinness would play it. It could easily have run longer.

Lucille stayed on in London until November 13. One day, between a matinee and evening performance, she was photographed on the set with Guinness. He is holding her left hand up in his and smiling broadly at the camera, and Lucille, wearing a white hat, looks tired but pleased.

That was the time, according to Sandy Starr, when Guinness said to her, "Lucille, you're coming so often," and she replied, "Yes, I'm understudying the Russian." Then there was the day Lucille decided to give a tea at Arlington House, and she and Marge Farwell walked to Fortnum and Mason to buy smoked salmon. On the way back they ran into Sir Alec on Jermyn Street. Apparently surprised to see her on foot, the actor said, "Lucille, you're walking." She answered vivaciously with her own version of one of Botvinnik's lines, "I'm walking, I'm sitting, I'm walking again."

"Alec Guinness on the star side was number one," said Ben Sprecher, who had also traveled to London for the opening. "Nobody was higher than Guinness."

It is hard to determine how the idea of taking *A Walk in the Woods* to the Soviet Union formed in everyone's minds, although it seemed a logical step. The concrete plan evolved through the American/Soviet Theatre Initiative (ASTI), which was signed in Moscow in December 1987 and ratified in April 1988, to encourage cultural exchange. An outgrowth of the reform movement that Gorbachev was nurturing in the Soviet Union, it had been spearheaded on the American side by George C. White, founder of the Eugene O'Neill Memorial Theatre Center in Waterford, Connecticut, and by a Soviet named Grigori Nersesyan, who became ASTI's executive director in Moscow. White recalled that "*A Walk in the Woods* seemed an opportune play in terms of U.S.-Soviet relations. It was symbolic of what we at ASTI were trying to do." He told Lucille, "not only will you be the queen of Off Broadway, you will be the czarina of Gorky Street."

She needed little persuading. Taking *A Walk in the Woods* to the Soviet Union was the sort of uncommon gesture she loved. Not only would it bring additional attention to the play, it would reflect well on her for supporting it. She turned to Sprecher for help in negotiating her contract with Yale, which would organize and manage the production arrangements, and to her accountants for the financial leeway. The cost at the American end would be around $184,000, which would include bringing Soviet actors to the United States as part of an exchange. Lucille raised some money from outside sources, but mostly she underwrote the expense herself.

From several cities and across thousands of miles, artists, technological support and Americans converged on Moscow's Pushkin Drama Theatre for the opening on May 19, 1989. The actors rehearsed with Des McAnuff in Budapest, where Sam Waterston was wrapping up work on a television miniseries. From Vilnius, Lithuania, which had supplanted Leningrad as the second stop on the play's tour, came the set: trees with twenty thousand leaves handcrafted in fabric by Russian women and trucked to Moscow. From New York came people connected with the production, including press agent Jeffrey Richards. Also from New York came the group who had signed on for the ASTI cultural tour of Moscow and Leningrad, mostly Lucille's friends.

Lucille, Ben Sprecher, a Florida-based reporter named Jeanette Kamins, and Sandy Starr left John F. Kennedy airport on Saturday, May 13, and flew to Helsinki, Finland, where they spent one night. They arrived in Moscow on May 15. Inadvertently Kamins had irritated Lucille by showing up with an identically styled hat and was relegated to the tour group, the social equivalent of Siberia, so Blanche Marvin replaced her as Lucille's traveling companion.

In Moscow, Sam Waterston recalled that a revolution seemed underway, nearly around the corner from the theatre where they were performing. "Students, reformists—people were demonstrating on a regular basis," he remembered. "There was a lot of excitement going on."

Moscow shocked nearly everyone. Gorbachev was esteemed in the West, but in the Soviet Union his restructuring of the economy, or perestroika, had led to shortages of everything from food to soap. Disorganization and the black market reigned on the streets. Robert Prosky, who had been to Moscow ten years before with the first American company to play the U.S.S.R., felt astounded by the difference. "The first time, the waves parted in front of us," he remembered. "This time we were lucky to get lunch." The food was so poor that the actors bought eggs, which their wives boiled in a samovar. Neither Prosky nor Waterston smoked, but they purchased cigarettes. "If you stood on a corner and waved a pack, you got a taxi," Prosky said.

As for the members of the ASTI tour, they landed up at a hotel far from the heart of Moscow, in which the rooms were infested with bedbugs and mice. Their guides were poor. Two of Lucille's friends actually turned around and flew home, although those who braved it developed a troupers' attitude about the adventure and derived pleasure in spite of everything.

Lucille was cushioned from most of these discomforts, although not all. A car, a driver and a female interpreter were at her disposal, but her first encounter with a Soviet hotel was a standoff. Benjamin Mordecai had reserved a suite for her at the Rossiya Hotel, near the center of Moscow. But when she and Sandy Starr arrived, the hotel wanted to put them into one room with twin beds, which Lucille would not accept. Back straight, head erect, she sat in the lobby with Starr and the interpreter from 1:30 P.M. to 5:30 P.M. and would not register until Mordecai and Gregori Nersesyan arranged for the suite she had expected: a bedroom, bath, kitchen, dining room, a living room with a television set, and a kind of den that contained a piano. Starr slept on a pad of blankets, because apparently only one box spring and one mattress were available.

Arrival day was Monday. By Thursday Lucille had adjusted, although she felt tired and her feet were hurting badly. She and Starr shopped for a hat, so that Lucille and Jeanette Kamins would not be wearing the same one to the press conference, and somewhere they unearthed a man's fedora made out of plastic. They had traveled with tea bags, hot chocolate and boxes of milk, and on one of their sorties discovered a bakery and purchased black bread, which they took back to their suite for tea. Dinner they occasionally ate with the tour in the hotel's restaurant, at other times with Mordecai and his Russian friends. They visited a circus and attended a ballet. Curious about little except theatre, Lucille had never been one to go sightseeing—even when she and Lou took cruises, they usually stayed on the ship when it went into port.

On Friday, May 19, at 7:00 P.M., *A Walk in the Woods* had its Moscow opening.

The Pushkin Drama Theatre stands on Tsverskoi Boulevard, not far from Red Square. Its interior is a simple, rectangular space with a high stage at one end and about 950-red, fabric-covered seats in the slightly raked orchestra. That night the house was filled with Americans and Soviets, students and journalists, theatre critics and regular theatregoers. For the Americans, many of whom had seen the Broadway production, the performance was erratic. The simultaneous Russian translation wafted noisily from earphones and drowned out the actors, who were not projecting loudly enough. The pace felt slow, and the actors were not getting the laughs they had come to expect in New York. "In rehearsal in Budapest," said Prosky, "we changed the style to less theatrical and more realistic, if you will, which didn't go in that large theatre. It was a little rocky."

While th\ Americans were restless, the Soviets listened and watched intently. Some found the acting fine and the play an accurate portrayal of a negative but charming Soviet negotiator. Others thought the script didactic or the Soviet diplomat too war-mongering to be credible. Generally they found the drama out of date. The relationship between the United States and the Soviet Union had improved so markedly between the time Blessing wrote his play and when it was presented in Moscow, that, to the surprise of many of the American organizers, the script's situation no longer felt timely to the Soviets. In Vilnius two weeks later, perhaps because of Lithuania's strained relationship with the U.S.S.R., audiences would be more appreciative, although Lucille, who had never planned to go on to Lithuania, would not be there to experience it.

Lucille and Starr did not watch the second act, but talked in the lobby with members of the tour. Then it was on to a party at Spasso House, the residence of the Honorable Jack F. Matlock, American Ambassador to the Soviet Union, and his wife. Hot dogs with catsup were on the menu, to the delight of Lucille, who loved frankfurters, and the relief of the other American visitors, who were wearying of chicken Kiev. She looked quietly pleased whenever Nersesyan offered her his arm and she talked animatedly with young Soviet actors to whom she was introduced. The next night Lucille, Blanche Marvin and Starr went to the equivalent of an Off-Broadway basement theatre to see a play directed by Oleg Tabakov, one of the cofounders of the politically liberal Sovremennik Theatre. If Lucille was surprised that *A Walk in the Woods* did not prove the blockbuster everyone expected, she never said so. She would have dismissed the reaction in any case. From her point of view, bringing play and people together was significant enough.

CHAPTER 11

On the Wings of a Dream

*T*he leaves were forming a green haze in Central Park when Lucille returned from the Soviet Union late in May. Her elation from producing *A Walk in the Woods* merged with the city's springtime and carried her through the rest of 1989, to Anna Strasberg's party on December 15, which celebrated "The Czarina of Gorky Street."

With a light schedule in June, she resumed going to the theatre: she saw A.R. Gurney's *Love Letters* and Alfred Jarry's *Ubu*. On the 22nd she attended the annual Senior Concert in Carnegie Hall and later that afternoon threw a party for the Soviet tour at the Russian Tea Room, where the food was better than any they had tasted on their trip.

Her business enterprises included *Steel Magnolias* at the Lortel, which had transferred from the not-for-profit WPA Theatre and which Lucille did not like, even though it had graduated to its second successful year. At the White Barn the season began in August with only three entries, the most stimulating being *Margaret Sanger—Unfinished Business*, a one-person play starring Eileen Heckart as the pioneering exponent of birth control in the United States.

For a woman on the cusp of her nineties, whose only exercise was a brief, occasional walk and whose idea of a healthful meal was the delicious spinach quiche that actor Drew Eliot brought her, Lucille's health was generally good. Still, it caused her apprehension. She suffered from an irregular heartbeat and digestive problems, for which she took a battery of medicines, several simply to help her relax or sleep. At the slightest pain or cough she called her physician, Theodore Tyberg, no matter where he was, and by the late 1990s he would often be summoned to sit behind her at the theatre, where he could periodically test her pulse and reassure her that she was fine. She decided that in the event she was incapacitated physically or mentally, she did not want medical treatment to prolong her life and in July 1991 she signed a Health Care Proxy and Declaration. In 1994 she added a new directive: she wanted to be cared for in her own apartment and never see the inside of a nursing home.

She had begun to wear hearing aids in the late 1980s. But her biggest day-to-day concerns were painful feet and arthritis in her knees, which forced her, much as she disliked it, to use a cane and to take stairs one step at a time. She also suffered from diminishing bladder control, which often obliged her to sit in a back row when she went to the theatre, so that even when moving slowly she could be among the first to the bathroom during intermission. At The Players Club her dilemma inspired a practical solution. The Players had finally admitted women in 1989—Lucille was among the first to be inducted—but as late as 1994 it still had no ladies room either on the main floor near the dining room or downstairs near the Grill Room. To reach a bathroom a woman had to ride a rickety, unreliable elevator, which barely accommodated two people, or walk up a long flight of stairs. So in 1994 Lucille donated $10,000 for the construction of a ladies room near the grill. The result was a small, cheerful white, black and red lavatory, decorated inside with theatre posters and on the outside with a brass plaque proclaiming this "Lucille's Loo."

. . .

Around the middle of the 1960s, Betty Corwin, a Weston, Connecticut, homemaker with a passion for theatre, had gone to the New York Public Library (NYPL) for the Performing Arts with a simple but revolutionary idea. She would arrange for live theatrical performances in and around New York City to be filmed or videotaped for an archive. Corwin single-handedly pursued her goal during the 1970s on a volunteer basis, often taping productions at the White Barn and the de Lys.

Why Lucille became so enamored of what came to be known as Theatre on Film and Tape, or TOFT, Corwin did not really know. "I think originally it was because she liked her own work preserved," Corwin said. In addition film lived in Lucille's personal history. Not only had she wanted to be a movie actress, but also for many years Lou had equipped the White Barn with state-of-the-art television technology. TOFT afforded another chance for Lucille to be in the vanguard—and to give strategic support to Corwin, who was working with little help from the library. Over the years, whenever Lucille wanted something videotaped, a production or one of her celebratory events, she donated anywhere from $3,500 to $7,500 for the job.

The New York Public Library had been wooing Lucille for a sizable contribution since 1985, when Vartan Gregorian, then the library's president, wrote to thank her effusively for a gift; to master fundraiser Gregorian, no donation was too small to merit a grand thank-you.(After Gregorian moved on to the presidency of Brown University, he would again court Lucille). Andrew Heiskell, NYPL's chairman of the board, invited Lucille in 1987 to join him for drinks and a private tour of the Performing Arts Research Center, and two years later, shortly after she returned from the Soviet Union, the library honored her at a dinner for twenty-one "Lions of the Performing Arts."

It is possible that the library hoped its private tours would induce Lucille to give to the Research Center generally; TOFT was not at the top of its agenda. "They really wanted her to give to a lot of other things, too," said Betty Corwin. "But she felt that TOFT was her baby. It was a unique archive, and she knew what it meant to have her work preserved." She also knew what it would mean for her reputation and for TOFT if she were to give the archive its first major endowment. If the NYPL wanted her money, they would have to take it the way she wanted to give it.

The library's trustees and administrators lavished personal attention on her. "I've done a lot of fundraising," said Corwin, "and if you write a letter explaining a need, you usually focus on how important the issue is; you don't have to stroke the way people did with Lucille. Everybody knew that she needed to be stroked." After private meetings with her, the NYPL proposed that she donate $1,000,000 over four years to establish the Lucille Lortel Room and create the Lucille Lortel Endowment Fund for Theatre on Film and Tape. "The library needs you to be the angel of the Theatre on Film and Tape (TOFT) Archive," Andrew Heiskell wrote Lucille on December 9, 1989. "Yours would be a gift of surpassing generosity, for the benefit of the entire theatre community of which you are such an important part." She gave $100,000 to construct the room, $900,000 for an endowment.

Lucille sat down with her lawyers and with historian Mary Henderson to work out the arrangement. A portion of the Billy Rose Theatre Collection Reading Room would become a separate room with a separate entrance, to be known as the Lucille Lortel Room/Theatre on Film and Tape Archive, even if, as eventually happened, the Reading Room was torn apart and redesigned. "We had never had a room before," said Betty Corwin, "We just had television sets in the corners." The interest from the endowment would go toward paying much-needed salaries. "However, as always with Lucille," said Corwin, "the stipulation was, 'What am I going to get out of this?' There had to be a display about her life." The NYPL agreed that Lucille's memorabilia would be exhibited for three months in the Vincent Astor Gallery and that from then on the Lucille Lortel Room itself would contain a permanent display about her life. In addition her name would be carved on one of the marble pylons at the Central Research Library at Fifth Avenue and 42nd Street. "She was into monuments in the 1990s," curator Robert Taylor acknowledged, although he did not object to what he saw as a natural desire on Lucille's part to be remembered for her gift. When the Room was dedicated on November 28, 1990, it brought Lucille public acclaim, Corwin public credit for the archive she had worked so hard to accumulate, and TOFT finally received the attention this exceptional resource deserved.

With *A Walk in the Woods* behind her, Lucille reverted to her low-key style of producing. By 1988, arrangements with Equity regarding the White Barn had once again fallen apart. Lucille had refused to pay actors pension and welfare benefits. Equity responded by ruling that she could only produce work in which a single actor was essentially performing his or her own play. Every summer now she told reporters that she had considered calling off the season, but then someone would come to her with an idea for a project—singers Liliane Montevecchi, Julie Wilson or Donna McKechnie—and she could not say no. August weekends at the White Barn turned into an appealing series of musical evenings, one-person plays and staged readings, largely organized by Vincent Curcio, but were far from the adventuresome roster of new work that had occupied the stage nearly fifty years earlier. One exception was a staged reading of Lanford Wilson's new drama *Redwood Curtain* in August 1991. For that, Marshall Mason, who was directing, received permission from Actors' Equity to do the reading as a benefit for Circle Repertory Company.

The White Barn Theatre Museum had opened its new home adjacent to the theatre on September 26, 1992, with an exhibition devoted to Sean O'Casey, the first of many exhibitions curated by Mary Henderson, and some of the most stimulating offerings occurred arm-in-arm with the tiny museum. That September afternoon the White Barn hosted a benefit for the O'Casey Theater Company, which was headed by Eileen and Sean's daughter, Shivaun. The audience gazed at O'Casey memorabilia and heard Kim Hunter, Anne Meara and Dermot McNamara read letters and stories by and about the Irish playwright. Shivaun reported that Eileen was not well and had been in the hospital, but sent her love. Subsequent exhibitions commemorated the work of other artists whose careers had entwined directly or indirectly with Lucille's: composer Marc Blitzstein; Athol Fugard; Ralph Alswang and Eva Le Gallienne, who had died in 1991; Kurt Weill, Bertolt Brecht and Lotte Lenya. In conjunction with the Fugard exhibit in August 1994, the South African playwright came to the White Barn and read from his autobiographical book *Cousins*, after which Lucille presented him with a check for $5,000. In a note afterward, Lucille said, "I just want to thank you for all your sweetness and the love you have given me over the years." Fugard, genuinely surprised and touched by the check, and sensitive to Lucille's need for appreciation, wrote back:

> The occasion itself—my reading from *Cousins*—was one I person-
> ally enjoyed immensely and principally because it allowed me to
> share with you my beginnings as a writer—You after all did launch
> my American career. Is it possible for a playwright to have a
> greater debt to anyone?

Writing later that month to longtime friend Victoria Oakie in California, Lucille said, "I am particularly pleased by Fugard's letter and by the letter of Shivaun O'Casey (Sean's daughter). They both affirm that I really did make a difference in their careers . . . "

Lucille's return to her behind-the-scenes mode of coproducing did not lessen her emotional involvement, especially when she liked a play as much as she did Jane Anderson's *The Baby Dance*.

Connecticut theatre reviewer Fran Sikorski had seen *Baby Dance* at the Williamstown Theatre Festival during the summer of 1990 and wrote

Lucille to watch for the play when Long Wharf Theatre produced it the following spring. Lucille attended the opening night and, ignoring the script's contrivances, responded directly to the story and the relationships. The central character, a middle-class woman named Rachel, is unable to have a child and locates a couple named Al and Wanda, who live in a trailer and have more children than they can afford to raise. Wanda is pregnant again, and she and her husband agree to have the baby and essentially sell it to Rachel and her husband. Unfortunately the birth is difficult, the baby possibly brain-damaged, and Rachel's husband insists that they back out of the agreement.

Perhaps Lucille heard an echo of the conflicts that she and Lou experienced when they considered adopting during the 1940s. In any case, the Lortel looked as though it was going to be available in September 1991; the current rental, Charles Busch's *Red Scare on Sunset*, an entertaining satire of Hollywood in the blacklist era, had run its course. *The Baby Dance* was capitalized at $350,000, and although Sprecher questioned the production's high weekly operating expenses, and issues relating to its lead producer, John A. McQuiggan, Lucille wanted the play to come into the Lortel and she became a limited partner.

Another coproducer was a woman named Daryl Roth.

The slim, blonde Roth had come to producing out of a love for theatre. Unlike Lucille, Roth had never been an actress but had raised a family in New Jersey and established an interior design business. Like Lucille she was married to a wealthy man, and in middle age, when her children no longer needed her to drive them to school each day, she decided to try her hand at producing commercial theatre. *The Baby Dance* was only the second production she had attempted.

The two women had met shortly before *Baby Dance* opened, when Roth, who at the time was living up the block at the Pierre Hotel, went to the Sherry for tea. "I so enjoyed meeting you yesterday," she wrote her neighbor. "I knew I would adore you, since I have always admired your passion for theater and your desire to help make plays happen! We share that enthusiasm and love ..."

If *Baby Dance* had opened to glorious reviews on October 17, maybe Roth and Lucille would not have become so friendly. But yet again Frank Rich served up a damning critique—"vicious" was how Roth described it. Other New York critics were also less than ecstatic. Roth, Stephanie Zimbalist, who played Rachel, and the director, Jenny Sullivan, made a pilgrimage to the Sherry-Netherland to ask Lucille for concessions regarding the Lortel and for her continued support. "We went to tell her why we thought we could make this work," said Roth. "And she loved that."

With Lucille's encouragement, and as Lucille had done in the past, Roth mounted a fierce campaign to bring in an audience: a 600-piece mailing to friends and colleagues; a letter to schools, clubs and charities urging groups and theatre parties; contact with an adoptive parents' convention at Fordham University. "I've felt a kinship to you," Roth wrote Lucille on October 28. "You are surely an inspiration to me....It will take additional hard work but I will persevere. I continue to call, write and talk to everyone I meet....My energy will be spent in every way I know how to keep it going."

Lucille responded the next day, "You've got guts and that's what this play needs. To have someone like you fighting for it....Daryl, you have what it takes, and I think that if we could...put our noses to the grind stone we could get beyond that one critic that was so cruel to criticize this play as he did." She added, perhaps with a bit of long-standing resentment, "Nothing would please me more than that we could rise above his criticisms and make a go of it..."

"Daryl Roth wants to be Lucille Lortel," Ben Sprecher concluded. Roth in fact bought a former bank building near Union Square, gutted it, turned it into an Off-Broadway performance space, and named it after herself. "The lessons I learned from Lucille and that I have kept in my heart," she said, "are that if you believe in something and see people responding, by hook and by crook you keep a play going. Which flips back to the philosophy Lucille had, and that I hope I have, which is never do anything you don't feel passionately about."

Sprecher believed that Lucille thought Roth "kind of a neophyte" and that "to the extent Lucille felt capable, she took Daryl under her wing." But Sprecher perhaps was discounting Lucille's need to feel admired and be part of a project. The group involved with trying to save *Baby Dance*— Roth; Ann Sheffer, a wealthy Westport resident who had invested in the production; Sullivan; and its two female stars, Zimbalist and Linda Purl—formed a sort of family. Roth brought Lucille into this family. "She sort of became one of the gals with us," said Sullivan. They became a group of women fighting for a play that evidently spoke more to women than men, and Lucille, who usually did not make common cause with women, became a member of their band. She, the nonpolitical one, even signed a statement of affirmation from Planned Parenthood, that the way to make abortions unnecessary was not to close abortion clinics but to help men and women prevent unintended pregnancies.

The women's efforts eventually ran aground. *Baby Dance*, after sixty-one performances, gave its last on December 8, 1991. But by involving Lucille in this fight, Roth had not only extended the life of the project but had momentarily rejuvenated her.

Lucille's next producing adventure, in the fall of 1992, was not to be nearly so comradely.

It had started out pleasantly enough. Lucille had gone to the New York Public Library for the Performing Arts in 1990 to hear Colleen Dewhurst, George Grizzard and Brad Davis read a lengthy autobiographical play by Larry Kramer called *The Destiny of Me*. She adored the script, a memory play that traces a young man's acceptance of his homosexuality and his family's rejection, his lover's recent death from the virus that causes AIDS and the discovery that he, too, is HIV-positive. Marshall Mason had directed, and Lucille had told him that she would love to see the play at the Lortel. When Circle Repertory Company decided to mount a production, Lucille became involved.

Lucille's agreement with Circle Rep called for it to produce the play at the Lortel for six weeks in 1992, during which time Circle Rep's subscribers would see the production; Lucille would donate her theatre and $100,000. Then, as a dubious Lucille explained to Blanche Marvin in a September 1 letter, the production would become commercial. "I take over with two men—novice producers—who run Broadway Cares/Equity Fights Aids. They put in $50,000 and one is the lover of Larry Kramer."

It soon became apparent how much Kramer's lover, Rodger McFarlane, and Tom Viola were novices. In Sprecher's and Lucille's view they had undercapitalized the production. *The Destiny of Me* opened on October 20 to phenomenal reviews—even Frank Rich praised the writing, the acting, the direction. But after Circle Rep's subscribers had seen it and the producers needed to attract a general audience, McFarlane and Viola did not know how to market the play. They didn't have enough money in the bank for a fresh advertising campaign or to carry the show while waiting for an audience to appear, nor were they able to raise additional cash. It looked as though the production would have to close.

Sprecher sputtered in indignation as he remembered it. "Basically, Larry Kramer's two friends didn't know anything about running a show. The show opened and after six weeks it converted, and then these characters, who had also promised to provide funding—can you imagine, fifty thousand dollars? Meanwhile the show is doing 'eh' business." Sprecher told Lucille that, if she wanted the production to run, she would have to take it over herself.

Lucille sent a letter to Marshall Mason on October 30 indicating her concern and that she was bringing a friend, the producer Elliot Martin, to see the show. "It was a powerful play," said Martin. "It should have been on Broadway. But what happened was that whatever they could get in terms of interviews and promotion was done for that six-week period, and Lucille was left hanging out to dry at the end of the six weeks. I said, 'Well, Lucille, you have to find an entire new audience for this. You haven't tapped the Jewish audience. It's pretty late now, but that's one way to go.' "

In the meantime tensions flared among the people connected with the production, whom Larry Kramer, in one anguished and irate memo, called "an unholy alliance." Everyone accused somebody else of falling down on the job. Kramer blamed Circle Rep's inexperience, and McFarlane-Viola believed they were always cleaning up after Circle Rep's mistakes. That company was struggling with its own fiscal difficulties. Kramer and Ben Sprecher loathed each other. Lucille, who had not yet met Kramer in person, tried to soothe him by letter. "I love your play so much that nothing will keep me from doing whatever I can to keep it running," she wrote on November 21. "But, I can't ask people to invest in it now because as a limited partner I do not have the control I'd need to get things done."

McFarlane and Viola finally assigned her that control on December 15. "Not only did we put up a hundred thousand dollars and provide the theatre rent free," said Sprecher, "I had to *buy* the show from them. That was an example where I thought Lucille really got taken advantage of, even though she agreed to it." Basically, Lucille bought out McFarlane and Viola and assumed responsibility for the operating deficit and any liabilities. Paying Elliot Martin out of her own pocket, she hired him as a consultant, and he brought on board new management and a new press agent, for which she also paid.

Kramer was temporarily calmed when he arrived at Anna Strasberg's *Destiny of Me* party on December 18 bearing four hats for Lucille: a plaid one that she never wore; a mossy green cloche with feathers that she rarely wore; a luscious, large-brimmed purple confection that she gave to singer Julie Wilson, who had a suit to match; and a raffish scarlet fedora with a black band and a black feather, which Lucille took to instantly.

"How delightful it was for me to meet you," she wrote to Kramer on the twenty-second. "The charming, soft-spoken, lovable pussy cat that I met certainly didn't live up to your advance press."

With Jeffrey Richards now handling publicity for *Destiny of Me,* they pursued the Jewish audience that Martin had targeted, despite derisive comments from Bruce Weber in his *New York Times* column: "A tender family drama with a special appeal for Jewish audiences. If you've seen Larry Kramer's play 'The Destiny of Me,' this may not be how you remember it. If you haven't, however, this is how the Off-Broadway grande dame, Lucille Lortel, wants you to think of it."

Most people who had seen the play and been touched by it encouraged Lucille in her fight. But she waged an uphill battle. She was unable to attract additional investors, and whether because of the play's subject matter, its length (over three hours), Weber's disparaging column, or all three, audiences stayed away. It did not help that the popular actor Ralph Waite considered leaving the show earlier than planned. The production continued to lose money each week. Finally Lucille acknowledged that she could no longer sustain it. On Sunday, March 21, 1993, *Destiny of Me* closed, having played 198 performances.

Word got to Kramer that Lucille was dismayed because he was not displaying enough gratitude for all she had done. On April 7 he wrote to assuage her distress:

> This play has meant a great deal to both of us and both of us wished it to run forever. Well, it did not, for whatever reason. And there is nothing to be done about it. You did your best. You did better than your best. You kept it running longer than any other producer would have kept it running. And you will be blessed in that theatrical heaven where such heroic and generous deeds are recorded. I will make the entry in the Big Book myself, when I get there. So stop torturing yourself, and me, by even allowing yourself

to think that I have forgotten you or your generosity. You have been incredible. Now stop being such a Jewish mother!

Lucille continued to invest in plays that came into the Lortel—notably *Mrs. Klein* starring Uta Hagen in 1995—and she produced the occasional one-person show, such as Liliane Montevecchi's *Back on the Boulevard* in 1996, in memory of her friend Martin Kaufman, who had produced Montevecchi's *On the Boulevard*. Nor did she lose her sense of humor. "I'm a desperate playwright," Rich Orloff wrote her in September 1993, "and I thought you could help me." "I'm a desperate old lady now. Cannot read," Lucille dictated to Sandy Starr. But *Destiny of Me* was the last major production that Lucille would take over or to which she would dedicate her energy and financial resources. As she wrote Larry Kramer, "I get too emotionally involved. It keeps me up at night. I think of all the things that should be done that aren't being done." Her physical stamina no longer matched her passions.

Her life became both a casting off and a fight to hold on. She resigned from most of the boards on which she served, including Circle Rep in 1991. Cranbury Farm was sold in 1993. She continued to disperse money to dozens of nonprofit organizations. She endowed a chair in theatre at the Graduate Center of the City University of New York. Brown University under Vartan Gregorian had been wooing her since 1990 to underwrite a physical space or a fellowship that would bear her name. Anna Strasberg, whose two sons were undergraduates there, cleverly functioned as matchmaker by setting up a playwriting fund to honor Lucille and donating its inaugural gift. The Brown development staff and alumni then swooped in to finalize the marriage, with Timothy C. Forbes, class of '76, inviting Lucille to join Gregorian, himself and other alumni aboard the Highlander, the grand yacht owned by Forbes family. Advised that a playwriting fund might last longer than a building, which could be torn down or renamed, in 1995 Lucille endowed the fund with $225,000.

But as always for Lucille, divesting was fraught with issues of control. Who would receive what, and how much? Who would be in charge once she was no longer there? She and her lawyers drew up numerous versions of what she referred to as "my goddamn will," and with each version she changed the amounts of the bequests and the recipients, depending upon who was in her favor, who not. When it came to which person or organization should run the White Barn and the Lucille Lortel Theatre when she died, the same fluctuations reigned. But it was the Lortel Foundation, which had been set up in 1980, that particularly concerned her, and she sought the views of friends, colleagues, employees, even a consulting firm, to advise her about its future operation.

By 1996, there seemed to be an understanding that, after Lucille died, the Foundation was to be run by her accountant Michael Hecht, the financial advisor George Shaskan, and her attorney James Ross, who supposedly would seek and receive the advice of a rotating artistic advisory board regarding both the White Barn and the Lucille Lortel Theatre. After adding and discarding names, Lucille finally decided that she wanted the initial artistic board to consist of Marshall Mason, Lanford Wilson, Arvin Brown, and Anna Strasberg, with Mason the first artistic director, particularly entrusted with overseeing the Lortel Theatre. The Foundation was not to be a producing organization. It would subsidize programs such as the Lucille Lortel Awards and the annual Senior Concert, bring the Lortel Theatre "good and serious theatrical productions" and ensure "high quality experimental and other theatrical productions" at the White Barn Theatre. Somewhat later she decided to set up a separate artistic advisory board for the White Barn Theatre Foundation, consisting of Vincent Curcio, Mary Henderson and Donald Saddler.

If it occurred to Lucille that she was vesting the real power in attorneys and financial advisors who did not share her commitment and zeal, that did not seem to trouble her. She had always looked to lawyers, investors and businessmen for advice, beginning with her husband. She trusted them. Ultimately they always did her bidding, since she controlled the financial assets as well as the theatres.

But as she and her lawyers were structuring it, the artistic advisory boards of the Lortel Foundation and the White Barn Theatre Foundation would have no such control. Quite the opposite. Perhaps out of her innate wariness about spending money, or a concern that others would bankrupt her estate if they had access to it, Lucille separated the assets from the artists. Under this arrangement, the artistic advisors would never be able to decide how much money to spend where—they would only be able to make recommendations to men who supposedly were smart about managing an estate but possessed little artistic sophistication. But at least when it came to productions at the Lortel Theatre there would be one dominant artistic voice.

Mason had lobbied hard for the position that she had promised him in the early 1980s when he was artistic director of Circle Repertory Company and he tried to remain uppermost in her attention. From California, where he was striving unsuccessfully to jump-start a career as a film director, he kept in touch. Hearing early in 1994 that she was considering others to run the Lortel Theatre after her death, he wrote her that he "was alarmed" by the people in question and that "I just want you to know that I am steadfast in my devotion to you and your vision, and I will be available to keep your star shining on Christopher Street long after this Century has ended." However, he also told her that he would be able to do that only if he received adequate yearly compensation.

While Lucille wrestled with the future of her theatres, a generation of theatre people whom she had known or with whom she had worked seeped from her life. Paul Shyre, with whom she had collaborated to produce Sean O'Casey's plays, had died in 1989, and Robert Breen, who had rejuvenated ANTA back in the 1940s, had passed away in 1990. Willard Swire, for so long one of Lucille's defenders at Equity, died in 1991.

To Lucille, even those around her who were active seemed to betray her. In 1991 Ben Sprecher married and became less accessible. He now co-owned and operated two theatres, the Variety Arts on Third Avenue near 14th Street and the Promenade on the Upper West Side; as Sprecher's business expanded, his assistant George Forbes, whom he had hired in 1989, took over the Lortel's day-to-day operation. Lucille, always alert to disloyalty among her employees, feared that Sprecher was funneling plays to his own theatres rather than to hers, and she seriously considered firing him. "We walked a fine line," Sprecher recalled. "She would get jealous of something I was doing or trying to do. My solution was: apologize and work it out later. Just neutralize it, because at that point she could not deal with any kind of disagreement." The days when Lucille and Sprecher could argue productively were past. As she aged, she found their disagreements so upsetting, according to Sprecher, that she would just fall silent and cut him off. Finally, around 1998, their relationship ruptured. "She accused me of lying," said Sprecher, "and I was so upset that I yelled at her and hung up the phone, and that was it. I tried apologizing for my behavior, but we never really reconnected."

She clung to those whom she trusted: Anna Strasberg, Vincent Curcio, Donald Saddler. Marge Farwell had suffered a devastating stroke in 1993, but Lucille talked by telephone with Mimi Bochco in California and frequently sent her announcements about the Lortel. "You are my 'Ruthie,'" she wrote Bochco. "So, anything I get I send to you as you're the person who is nearest to being my sister that I have."

Perhaps out of the desire for family, during the 1990s she began to see more of her nephew Michael Mayo, his wife and children. During the summers she brought them up from Florida to Westport, to give their daughter Angela a birthday party at the beach around July 4 and the rest of them, including their son Waldo, a vacation. Michael was dependent on Lucille financially and he brought his family at her call, not only during the summer but also around Christmastime and in the spring for the

Senior Concert that honored his late father. Michael's brother, Rodney, whom Lucille had also helped financially, was busy acquiring a string of Palm Beach nightclubs and hardly ever visited.

By 1995 Lucille was slowing down. Now she rarely scheduled an appointment until two in the afternoon or later. That spring her calendar was largely empty except for the Lucille Lortel Awards on April 24, which also celebrated the Lortel Theatre's fortieth year. She attended a memorial with Anna Strasberg on May 19 at The Players for Sidney Kinglsey, who had died on March 20. More and more, rather than going out, she invited friends to tea at the Sherry. One night in 1996 she fell in her bedroom, and at Dr. Tyberg's urging she hired a night nurse, who slept in a Barcalounger near Lucille's bed. In 1997 she began keeping nurses around the clock, to sit with her and accompany her outdoors.

But her innate feistiness battled with her fear of accidents and illness. Increasing frailty did not stop her from sallying forth to attend the Helen Hayes gala for St. Clare's Hospital in December 1996, when she received the Helen Hayes Award and was photographed nestling close to the towering heavyweight prize fighter Joe Frazier. "Dear Helen," Lucille recalled fondly for a *New York Post* columnist at Anna Strasberg's party two weeks later, "we used to compare our breast sizes backstage at the Guild Theatre."

In March 1997 she ventured with Anna Strasberg to Paula Vogel's *How I Learned to Drive* and appeared at the thirty-fifth anniversary of the Vera Institute of Justice. When Signature Theatre Company threw a celebratory dinner at the Laura Belle Supper Club, to honor Lucille and playwright Horton Foote, Lucille was there. She did, however, instruct the organizers that she wanted to be able to see Sandy Starr from her table, and that Starr should be able to hear if Lucille called her, in case Lucille needed to be taken to the bathroom or wanted to go home. She did not have the energy to go to the Longacre Theatre afterward to see Foote's *The Young Man From Atlanta*.

But she could not miss the fiftieth anniversary of the White Barn on

Sunday, August 31, 1997, an evening of reminiscence, performance and loving commendations. The evening started with the White Barn curtain opening to reveal Lucille standing in front of a microphone. For many years now she had stopped dyeing her hair, and it had gone silvery gray, which made her look distinguished, if fragile. After the applause ended, Donald Saddler, who had directed the celebration, joined her on stage. Lucille momentarily forgot to introduce Vincent Curcio, but he, too, walked on and gave her a gold pin engraved with the image of the White Barn. Then Saddler gracefully stepped forward. "Lucille," he said, "I don't have any present for you, just two arms to dance with you," and with that he gently and lightly led a smiling Lucille into a few bars of a foxtrot. "The highlight was dancing with you," Saddler wrote her the next day. "It is a memory I shall cherish."

That year she signed what would turn out to be the last version of her will. In 1998, with Lucille's agreement, her lawyers established the not-for-profit Lucille Lortel Theatre Foundation, which would run the Lortel and, like the White Barn Theatre Foundation, go to the mother source, the Lucille Lortel Foundation, for money. Attached to this new Lucille Lortel Theatre Foundation was the old artistic advisory board—growing in size and diminishing in power, for Lucille had invited Elliot Martin to join and considered asking Al Pacino.

Just as Lucille determined to venture forth when she could, so she needed to feel that she was still working and busy, still necessary. Despite her frailty, the impulse to start new projects, which she had followed for the last fifty years, carried her forward almost automatically, and in 1998, at the age of 97, she embarked on what became known as the Playwrights Sidewalk in front of the Lortel Theatre.

Like other ideas for which Lucille took credit, the origin of this one is lost amid competing egos and memories. Lucille herself said that she was inspired by seeing a television report of Al Pacino putting his hands in the cement outside of Grauman's Chinese Theatre in Hollywood. Ben

Sprecher, who several times had to replace the sidewalk in front of the Lortel, said that he once suggested it might be fun to put playwrights' names there, much as the Walk of Fame on Hollywood Boulevard immortalized actors with bronze stars imbedded in the sidewalk. George Atty, a photographer who often videotaped Lucille's events for her, believed that he was the one who first approached Lucille with the idea of a star-studded sidewalk, where each star enclosed a playwright's name and the biggest star of all was reserved for Lucille. He generated a computer drawing, and most likely this was the sketch that Lucille handed to Sprecher one day, during a rare moment of renewed communication, and said, "I really want to do this. Why don't we do this, darling?" In November 1998, after the sidewalk was constructed and dedicated, Atty wrote Lucille how hurt he was that no one had acknowledged his contribution. "You deserve to be acknowledged and publicly thanked," she wrote back. "It was your rendition of playwrights' names in stars that gave my idea a tangible being. I remember . . . how it excited everyone I showed it to."

Whether the idea was Lucille's or not, the insistence on making it happen certainly was hers. Suddenly in 1998 she had a task to which she could commit her attention and summon her energy, even if only from her bedroom at the Sherry.

The project turned out to be bigger than anyone expected. Sprecher hired architect John Harding to draw up plans, then found that the New York City Landmarks Commission needed to approve them, because the Lortel Theatre was in a landmark district. While Lucille polled colleagues for playwrights' names and assembled a list, Sprecher asked well-known theatre people to write letters of support to the Landmarks Preservation Commission. In the meantime, the physical concept mushroomed. One day when Sprecher and George Forbes were toying with the design, they decided to put empty stars along the side of the building, so that each year, when a playwright received a Lortel Award, his or her name could be added. And although Sprecher never told Lucille,

inscribed on the back of her bronze star were the words, "This sidewalk
was created by Ben Sprecher, John Harding, Architect, and Martin
Rodow"—the construction manager.

The sidewalk cost a quarter of a million dollars. At its dedication, on
Monday evening, October 26, 1998, the names of forty-three playwrights, from Edward Albee to Paul Zindel, shone beneath the marquee
lights. The day before, Donald Saddler, who was staging the ceremony,
had gone to the Sherry in the late afternoon to walk through the program with Lucille, but she still felt anxious. Watching her outside the
Lortel on Monday evening, Sprecher remembered thinking that she was
"almost not there." Still, she looked dashing standing in front of the theatre, wearing a black dress with an outsized scarlet collar and the scarlet
hat that Larry Kramer had given her, and cradling a bouquet of pink
roses. And once she had said her few prepared words she smiled and felt
more relaxed and spoke into reporters' microphones. Afterward she
went up to the mezzanine for a reception, where playwrights Paula
Vogel, Lanford Wilson and William Hoffman, among others, stopped to
say hello and chat. Then around 10:00 P.M. Sandy Starr and Olive
Wright bundled Lucille into a car and took her home.

During the fall Lucille's world alternated between the Sherry, where
she still received people for tea, and the occasional outing: to doctors; to
Anna Strasberg's for an election night party in November; to the Lortel
on November 16 for a memorial for Paul Berkowsky, who had died of
leukemia; to Anna's again at Thanksgiving, accompanied by Robert
Buzzell and her nurse Erlah Hackett.

Strasberg went to California that Christmas, to take care of her son
David and was unable to give Lucille her usual holiday celebration. Lucille
scheduled nothing herself for her ninety-eighth birthday, although Blanche
Marvin and her family sent balloons, and flowers arrived by the cartload.
On December 21 Lucille gave her own holiday party at the Lortel. Begin-
ning at 5:30 in the afternoon, about thirty-six guests arrived to admire the

sidewalk and join Lucille in the mezzanine for a cozy reception. She went as usual to Isabelle and John Stevenson's that Christmas Eve, and on Christmas Day, Michael Mayo and his family, and Hope Alswang and her family, dropped by the Sherry at around five for tea and cake.

It is hard to know how Lucille felt as her world receded. George Forbes remembered being called to the Sherry to settle arguments between Lucille and Sandy Starr, because Starr would insist on her taking certain medicines or not eating certain food, and Lucille, in frustration, would cry and shake her fists and say "Sandy is trying to kill me," and Starr herself would be in tears.

At other times she displayed a touching persistence. The last time Elliot Martin saw Lucille, he was crossing 59th Street near Fifth Avenue and Lucille was on the sidewalk, with Starr on one side and Olive Wright on the other. "They were holding her," said Martin, "and her little feet were barely touching the ground. They stopped, and she saw me, and she said, 'Darling, darling,' and then she said, 'Sandy, give me my purse,' and she pulled out this flyer and said, 'This is my next play.' "

And she preserved her sense of humor, even in unlikely situations such as Frankie Godowsky's funeral in January 1999. She arrived at Frank E. Campbell's just as the funeral was starting, and David Hays gave her his seat. "Oh, Leonora," Lucille said after she had sat down beside Hays' wife, "do you come here often?"

Early in March 1999 Lucille had the flu, but seemed to recover. Then on Thursday, March 25, she began to complain of intestinal pain. Dr. Tyberg was in Aruba on vacation, and Lucille did not want to go to the hospital. But by Sunday night the pain had intensified and there was severe diarrhea, and around eight o'clock Monday morning, March 29, Sandy Starr reached George Forbes at the Lortel and asked him to come to the Sherry immediately, to help take Lucille to the emergency room. Olive Wright and a nurse, Lucille Williams, dressed Lucille and put on her makeup, and when Forbes arrived they took her downstairs, put her in a town car and brought her to New York Hospital. "She was definitely in pain," Forbes said, "but she was holding it together."

At the hospital, others began to arrive: Ben Sprecher, Michael Hecht, James Ross, Anna Strasberg. Williams dressed Lucille in a hospital gown and braided her hair. Hospital aides put her on a gurney and took her to be X-rayed, and they brought her back to a little room off the emergency area. There Lucille asked to have the lights turned off, because the glare was hurting her eyes, so Forbes and Starr sat on either side of Lucille in the dark, holding her hands.

They spent all day in the ER, while the doctors conversed with Hecht and Ross and dickered with each other about whether to operate and remove the intestinal blockage—surgery from which Lucille might die— or not operate, in which case Lucille might die in enormous pain. Finally, late Monday afternoon, they decided on surgery, and at around eight o'clock that night Lucille was wheeled into the operating room. "She was absolutely terrified," said Sprecher.

Lucille survived the surgery and woke up later that night in the recovery room. "I want to go home," she told Sandy Starr, gripping her hand tightly. But the next day she floated in and out of consciousness, and sometime late Wednesday night or early Thursday morning, while she was in a private room in the surgical wing, she suffered a massive cerebral hemorrhage and never regained consciousness.

All that week relatives and friends drifted in and out. Michael Mayo and his family flew up from Florida. Blanche Marvin arrived from London. Late in the afternoon on Easter Sunday, April 4, a number of people gathered in Lucille's hospital room: Marvin, Anna Strasberg, Drew Eliot, nurse Williams, Olive Wright and Sandy Starr. Dr. Tyberg had cut short his vacation and returned that afternoon and shortly before four o'clock he walked into Lucille's room and said, "Lucille, it's Dr. Tyberg." She breathed a deep sigh and minutes later she was gone.

Afterword

Tuesday morning, April 6, 1999, was sunny when friends and relatives and colleagues walked slowly into Frank E. Campbell's funeral home for Lucille Lortel's service. Anna Strasberg and Ben Sprecher had organized the ceremony. A blanket of red roses draped Lucille's casket, and a chamber orchestra played music at the back of the room. Rabbi Joseph Potasnik officiated. Potasnik was Strasberg's rabbi and had not known Lucille, so he delicately turned over the rostrum to those who had. Five people spoke: Hope Alswang, Lynne Mayocole, Ben Sprecher, Mimi Bochco, and Strasberg. Later there would be public memorials at the Lortel Theatre and the White Barn— the first cloyingly sentimental, the second more lighthearted. But none was so brief, intimate or honest as this. Sitting there and listening to Hope Alswang, Albert Poland heard her describe "the Lucille I knew": generous but parsimonious, friendly but blunt sometimes to the point of being hurtful, coquettish rather than maternal, and always active—"A woman," said Alswang, "who lived ten lives." Mayocole called her aunt "tough, feisty and smart," and Ben Sprecher, his voice tearful, said "I loved Lucille and she had a great deal of sway over me. No one could make me more miserable or angry when she was upset with me, or make me happier when she was pleased with me."

When the service ended, ten pallbearers escorted the casket out the door and into a waiting hearse. Lucille had always stated she wished to be cremated, as her parents, brothers and sister had been. In an early version of her will she had directed that her ashes be buried in Lou's family plot in Queens. But at some point after 1993 she changed her mind about the site. She had noted that on Sundays Anna visited Lee Strasberg's grave at the Westchester Hills Cemetery of the Stephen Wise Free Synagogue, and one day she called Anna and said, "I've decided I want to be buried near Lee, because I know you will visit on Sundays and you'd put flowers on my grave." And there, in the uppermost corner of a hillside, beneath some trees, Lucille Lortel's ashes are buried. A flared, reddish granite gravestone reads

Lucille Lortel

Theatrical pioneer, patron of

the arts,

loving mentor to all who

worked with her.

HER THEATRES WERE HER CHILDREN

In front of the grave and to the side is a narrow granite bench with the words "The Queen of Off-Broadway" carved along the edge of the seat. About two yards down the slope the composer and lyricist Arthur Schwartz lies buried, and a bit further down the hill lies Lee Strasberg. A mausoleum near the entrance to the cemetery is for the Gershwin family and contains the ashes of Leopold Godowsky, Jr.

The will that Lucille had labored to perfect left an estate worth over $37 million. She endowed the Lucille Lortel Foundation with $5 million and also entrusted it with the Lucille Lortel Theatre and her Connecticut real estate. She gave over $1 million dollars in outright bequests to friends and employees, including her nurses. More than $1 million dollars was designated for nonprofit theatre companies and other charitable organizations, including the Eugene O'Neill Memorial Theater Center, the Goodspeed Opera House Foundation, the Lee Strasberg Creative Center, and New Dramatists, each of which received $50,000. The Actors' Fund received $100,000 for her theatre at the long-term care facility in New Jersey, and she earmarked $500,000 for continuing the Lucille Lortel Awards.

There were bequests for Mayo's two daughters and tightly controlled trusts for Michael and Wilmien Mayo and their children. Michael Mayo also received most of the furniture and clothing in the Sherry-Netherland apartment and in Fairweather, which he sold at auction. To Rodney Mayo she left nothing, with the message that she had confidence in his abilities as a businessman.

Lanford Wilson was the only playwright she had produced to whom she left money—$50,000—and the only theatre critic was Clive Barnes, who always said he was mystified by his $50,000 bequest. But George Forbes, who used to attend the meetings of the Lucille Lortel Awards committee, on which Barnes served, said that every time Lucille left a meeting she would ask, "Is he poor? He wears horrible clothes. I think I'll leave him something."

Her memorabilia she gave to the Lucille Lortel Foundation. Her papers would eventually be removed from the Westport Public Library and donated to the Billy Rose Theatre Collection of the New York Public Library for the Performing Arts.

Anna Strasberg received Lucille's ruby necklace, earrings and ring. Ben Sprecher received $50,000. To Sandy Starr, who had served Lucille slavishly for sixteen years, as secretary, chauffeur and nursemaid, she left $25,000. Pointedly she gave no money to Marshall Mason, nor any directive that he be artistic head of the Lortel Theatre. Instead she instructed the Lortel Foundation's directors to operate the theatre as a not-for-profit entity, with artistic leadership from the board of advisors.

The Lucille Lortel Foundation and the two theatres seemed to float in a kind of executive and artistic limbo after Lucille's death. The Foundation eventually began disbursing money to not-for-profit theatres, and in 2001 Vincent Curcio renegotiated a contract with Equity for the White Barn and, as artistic director, began producing the first full-scale productions there since 1987. But running the White Barn proved expensive, and all the buildings at Fairweather needed repair. By 2003 the board and the executive director, George Forbes, were questioning whether to keep the theatre going, to use the property for another purpose or to sell it.

As for the Lortel Theatre, its operation floundered for a while, until the Foundation began renting the space to nonprofit theatre companies. Without the Queen of Off Broadway's presence and vitality, the Lortel seemed to belong less and less to Lucille, and more and more to the groups that now called it a temporary home.

Enid Nemy quoted Lucille in her *New York Times* obituary: "If you love the theater you must be innovative. You must try new ideas and new faces. That's the only way theater can develop. You can't do it on Broadway because it costs too much. The costs are lower Off Broadway, so you can afford to take a chance, and you *must* take a chance."

Throughout more than fifty years of producing plays and owning theatres, Lucille Lortel risked. Instinctive and canny, she preferred the club theatre to run-of-the-mill summer stock, Greenwich Village to Broadway, the innovative playwright to the conventional, a drama with something to say before a piece of frivolous entertainment. She was a middle-class woman with a bohemian streak, which she expressed through the plays she selected and the artists she supported.

She grew up when theatre was solely a commercial enterprise and so she naturally became a commercial producer. But she possessed the inclinations of an artistic director who valued quality over profits. Sensing that Broadway's forms were stale and its content empty, she turned for vibrancy to avant-garde Europeans and youthful Americans, and helped revolutionize New York theatre. But she never embraced the new for its own sake. She stuck by her inner standards, which drew her to humanism, social meaning and coherent language.

An interviewer once asked Lucille if she felt discriminated against as a female producer. She replied that she never felt slighted because of being a woman. If she had been asked whether she was a feminist, she probably would have sidestepped the question—she distrusted terms that she did not understand. But in the trajectory of her nearly one hundred years, one sees a woman taking control of her life and her immediate world, and defining herself.

Her wealth was both a benefit and a drawback. Money brought her the freedom to produce as she wished but to her distress, also the label of dilettante. As hard as she worked, and as many professional awards as she accumulated, she still felt the need to convince both the theatre community and herself of her significance. The irony is that someone who so loved theatre did not accept its ephemeral nature. The beauty is that she persisted, and in persisting gave opportunities to hundreds of playwrights, actors and directors who created a vigorous new theatre during the second half of the twentieth century.

At the public memorial in the Lortel Theatre on May 24, 1999, Eli Wallach and Anne Jackson paid tribute to Lucille, and Wallach spoke a line from Tennessee Williams' *Camino Real*: "*Make voyages!—Attempt them!*—there's nothing else..."

Bibliography

Atkinson, Brooks. *Broadway*. New York, 1970.

Belasco, David. *The Theatre Through Its Stage Door*. New York, 1919.

Brecht, Bertolt. *Brecht on Brecht*. Typescript, Cheryl Crawford Collection, NYPL.

Bronx Museum of the Arts. *Building a Borough*. Bronx, New York, 1986.

Brown, Alice. *Joint Owners in Spain*. Chicago, 1914.

Brinnin, John Malcolm. *Beau Voyage: Life Aboard the Last Great Ships*. New York, 1981.

_____. *The Sway of the Grand Saloon*. New York, 1971.

Burrows, Edwin G., and Wallace, Mike. *Gotham*. New York, 1999.

Chelik, Michael. *The Bronx Apartment House*. Bronx, New York, 1978.

Colton, John. *The Shanghai Gesture*. New York, 1926.

Comfort, Randall. *History of Bronx Borough, City of New York*. New York, 1906.

West End Association (New York, N.Y.), Committee on Law and Legislation. *Riverside Park and Hudson River Waterfront; origin and development of existing conditions, with maps and photographs*. New York, 1915.

Cook, Harry. *The Borough of the Bronx, 1639-1913: Its Marvelous Development and Historical Surroundings*. New York, 1913.

Cron, Theodore O., and Burt Goldblatt. *Portrait of Carnegie Hall*. New York, 1966.

Cugat, Xavier. *Rumba Is My Life*. New York, 1948.

D'Annunzio, Gabriele. *The Honeysuckle*. Tr. by Cecile Sartoris and Gabrielle Enthoven. London, 1915.

Derwent, Clarence. *The Derwent Story*. New York, 1953.

Dolkart, Andrew S. *Morningside Heights: A History of Its Architecture and Development*. New York, 1998.

Eaton, Walter Prichard. *New York, A Series of Wood Engravings in Colour with Prose Impressions by Walter Prichard Eaton*. New York, 1915.

Ellis, Edward Robb. *The Epic of New York City*. New York, 1966.

Farneth, David. *Lenya the Legend*. New York, 1998.

Fitch, Clyde. *Girls*. Typescript, NYPL, n.p. 1908.

Freedley, George. "The American National Theatre." *The Southwest Review*, Autumn 1946.

Fugard, Athol. Introduction to *Three Port Elizabeth Plays*. New York, 1974.

Gassner, John. *Masters of the Drama*. New York, 1954.

Godowsky, Dagmar. *First Person Plural*. New York, 1958.

Goldstone, Harmon H., and Martha Dalrymple. *History Preserved: A Guide to New York City Landmarks and Historic Districts*. New York, 1974.

Goodman, Edward. *Make-Believe: A primer of Acting*. Typescript, NYPL, n.d.

Gordon, E.A. *Mark the Music: The Life and Work of Marc Blitzstein*. New York, 1989.

Gordon, Max W. with Lewis Funke. *Max Gordon Presents*. New York, 1963.

Gordon, Ruth. *Myself Among Others*. New York, 1971.

_____. *My Side*. New York, 1976.

_____. *Ruth Gordon, An Open Book*. New York, 1980.

Gould, Eleanor Cody. *Charles Jehlinger in Rehearsal*. n. p. 1958.

Greene, Alexis. *Revolutions Off Off Broadway, 1959-1969*. Unpublished dissertation, City University of New York, 1987.

Heinze, Andrew R. *Adapting to Abundance: Jewish Immigrants, Mass Consumption, and the Search for American Identity*. New York, 1990.

Henderson, Mary C. *The City and the Theater: New York Playhouses from Bowling Green to Times Square*. Clifton, New Jersey, 1973.

Hewitt, Barnard. *Theatre U.S.A., 1665 to 1957*. New York, 1959.

Hopwood, Avery. *The Demi-Virgin*. Typescript, n.d., NYPL.

_____. *The Gold Diggers*. Typescript, 1919, NYPL.

Howe, Irving. *World of Our Fathers*. New York, 1976.

Jablonski, Edward. *Gershwin*. New York, 1987.

Jablonski, Edward, and Lawrence D. Stewart. *The Gershwin Years*. New York, 1958.

Kessner, Thomas. *The Golden Door: Italian and Jewish Mobility in New York City, 1880–1915*. New York, 1977.

Klein, Woody. *Westport, Connecticut: The Story of a New England Town's Rise to Prominence*. Westport, 2000.

Knoblauch, Edward. *My Lady's Dress*; a play in three acts; with an introduction by Frank Chouteau Brown. Garden City, N.Y., 1916.

Krause, David, ed. *The Letters of Sean O'Casey*, Volume I. New York, 1975.

_____. Volume II. New York, 1980.

_____. Volume III. Washington, D.C., 1989.

Kuler, James M. "Classical Music." In *The Encyclopedia of New York City*, Kenneth T. Jackson, ed. New Haven, 1995.

Little, Stuart W. *Off-Broadway: The Prophetic Theater*. New York, 1972.

Lockwood, Charles. *Manhattan Moves Uptown: An Illustrated History*. Boston, 1976.

Mack, Willard. *Kick In*. Typescript, n.d., NYPL.

Maney, Richard. *Fanfare: The Confessions of a Press Agent*. New York, 1957.

Mantle, Burns. *The Best Plays*. New York, 1919/20–1988/89.

McCready, Sam. *Lucille Lortel: A Bio-Bibliography*. Westport, Connecticut, 1993.

Miller, Michael B. *Theatres of the Bronx*. 1972.

Moore, Carlyle. *Stop Thief, A Farcical Fact in Three Acts*. New York, 1917.

New York State Consolidated Laws Service. Volume 3A. Rochester, NY, 1983.

New York (State). Court of Appeals. *Reports of Cases Decided in the Court of Appeals of the State of New York*. New York, 1956–1997.

New York (State). Supreme Court. *Reports of Cases Decided in the Appellate Division of the Supreme Court of the State of New York*. New York, 1955–1998.

Nicholas, Jeremy. *Godowsky, The Pianist's Pianist*. Wark, Hexham, Northumberland, 1989.

Peyser, Ethel. *The House That Music Built*. New York, 1936.

Pillot, Eugene. *Two Crooks and a Lady*. New York, c. 1918.

Polk's (Trow's) New York Copartnership and Corporation Directory, Boroughs of Manhattan and the Bronx. New York, 1898–1925.

Quinn, Arthur Hobson. *A History of the American Drama.* New York, 1945.

Rampersad, Arnold. *The Life of Langston Hughes,* Volume I. New York, 1986.
____. Volume II. New York, 1988.

Salwen, Peter. *Upper West Side Story: A History and Guide.* New York, 1989.

Sanders, Ronald. *The Downtown Jews: Portraits of an Immigrant Generation.* New York, 1969.

Schickel, Richard. *The World of Carnegie Hall.* New York, 1960.

Sheehy, Helen. *Eva Le Gallienne.* New York, 1996.

Soyer, Daniel. *Jewish Immigrant Associations 1880–1939 and American Identity in New York.*

TenEick, Virginia Elliott. *The History of Hollywood (1920–1950).* Hollywood, Florida, 1966.

White, Edmund. *Genet.* New York, 1993.

White, Michael. *Empty Seats.* London, 1984.

Whitelaw, Billie. *Billie Whitelaw . . . Who He?* New York, 1995.

Williams, Tennessee. *Camino Real.* In *The Theatre of Tennessee Williams,* Volume II. New York, 1971.

Woolf, Edgar A. *The Man Who Laughed.* Typescript, n.p. LL Collection, NYPL.

Filmography

Woolf, Edgar A. *The Man Who Laughed Last.* LL Collection.
Everything Happens to Me. Library of Congress.
Grounds for Murder. Library of Congress.

Notes

Abbreviations

AG   Alexis Greene
AW   Anny Wadler
C-C   Francis Coradal-Cugat
HW   Harry Wadler
LL   Lucille Lortel
LS   Louis Schweitzer
LW   Lucille Wadler
NYPL   New York Public Library
RW   Ruth Wadler

Chapter 1—A Young Woman of the Theatre

ARCHIVES: American Academy of Dramatic Arts; Billy Rose Theatre Collection, NYPL; LL Collection, NYPL; Municipal Archives, New York City; NYPL.

BOOKS, DOCUMENTS AND PLAYS: Atkinson, *Broadway;* Becker, *The Fight for Space;* Belasco, *The Theatre Through Its Stage Door;* Henderson, *The City* *and the Theater;* Bronx Museum of Arts, *Building a Borough;* Burrows & Wallace, *Gotham;* Brown, *Joint Owners in Spain;* Chelik, *The Bronx Apartment House;* Comfort, *History of Bronx Borough;* Cook, *The Borough of the Bronx;* Cron, *Portrait of Carnegie Hall;* D'Annunzio, *The Honeysuckle;* Dolkart, *Morningside Heights;* Eaton, *New York;* Fitch, *Girls;* Goldstone and Dalrymple, *History Preserved;* Goodman, *Make-Believe;* Gould, *Charles Jehlinger in Rehearsal;* Heinze, *Adapting to Abundance;* Hewitt, *Theatre U.S.A.;* Howe, *World of Our Fathers;* Jablonski, *Gershwin;* Kessner, *The Golden Door;* Kuler, "Classical Music"; Knoblauch, *My Lady's Dress;* Levy, *Art Education in the City of New York;* Lockwood, *Manhattan Moves Uptown;* Mannes, *The New York I Knew;* Miller, *Theatres of the Bronx;* Moore, *Stop Thief;* Peyser, *The House That Music Built;* Pillot, *Two Crooks and a Lady;* Polk's (Trow's) *New York Copartnership and Corporation Directory;* Salwen, *Upper West Side Story;* Sanders, *The Downtown Jews;* Soyer, *Jewish Immigrant Associations;* West End Association, *Riverside Park and Hudson River Waterfront.*

INTERVIEWS: Mimi Bochco; Concetta Clark; Vincent Curcio; Elizabeth Goodyear; Portia Waldman Laveman; Martine Lund; Lynne Mayocole; Paul Moss; Anna Strasberg; Joel A. Weiner.

NOTES

It seems strange: Ruth Wadler to Lucille Wadler, March 5, 1931.

Lu: LL Collection.

Here, at night, the Great White Way: Eaton, pp. 77–78.

Every character has a heart: Eleanor Cody Gould was an aspiring actress when she sat in Charles Jehlinger's classes at the Academy in 1918 and 1919 and transcribed his maxims verbatim; she graduated in 1920, the year Lucille Wadler entered AADA. Gould sat in on Jehlinger's classes again in 1934, and from 1950 to 1952.

Mayo Wadler's sister: *Musical Leader,* Feb. 3, 1921.

What would I not do: *Honeysuckle,* p. 91.

Light and vivacious: *Honeysuckle,* p. 3.

Lucille Wadler, an exquisite little creature: *Musical Leader,* March 31, 1921.

A turgid, dour, oratorical: *Morning Telegraph,,* March 22, 1921.

Chapter 2—Breaking In

ARCHIVES: Billy Rose Theatre Collection, NYPL; LL Collection, NYPL; Municipal Archives, New York City.

BOOKS, DOCUMENTS, PLAYS, AND FILMSCRIPTS: Anon., *Freddys Liebestod;* Brinnin, *Beau Voyage;* Brinnin, *The Sway of the Grand Saloon;* Cugat, *Rumba Is My Life;* Colton, *Shanghai Gesture;* Derwent, *Derwent Story;* Godowsky, *First Person Plural;* Gordon (Max), *Max Gordon Presents;* Gordon (Ruth), *Myself Among Others;* Gordon (Ruth), *My Side;* Gordon (Ruth), *Ruth Gordon;* Jablonski, *Gershwin;* Jablonski and Stewart, *The Gershwin Years;* Hopwood, *The Demi-Virgin;* Hopwood, *The Gold Diggers;* Mack, *Kick In;* Maney, *Fanfare;* Woolf, *The Man Who Laughed.*

FILMS: *The Man Who Laughed Last* (1928), LL Collection; *Everything Happens To Me,* n.d., Library of Congress; *Grounds for Murder,* n.d., Library of Congress.

ORAL HISTORIES: Francis Gershwin Godowsky, transcript of an interview by Dorothy Horowitz, October 23, 1980, NYPL; Leopold Godowsky, Jr., transcript of an interview by Alan Green, April 16, 30, 1971, NYPL; Lucille Lortel, interview by Corinne Jacker, c.1982, LL Collection, Rodgers and Hammerstein Archives.

INTERVIEWS: Hope Alswang; Mirel Bercovici; Mimi Bochco; Vincent Curcio; Lisa Fabietti; Leopold Godowsky III; Alexis Gershwin Godowsky; Elizabeth Goodyear; Lynne Mayocole; Donald Saddler; Sandra Starr.

NOTES

My brother was studying: *New Haven Register,* July 3, 1983.

The men are so nice to me: LW to Marvine Maazel, April 26, 1921.

The bliss that was mine: Leopold Godowsky, Jr., to LW, April 20, 1921.

This is the 3rd day: LW to Marvine Maazel, April 22, 1921.

Leo of all things: LW to Leopold Godowsky, Jr., April 25, 1921.

I love you for your sincere and noble character: Leopold Godowsky, Jr., to LW, May 11, 1921.

Happy days…: Leopold Godowsky, Jr., to LW, June 14, 1921.

It is very sweet of you: LW to Leo Godowsky, Jr., July 1, 1921.

Don't believe what you said: LW to Marvine Maazel, August 8, 1921.

Do you fail to realize: Marvine Maazel to LW, undated but probably September 1921.

Come home: C-C to RW, n.d.

Dearest, Darling—Lu: RW to LW, November 1, 1921.

Miss Wadler, of the New York Dramatic Academy: *The Daily Mail,* July 30, 1921.

Working on a picture in Berlin: RW to LW, December 23, 1921.

It was the first time: RW to LW, June 8, 1922.

Lucille Lortel, talented young American: *Apparel Producer,* undated but probably early 1923.

You know that five dollars: AG interview with Vincent Curcio.

Dearest folks: n.d., LL Collection.

Say kidd: AW to LL, May 4, 1924.

The boxes, draped with the national colors: *Lewiston Journal,* July 1, 1924.

Dressed up like a house: *Kick In,* LL Collection.

Benny's in trouble: *Kick In, Act* 1, pp. 6 and 7.

Miss Lortel goes back to New York: *Lewiston Journal,* July 1924.

Premature and abortive: *Variety,* February 25, 1925.

Lacked one solitary bright line: *American,* February 25, 1925.

I did the harpist: LL interview by Corinne Jacker, LL Collection. The production of *Caesar and Cleopatra* opened the new Guild Theatre on West 52nd Street. Lucille was apparently unaware that at eight o'clock on opening night, April 13, 1925, President Calvin Coolidge pressed a button in the White House, and the resulting vibration rang a bell and raised the new theatre's first curtain.

I had long dark hair: Interview with LL, May 31, 1985, LL Collection, Rodgers and Hammerstein Archives.

It is still raining: *Telegram,* May 26, 1926.

The banalities of old-time theatricalisms: *New York Times,* May 26, 1926.

Destined for a short stay: *Evening Graphic,* May 26, 1926.

Press agentry is no business: Maney, p. 19.

By such dodges: Maney, p. 119.

Other items raided: *New York World,* February 17, 1927.

On less than twenty-four hours notice: "Along Broadway" column in unidentified newspaper, LL Collection.

Exquisite as a summer morning: Colton, p. 34.

Oh, I am a bad one!: Colton, p. 188.

Lucille Lortell . . . won a deserved hand: *Kansas City Star,* October 3, 1927.

Lucille Lortell gave the part full measure: *The Independent,* October 8, 1927.

Lucille Lortell is Poppy: *Kansas City Times,* October 3, 1927.

The dirty dog: Woolf, *The Man Who Laughed.* Albert Lewis, with his partner Max Gordon, produced the Hayakawa vehicle; Lucille recounted that they had seen her in *The Shanghai Gesture.* Before becoming producers they were known as the vaudeville team of Lewis and Gordon and subsequently they developed the idea of presenting short plays in vaudeville. Gordon would eventually become a prominent agent and producer in his own right.

At a wholesale rate: Sidney Phillips of Albert Lewis Incorporated, Theatrical Enterprises, to Van Raalte & Co., 295 Fifth Avenue, March 7, 1928.

Your letter to hand: David Mendoza to LL, July 17, 1928.

Chapter 3—An Unlikely Marriage

ARCHIVES: Billy Rose Theatre Collection, NYPL; LL Collection, NYPL; Municipal Archives, New York City; NYPL; Raymond H. Fogler Library, Univeristy of Maine, Orono; Records of the Actors' Equity Association 1913–1986, Tamiment Institute Library and Robert F. Wagner Labor Archives, New York University.

BOOKS: Klein, *Westport;* McCready, *Lucille Lortel;* TenEick, *History of Hollywood.*

ORAL HISTORIES: LL by Corinne Jacker, LL Collection, Rodgers and Hammerstein Archives.

INTERVIEWS: Hope Alswang; Mimi Bochco; Vincent Curcio; Tina Howe; Lily Lodge; Lynne Mayocole; Leo Nevas.

NOTES:

Lou looked at that cold Russian winter: *Lou's Saga*, 1944. LL Collection

If you want to see egoism: *The Prism*, Volume XXV, p. 49.

Lucille told: The story of how Lucille and Lou met is related in McCready's bio-bibliography.

It was harder and harder: McCready, p. 5.

You know what I think of married men: LL to LS, February 17, 1941.

You persist in behaving: LL to LS, February 5, 1931.

Be patient my sweet: LL to LS, February 17 or 18, 1931.

God kid: LS to LL, February 19, 1931.

This vacation: LS to LL, February 19, 1931.

If you really want me: LL to LS, March 5, 1931.

Lucille Wadler prof. known: LL Collection.

I was very naïve in those days: *The Hour,* July 21, 1989.

Really kid: RW to LL, March 13, 1931.

You can't imagine: AW to LL, March 13, 1931.

Welcome home: LS to LL, March 13, 1931.

Has gone a good deal further: LS to LL, February 19, 1931.

Darling Everyone is at church: LL to LS, March 22, 1931.

Two young U.S. paper men: *Time,* April 13, 1931.

Linen rags: *Business Week,* March 25, 1931.

Hope you maid good: LS to LL, September 8, 1932.

I don't have to tell you: LS to LL, P.M. March 21, 1933.

Volly dear: LS to LL, P.M. March 21, 1933.

Lucille Lortel: *Daily News,* November 20, 1935, p. 62. Most likely Gross was referring to *House on the Hill*. According to Lucille's published credits, which she approved, during this time she also appeared on a radio program called *Advice to the Lovelorn*, which supposedly also aired on WHN. The author was unable to find any record of this program, although during the golden age of radio hundreds of programs came and went, and it is possible that it existed and that she appeared on it.

By the way: LS to LL, March 27, 1933.

You don't like me around your neck: LS to LL, 1930s.

Older sisters: LS to LL, August 12, 1935.

I never thought I would like a girl: LS to LL, 1930s.

To a crazy guy: LL to LS, 1930s.

To Lou: LL to LS, 1930s.

A cold bitch of a woman: LL fax to Blanche Marvin, October 30, 1998.

Bon voyage honey: LS to LL, February 7, 1941.

Lou dear: LL to LS, February 17, 1941.

Tell her that you heard: LL to LS, February 17, 1941.

Darling Lou: LS to LL, February 20, 1941.

Look honey: LL to Elizabeth Licht, February or March 1941.

You two still have: Carl Reifenberg to LL, March 8, 1941.

The first ten years: LS to LL, March 23, 1941.

What made me really happy: Carl Reifenberg to LL, August 21, 1941.

Dear Louis: LL to Louis Berlin, July 6, 1942.

Wanted children: On September 5, 1994, she wrote to Mimi Bochco's daughter Joanna: "I never really wanted children—the theatres have been my children—but, I wish I had a daughter like you."

You know, this could make: AG interview with Vincent Curcio.

Chapter 4—The Making of a Producer: The White Barn Theatre

ARCHIVES: Billy Rose Theatre Collection, NYPL; LL Collection, NYPL; Records of the Actors' Equity Association 1913–1986, Tamiment Institute Library and Robert F. Wagner Labor Archives.

BOOKS: Atkinson, *Broadway;* Mantle, *Best Plays;* Hewitt, *Theatre U.S.A.*

ORAL HISTORY: Anne Meacham by Susan Richardson, during several months in 2001.

INTERVIEWS: Hope Alswang; Eloise Armen; Eric Bentley; Sheala Berkowsky; Ira Cirker; Maude Davis; Nancy Franklin; Gene Frankel; Robert Glenn; Elizabeth Goodyear; Henry Hewes; Geoffrey Holder; Paula Laurence;

Tina Louise; Marshall W. Mason; Lynne Mayocole; George Morfogen; Leo
Nevas; Milo O'Shea; Nancy Riegel; Rita Fredricks Salzman; Marian Seldes;
Elizabeth Stearns; Herbert Sturz; Janet Swire; Michael Tolan; Sada Thompson.

NOTES:

Two hundred productions: These figures are drawn from Burns Mantle's *Best
Plays* series.

Lucille found more opportunity: A squib that ran in the June 26, 1947 issue of
the *Westporter-Herald* referred to "Lucille Lortel Schweitzer, assistant producer of the Ridgefield repertory company," but quite possibly this was
her own characterization of her role there.

In Paris...making hanky-panky: LL fax to Blanche Marvin, October 30,
1998.

Waldo [Mayo] lives in New York: *Bridgeport Sunday Post,* July 29, 1947.

I wish to announce: LL Collection.

The thought of speaking in public: Excerpted from a talk, LL Collection.

Something new in the way of a summer theatre: *New York Post,* July 29, 1947.

Miss Lortel probably: *New York Post,* July 29, 1947.

Stated that they had devised: Actors' Equity Association Collection.

The white barn is hoping: *Actors Cues,* September 9, 1947.

One exasperated councilor: *New York Times,* September 3, 1947.

Readings of plays: *Variety,* September 10, 1947.

Thanks for all the help: LL to LS, n.d. but probably September 1947.

Lou wanted to go: Travel diary, LL Collection.

I have as yet not found anything: LL to RW, April 22, 1949.

In England I was particularly interested: *Show Business,* May 31, 1949.

I'm not in the theater business: *New York Herald Tribune,* September 18, 1955.

I would have thought: Somerset Maugham to LL, June 22, 1951.

Heavy-handed pacing: *Variety,* July 22, 1953.

Judicious cutting: *Show Business,* August 17, 1953.

Had the story been told: *Bridgeport Post,* July 30, 1954.

Everybody went around: *New York Post,* August 6, 1951.

Couldn't you use: Basil C. Langton to LL, October 17, 1958.

I find reading Fugard is very simple: October 20, 1993, Videotape, LL Collection.

Imaginative, highly stylized: *Westporter-Herald,* July 15, 1954.

The set: *Westport Town Crier,* July 15, 1954.

Could get some publicity: LS to Benjamin Sonnenberg, August 23, 1951.

Beloved husband of Anna, devoted father: *The New York Times,* April 26, 1955. Harry Wadler had died on April 24, 1955. On Wednesday, April 27, there was a small private service at the Riverside Memorial Chapel on Amsterdam Avenue at 76th Street.

Chapter 5—A Theatre in Greenwich Village

ARCHIVES: Billy Rose Theatre Collection, NYPL; LL Collection, NYPL; New York State Library, Records and Briefs, Albany.

BOOKS AND DOCUMENTS: Gordon, *Mark the Music;* Hewitt, *Theatre U.S.A.;* Little, *Off-Broadway; New York State Consolidated Laws;* New York (State), *Reports of Cases Decided in the Appellate Division of the Supreme Court of the State of New York;* New York (State), *Reports of Cases Decided in the Court of Appeals of the State of New York;* Transcript, Max Eisen against John Post, Jr., Anita Post Litsky, Louis Schweitzer, Senior Estate, Ltd., and Joseph Feldman..

DISSERTATION: Greene, *Revolutions Off Off Broadway.*

ORAL HISTORY: Nan Krulewitch by Elizabeth Stearns; LL by Corinne Jacker; Anne Meacham by Susan Richardson.

INTERVIEWS: Hartney Arthur; Carmen Capalbo; Max Eisen; Jane Connell; Mary C. Henderson; Floria V. Lasky; Stuart Little; Jo Sullivan Loesser; Jerry Orbach; Ben Sprecher; Elizabeth Stearns.

NOTES:

As staged by the talented new director: Hewitt, p. 458.

Theatrical art center: *New York Times,* October 26, 1952.

What William de Lys: *New York Journal American,* October 29, 1952.

William Hawkins: *New York World-Telegram,* October 29, 1952.

The results are fairly frightening: *New York Herald Tribune,* October 29, 1952.

Candied up with some fake: *Morning Telegraph,* October 30, 1952.

The score of 'The Threepenny Opera': *New York Times,* May 11, 1954.

Brooks Atkinson thought it: *New York Times,* 1954.

Pending the signing of papers: *New York Times,* March 23, 1955.

At the Daily News: *Daily News,* March 24, 1955.

The thought of your project: Hazel Vincent Wallace to LL, April 27, 1955.

I consider the De Lys simply an extension: *New York Herald Tribune,* September 18, 1955.

The author is concerned: *Westport Town Crier,* August n.d., 1955.

The play…is considerably closer: *Westport Town Crier,* August n. d., 1955.

'The River Line' is a three-act drama: *Variety,* August 3, 1955.

It was apparent: *Show Business,* September 5, 1955.

Ably maintains and projects: *Show Business,* September 5, 1955.

Dress king: *Sunday Herald,* September 4, 1955.

Lucille Lortel will receive: LL Collection.

'The Threepenny Opera' is back: *New York Times,* September 21, 1955.

Conceivably the decision could threaten: On July 20, 1957, five months before the Court of Appeals ruled, the *New York Herald Tribune* ran the following item: "Ethel Watt and Max Eisen are still looking for an Off-Broadway house for their production of 'Steps on Toes,' but Mr. Eisen is now setting late October as a starting date. He also said bluntly he would like to bring it into the Theater de Lys where 'The Threepenny Opera' is racking up one of Off Broadway's long-run records."

He always asserted: Justice Stanley H. Fuld wrote the cogent minority opinion for the Court of Appeals. "A corporation empowered to buy, sell and generally trade in real estate may not be said to be carrying on that 'business' if its entire corporate life has been devoted to owning, managing and operating but a single piece of property….It is difficult to understand how a sale effectively terminating the corporation's 'business' may be regarded as one made in its regular course, no matter how extensive the recitals of its charter." *New York Reports,* 2d Series, pp. 526-531.

In 1965 the New York State legislature passed new business corporation law to take into account selling all or substantially all of a corporation's assets outside the regular course of business *actually conducted* (italics
author's). "The following changes in law should be noted: (a) The minority position in Eisen v. Post, 3NY2d 518 (1957) has been adopted..." *New
York State Consolidated Laws Service*, pp. 63-72.

Chapter 6—The Queen of Off Broadway

ARCHIVES: Billy Rose Theatre Collection, NYPL; Cheryl Crawford Col-
lection, NYPL; LL Collection, NYPL; The History Factory; Records of the
Actors' Equity Association 1913–1986, Tamiment Institute Library and
Robert F. Wagner Labor Archives, New York University.

BOOKS, DOCUMENTS AND PLAYS: *American National Theatre and
Academy By-Laws;* Brecht, *Brecht on Brecht;* Farneth, *Lenya the Legend;* Freedley,
"American National Theatre"; Krause, *Letters of Sean O'Casey;* Little, *Off-
Broadway;* Rampersad, *Life of Langston Hughes;* Sheehy, *Eva Le Gallienne;* White,
Edmund, *Genet;* White, Michael, *Empty Seats.*

ORAL HISTORY: Lucille Lortel by Corinne Jacker; Anne Meacham by
Susan Richardson.

INTERVIEWS: Eloise G. Armen; Howard Atlee; Sheala Berkowsky;
Jacqueline Brookes; Saraleigh Carney; Helena Carroll; Merle Debuskey; Mar-
jorie L. Dycke; Gene Frankel; Robert Glenn; Alice Griffin; Terese Hayden;
David Hays; Henry Hewes; Earle Hyman; Anne Jackson; Michael Kahn;
Susan Komarow; Paula Laurence; Stuart Little; Theodore Mann; Shivaun
O'Casey; Stephen Porter; Daniel Sullivan; Stuart Vaughan.

NOTES:

We got the charter but not the money: *Morning Telegraph,* January 19, 1954.
Because it was thought: Freedley, p. 4.
Will be to the theatre: Freedley, p. 1.

ANTA **would bring:** Freedley, p. 1.

The stimulation of public interest: American National Theatre and Academy By-Laws, Article II.

To get together a group: Executive Committee Minutes, ANTA, November 14, 1955.

Scores were turned away: *Morning Telegraph,* June 5, 1956.

Le Gallienne's biographer: Helen Sheehy letter to AG, May 2, 2000.

John Dos Passos' 'U.S.A.' : *New York Post,* December 19, 1956,

If Paul Shyre's concert-reading: *New York Times,* December 19, 1956.

Representative repertory company: *Variety,* January 2, 1957.

In London: This description of Genet's reaction to the London production is drawn from Edmund White's biography, *Genet.*

I was really rather shocked: Hazel Vincent Wallace to LL, May 23, 1969.

It is very unusual: LL to Meade Roberts, LL Collection.

From the weather: *Westport Town Crier and Herald,* August 29, 1957.

The tenderness, the humor: *New York Times,* September 30, 1957.

Would you rent me your theatre?: John Wilson to LL, n.d., but probably August or September 1957, judging by LL response on September 16, 1957. Although Lucille asked for the scripts, there is no record that she heard a reading of the plays. In 1958, under the title *Garden District,* Wilson produced the one-acts *Something Unspoken* and *Suddenly Last Summer* with Warner LeRoy at the York Playhouse.

I live in a world: Katherine Anne Porter to LL, December 19, 1957.

Perhaps the most poignant aspect: *New York Times,* May 21, 1958.

It was a pity: Minutes of ANTA Executive Committee meeting, October 20, 1958.

Doing a number of major revisions: Peter Brook to LL, November 11, 1957.

At present feeling: LL to Bernard Frechtman, November 20, 1957.

If Peter Brook turns out: Alan Schneider to LL, November 11, 1957.

If any publicity: The story about the Toronto opening appears in Krause's *Letters of Sean O'Casey.*

Celtic tone: *New York Times,* November 13, 1958.

I have thought of you & Louis: Eileen O'Casey to LL, December 3, 1958.

Each character: Paper not identified, n.d.

About the loveliest show: Rampersad, Volume II, p. 303.

'Shakespeare in Harlem': *New York Times,* February 10, 1960.

Doesn't Sean have any new: LL to Eileen O'Casey, December 29, 1959.

I hope that it will receive: LL to Eileen O'Casey, December 29, 1959.

How does one go about it?: LL to Hazel Vincent Wallace, LL Collection.

So she took the script: Mann, in an interview with the author, denied that
   Quintero ever sought out Lucille through Audrey Wood, since he claimed
   there was never any question about Quintero's directing the production.
   But several letters from LL in her collection attest to the other version.
   Mann also questioned whether LL had actually put up the $14,000 speci-
   fied in the production agreement. One suspects Mann of wishing to take
   complete credit here; there is no record of her reneging on the deal.

It is not photography, but imagery: *New York Times,* February 8, 1960.

Lady producer Lortel: *Daily News,* January 9, 1960.

This got strange reviews: LL to Eileen and Sean O'Casey, March 24, 1960.

A plaster-of-Paris play: *New York Herald Tribune,* March 4, 1960.

It would take a committee of alienists: *New York Times,* March 4, 1960.

The most profound: *Saturday Review,* March 26, 1960.

Genet belongs to a category of artists: *Nation,* March 26, 1960.

Selling out: LS to Bernard Frechtman, March 22, 1960.

He donated WBAI: *Time,* January 25, 1960.

President Lyndon Baines Johnson: Press Release, Office of the White House
   Press Secretary, June 22, 1966.

Lucille is still very anxious: LS to Bernard Frechtman, March 22, 1960.

Literally flung a sandwich: Records of Actors' Equity Association.

Since you seem to be fond: Felix Munso to George S. Kaufman, July 26, 1957.
   Records of Actors' Equity Association.

A slow-starting, but ultimately absorbing: *New York Times,* October 26, 1960.

A mildly diverting spoof: Edward Albee, according to a letter to the author
   on October 3, 2002, did not remember how *Fam and Yam* reached Lucille
   but surmised that Richard Barr brought it to her. Albee had no memory
   of the disastrous post-play discussion in Washington, D.C. "It was clear to
   me that Lucille was a self-generating engine who accomplished a great
   deal of good for the theatre in her long lifetime," he wrote. "Like most

producers, very little of what she did was of any lasting value but much was provocative and needed to be done."

Plays the bizarre: *New York Times,* November 16, 1960.

De tout coeur: Eugene Ionesco to LL, "Nov. 1960, Jeudi." (November 24, 1960).

The curtain went up: *Time,* December 12, 1960.

M. Ionesco: *New York Herald Tribune,* November 30, 1960.

Now she rarely/shops for diamonds: Copyright Marc Blitzstein, March 11, 1961.

The performance: LL Collection.

The sole purpose: LL to Theodore Bikel, August 28, 1961.

The White Barn: *Equity,* October 1961.

Having just had a very pleasant: *Equity,* October 1961.

The moment: *Equity,* October 1961.

While it was felt: Records of Actors' Equity Association.

I think the show should be called: George Tabori to LL, October 21, 1961.

A very good translator of Brecht: Farneth, p. 174.

Eight people on stools: *Village Voice,* November 23, 1961.

There is a cult about Brecht: *New Yorker,* June 16, 1962.

Everyone has long faces: *Norwalk Hour,* December 18, 1961.

Business continues hot: Cheryl Crawford to LL, January 9, 1962.

Continues most faithfully: "The Margo Jones Award," LL Collection.

Dear Audrey: LL to Audrey Wood, October 5, 1961.

I certainly think: Audrey Wood to LL, October 8, 1961.

I shall make sure: George Freedley to LL, October 31, 1961.

I will submit your name: Robert Glenn to LL, October 16, 1961.

I have always had: Robert Brustein to LL, November 17, 1961.

A producer's award: LL to Robert Brustein, November 21, 1961.

It is my understanding: LL to Committee, The Margo Jones Award, January 4, 1962.

We are delighted to announce: Signed "Margo Jones Award Committee Jerome Lawrence," February 8, 1962.

The theatre executive: Press release, LL Collection.

The White Barn Theatre in Westport: Abner W. Sibal to LL, February 20, 1962.

I worked for Margo: Nina Vance to LL, February 24, 1962.

It seems to be my year for awards: LL to Jerome Lawrence, March 1962.

Lucille Lortel: *Washington Post,* April 3, 1962.

Aside from the above: LL to Angus Duncan, April 12, 1962.

In no way: Actors' Equity Association inter-office correspondence addressed
to Council from the Stock and Off-Broadway Committee, May 8, 1962.

This will acknowledge receipt: LL to Angus Duncam, June 27, 1962.

Chapter 7—Passages

ARCHIVES: Billy Rose Theatre Collection, NYPL; LL Collection, NYPL;
National Library of Ireland; NYPL; Records of the Actors' Equity Associa-
tion 1913–1986, Tamiment Institute Library and Robert F. Wagner Labor
Archives, New York University.

BOOKS: Fugard, *Three Port Elizabeth Plays.*

INTERVIEWS: Sheala Berkowsky; Mimi Bochco; Athol Fugard; Robert
Glenn; Kim Hunter; James Earl Jones; Shivaun O'Casey; Albert Poland;
Haila Stoddard.

NOTES:

My dear Lucille: Sean O'Casey to LL, August 23, 1962.

I go there daily: LL to Eileen O'Casey, October 12, 1962.

The plays came off: LL to Eileen O'Casey, November 2, 1962.

'Put It in Writing': *New York Herald Tribune,* May 14, 1963.

Decrease our Operating Cost: Harlan P. Kleiman to the Futz Company, July
15, 1968.

You've done more: Harry Tierney, Jr. to LL, June 13, 1962.

Each actor will receive: LL to Angus Duncan, July 1, 1963.

The shepherd would not have: Bernard Frechtman to LL, June 22, 1962.

I decided not to do: LL to Sol Jacobson, May 29, 1962.

When Leonard White was here: LL to Michael White, November 26, 1963.
Michael White had been an intern at the White Barn and subsequently
made a theatre career in England. Leonard White had been in the British

production of *A Sleep of Prisoners* and also acted in LL's American production. He went on to direct and to work at the British Broadcasting Corporation.

Dumping ground: Fugard, p. ix.

It was still possible: Fugard, p. xi.

No play in town: *New York Times*, March 2, 1964.

Dear Miss Lortel: Athol Fugard to LL, n.d., but probably June 1964.

I can't tell you: LL to Athol Fugard, June 15, 1964.

Your warm, generous and forgiving letter: Athol Fugard to LL, n.d., June or July 1964.

On my side: Athol Fugard to LL, n.d., June or July 1964.

I do hope: LL to Eileen O'Casey, November 6, 1964.

My dearest Lucille: Eileen O'Casey to LL, dated October 1964.

Darling Eileen: This letter had originally been read at a tribute to Sean O'-Casey at the New York Shakespeare Festival on October 11, 1964. Eileen, at first concerned that LL wanted the letter read from the stage at the start of each performance, at first asked her not to have the letter read at all. But when she learned that LL only wanted Peggy Wood to read it on opening night, Eileen relented.

Took the warm poetic words: *New York Times*, November 27, 1964.

Made their characters: *New York Herald Tribune*, November 26,1964.

Too old, too fat: *New Haven Register*, August 14, 1967.

Throughout I feel: LL to James Bohan at the Ashley Famous Agency, December 4, 1965.

'The anta Matinee Series': *New York Times*, December 10, 1968.

'Brecht's little play' : *New York Times*, December 10, 1965.

I hope that your Sabbatical: Barney Simon to LL, April 5, 1968.

Theaters: *The Miami Herald*, April 9, 1966.

I've been thinking about you both: William Liebling and Audrey Wood to LL and LS, November 9, 1969.

You both live and work: Herbert Biberman to LS and LL, January 3, 1970.

You and Lou did everything: Albert Dickason to LL, February 7, 1970.

In 1931: LL Collection.

When I asked you yesterday: LS to LL, December 16, 1970.

Chapter 8—On Her Own

ARCHIVES: LL Collection, NYPL; NYPL; Surrogate's Court, New York County.

INTERVIEWS: Hope Alswang; Eloise G. Armen; Sheala Berkowsky; Mimi Bochco; Gavin Choi; Vincent Curcio; Robert Glenn; June Havoc; Lynne Mayocole; Evangeline Morphos; Genevieve Murray; Ben Sprecher; Anna Strasberg; Herbert Sturz; Lilian K. Swartburg.

ORAL HISTORY: LL by Corinne Jacker.

NOTES:

It has been a glorious trip: LL to Mimi Bochco, p.m. August 31, 1971.

Was looking very frail: Kitty Black to LL, September 26, 1971.

Lou passed away: LL Collection.

Lou Schweitzer believed passionately: Eulogy by Nicholas deB. Katzenbach, September 23, 1971. LL Collection. According to Herbert Sturz, Katzenbach's eulogy had been drafted by Patricia Wald, who later became a United States Appeals Court judge.

Silent Key: Vincent J. Skee to Editor *QST,* September 27, 1971. LL Collection.

My dearest: Eileen O'Casey to LL, October 14, 1971.

I simply cannot concentrate: Peter Cotes to LL, November 5, 1988.

I am involving myself: LL to Lyn Mosten, October 21, 1971.

My only salvation: LL to Marjorie Dycke, October 29, 1971.

I shall have to learn: LL to Gale Sondergaard (Mrs. Herbert J. Biberman), December 3, 1971.

An outright marital bequest: LL Collection; Surrogate's Court.

I cannot tell you: LL to Robert Koesis, January 12, 1972.

As is often the case: *New York Times,* January 1, 1973.

Life has been pretty cruel: LL to Betty Gardner (Mrs. John H. Gardner), October 15, 1971.

Bubbie: Carl Schaeffer to LL, LL Collection.

To the sweetest sweetheart: Carl Schaeffer to LL, December 16, 1975.

Sweetheart: Carl Schaeffer to LL, n.d., 1975.

On behalf: Office of the Council President, City of New York, Proclamation, December 1, 1975. LL Collection.

My personal thought: Carl Schaeffer to Leland Miles, December 7, 1977.

After 4 p.m.: LL Collection.

I am worried about you: Philip Huston to LL, December 3, 1978.

Chapter 9—Of Renewal, Honors And Gifts

ARCHIVES: LL Collection, NYPL; NYPL; Rodgers and Hammerstein Archives, NYPL.

BOOKS: Whitelaw, *Billie Whitelaw*.

INTERVIEWS: Sheala Berkowsky; Mimi Bochco; Ira Cirker; Betty Corwin; Vincent Curcio; Suzanne Daché; Tom Dillon; Drew Eliot; Burry Fredrik; Ciro A. Gamboni; John Hawkins; David Hays; Michael Hecht; Mary C. Henderson; William M. Hoffman; Frances Koll; Marshall W. Mason; Beatrice Milwe; Wallace Monroe; Evangeline Morphos; Nelle Nugent; Dorothy Olim; Bob Phillips; Albert Poland; Daryl Roth; Marian Seldes; Ben Sprecher; Isabelle Stevenson; Sandra Starr; Haila Stoddard; Anna Strasberg; Robert Taylor; Charles D. Webb.

NOTES:

I like to lean on a man: *Playbill*, March 21, 1986.

The two dominant forces: Charles D. Webb to LL, June 25, 1981.

I feel I should put: LL to Michael Hecht, July 13, 1981.

I do feel that Circle Repertory: LL to Porter Van Zandt, July 13, 1981.

Some ideas: Charles D. Webb to LL, July 28, 1981.

The memorandum noted: June 30, 1983, LL Collection.

O give me something: "Something to remember you by." Copyright Arthur Schwartz, 1930.

We're paying tribute to one woman: Videotape, LL Collection.

I have no recollection: LL to Joseph Veach Noble, November 15, 1982.

The Stars Salute: Videotape, LL Collection.

I am not in a position: Robert M. Zarem to LL, March 7, 1985.

Nancy joins me: Ronald Reagan, The White House, to Miss Lucille Lortel, March 13, 1985.

I feel that this theatre: Videotape, LL Collection.

If Lee were present: Sidney Kingsley to LL, May 20, 1985.

This is the first time: Audiotape, LL Collection, Rodgers and Hammerstein Archives.

I just can't tell you: Audiotape, LL Collection, Rodgers and Hammerstein Archives.

Is there anyone more deserving: Raymond R. Rebhann to "Alex and Hildy," May 12, 1981.

Felt that I should be getting a Tony: LL to Richard Coe, October 13, 1981.

Since I've had two shows on Broadway: LL to Isabelle Stevenson, January 11, 1985. The production of *Blood Knot* was the revival staged by Yale Repertory Theatre.

All of us: Richard Barr to Mary C. Henderson, April 8, 1985.

In my will: LL to Nedda Harrigan Logan, December 3, 1986.

A beautiful little theater: Nedda Harrigan Logan to LL, September 17, 1987.

As soon as you have: LL to Jane M. Gulong, December 5, 1984.

In the name of: Bernard Gersten to LL, April 22, 1986.

And, I'm really tired: LL to Max Wilk, May 7, 1987.

As honorary chairman: Isobel Robins Konecky to LL, December 9, 1991.

If there's anything that riles me: LL to Isobel Robins Konecky, December 13, 1991.

If ever I thought I had a hit: LL to Blanche Marvin, November 30, 1983.

Looks extremely interesting: LL to Blanche Marvin, May 9, 1985.

This is the first time: LL to Lawrence A. Wien, October 29, 1985.

Miner is all hearty assurance: *Daily News,* January 10, 1986.

We learn more about Stein: *New York Post,* January 10, 1986.

Largely a stilted colloquy: *New York Times,* January 10, 1986.

Thank you for being 'Alice': LL to Marian Seldes, February 24, 1986.

Chapter 10—A Walk on Broadway

ARCHIVES: Billie Rose Theatre Collection, NYPL; LL Collection, NYPL; NYPL.

INTERVIEWS: Emanuel Azenberg; Irene Backalenick; Lee Blessing; Susan Chicoine; Vincent Curcio; Lindsay Law; Benjamin Mordecai; Robert Prosky; Lloyd Richards; Ben Sprecher; Sandra Starr; Duncan Weldon; George White.

NOTES:

An exhilharating play: *Variety*, March 4, 1987.

Because of its compactness: *New York Times*, March 8, 1987.

I cannot get: LL to Lloyd Richards, February 24, 1987.

I'd love to put [*A Walk in the Woods*]: LL to Lloyd Richards, February 24, 1987.

Thank you for your note: Lloyd Richards to LL, March 2, 1987.

I believe you are aware: Benjamin Mordecai to LL, March 2, 1987.

I think this would be: Robert G. Donnalley, Jr., to LL, June 24, 1987.

How can you help me: LL to Lois Berman, April 2, 1987.

It is possible at this time: LL to Lloyd Richards, April 2, 1987.

I wanted to take this opportunity: Lloyd Richards to LL, June 29, 1987.

Endless conference rooms: *Los Angeles Times*, July 21, 1987.

Had a little talk: LL to Lois Berman, August 20, 1987.

I feel this play: LL to Lawrence Wien, August 25, 1987.

To affirm for ourselves: Lloyd Richards to LL et al, September 22, 1987.

Discounts and discards: Lloyd Richards to LL, October 6, 1987.

Lucille, when you first: Lloyd Richards to LL, October 6, 1987.

In one of several funny passages: *New York Times*, February 29, 1988.

A work of passion: *Time*, March 14, 1988.

Always satisfying: *The New Yorker*, March 14, 1988.

Came up with a money deal: LL to Vincent Curcio, March 8, 1988.

My manager: LL to Howard Taubman and Lori March, March 3, 1988.

I finally got Lee Blessing: LL to Vincent Curcio, March 8, 1988.

Considering the cost: LL to Julia Hansen, April 23, 1988.

Mel Gussow: *New York Times*, March 6, 1988.

Speak directly to an affluent generation: *New York Times,* May 22, 1988.
Privately she was fuming: *New York Times,* June 5, 1988
A producer cannot ask: LL to *New York Times,* June 9, 1988. LL sent copies of this letter to Max Frankel, the *Times'* executive editor; Arthur Gelb, the managing editor; and Michael Leahy, editor of Arts and Leisure.
Our handling of feature articles: Max Frankel to LL, June 20, 1988.
You never quite see: *Financial Times,* November 4, 1988.
Interview: *New York Times,* January 29, 1988.

Chapter 11—On the Wings of a Dream

ARCHIVES: Billy Rose Theatre Collection, NYPL; LL Collection, NYPL; NYPL.

INTERVIEWS: George Atty; Betty Corwin; Vincent Curcio; Drew Eliot; Athol Fugard; Michael Hecht; Mary C. Henderson; Elliot Martin; Marshall W. Mason; David Richenthal; Daryl Roth; Donald Saddler; Ben Sprecher; Sandra Starr; Anna Strasberg; Jenny Sullivan; Robert Taylor; Dr. Theodore Tyberg.

NOTES:
The library needs you: Andrew Heiskell to LL, December 9, 1989.
I just want to thank you: LL to Athol Fugard, August 26, 1994.
The occasion itself: Athol Fugard to LL, September 8, 1994.
I am particularly pleased: LL to Victoria "Vickie" Oakie, September 24, 1994.
I so enjoyed meeting you: Daryl Roth to LL, September 21, 1991.
I've felt a kinship: Daryl Roth to LL, October 28, 1991
You've got guts: LL to Daryl Roth, October 29, 1991.
I take over with two men: LL to Blanche Marvin, September 1, 1992.
Unholy alliance: Four-page memorandum from Larry Kramer to Tanya Berezin, Abigail Evans, Bill Evans, Stuart Howard, Lucille Lortel, Marshall Mason, Rodger McFarlane, George Sheanshang, Ben Sprecher, Tom Viola, and Jon Wilner, December 5, 1992.

I love your play: LL to Larry Kramer, November 21, 1992.

How delightful it was: LL to Larry Kramer, December 22, 1992.

A tender family drama: *New York Times,* January 1, 1993.

This play has meant a great: Larry Kramer to LL, April 7, 1993.

I'm a desperate playwright: Rich Orloff to LL, September 28, 1993.

I get too emotionally involved: LL to Larry Kramer, November 21, 1992.

Good and serious: Memorandum to Board of Directors and Artistic Advisory
    Board from James Ross, March 14, 1996, LL Collection.

I just want you to know: Marshall W. Mason to LL, February 24, 1994.

You are my 'Ruthie': LL to Mimi Bochco, February 19, 1994.

Dear Helen: *New York Post*, n. d.

Lucille: Video, LL Collection.

The highlight: Donald Saddler to LL, September 1, 1997.

You deserve: LL to George Atty, November 11, 1998.

Minutes later: Lucille died at 4:13 P.M.

Afterword

ARCHIVES: LL Colleciton, NYPL; LL Collection, Rodgers and Hammerstein Archives, NYPL.

INTERVIEWS: Hope Alswang; Clive Barnes; Mimi Bochco; George
Forbes; Lynne Mayocole; Albert Poland; Ben Sprecher; Sandra Starr; Anna
Strasberg.

PLAYS: Williams, *Camino Real.*

NOTES:

Public memorials: Videos, LL Collection.

If you love the theater: *New York Times*, April 6, 1999.

An interviewer once: LL Collection, Rodgers and Hammerstein Archives.

Make voyages: *Camino Real*, p. 508.

Index

Abel, Walter, 175, 232
Actors' Equity Association, 4, 35, 39, 93, 95, 96, 98, 108, 110, 114, 171, 172, 309, 319; antidiscrimination boycotts by, 83; Curcio contract renegotiation with, 330; LL dealings with, 34, 86–88, 91, 149–50, 176–80, 184, 188–90, 194, 206, 207, 233, 309, 319
Actors' Fund of America, 257, 258, 267–68, 329
Actors Studio, 250
Adams, Mason, 231
Adams, Maude, 13
A-Day (R. White), 89–90
Adler, Luther, 33, 80, 194
Adler, Stella, 88
After Dinner Opera Company, 139
"Afternoon of Poetry, An," 175
Aiken, Conrad, 175
Albee, Edward, 167, 170, 172, 187–88, 324
Alive and Kicking (Carmichael), 90
Allen, Rae, 202
Alswang, Betty, 97
Alswang, Frances, 248
Alswang, Hope, 33, 76, 97, 103, 106, 226, 228, 248, 325; LL's funeral and, 327
Alswang, Ralph, 76, 80, 97, 103, 106, 107, 111, 207, 228, 233, 234, 239, 310
Alswang, Ralph, Jr., 97, 248
Alton, Zohra, 126
American Academy of Dramatic Arts, 15–20, 21, 23, 32

American Mime Theatre, 104
American National Theatre and Academy (ANTA), 39, 81, 87–88, 97, 105, 184, 187, 188, 208–9, 211, 212, 225, 231, 257, 273, 288, 319. See also Matinee Series
American Playhouse (TV series), 288, 291, 297
American Playhouse Theatre Productions, 288, 295
American/Soviet Theatre Initiative (ASTI), 300, 301, 302
American Theatre Critics Association (ATCA), 264, 265
American Theatre Wing, 265, 267
Anderson, Jane, 310–15
Anderson, Judith, 40, 120
Anderson, Maxwell, 80
Angels Fall (L. Wilson), 254, 264
Anglin, Florence, 224
Animal Keepers (Winters), 208
ANTA. See American National Theatre and Academy
ANTA Matinee Series. See Matinee Series
Antoinette Perry Awards. See Tony Awards
Antonio, Lou, 194
Apollo and Persephone (Cockshott), 139
Archipenko, Alexander, 50
Aria da Capo (Millay), 148
Armen, Eloise G., 90, 139, 234–37
Arnold Weissberger Award, 259
Arrick, Lawrence, 145

Arthur, Beatrice, 141
Arthur, Hartney, 128
Arthur, Jean, 63
As Is (Hoffman), 263–65, 270, 272
*Asylum, or What the Gentlemen Are Up To,
  Not To Mention the Ladies* (Kopit), 193
Atkinson, Brooks, 42, 122, 142, 154, 158,
  166, 193
Atlee, Howard, 160–61, 163, 172–73, 175
Atty, George, 323
Atwill, Lionel, 40
Auden, W.H., 149
Audrey Wood Scholarship, 278
Awake and Sing! (Odets), 79
Aymé, Marcel, 91, 279
Azenberg, Emanuel (Manny), 282, 285,
  289, 291

Baby Dance, The (J. Anderson), 310–15
Back on the Boulevard (Montevecchi), 317
Balcony, The (Genet), 144–47, 151–53,
  163–67, 175, 210; French production
  of, 168, 169, 170
Ball, William, 141
Balzac, Honoré de, 24, 129
Banks, Danny, 242
Barnes, Clive, 212, 224–25, 275; LL's be-
  quest to, 329
Barr, Richard, 170, 265
Barrault, Jean-Louis, 91
Bart, Jean, 63–64
Baruch, Amalie, 58
Beame, Abraham D., 232
Beckett, Samuel, 153, 167, 170, 172, 176,
  194, 195, 255, 256
Before Breakfast (O'Neill), 232
Beggars Are Coming to Town (Reeves), 80
Behan, Brendan, 147, 155
Belasco, David, 35, 40
Belonogov, Alexander, 289
Beloved (Victor), 85
Ben-Gurion University, 266
Benincasa, Joseph P., 267
Bennett, Rosamund (Rozzie), 76, 84,
  128, 247
Benter, Richard, 179
Bentley, Eric, 181, 182, 183
Bercovici, Konrad, 32–33
Berezin, Tanya, 252
Berghof, Herbert, 80
Berkowsky, Paul B., 110, 204–66, 209,
  217, 228–30, 241, 242, 246, 324

Berkowsky, Sheala, 110, 205, 217, 241
Berlin, Louis, 75
Berlin to Broadway with Kurt Weill, 228
Berman, David, 248
Berman, Lois, 248, 279, 281, 285
Bernstein, Sidney, 197, 198, 200
Berry, John, 197, 198, 200
Biberman, Herbert J., 63, 64, 214, 222
Biel, Nicholas, 139
Bikel, Theodore, 177, 178, 180
Billie Whitelaw...Who He? (Whitelaw), 255
Billy Rose Theatre Collection (NYPL),
  308, 329
Bilowit, Ira, 128
Birthday of the Infanta, The (Wilde), 141
Black, Kitty, 218, 299
Black Girl (Franklin), 228
Blaine, Vivian, 261
Blake, Lisabeth, 99–100
Blessing, Lee, 277–78, 279, 280, 286, 287,
  290, 293, 296, 298, 303
Blinn, Holbrook, 40, 41
Blitzstein, Marc, 121–22, 155, 175–76, 310
Blood Knot, The (Fugard), 196–202, 213,
  264, 265
Blossom, Roberts, 145
Bochco, Mimi, 11, 12, 59, 61, 63, 89, 98,
  213, 215, 218, 221, 227, 237, 242,
  263–64, 266, 320, 327
Bochco, Rudolf, 12
Boettcher, Henry, 142
Bolton, Whitney, 118–19
Booth Theatre, 285, 289, 290, 295
Boren, David L., 294
Bourdet, Edouard, 44
Bowden, Charles, 103
Bowes, Major Edward, 43, 69, 77
Braggiotti, Francesca, 77–78, 83
Braggiotti, Stiano, 83
Branch, Anthony, 298
Brecht, Bertolt, 120–22, 131, 176, 180–84,
  194, 198, 212, 310
Brecht on Brecht (show), 181–84, 193, 194,
  232
Breen, Robert, 319
Brewsie and Willy (Stein; Violett adapt.),
  100
Broadway Cares/Equity Fights Aids, 314
"Broadway Salutes Off-Broadway," 257
Bromberg, Conrad, 211
Brook, Peter, 152, 153, 163, 170
Brooke, Rupert, 175

Brooks, David, 187, 188
Brown, Alice, 18
Brown, Arvin, 318
Brown, Scoogie, 105
Brown, William F., 289
Browning, Kirk, 297
Brownsville Raid, The (Fuller), 242
Brown University, 307, 317
Brustein, Robert, 167, 185, 186
Buried Child (Shepard), 242
Burrows, Vinie, 210, 232
Burton, Philip, 154
Burton, Richard, 175, 232
Bury, John, 198, 200
Busch, Charles, 312
Buzzell, Robert, 248, 324

Caesar and Cleopatra (Shaw), 40
Calta, Louis, 173
Cambridge, Godfrey, 156, 158
Camino Real (Williams), 331
Campbell, C. Lawton, 100, 136
Candida (Shaw), 141
Cannon, J.D., 198–200
Cantor, Arthur, 193
Capalbo, Carmen, 121, 122, 129–30, 131, 183
Capitol Grand Theatre, 43–44, 50, 68
Captive, The (Bourdet), 44
Caretaker, The (Pinter), 196
Carlino, Lewis John, 180, 193
Carmichael, Hoagy, 90
Carnegie Hall Playhouse, 139, 142, 154
Carnegie Lyceum Theatre, 6, 15–18
Carroll, Helena, 171, 176
Carroll, Paul Vincent, 159, 171
Carter, Mrs. Leslie, 41, 46
Casson, Lewis, 141
Catastrophe (Beckett), 255
Catholic School Girls (Kurtii), 252
Cerf, Kurt, 83
Chairs, The (Ionesco), 145–46
Chanler, Richard, 139
Channing, Stockard, 271
Chase, Stanley, 121, 122, 129–31, 183
Chatterton, Ruth, 96, 125, 127, 128
Choi, Felicia, 236
Choi, Gavin, 233–34, 235–36
Christmas Oratorio (Auden), 149
Christofer, Michael, 271
Churchill, Caryl, 243–44
Circle in the Square, 114, 155, 164, 175

Circle Repertory Company, 252–54, 269–70, 272, 289, 309, 314–19
Cirker, Ira, 112, 273–76
Cisney, Marcella, 237
Clancy Brothers, 148
Clarke, Bill, 283, 290
Clarke-Laurence, Michael, 176
Clark School for Concentration, 11, 262
Cloud 9 (Churchill), 243–44, 246, 252, 258
Clurman, Harold, 40, 79, 80, 88, 166–67, 185
Cock-a-Doodle Dandy (O'Casey), 153, 155
Cockshott, Gerald, 139
Coco, James, 180, 208
Coe, Richard L., 188, 265
Coggerers, The (Carroll), 159
Cohen, Alexander, 264, 268
Cohn, Max (step-grandfather), 5, 8
Cohn, Miriam (aunt), 5
Cohn, Sidney, 258
Cole, Tom, 241–42
Coleman, Jackson, 266
Colt, Ethel Barrymore, 207
Colton, John, 41, 45–48
Comedy on the Bridge (opera), 110
Come Slowly, Eden (Rosten), 206, 232
Coming Forth by Day of Osiris Jones, The (Aiken), 175
Connell, Jane, 117, 130
Conner, Whit, 207
Constantine, Michael, 283, 297
Conway, Curt, 126
Cook, Shirley, 94
Coolidge Auditorium, 149, 294
Coradel-Cugat, Francis. *See* Cugat, Francis
Corbin, Clayton, 138
Corwin, Betty, 307–8, 309
Coster, Nicholas, 200, 201, 213
Cotes, Peter, 92, 220
Cotsworth, Staats, 147, 202
Cousins (Fugard), 310
Couture, Myrtle M., 145–46
Coveny, Michael, 299
Crawford, Cheryl, 184
Cricket Theater, 198
Cronkite, Walter, 261
Cry, the Beloved Country (Paton; Komai adapt.), 137–38, 149, 232
¡Cuba Sí! (McNally), 212
Cugat, Francis (brother-in-law), 28, 32, 33, 43, 49, 50, 57, 58, 64, 91, 98, 110, 125, 126, 155, 213, 257; death of, 215, 253

Cugat, Ruth Wadler (sister), 5–12, 21, 24, 28–33, 37, 43, 67, 71, 72, 91, 110, 125, 155, 213, 223; as artist, 49, 50–51, 126, 256, 257; death of, 227, 264; dementia of, 205; LL's bond with, 11; LL's marriage and, 57–58, 61; marriage of, 32, 33; Reifenberg and, 66

Cugat, Xavier, 33, 64, 71, 78

Cullum, John, 261

cummings, e.e., 149–50

Cuomo, Mario, 261

Curcio, Vincent, 6, 13, 48, 64, 97, 239, 242, 251, 260, 267, 273, 279, 283–85, 287, 293, 309, 318, 320, 321, 330

Curry, Virgil, 184

Curtis, Paul, 104

Daché, Suzanne, 247

Dalrymple, Jean, 207, 231, 257, 261

Damask Drum, The (Mishima), 170

Dana, Jeanne-Marie, 299

Dann, Sam, 223

D'Annunzio, Gabriele, 19–20

D'Arcy, Roy, 51

Dark Fire (Burrows), 210

Davis, Brad, 313

Davis, Owen, 41

Dear Columbia (radio series), 66

de Lavallade, Carmen, 98

Delsarte, François, 17

de Lys, William, 115–20, 123, 258

DeMille, Cecil B., 15

Demi-Virgin, The (Hopwood), 36

Depression-era theatre, 79

Derwent, Clarence, 39, 87–88, 95–96, 99, 108, 134, 141, 150, 157, 158, 177, 179, 225

Derwent, Elfrida, 108

Dessauer, Siegfried, 31

Destiny of Me, The (Kramer), 250, 313–17

Devine, George, 191

DeVine, Larry, 209

Dewhurst, Colleen, 313

Dickason, Albert A., 99, 101, 214

Dickinson, Emily, 206

Dignam, Alex, 191

Dogface Sonata (Harrity), 116, 136

Domingo, Placido, 261

Donnalley, Robert G., Jr., 281, 285

Dorin, Rube, 134

Dos Passos, John, 100

Dostoyevsky, Fyodor, 159

Douglas Fairbanks Theatre, 251

Dove, The (Mack), 40–41

Downey, Jim, 203

Drama League of New York, 293

Dream of a Blacklisted Actor (Bromberg), 211

Dream on Monkey Mountain (Walcott), 228

Dream Watcher, The (Wersba), 233

Drexler, Rosalyn, 210

Drums at Yale (Fairservis), 211

Dublin Players, 191

Dugan, William Francis, 44–45

Duke University, 285, 289

Duncan, Angus, 188, 189, 194

Dunham, Katherine, 94

Dunnock, Mildred, 211, 232

Dunphy, Jack, 180

Dycke, Marjorie L., 136, 221

Earle, Ralph, 289

Eaton, Walter Prichard, 14

Ebert, Joyce, 141

Effect of Gamma Rays on Man-in-the-Moon Marigolds, The (Zindel), 206

Egan, Jenny, 145

Eisen, Max, 119–25, 128, 131, 132

Elder, Eldon, 202

Eliot, Drew, 248, 306, 326

Eliot, T.S., 96

Elizabeth, The Bachelor Queen (Campbell), 100, 136

Elliott, Stephen, 202

Embers (Beckett), 170, 172

Emmy Awards, 276

Enough (Beckett), 255

Equity Library Theatre (ELT), 34, 95–96, 103, 177–78, 180, 189

Erdman, Jean, 224

Eugene O'Neill Memorial Theater Center, 329

Evans, Don, 224, 225

Everything Happens to Me (film), 51

Experimental Theatre Invitational Series, 87–88

Eyre, Ronald, 298

Fadiman, Mr. and Mrs. Clifton, 78

Fagan, James J., 60

Fairbanks, Douglas, Sr., 49

Fairservis, Walter J., Jr., 211

Fam and Yam (Albee), 170, 187

Fanfare (Maney), 42

Farentino, James, 229

Farwell, Margaret (Marge), 221, 298,
   300, 320
Feingold, Michael, 255
Fences (A. Wilson), 278
Feury, Peggy, 126
Fiedler, Arthur, 12
Field, Rachel, 99–100
Figuro in the Night (O'Casey), 192
Fischer, Bernd, 289
Fitch, Clyde, 13, 18, 64
Fitzgerald, F. Scott, 41
Flusser, Richard Stuart, 139
Foote, Horton, 321
Footfalls (Beckett), 255
Forbes, George, 320, 325–26, 329
Forbes, Timothy C., 317
Ford, Nancy, 207, 208
Ford, Ruth, 224
For Ladies Only (farce), 51
Forsythe, Henderson, 138
Foster, Phoebe, 51
Frankel, Gene, 95, 112, 129, 180–83, 232
Frankel, Max, 297
Franklin, J.E., 228, 229–30
Franklin, Nancy, 83
Frazier, Joe, 321
Frechtman, Bernard, 144, 153, 164, 169, 195
Freddys Liebestod (film), 31
Fredrik, Burry, 242, 251
Freedley, George, 133, 134, 138, 185–86
Freydberg, James B., 202, 280, 298
Friedman, Ben, 2
Friedman, Sanford, 139, 142
Frohman, Charles, 15
Frohman, Daniel, 15, 18
Fry, Christopher, 120, 152
Fugard, Athol, 104, 196–202, 212–13, 310
Fuller, Charles, 242
Funke, Lewis, 122, 130
Funny Kind of Evening with David Kossoff, A
   (show), 228–29
Futz! (Owens), 194, 211

Gaines, Frederick, 224
Gamboni, Ciro A., 270
Gardner, Betty, 227
Garfein, Jack, 254–55
Gaynes, George, 182
Geer, Will, 155
Gelb, Arthur, 147, 148, 161, 164, 165, 172
Genet, Jean, 144, 145, 152, 153, 159,
   163–67, 170, 176, 194, 195, 197, 210

Gershwin, Arthur, 28, 78
Gershwin, George, 12, 28, 50
Gershwin, Ira, 12, 28, 50
Gershwin, Rose, 71
Gersten, Bernard, 268
Gertrude Stein and a Companion (Wells), 103,
   112, 272–76, 285
Getting Out (Norman), 239
Ghosts (Ibsen), 139
Gibberson, William, 189
Gide, André, 103, 150
Gilder, Rosamund, 174, 188
Gilman, Sadie, 72
Gingerbread House (Cook), 94
Girls (Fitch), 18
Givot, George, 63
Glass Menagerie, The (Wilder), 80
Glenn, Robert, 111, 112, 152, 155–60, 185,
   186, 205, 206, 226, 230–31, 240
Glines, The, 272
Godowsky, Frances (Frankie) Gershwin,
   24, 28, 71, 78, 221, 325
Godowsky, Leopold, 22
Godowsky, Leopold, Jr., 12, 22–28, 71,
   78, 328
God's Trombones (Hughes), 158
Gold Diggers, The (Hopwood), 36
Golden Gate Quartet, 90
Goodspeed Opera House Foundation, 329
Goodyear, Elizabeth, 1, 82–83, 85
Gorbachev, Mikhail, 279, 286, 291, 300,
   302
Gossett, Louis, Jr., 200, 201
Gottfried, Howard, 146, 153, 158
Gottfried, Martin, 204
Gould, Eleanor Cody, 17
Gran Carpa de los Rasquachis, La (*Tent of the
   Underdogs*) (play), 228
Grant, Micki, 229–30
Great Gatsby, The (Fitzgerald; Davis
   adapt.), 41
Greenberg, Nat H., 84
Greene, Gayle, 239, 240
Greene, Luther, 120
Gregorian, Vartan, 307, 317
Gregory, Lady Isabella, 106
Grew, Mary, 92, 196, 218
Griffin, Alice, 162
Griffin, John, 162
Grizzard, George, 313
Gross, Ben, 66
Groucho (musical), 280

Grounds for Murder (film), 51
Guests of the Nation (O'Connor), 148
Guinness, Alec, 283–88, 293, 298–300
Gulong, Jane M., 268
Guns of Carrar (Brecht), 212
Gurney, A.R., 305
Gussow, Mel, 225, 275, 279
Guthrie, Woody, 231
Gypsy Code (film), 51

Haas, Dolly, 182
Hackett, Erlah, 324
Hagen, Uta, 317
Hale, Nathan, 211
Hall, Dorothy, 44
Hall, Norman, 140
Halligan, Maureen, 191
Hamlet (Shakespeare), 141
Hanjo (Mishima), 170, 172
Hansberry, Lorraine, 158, 201
Hansen, Julia, 293
Happy Ant-Hill, The (Spencer), 107
Happy As Larry (MacDonagh), 170, 172, 176–77
Happy Prince, The (Wilde), 141
Harding, John, 323, 324
Hare, Will, 231
Harold Clurman Theatre, 255
Harris, Rosemary, 229
Harrity, Richard, 116, 136
Hassan, Rita, 101, 128
Havoc, June, 226–27, 237, 239
Hawkins, William, 104–5, 118
Hayakawa, Sessue, 14, 35, 48–49, 52
Hayden, Terese, 145, 149, 152
Hayes, Helen, 22, 40, 140, 232, 268, 321
Hays, David, 165, 167, 248, 325
Hays, Leonora, 248, 325
Hecht, Michael, 230, 253, 270, 326
Heckart, Eileen, 232, 305
Heidt, Charles and Eidell, 225
Heiskell, Andrew, 307, 308
Helen Hayes Award, 321
Hello and Goodbye (Fugard), 212–13
Hemingway, Ernest, 272, 273, 274
Henderson, Mary C., 259, 260, 265, 308, 318
Henry, William A., III, 290
Henry V (Shakespeare), 140
Here Is the News (play), 96
Herrmann, Edward, 298, 299
Hess, Willy, 7

Hewes, Henry, 97, 137–41, 145, 151, 166, 185, 188, 265
Hilltop Musical Company, 104
Hirshfeld, Al, 260, 264
Hirson, Roger O., 193
Hoffman, William M., 263, 272, 324
Hofmann, Gert, 208, 211
Holder, Geoffrey, 97, 98, 104–5, 112, 289
Hollywood, Fla., 71
Honeysuckle, The (D'Annunzio), 19–20
Hopkins, Gerard Manley, 175
Hopwood, Avery, 36
Hornstein, Harold, 107
House on the Hill (Silver), 86
House on the Hill, The (radio series), 66
Howard, Edwin L., 70
Howard, Marc, 239
Howe, Quincy, 69
Howe, Tina, 69
How I Learned to Drive (Vogel), 321
Hughes, Langston, 156, 157
Hum, Susan, 274
Humphrey, Cavada, 224
Hunter, Kim, 89, 206, 213, 310
Hurley, Arthur, 51
Huston, Philip, 1, 82–83, 85, 88, 238
Hwang, David Henry, 295
Hyman, Earle, 138, 141, 211, 232

Ibsen, Henrik, 111, 139
If I Was Rich (McGuire), 44
I Knock at the Door (O'Casey; Perl adapt.), 139
I Knock at the Door (O'Casey; Shyre adapt.), 146–48, 153, 186, 202–4, 229
Inge, William, 170, 185, 186
Inness-Brown, Virginia (Mrs. H. Alwyn), 136, 138, 151–52, 187
Into the Woods (Sondheim), 285
Ionesco, Eugene, 145–46, 158–59, 173–76, 187, 194, 195
I Rise in Flame, Cried the Phoenix (Williams), 169
Irish Players, 171, 176
Irving, George, 261
Irving, Jules, 229
Isn't It Romantic (Wasserstein), 252
Ivory Tower (comedy), 86, 87, 88

Jacker, Corinne, 40, 63, 116, 119, 137, 141, 145, 175, 184, 233
Jackson, Anne, 182, 183, 221, 226, 232, 289, 331

Jackson, Shirley, 100
Jacobi, Derek, 296
Jacobson, Sol, 186, 195
Jaffe, Sam, 100
Jarry, Alfred, 305
Javits, Mr. and Mrs. Benjamin A., 78
Javits, Jacob, 84, 95
Javits, Lily, 84
Jehlinger, Charles (Jelly), 17
Jens, Salome, 166
Jewish Wife, The (Brecht), 180, 181, 182
Jim Dandy (Saroyan), 89
Johnson, Lyndon Baines, 169, 219
Joint Owners in Spain (Brown), 18
Jones, James Earl, 198–99, 200, 261, 262
Joyce, Henry, 248

Kafka, Franz, 97, 141
Kafka, Harry, 259
Kahn, Alex Bennett, 86
Kahn, Michael, 150–51, 210
Kallesser, Michael, 41–42
Kamins, Jeanette, 301, 302
Katzenbach, Nicholas deB., 219–20
Kaufman, Martin, 317
Kaye, Danny, 78
Kazan, Elia, 79
Keene, Donald, 170
Kennedy, Adrienne, 150, 206, 210
Kennel, Louis, 41
Kerr, Walter, 118, 142, 166
Khumalo, Leleti, 296
Kick In (Mack), 37–38
Kid, The (Aiken), 175
Kimmelman, Michael, 295, 296
King, Woodie, Jr., 229
Kingsley, Sidney, 79, 80, 249, 257, 262, 289, 321
Kirkland, Alexander, 81
Kirkland, Jack, 79
Kissel, Howard, 290–91
Kleiman, Harlan P., 194
Klein, Amanda J., 274
Kley, Dina, 230
Knickerbocker, Cholly, 88
Knoblauch, Edward, 18
Koesis, Robert, 223, 224
Koll, Frances, 267
Komai, Felicia, 137, 138
Komarow, Susan, 137, 151, 152, 162
Konecky, Isobel Robins, 269
Kopit, Arthur, 188, 193

Korff, Arnold, 30
Kossoff, David, 228–29
Kostelanetz, André, 78
Kramer, Larry, 250, 313–17, 324
Kruelewitch, Nan, 128
Kuchwara, Michael, 291
Kumin, Fran, 282
Kurtii, Casey, 252
Kvitsinsky, Yuli A., 277

Lady Akane, The (Mishima), 170, 172, 173
Lady and the Clarinet, The (Christofer), 271
La Jolla Playhouse, 277, 280, 281, 283
La Mama ETC, 228
Lampert, Zohra. *See* Alton, Zohra
Landis, Jessie Royce, 202, 203
Lane, Burton, 261
Langner, Lawrence, 81, 102, 113, 153
Langton, Basil C., 103
Last Sweet Days of Isaac, The (Cryer and Ford), 208
Latham, John, 230, 231
Latham, Leslie, 157
Laurence, Paula, 103, 104–5, 140
Laveman, Portia Waldman, 8
Law, Lindsay, 291, 294
Lawren, Joseph, 37
Lawrence, Jerome, 184–87
League of New York Theatres and Producers, 265
League of Off Broadway Theatres and Producers, 232, 256
Lee, Canada, 82, 83, 89
Lee, Gypsy Rose, 81, 184
Lee, Manfred, 102
Lee, Robert E. (playwright), 184–85
Lee Strasberg Creative Center, 329
Lee Strasberg Institute of the Theatre, 249
Lee Strasberg Lifetime Achievement in Theatre Award, 250, 260–61
Leffert, Sarah (sister-in-law), 222
Le Gallienne, Eva, 22, 109, 111, 139–41, 158, 178, 207, 227, 232, 233, 310
Legend of Charlie Parker, The (play with music), 206
Le Noire, Rosetta, 138
Lenthall, Franklyn, 248
Lenya, Lotte, 129, 181–83, 261, 310
Lerner, Alan Jay, 261
Levitt, Mortimer, 251
Lewis, Emory, 185
Lewis, Robert, 79, 153

Library of Congress, 149
Licht, Elizabeth Schweitzer (sister-in-
law), 73–74
Liebling, William, 84
Life and Times of J. Walter Smintheus, The
(White), 211–12
Life in the Theatre, A (Mamet), 242
Lincoln Center Theater, 288
Lindfors, Viveca, 180–81, 182, 194, 212,
232
Lindsay, Howard, 39, 185
Lipton, James, 126
Lissberger, Walter, 108
Lithgow, John, 296
Little, Stuart W., 114, 166, 174–75,
231–32
Littlewood, Joan, 129, 196
Livingston, Jock, 167
Loaves and Fishes (Maugham), 99
Lodge, John Davis, 77–78, 98, 102
Lodge, Lily, 78, 102
Loesser, Frank, 261
Loesser, Jo Sullivan, 86, 122, 261
Logan, Nedda Harrigan, 257, 267
Londonderry Air (Field), 99–100
Long Valley, The (Steinbeck), 230
Long Wharf Theatre, 311
Lorca, Federico Garcia, 94
Loren, Sophia, 261
Lortel, Lucille: as actress, 14–21, 28–58,
63–66, 67, 75, 105, 188; arts network-
ing by, 77–78; avant-garde playwrights
and, 195–96; awards and honors of,
148, 185–87, 188, 232, 250, 256,
257–59, 260–63, 276, 278; background
and youth of, 2–12, 34; birth of, 2, 4, 5,
6; Broadway debut of, 39–40; burial
site of, 328; as center of family, 110,
214; changed name of, 32–33; childlessness of, 62, 75–76; courtship of,
55–58; death of, 326; deaths and,
214–15, 236, 253, 264, 319, 321, 324,
325; declining health of, 305–6, 321,
325; education of, 11–12, 14; escorts of,
247–48; estate left by, 328–30; European trips of, 21–32, 90, 91, 105,
143–45, 169–70, 191, 217–18; film
about, 259–60, 261, 289, 298; first professional stage appearance of, 35–37;
food obsession of, 160; frugality of, 2,
33–34; funeral of, 327–28; gifts to
friends of, 249; giving linked with

need to control by, 97–98, 318; health
problems of, 12, 233–34, 238, 247,
305–6, 321; husband's death and estate left to, 218–23; last decade of,
305–26; later social life of, 34, 248–49;
London club theatres and, 92–93;
marriage of. *See* Schweitzer, Louis P.;
memorabilia of, 308–9, 329; men and,
9, 22–28, 42, 56, 247–48; New York
Public Library and, 250, 307–9;
ninety-eighth birthday of, 324; papers
of, 260; personal traits of, 2, 11, 12, 34,
76, 97–98, 250, 320; philanthropies of,
255–59, 265–70, 278, 288, 307–9,
317–18, 322, 328–29; as producer. *See*
Theatre de Lys; White Barn Theatre;
publicity and, 139, 152, 154, 160–61,
165; public memorial for, 331; puri-
tanism of, 61, 210–11, 227; as Queen of
Off Broadway, 188, 261; radio acting
by, 63, 65–66; recognition as need of,
2, 263–64; "rich matron" reputation
of, 90, 112, 214; Schaeffer relationship
with, 225–40 passim, 247; seating
arrangements and, 162; self-
promotion by, 2, 38, 43, 52, 105;
Sherry-Netherland apartment of,
256–58; shipboard wedding of, 60–61;
socializing by, 12, 43, 62, 64, 72, 84,
155, 247–49, 324–25; Soviet tour of,
300–304, 305; theatrical legacy of, 331;
theatrical risk-taking by, 330–31; Tony
Awards and, 264–65, 292, 294, 295,
296; trusted friends of, 320; Westport
home of, 68–71, 77–78, 317; as widow,
221–26; will and bequests of, 322,
328–30
Lortel Theatre. *See* Lucille Lortel Theatre
Lottery, The (Jackson; Violett adapt.), 100
Lou's Saga (poem), 53
Love Letters (Gurney), 305
*Love of Don Perlimpin and Belisa in the Gar-
den, The* (Lorca), 94
Lovers, Villains & Fools, 140
Love's Old Sweet Song, 233
Lucienne and the Butcher (Aymé), 91, 279
Lucille Lortel Awards, 256, 318, 321, 329
Lucille Lortel Distinguished Lecture Se-
ries, 276
Lucille Lortel Endowment Fund for
Theatre on Film and Tape, 307

Lucille Lortel Foundation, 252, 254, 267, 270, 318, 322, 328, 329, 330
Lucille Lortel Fund for New Drama at Yale, 282
Lucille Lortel Gallery and Museum, 259
Lucille Lortel Room, New York Public Library for the Performing Arts, 250, 308–9
Lucille Lortel's Theatre de Lys. *See* Theatre de Lys
Lucille Lortel's Theatre World, 260
Lucille Lortel Theatre, 254, 258, 261, 268, 271, 274, 280, 281, 305, 317–31; Playwrights Sidewalk and, 322–24, *See also* Theatre de Lys
Lucille Lortel Theatre Foundation, 322
Lucille Lortel Theatre Gallery, 258–59
Lucille's Showboat (houseboat), 168
Ludlow Fair (L. Wilson), 210
Lund, Martine, 4
Lyceum (theatre), 18, 20, 272, 284
Lyons, Gene, 142

Maazel, Marvine (Marvin), 22–27, 30
MacDonagh, Donagh, 170
Machiz, Herbert, 129, 224
Mack, Willard, 37–38, 40–41
MacKaye, Steele, 15
MacMahon, Aline, 147
MacVickar, Kitty, 58
Madame de Sade (Mishima), 224
Madrigal (show), 207
Maeterlinck, Maurice, 141
Maidens and Mistresses at Home at the Zoo (Roberts), 169
Maltby, H.F., 44–45
Maltz, Albert, 75
Mamet, David, 242, 295, 296
Mandel, Frank, 37
Maney, Richard, 42–43
Manhattan Bail Project, 169, 219
Manhoff, Joy, 201
Mann, Theodore, 114, 163, 164, 165, 166
Mannes, Leopold Damrosch, 23, 28
Man Who Laughed, The (Woolf), 14, 35, 48–49, 50
Man Who Laughed Last, The (film), 50, 51–52, 259
Man Who Reclaimed His Head, The (Bart), 63–64
Marat-Sade (Weiss), 225
March, Lori, 289, 292

Marchand, Nancy, 167
Margaret Sanger—Unfinished Business (play), 305
Margolys, Miriam, 272, 273
Marlowe, Alan, 231
Marsh, Calden, 157
Marsh, Donald, 146
Marshall, Armina, 81, 102
Marshall, E.G., 80
Martin, Elliot, 314–15, 316, 322, 325
Martin, Ian, 127
Martinique theatre, 176
Marvin, Blanche, 69, 81, 198, 221, 239–40, 244, 247, 250, 271–75, 295, 301, 304, 314, 326
Marvin, Mark, 89
Mason, Marshall W., 98, 252, 254, 270, 272, 309, 313–14, 318, 319, 329–30
Matinee Series, 97, 111, 133, 136–63, 169, 172–75, 179, 180, 185, 187, 192, 193, 195, 196, 204–6, 209–13, 221, 223–25, 229–32, 257, 273, 288
Matlock, Jack F., 304
Matz, Sidney, 65
Maugham, Somerset, 45, 99
Mayo, Frances Grace Jones (sister-in-law), 50, 69, 76–77
Mayo, Laura (sister-in-law), 215, 222
Mayo, Michael (nephew), 222, 320–21, 325, 326, 329
Mayo, Penelope (niece), 76, 77
Mayo, Rodney (nephew), 222, 321, 329
Mayo, Wadler (great-nephew), 320
Mayo, Waldo (Mayo Wadler) (brother), 5–12, 22, 26–33, 37, 41, 49, 110, 155, 215, 222, 223, 231; death of, 236; LL's memorials to, 265–66, 295, 321; marital problems of, 76–77; music career of, 5, 6–7, 8, 19, 21, 26–27, 43–44, 50, 68; name change by, 44; White Barn Theatre and, 81–87, 94, 111, 135
Mayocole, Lynne (Carolyn) (niece), 8, 9, 11, 53, 69, 226, 236; custody fight over, 77; LL's funeral and, 327
McAnuff, Des, 277, 280, 283, 286, 293, 301
McArt, Jan, 227
McCann, Elizabeth I., 271
McCarthy, Eugene, 217
McClain, John, 118
McClintic, Guthrie, 46
McCready, Sam, 104

McFarlane, Rodger, 314, 315
McGinn, Walter, 211
McGuire, William Anthony, 44
McHarry, Charles, 165
McKechnie, Donna, 309
McKenna, Siobhan, 141
McKenzie, James B., 297
McKenzie, Neil, 148–49
McLaughlin, Robert, 41
McNally, Terrence, 208, 212
McNamara, Dermot, 310
McQueen, Butterfly, 156–57
McQuiggan, John A., 311
Meacham, Anne, 96–97, 109, 127, 170, 172, 193, 273
Meara, Anne, 310
Medal of Honor Rag (Cole), 241–42
Mendelssohn, Felix, 95
Mendoza, David, 43–44, 49–50
Menotti, Gian-Carlo, 106
Merkel, Una, 39
Merrell, Richard, 107, 108
Metamorphosis (Kafka; Watson adapt.), 97, 141
Mielziner, Jo, 80
Miles, Leland, 237
Millay, Edna St. Vincent, 113, 148
Miller, Leo, 111, 186
Milwe, Beatrice, 248
Miner, Jan, 273, 274, 275
Minskoff, Jerome, 298
Mishima, Yukio, 161, 170, 172, 173, 224, 225
Mitgang, Herbert, 299
Moeller, Philip, 40
Mokae, Zakes, 197, 202
Molleson, John, 203
Monroe, Marilyn, 11, 128
Monroe, Wallace, 267
"Montage of a Drean Deferred" (Hughes), 157
Montevecchi, Liliane, 309, 317
Moonchildren (Weller), 223, 228
Moon Shines on Kylenamoe, The (O'Casey), 192
Mordecai, Benjamin, 280–84, 287, 288, 291, 293, 302, 303
Moreno, J. L., 88
Morfogen, George, 109
Morgan, Charles, 125, 126, 127, 139, 142–43
Morley, Sheridan, 298
Morphos, Evangeline, 239, 259

Morris, Mary, 137, 138
Moscowitz, Jennie (actress), 66
Moskowitz, Bertha (aunt), 28, 32
Moskowitz, Dibvra Minz (grandmother), 3–4
Moskowitz, Heiman (Hyman) (grandfather), 3–4
Moskowitz, Helen (aunt), 3
Moskowitz, Isidore (uncle), 4, 6, 7, 8, 9, 28
Moskowitz, Mildred (aunt), 3
Moskowitz, Philip (uncle), 4
Moskowitz, Rose (aunt), 4
Moskowitz, Sophie (aunt), 4
Moskowitz, Victoria (aunt), 3
Moss, Paul (cousin), 8
Mostel, Zero, 89, 173
Mosten, Lyn, 221
Mourning Becomes Electra (O'Neill), 79
Moveable Feast, A (Hemingway), 272
Mrs. Klein (play), 317
Munso, Felix, 171–72, 176–80, 222
Murder in the Cathedral (Eliot), 96
Murray, Arthur (Art), 110, 219
Murray, Genevieve, 219
Murray, Peg, 99–100
Museum of the City of New York, 258–60, 269
My Lady Friends (Nyitray and Mandel), 37
My Lady's Dress (Knoblauch), 18
Myrkle-Harder Players, 38–39

Nathanson, Irwin, 81
National Academy of Television Arts and Sciences, 276
Native Son (Wright), 83
Negro Ensemble Company, 242, 266
Nekros (Tierney), 170
Nemy, Enid, 330
Nersesyan, Grigori, 300, 302, 304
Nesbitt, Cathleen, 175, 232
Nettleton, Lois, 229
Nevas, Lou, 77, 94, 110, 206
New Dramatists, 329
New Federal Theatre, 228
New Lyceum. *See* Lyceum
Newman, Paul, 201
Newton, Willoughby, 248
New York City Landmarks Commission, 323
New York Public Library for the Performing Arts, 250, 307–9, 313
New York Shakespeare Festival, 266, 268

Next (McNally), 208
Neylin, James, 191
Ngemi, Mbongeni, 296
Nicholson, J. Kenyon, 37
Night Before Thinking, The, 228
Nitze, Paul H., 277, 294
Noah: The Voyage of the Ark (Obey), 100
Noble, Joseph Veach, 259
Noble, Ruth, 49
No Casting Today (revue), 86
Noguchi, Isamu, 50
Norman, Marsha, 239
Notes from the Underground (Dostoyevsky), 159
Now Is the Time for All Good Men (Cryer and Ford), 207
Nugent, Nelle, 271
Nunn, Sam, 294
Nyitray, Emil, 37

Oakie, Victoria, 310
Obaldia, René de, 180
Obey, André, 100
Obie Awards, 148, 149, 163, 167
O'Casey, Eileen, 154–55, 159, 166, 191, 193, 202–4, 218, 220, 299, 309, 310
O'Casey, Niall, 154
O'Casey, Sean, 89, 139, 146–47, 153, 154, 159, 166, 191–92, 202–4, 232, 319; White Barn memorabilia exhibit, 309–10
O'Casey, Shivaun, 309, 310
O'Connor, Frank, 148
Odets, Clifford, 79, 80
O'Dwyer, Paul, 232
Off Broadway, 2, 19, 35, 85, 113–15, 161, 167; LL as "Queen of," 188, 261; Obie Awards, 148, 149, 163, 167. *See also specific theaters*
Off-Broadway: The Prophetic Theatre (Little), 166
Off-Off Broadway, 209–10
Oh, What a Lovely War! (Littlewood), 196
Ohio Impromptu (Beckett), 255
O'Horgan, Tom, 211
Olim, Dorothy, 246–47
Oliver, Edith, 291
Olivier, Laurence, 297
Olmsted, Frederick Law, 9
O'Neill, Eugene, 79, 80, 92, 113, 137, 163, 232
One Man's Woman (Kallesser), 41–43, 44
On the Boulevard (Montevecchi), 317

Ormandy, Eugene, 44
O'Shaughnessy, John, 89, 90
O'Shea, Milo, 98, 109, 191
Osterman, Lester, 239
Our Man in Madras (Hofmann), 208
Owens, Rochelle, 194, 211
Owl Answers, The (Kennedy), 150, 206, 210

Pacifica Foundation, 168
Pacino, Al, 251, 322
Painted Wagon (Goodyear and Huston), 1, 82–85
Palace Theatre, 48–49
Pale Horse, Pale Rider (Porter; Jacker adapt.), 145, 148, 232, 288
Palmer, Lilli, 84
Papp, Joseph, 248, 261, 262, 289
Paris, Ronnie, 224, 225
Parks, Hildy, 264
Pascone, Tere, 81
Pastures of Heaven, The (Steinbeck), 230
Paton, Alan, 137
Patton, Lucille, 224
Pearl of Great Price, The (McLaughlin), 41
Pell, Claiborne, 294
Pelleas and Melisande (Maeterlinck; Watson adapt.), 141
Père Goriot (Balzac; Littlewood adapt.), 129
Performing Arts Research Center, 307
Perl, Arnold, 139, 146
Peter der Grosse (film), 30
Petrides, Avra, 224
Phillips, Bob, 274
Phillips, Bradley, 148
Philoctetes (Gide), 150
Philoctetes (Sophocles), 150
Picasso, Pablo, 273, 275
Picon, Molly, 233
Pictures in the Hallway (O'Casey), 202
Pinter, Harold, 191, 195–96
"Pirate Jenny" (song), 183
Piscator, Erwin, 78, 83, 91, 113
Piscator, Maria-Ley, 78, 91
Place Without Mornings, A (Koesis), 223, 224
Playbill (program), 247–48
Players, The (club), 262, 264, 321; LL's ladies room donation, 306
Playhouse Theatre (Toronto), 154
Playwrights Sidewalk, 322–24
Poland, Albert, 211, 255, 263, 327
Pons, Lily, 78
Poons, Marvin, 207

Porter, Katherine Anne, 145, 148
Porter, Stephen, 150
Potasnik, Rabbi Joseph, 327
Pot of Fat (Chanler), 139
Premice, Josephine, 94
Pressman, Lawrence, 283, 297
Price, Gerald, 175
Price, Roger, 94
Proctor, Frederick Francis, 35–36
Proctor Players, 35–37
Prodigal Sister, The (Franklin and Grant), 229–30
Promenade (theatre), 246, 320
Prosky, Robert, 288, 290, 294, 296, 302, 303
Provost, William, 86
Purl, Linda, 313
Pushkin Drama Theatre (Moscow), 301, 303
Put It in Writing (revue), 193

Quare Fellow, The (Behan), 147, 155
Queen of Off-Broadway, The (exhibition), 259
Queen of Off-Broadway, The (film), 259–60, 261, 289, 298
Quintero, José, 114, 115, 163–65

Rabb, Ellis, 141, 150, 229
Rain (Colton and Randolph), 45
Rainer, Luise, 251
Rains, Claude, 63
Randall, Albert B., 60–61
Randolph, Bryson, 107
Randolph, Clemence, 45–48
Rattigan, Terence, 243
Reagan, Nancy, 261
Reagan, Ronald, 261, 279, 286, 291
Rebhann, Raymond R., 257, 264
Red Roses for Me (O'Casey), 89, 90, 119, 147
Red Scare on Sunset (Busch), 311
Redwood Curtian (L. Wilson), 309
Reed, Florence, 46, 48
Reeves, Theodore, 80
Regan, Joe, 170
Reifenberg, Carl, 66, 71, 74–75
Reiner, Fritz, 78
Reisner, Robert, 206
Reldaw, John R., 31
Rella, Ettore, 96, 125, 127–28
Repertory Theatre of Lincoln Center, 229

Rice, Vernon, 84, 85, 101, 102, 161, 163
Rich, Frank, 271, 290, 291, 294, 295–96, 312, 314
Richards, Jeffrey, 276, 282, 289, 301, 316
Richards, Ken, 295
Richards, Lloyd, 278, 280–88, 291, 293, 297
Richardson, Ralph, 297
Ridgefield Summer Theatre, 81
Rip Van Winkle (show), 81
Rising of the Moon, The (Gregory), 106
River Line, The (Morgan), 125, 126, 128, 139, 142–43, 147
Riverside Drive (N.Y.C.), 7, 9–11
Riverside Drive (play), 198
Roberts, Meade, 144, 169
Robertson, Nan, 289
Rockaby (Beckett), 255
Rodow, Martin, 324
Rogers, Ronald, 227
Romoff, Colin, 261
Rosen, Max, 12
Rosenfield, John, 185, 186
Ross, Daniel G. (Danny), 221–22
Ross, David, 147
Ross, Don, 99, 125
Ross, Grace, 221–22
Ross, James, 326
Rosten, Norman, 206
Roth, Daryl, 246, 311–13
Roth, Wolfgang, 142
Roundabout Theatre, 243
Royale Theatre, 228
Rubin, Don, 208
Rubin, Jane, 159
Russell, Fred H., 84, 90, 101
Russian Tea Room, 305

Saddler, Donald, 51, 248, 318, 320, 322, 324
Saint, Eva Marie, 86
St. James Church, 120
St. James Theatre, 229
Saints Day (Whiting), 145
Sally, George and Martha (Dann), 223
Salzman, Herbert, 299
Salzman, Rita Fredricks, 103, 299
Sands, Diana, 194
Sanford, Isabel, 156
Sanger, Margaret, 58, 305
Santa Claus (cummings), 150
Sarafina! (musical), 264, 288, 296
Sargent, Franklin Haven, 15–16, 17
Saroyan, William, 89

Sartre, Jean Paul, 91, 114
Saunders, Rai, 127
Schaeffer, Carl, 225–40 passim, 242, 247
Schechner, Richard, 201
Schippers, Thomas, 106
Schisgal, Murray, 180
Schlamme, Martha, 227
Schmidt, Sandra, 183
Schmitt, William. *See* de Lys, William
Schneider, Alan, 153, 196, 255
Schnitzler, Robert, 237
Schoenfeld, Jerry, 280
Schwartz, Arthur, 56, 257, 328
Schweitzer, Gertrude (sister-in-law), 223
Schweitzer, Louis (taxi driver), 143
Schweitzer, Louis P. (Lou) (husband), 91,
  98, 103, 118, 129, 138, 155, 167, 175,
  176, 189, 191, 192, 202, 204, 206, 208,
  215, 222, 237, 241, 247, 256, 257, 264,
  265, 267, 274, 279, 303, 307, 328; background of, 53–55; Bail Project and,
  169, 219, 222; business activities of, 55,
  62, 65, 68, 143, 162, 205, 318; childlessness and, 62, 75–76; death of, 204,
  218–27, 249; eccentricities of, 59,
  143–44; estate and bequests of,
  222–23; ham radio and, 55, 76, 109,
  138, 168, 207, 220; health problems of,
  109, 132, 138, 143, 168, 192–93, 205,
  213–18; houseboat purchase by, 168;
  LL contrasted with, 55–56; LL
  courtship by, 55–58; LL marriage to,
  58–62, 91, 108, 168, 169, 216; LL's acting and, 63, 64, 67; LL's feelings
  about, 59–60; LL's marital conflicts
  with, 56, 62–68, 71–74, 81, 88–89, 238,
  311; LL's producing ventures and, 164,
  171, 185, 229; poem by, 216; Theatre
  de Lys purchase by, 119, 122–25, 128,
  131, 132, 257; Wadler family and, 31,
  67–68, 110; wealth of, 2, 68; Westport
  home of, 68–70, 77–78; womanizing
  by, 76, 81, 88–89, 109, 168, 221. *See also*
  White Barn Theatre
Schweitzer, M. Peter (brother-in-law),
  217, 222
Schweitzer, Peter J. (father-in-law), 53, 54
Schweitzer, Vera Gorodnitzky (mother-
  in-law), 53, 54, 64, 66, 68, 169
Schweitzer, William (brother-in-law), 55,
  62, 217, 223
Seldes, Marian, 103–4, 273, 274, 275, 276

Senior Concert, 266, 295, 318, 321
Serlin, Oscar, 80
Sex (West), 44
Shakespeare, William, 102, 111, 139, 152,
  207
Shakespeare in Harlem (Hughes material),
  111, 156–57, 158, 160, 232
Shanghai Gesture, The (Colton), 41, 45–48
Shaskan, George, Jr., 230, 270
Shaw, George Bernard, 40, 141
Shearer, Norma, 50
Sheehy, Helen, 139
Sheffer, Ann, 313
Sheffer, Ralph, 260
Shepard, Richard F., 203
Shepard, Sam, 242, 248
Shepherd's Chameleon, The (Ionesco),
  173–74, 187, 195
Sheridan Square Playhouse, 193, 213
Sherry-Netherland, 256–58
Sherwood, Robert, 80
Shipley, Joseph T., 185
Shubert Organization, 272, 285
Shultz, George, 294
Shyre, Paul, 96, 100–101, 126, 140, 141,
  146, 147, 153, 155, 202, 319
Sidney, Sylvia, 198
Signature Theatre Company, 321
Sign of Winter (Rella), 96, 125, 128
Sikorski, Fran, 310–11
Silberman, John, 289, 291, 293
Silver, Ron, 296
Silver, Warren, 86
Silvera, Frank, 139
Simenon, Georges, 101
Simon, Barney, 212–13
Simon, John, 291
Simon, Meg, 282
Skee, Vincent J., 220
Sklar, George, 75
Sleep of Prisoners, A (Fry), 120, 125, 197
Smith, Liz, 264
Smith, Michael, 210
Snow Was Black, The (Simenon), 101
Sokolow, Anna, 139
So Long, 174th Street (musical), 261
Sommer, Josef, 277
Sondergaard, Gale, 64, 222
Sondheim, Stephen, 284–85
Sondheimer, Hans, 93
Sonnenberg, Benjamin, 110
Sophocles, 150

Soul Goes Home (Hughes), 158
Sound on the Goose (Biel), 139
Soviet Union, 279, 286, 291, 300–304, 305
Speaks, Charmé and Charles, 77
Spencer, Franz, 107
Spoleto Festival of Two Worlds, 169
Sprecher, Ben, 131, 218, 241–47, 250, 252, 255, 258, 264, 265, 271–72, 275, 277–84, 288, 291, 300, 301, 312–15, 320, 322–24; LL's death and, 326, 327, 329
Stage a Number (TV series), 104
Stage Struck (film), 63
Starr, Sandra (Sandy), 247, 262, 276, 277, 283, 287, 298, 300–304, 317, 321, 324, 325–26, 329
"Stars Salute the Queen of Off-Broadway, The" (gala), 261
Stearns, Elizabeth, 112
Steel Magnolias (play), 305
Stein, Gertrude, 100, 103, 272–76
Stein, Leo, 273
Steinbeck, John, 230–31
Stephen Wise Free Synagogue, 328
Stevens, Roger L., 193
Stevenson, Isabelle, 248, 265, 289, 325
Stevenson, John, 248, 325
Stoddard, Haila, 207, 208, 251, 257, 299
Straight, Beatrice, 142
Stranger, The (Mendelssohn), 95
Strasberg, Adam Lee, 250
Strasberg, Anna, 17, 237–38, 239, 259, 260, 262, 266, 271, 289, 299, 317, 318; LL's death and, 326, 327, 328, 329; LL's friendship with, 249–51, 320; parties of, 223, 248, 249, 305, 315, 321, 324
Strasberg, David Lee, 250, 324
Strasberg, Lee, 79, 155, 223, 238, 249, 250, 251, 260–62, 328
Strasberg, Paula, 155, 223
Strasberg, Susan, 155
Streetcar Named Desire, A (Williams), 89, 229
Strindberg, August, 104
Stronger, The (Weisgall opera), 104
Stuart, Michel, 244, 258
Sturz, Herbert, 109
Sullivan, Jenny, 312, 313
Sullivan, Jo. *See* Loesser, Jo Sullivan
Sulzberger, Arthur Ochs, 296
Swartburg, Lilian K., 218–19

Swartburg, Robert, 218, 219
Swire, Willard (Bill), 96, 289, 319
Symphony Pastoral (Gide), 103

Tabakov, Oleg, 304
Tabori, George, 180–81, 182, 183
Tallmer, Jerry, 204
Tamarin, Alfred H., 89, 90
Taubman, Howard, 199, 289, 292
Taylor, Markland, 21, 251
Taylor, Robert (curator), 248, 309
Teatro Campesino, El, 228
Teitel, Carol, 178
Theater Hall of Fame, 259
Theatre de Lys, 2, 110, 113, 116–64, 168, 173, 174, 182, 183, 184, 193, 194, 198, 199, 203–11, 224, 225, 228, 229, 231, 232, 238, 239, 242–46, 253, 254; name change of, 258; Schweitzer's purchase of, 119, 122–25, 128, 131, 132, 257; videotaped productions of, 307. *See also* Lucille Lortel Theatre
Theatre Guild, 40, 63, 79, 81, 95, 113, 126
Theatre of the Open Eye, 224
Theatre on Film and Tape (TOFT), 307–8
They Shall Not Die (play), 95
Thirkield, Robert, 252
Thomas, Dylan, 175
Thompson, Sada, 96, 101, 140, 142
Thorndike, Sybil, 141, 232
Threepenny Opera, The (Brecht and Weill), 117, 120–22, 129, 130–33, 136–39, 143, 153–54, 164, 183–84, 193, 245, 261
Tibor-Nagy Marionettes, 97
Tierney, Harry, Jr., 170, 172, 194
Ti-Jean and His Brothers (Walcott), 228
Time To Go (O'Casey), 159, 232
Tippit, Tina, 289
TOFT. *See* Theatre on Film and Tape
Toklas, Alice B., 272–76
Tolan, Michael, 96
Tony Awards, 264–65, 292, 294, 295, 296
Touring Players, 99
Trimble, Jessy. *See* Turner, John
Trinidad Theatre Company, 228
Trixie True, Teen Detective (musical), 243
Tulane Drama Review, 201, 210
Tune, Tommy, 244
Turner, John, 39
Twin City Players, 37–38

Two By Two (Turner and Woodward), 39
Two Crooks and a Lady (play), 19
Tyberg, Theodore, 266–67, 306, 321, 325, 326
Typists, The (Schisgal), 180

Ubu (Jarry), 305
University of Alabama, 279
University of Bridgeport, 237, 262, 276
U.S.A. (Dos Passos; Shyre adapt.), 96, 100–101, 140–41, 142, 232

Vacation in Miami (Hofmann), 208
Vance, Nina, 187
Van Zandt, Porter, 253
Variety Arts Theatre, 320
Vaughan, Stuart, 142, 146, 147, 279
Vera Foundation, 109, 169, 219, 222
Vera Institute of Justice, 321
Victims of Duty (Ionesco), 158–59, 195
Victor, Jay, 85
Village Voice, 161. *See also* Obie Awards
Vincent Astor Gallery, 308
Viola, Tom, 314, 315
Violett, Ellen, 100
Virgin Man, The (Dugan and Maltby), 44–45
Vogel, Paula, 321, 324
Voskovec, George, 182, 232
Vreeland, Frank, 41–42

Wadler, Anna (Anny) Moskowitz (mother), 2–15, 19, 21, 28–34, 37, 43, 50, 54, 62, 65, 67, 70, 72, 76, 81, 91, 110, 126, 138, 206, 208, 214; death of, 214–15, 227; dominance of, 8, 9; eighty-second birthday of, 155; LL's marriage and, 57, 58–59, 68, 72, 110
Wadler, Annie (aunt), 5
Wadler, Augusta (Gussie) Polimer (grandmother), 4–5, 8
Wadler, Harris (Harry) (father), 2–15, 34, 57, 67, 91, 214; business affairs of, 28, 29, 54; daughters and, 29, 31–33; death of, 110; womanizing of, 8, 21, 56
Wadler, Lisa Glauber (sister-in-law), 155
Wadler, Lucille. *See* Lortel, Lucille
Wadler, Mayo (brother). *See* Mayo, Waldo
Wadler, Meier (grandfather), 4
Wadler, Ruth (sister). *See* Cugat, Ruth Wadler

Wadler, Seymour (brother), 5, 7, 8, 21, 31, 33, 110, 155, 215, 236
Wadler, Willie (uncle), 5
Wager, Michael, 182, 183
Waite, Ralph, 316
Walcott, Derek, 228
Waldo Mayo Memorial Violin Competition, 266
Walker, Robert, 202
Walk in the Woods, A (Blessing), 264, 277–80, 285–88, 290, 293, 295–98, 305, 309; Soviet tour of, 300–304
Wallace, Hazel Vincent, 92, 125, 144, 145, 160, 232, 299
Wallach, Eli, 182, 221, 226, 289, 331
Wallis, Hal, 80
Ward, Douglas Turner, 210
Wasserstein, Wendy, 252
Waterston, Sam, 288, 290, 294, 301
Watson, Douglass, 97, 141
Watson, Lucille, 32
Watt, Douglas, 275
Wax, Emanuel, 191–92, 195–96
WBAI-FM, 143, 162–63, 168
Webb, Charles D., 252–54, 270
Weber, Bruce, 316
Weill, Kurt, 120–22, 131, 176, 181–82, 228, 310
Weisgall, Hugo, 104, 106
Weiss, Peter, 225
Weissberger, L. Arnold, 258, 259
Weldon, Duncan, 283, 285–86, 293, 298
Weller, Michael, 223, 228
Wells, Win, 272, 275
Welsh, Kenneth, 277
Wersba, Barbara, 233
West, Mae, 44
Westchester Hills Cemetery, 328
Westport, Conn., 69–71, 77–78, 83. *See also* White Barn Theatre
Westport Country Playhouse, 70, 80–81, 83, 90, 102, 103, 106, 112, 113, 236, 297–98
Westport Public Library, 260, 329
What Where (Beckett), 255
Wheeler, David, 148
White, Edgar, 211–12
White, George C., 267, 300
White, Leonard, 196, 197
White, Michael, 196
White, Robertson, 89–90
White Barn Club Theatre, 94
White Barn Revue (Dickason), 101

White Barn Theatre (Westport), 6, 18,
19, 58, 59, 116, 120, 125–29, 135, 136,
139–41, 145, 148–50, 156–58, 160, 170,
173, 176, 177, 181, 185–88, 191, 194,
201, 213, 224, 227–29, 233–39, 251–54,
257, 265, 273, 274, 276, 284; Actors'
Equity and, 86–88, 91, 171, 172,
177–80, 188, 189–90, 206, 233, 309–10,
330; Derwent House at, 34, 98, 108,
111, 132, 171, 178, 234; fiftieth anniversary celebration, 321–22; future of,
318, 327, 330; growth and style of,
111–12; launching of, 1–2, 81–112; London club theatres and, 93, 135; politics
and, 95; Schweitzer and, 88, 90, 99,
107–10, 172, 177–79, 186, 190, 207;
stage design and, 106–8; Summer Apprentice program of, 99, 101–2, 106; as
talent showcase, 196–97; twentieth anniversary of, 207–8; videotaped productions of, 307
White Barn Theatre Foundation, 98–99,
108, 178, 190, 221, 318, 322
White Barn Theatre Museum, 309–10
White Barn Tryout Theatre, 81–89
Whitelaw, Billie, 255
Whiting, John, 145
Wickwire, Nancy, 100, 136
Wien, Lawrence A., 274, 285, 295
Wilde! (Gaines), 224
Wilde, Oscar, 141
Wilk, Barbara, 299
Wilk, Max, 268–69, 298–99
Willamstown Theatre Festival, 310
Williams, Lucille, 325–26
Williams, Tennessee, 80, 115, 147, 169,
185, 186, 188, 229, 278, 331
Willie Doesn't Live Here Anymore (Hof-
mann), 211
Willis, John, 259
Wilson, August, 278, 296
Wilson, Clerow (Flip), 206
Wilson, Edwin, 289, 291
Wilson, Forrest, 70
Wilson, John C., 147–48

Wilson, Julie, 309, 315
Wilson, Lanford, 210, 252, 254, 289, 309,
318, 324; LL's bequest to, 329
Winslow Boy, The (Rattigan), 243
Winter, Wales, 35
Winters, Marian, 208
Wise, Rabbi Stephen Samuel, 54
Witcover, Walt, 173
Woman Pays Club, 155
Women's Project, 263
Wood, Audrey, 84, 86, 163, 178–79, 185,
186, 214, 278
Wood, Peggy, 140, 141, 151, 177, 193, 202,
203, 207, 210
Woods, A.H., 35, 41, 46
Woods, Donald, 198
Woodward, Eugenie, 39
Woodward, Joanne, 201
Woolf, Edgar A., 48–49, 51
Words Upon the Window Pane, The (Yeats),
106
World War II, 69, 70, 76–78, 80
WPA Theatre, 305
Wright, Olive, 247, 324, 325, 326
Wright, Richard, 83

Yale Repertory Theatre, 277, 278,
280–82, 293–94, 296, 301, 302
Yale University School of Drama, 278,
282
Yeats, William Butler, 106
Yi-Kwei Sze, 94
Young, Joseph Wesley, 71
Young Ireland Theatre Company, 97,
98, 106, 109
Young Man From Atlanta, The (Foote), 321
Yurka, Blanche, 151

Zacharias, Steve, 107
Zarem, Robert M. (Bobby), 261, 289
Zero Hour (Sklar and Maltz), 75
Zimbalist, Stephanie, 312, 313
Zindel, Paul, 206, 324
Zipprodt, Patricia, 165–66
Zolotow, Sam, 87